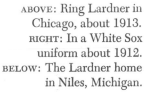
ABOVE: Ring Lardner in Chicago, about 1913.
RIGHT: In a White Sox uniform about 1912.
BELOW: The Lardner home in Niles, Michigan.

CO.

RING LARDNER

Ring Lardner

A BIOGRAPHY BY

DONALD ELDER

DOUBLEDAY & COMPANY, INC.

Garden City, New York, 1956

Library of Congress Catalog Card Number 56–7656

Designed by Alma Reese Cardi

ACKNOWLEDGMENTS

I am deeply indebted to Mrs. Ring Lardner, John Lardner,
and Ring Lardner, Jr., and to Miss Lena Lardner and Mrs.
Anna Lardner Tobin, for making available to me manuscripts, letters, family documents, and most of the significant information that
is contained in this book; and I am also grateful for their generous
and patient assistance at various stages of its writing. I am only less
indebted to the late Grantland Rice and to Mrs. Rice, to Mr. and
Mrs. Arthur Jacks, and to Miss Gusti Feldmann, for their recollections of Ring Lardner.

I am indebted to Mr. Edmund Wilson for permission to quote
from his notes on Ring Lardner and on Scott Fitzgerald, and from
private letters. I also wish to thank Mr. Burton Rascoe and Mr.
Quin Ryan, not only for information, but for directing me to many
other fruitful sources. To Mr. Maxwell Geismar I owe a special debt
for having turned over to me a great deal of material on Ring
Lardner; and to Mr. James R. Frakes and Mr. Howard W. Webb,
Jr., for generous and expert assistance in problems of research. The
list of writings appended to this book is taken from Mr. Webb's
complete bibliography of Ring Lardner's writings, a work of diligent
scholarship and indispensable to any student of Lardner.

Literally scores of Ring Lardner's friends and colleagues provided
me with valuable material, often at the cost of much time and effort.
I cannot hope to name them all here, but I am nonetheless grateful
for their kind help.

5

Thanks are due to the following publishers, agents, and authors for permission to use the material indicated:

Charles Scribner's Sons for the passages from the following works of Ring Lardner:

Symptoms of Being 35. Copyright 1921 by The Crowell Publishing Company and Charles Scribner's Sons, 1948, 1949 by Ellis A. Lardner.

You Know Me Al. Copyright 1916 by Charles Scribner's Sons, 1944 by Ellis A. Lardner.

"My Roomy." From *How to Write Short Stories.* Copyright 1924 by Charles Scribner's Sons, 1952 by Ellis A. Lardner.

"I Gaspiri," "Clemo Uti—the Water Lilies." From *What of It?* Copyright 1925 by Charles Scribner's Sons, 1953 by Ellis A. Lardner.

"Dinner Bridge," "The Democrats in 1924," "Night and Day," "Off Color," "A Crooner." From *First and Last.* Copyright 1934 by Ellis A. Lardner.

Harcourt, Brace & Company, Inc., and Leonard Woolf for permission to use two pages from "American Fiction" from *The Moment and Other Essays* by Virginia Woolf.

The Sporting News for use of two excerpts from "Pullman Pastimes" by Ring Lardner.

The New Yorker for material appearing on pages 225, 351–57, which originally appeared in *The New Yorker.*

Liveright Publishing Corporation for permission to use material from *Sherwood Anderson's Notebook,* by Sherwood Anderson. Copyright 1926 by Boni and Liveright, Inc.

Farrar, Straus & Cudahy, Inc., for permission to use material from *The Shores of Light,* by Edmund Wilson. Copyright 1952 by Edmund Wilson.

Music Publishers Holding Corporation for permission to use the lyrics of the following three songs: "June Moon," copyright 1929 by Harms, Inc., reprinted by permission. "Montana Moon," copyright 1929 by Harms, Inc., reprinted by permission. "Prohibition Blues," copyright 1919 by Jerome H. Remick & Company. Copyright renewed and assigned to Remick Music Corporation, reprinted by permission.

The Bell Syndicate, Inc., for permission to use excerpts from Ring Lardner's column written for the Bell Syndicate.

DONALD ELDER

RING LARDNER

CHAPTER ONE

At the height of his fame in the middle twenties Ring Lardner was known as a humorist, a newspaper columnist, and a writer of brilliant short stories; but to millions of his wide audience he was first of all a baseball reporter. His passion for the game began early in his childhood in Niles, Michigan, where he had every chance to gratify it. His father often took the Lardner children to big-league games in Chicago; Ring and his brother Rex drove the Lardner horse and buggy to South Bend to see the games of the Central League and the Notre Dame varsity team; and there were many semiprofessional teams around Niles. The Lardner boys followed national baseball closely in the newspapers, they worked on baseball statistics in the schoolroom, and when they sang in the choir of Trinity Church, they carried the Sunday sports pages folded under their vestments to read during the sermon. At one time Ring was intended for the ministry, but apparently his interest in sports superseded whatever vocation he was thought to have.

The other passion of his youth was music, but he was never to have any conspicuous professional success in that field. Baseball was the springboard to his ultimate achievement in journalism and fiction. The game was somewhat rustic in Niles in Ring's childhood, but by the time he graduated from high school at the age of sixteen, he probably knew the game as well as a professional reporter. It had not occurred to him yet to become a newspaperman; that happened almost by accident. After a brief and unenthusiastic attempt at higher education and four years of footless employment around

9

Niles he was hired as a baseball reporter and general handy man on the South Bend *Times*, and he remained a newspaperman nearly all his life, in spite of his success in other endeavors. After two years in South Bend he went to Chicago, and for six more years his exclusive occupation was covering baseball. Then his "Busher's Letters," which first appeared in *The Saturday Evening Post* in 1914, and his Chicago *Tribune* column, "In the Wake of the News," made him nationally famous, and he moved on to New York, where he became an almost legendary figure as a short-story writer, humorist, and playwright. But it was his baseball experiences that launched him as a writer and provided the milieu in which he first observed his American characters in action; and it was the language of baseball players and fans on which he based his distinctive style.

Everything Ring was to become in his professional life is foreshadowed in his early childhood and has its roots in his family background—his love of sports, music, theater, writing, and literature. The youngest son of wealthy and indulgent parents, he was given every advantage and diversion, and he was allowed every opportunity to display his native talents to the most appreciative audience a child could have, a large and doting family of acutely sensitive and highly cultivated people. Within that circle of security and affluence, of benevolence and amiability, the three youngest Lardner children seem to have had enchanted childhoods.

Ring was born in Niles, Michigan, March 6, 1885, the youngest of the nine children of Henry Lardner and Lena Phillips Lardner. Of their first six children three had died in childhood. The three eldest who survived were William, Henry, Jr., and Lena. The three youngest were Rex, born 1881; Anna, born 1883; and Ringgold Wilmer, later known as Ring. Rex was born some twelve years after Lena; to the younger Lardners their older brothers and sisters seemed to belong to another generation.

Ring was named for his father's first cousin, the son of Admiral James Lardner of Philadelphia, whose wife's maiden name was Wilmer. The first Ringgold, who died unmarried at the age of thirty, only a short time before the birth of his namesake, was named after Rear Admiral Cadwallader Ringgold, U.S.N. (d. 1867), a friend of the Lardner family. The reason for shortening Ringgold to Ring is obvious; it was odd and unwieldy. For years Ring signed his work Ring W. Lardner until he dropped the W., thereby achieving without changing his name the most distinctive *nom de plume* in American letters since Mark Twain.

The Lardner family ranked as an old one in Niles, having come

10

there from Philadelphia in 1836, only a few years after the town had been established. The founder of the family in America was Lynford Lardner, son of a wealthy London physician whose fortune was lost by his heirs in South Sea speculation. His sister had married Richard, third son of William Penn and a joint proprietor of the colony of Pennsylvania. Lynford came to Philadelphia in 1740 under the sponsorship of the Penns, distinguished himself in the many offices to which he was appointed, and became one of the foremost citizens of the colony. For one hundred seventy years Lardners were prominent as civic and social leaders, members of learned societies, cofounders of what is now the University of Pennsylvania, soldiers, naval officers, and men of affairs. Although they devoted a good part of their talents to public service, they also lived the lives of country gentlemen at their several estates in the colony.

Henry Lardner, of the third generation of the family in Pennsylvania, was born in Philadelphia in 1804 and graduated from the medical school of the University of Pennsylvania. Instead of entering into practice he came to Niles in 1836 with two cousins, who later moved farther west. On the way they had stopped in Cincinnati, where they built a sawmill and acquired land and timber holdings. Then they joined the westward migration that took place after the end of the Black Hawk War of the early 1830's, when the territory around the southern end of Lake Michigan became safe for permanent settlement.

Niles, which had been a regimental headquarters during the Black Hawk uprising, was not a prairie village. It was situated in the heart of the St. Joseph River valley, whose fame as a Promised Land had long since reached the East. Fort St. Joseph, a mile south of the town near the crossing of two great Indian trails, had been founded by French explorers in the seventeenth century. Charlevoix, approaching the fort in 1721, was overwhelmed by the natural beauty of the valley, and Sieur Cadillac was equally impressed. James Fenimore Cooper, who lived for a time near the region, called it the Garden of America, and Harriet Martineau, the indefatigable English traveler, who forded the river at Niles in June 1836, declared that Milton must have gone there before he wrote of the Garden in *Paradise Lost*.

Here Henry Lardner purchased a beautiful and fertile tract of timbered land on Dowagiac Creek, four miles north of the village, and named it Glenford. In 1838 he married Mary Keys of Philadelphia, who brought him a dowry of $10,000, a considerable sum. Ring's father, Henry Lardner, was born at Glenford in 1839. Mary

11

Keys Lardner died a few weeks after his birth, and Henry Lardner's eldest sister Elizabeth came from Philadelphia to take care of the child. She too purchased land in the vicinity of Niles and increased the family holdings, which in time were to devolve upon Ring's father and become the basis of the Lardner fortune in Michigan. The Lardners wrote about their new home to their brothers and sisters in Philadelphia; their letters were enthusiastic. They were also vivid, humorous, and written with style.

When young Henry was five years old, he was taken back to Philadelphia to be educated, and he did not return to Niles to live until he was eighteen. His father died in 1852, leaving him Glenford, now a prosperous farm. In 1861 he married Lena Bogardus Phillips, daughter of the Rev. Joseph Phillips, rector of Trinity Church, of which Henry Lardner was a zealous supporter. Phillips, who came from New York State, was a fine scholar and a man of far greater intellect than was common among clergymen in small Midwestern parishes. His daughter, who taught school in Niles before her marriage, shared his qualities and interests. She was deeply religious and active in church affairs, but by no means unworldly. She had an acute, in fact a rather wild, sense of humor and great personal charm as well as beauty, and she loved conviviality. Her chief interests were music, literature, education, and private charities; and she had a benevolent eye for other people's business.

The young Lardners were rich, handsome, and were bulwarks of everything solid and commendable in the community, and their fortunes and their family increased. They left Niles for a time to live near Cincinnati, where Henry Lardner had business interests; then they returned and bought a large and attractive house which had been built by a local banker. Mr. Lardner was doing well in real estate and investments outside Niles. He was a speculator, but so was everyone else; and so far western land had proved profitable.

The Lardner house stood on Bond Street, on what was then the southern edge of town, near the steep, wooded bank of the St. Joseph River. The immense yard covered a whole block of several acres and was enclosed by a rail fence. The land sloped gently down from the eastern boundary toward the river; behind the house were fields and gardens, which were Mr. Lardner's special interest—his roses were famous locally—and on the lawn in front were tall pine trees. There were also a baseball diamond, tennis court, and a coach house with a stable of horses. The house was dark gray stucco with steeply gabled roofs which shone on moonlight nights like some fairy-tale castle; and the eaves and porches were adorned with

12

wooden scrollwork. In its spacious grounds it stood apart from the town, a place of quiet charm and good taste, in an age when ostentatious and hideous piles were being erected on Main Street by prosperous merchants and businessmen.

Here, with the freedom and ease that long-established wealth, gentility, and culture bring, Mrs. Lardner wielded her benign authority over her family, the church, and Niles society. The town, in the center of rich farmlands, with ample water power for industry, was growing prosperous. Like most towns of the region, it had not been settled by immigrants from Europe but by families who had lived in the East for several generations and who brought money and culture West with them. Niles had boasted a "society" at a time when it regarded Chicago as a straggling sand patch inhabited by teamsters, drovers, and raw traders. Chicago does not seem to have felt this slight very deeply, but Niles, rightly or wrongly, did (and still does) take satisfaction in once having been bigger and more civilized than the metropolis. Rich Chicagoans built their summer homes along the St. Joseph River; it was civilized, and besides Niles real estate was a good investment; it was solid earth, while Chicago was a sandy shore at which the lake kept nibbling away.

Niles had its upper crust of a dozen families of Anglo-Saxon ancestry, and its poor, who were mostly German and Irish, and the objects of Mrs. Lardner's unbridled largess. (Ring called it a "pie," and once said to a newcomer, "I hope you don't find the upper crust too brittle or the lower crust too soggy"; he was very young then.) It also had its opera house, its musicales, and literary societies which were devoted to everything but literature. Its amenities are not to be compared to those of the East. Its streets were mud, the coaches were really buggies or "platforms" (simply planks on wheels), and its big social functions were apt to be picnics or corn roasts. Sports of all kinds flourished, and, because there was money, so did gambling. Compared to other small towns in the region, Niles was for decades wide-open. Social life even among the upper crust was marked by informality; in fact it was really quite homely. Mrs. Lardner, who wrote poems, short stories, and essays, described it in some verses on The Oaks, the large and comfortable home of a local merchant:

> *A home quite ancient! (from a Western view:)*
> *Whose genial warmth enwraps the happy guest;*
> *Outside may fall the snow, or gentle dew;*
> *Within these walls the season is the best!*

13

Here find we blent the charm of middle-age
  With youth; and all accord us welcome kind.
In "old-time" sports the lively guests engage,
  And each finds something "suited to his mind."

We make a "love-feast" of the viands spread;
  (Not one false note disturbs life's harmony:)
O'er all the spice of harmless mirth is shed,
  While like ambrosia tastes our cup o' tea!

With Eastern courtesy and Western fun
  Mingled in graceful and harmonious whole
Too swift the wingèd-footed moments run;
  Vainly we wish that Time would backward roll!

This exemplifies not only social life in Niles during Ring's child-hood, but also Mrs. Lardner's unquenchable optimism. Not one false note disturbed life's harmony, inside the home; and if it did, it was suppressed. Through ceaseless activity and a natural ebullience she maintained a happy disposition; and she had the faculty of shutting from her sight what she did not want to see. Life in the Lardner home was high-spirited, for she was witty, she loved fun, and she had an inborn gift for entertaining others, grownups and children alike. She kept up a running conversation with constant laughter when she had company or was amusing her children, and her own resources for diversion were unlimited. There was a steady stream of guests, of all sorts—Episcopal clergymen whom she knew through her father, prominent laymen, the ladies of the church guilds, the choir, the football team, the Senior Class, distinguished visitors from out of town, the district congressman, and a great many odd people who had no sort of social position but who were good companions. Among her friends was the local telegraph operator, an eccentric hunchback who had a mind and wit of his own, which did not make him socially acceptable anywhere else. Some Niles residents consid-ered Mrs. Lardner a little too democratic, but it is not possible that she could have cared. Orthodox as they were in religion, business, and politics, the Lardners' home was in many ways unconventional for a town like Niles. Their hospitality was lavish; there was plenty of food and drink. (Casey, a saloonkeeper who supplied their cellar, threw in a bottle of whiskey every week as lagniappe.) Mrs. Lard-ner had high and unrestrained qualities of imagination, and anyone who appealed to them, or to her kind heart and her genuine interest in people, was welcome in her house.

14

Her charity extended far beyond her family and the church, for which she worked in every possible way, organizing the first choir, teaching Sunday-school classes, and presiding over the guilds. She also undertook to provide for the sick and afflicted and her servants were kept busy taking baskets of food all over town. No starving family, no unwed mother seemed to escape her eye. Her generosity was spontaneous and unfeigned, and, having the means to indulge it, she probably took good works as part of her Christian duty. She was always looking for underdogs to succor, and sometimes she strayed outside the path of strict charity and laid herself open to the charge of meddling; she managed things with a firm and authoritative air.

Mr. Lardner, kindly, indulgent, and quiet by nature, was not so close to the younger children as their mother was. He seems to have remained in the background, while Mrs. Lardner's personality dominated the house and she was the center of conviviality. As he grew older and his health failed, he grew more taciturn. Later he endured the loss of his fortune with stoicism, allowing his wife and family every luxury he could afford until his resources were depleted. But when Ring was growing up, his father was already an elderly man; he did not leave so powerful an impression on Ring as his mother did.

Rex, Anna, and Ring were the children of her middle age, and on them she lavished a particular devotion. Mr. Lardner indulged her and she in turn indulged the children. While they were small, each child had his own Irish nursemaid, an uncommon extravagance even for people of the Lardners' circumstances. Although the parents were active in the life of the community, the children saw little of it; they were not allowed to go out of the yard until Ring was eight years old, except in the company of the family or servants. They all slept upstairs in the large nursery with Mrs. Rattigan, the oldest of the nurses, who stayed on after the others had gone; she told them the same Irish fairy tales night after night, long after they knew them by heart. By day they were bundled up and taken out for a two- or three-hour ride on the platform, a horse-drawn wagon driven by Ed Donnelly, the coachman, one of Ring's early childhood heroes. Their restricted life, hardly typical of a Midwestern upbringing, does not seem to have been at all oppressive. Other children could come to play with them, and there was plenty to do. They could play all kinds of games in the yard; in the winter there was a long toboggan run at the north side of the yard; and on the river below Mr. Lardner kept a launch for boat rides and picnics. The three children, remarkably alike in temperament, had an uncanny rapport with each other, and were quite self-sufficient; Mrs. Lardner spent a great deal of time with them.

In games Ring was somewhat handicapped by a metal brace, which he wore on his leg until he was eleven years old. He was born with a deformed foot, and in his infancy underwent an operation to correct it, and the brace was applied. The treatment was successful, and Ring was able to join in sports with other children even though he limped slightly and clanked when he ran. After he was grown, there was no trace of the defect except that his left leg was thinner than his right. He was not symmetrical, he said. As a child, he is said to have shown no self-consciousness about it, but it is probable that he played harder at ball than he would normally have done to keep up with other children, and it may be that his inordinate admiration for athletic virtuosity owed something to his own early incapacity.

The Irish servants amused the children and also provided an audience for their performances—and they were continuous performers. Ed Donnelly, the coachman, was a dandy with a waxed and perfumed mustache and a fondness for gaudy neckties, and Ring used to emulate his hero by stealing his mother's perfume and holding under his chin colored Easter eggs in imitation of Ed's ties. This, like much of Ring's childhood drollery, sent his brother and sister, not to mention himself (he appreciated his own jokes), into uncontrollable giggles, a habit which all three children developed to an almost pathological degree. Ed also impressed the children by taking them on the platform to see his sweetheart Nellie Flynn, bearing roses surreptitiously taken from Mr. Lardner's garden. Nellie is said to have exclaimed, "Look at them roses! How they stink!" This remark, which seemed to them notable for its grammar and diction, stuck in the children's minds. Even at an early age Ring had an ear for common speech.

The servants were also called in to witness the dramatic spectacles the children put on. Ring's nurse, Rose Flood, who was a Roman Catholic, was so devoted to him that she even took him to church with her. When he was four or five years old, Ring held a High Mass at home, intoning a Latin of his own invention. The children also gave a dramatic recitation of Poe's *The Raven*, spoken with flourishes by Rex and Anna, while the owl-eyed Ring, perched on a bookcase, quoth "Nevermore" at appropriate intervals; and an extravagant version of *Bluebeard* with Ring swaggering in the title role. Later, when they had been taken to see the Eden Musée wax-

16

works at the Chicago World's Fair, which featured the latest and most sensational murders, with realistic scenes of violence and corpses splashed with red paint, Ring was inspired to compose horror plays, which the three children acted out for the edification of the household staff. Ring and Anna played their gory roles boldly, while Rex, the shyest of the three, hardly managed to speak a word, usually disappearing before the show was over. Ring also "entertained" the long-suffering servants whenever the Lardners had company and the younger ones ate in the kitchen.

In fact Ring was an excruciating exhibitionist, and everyone's delight. As a small boy, he was smiling and friendly and quite fat (he had weighed fourteen pounds at birth). It was he, more than Rex or Anna, who made acquaintances among the townspeople whenever he was taken out. He was droll and amusing, and seems to have been aware of it. No one ever discouraged him.

Dancing lessons were another diversion provided for the children, who were entertained for the wrong reasons. Each Thursday afternoon a Mr. William Peake arrived on the platform with his harp and his son, Peake, Jr. While he played the harp, Peake, Jr., instructed the children in the polka, schottische, and minuet; no "vulgar" dancing was even thought of. The children went through the steps, which they thought rather quaint, with suppressed laughter, until the effeminate manners of the dancing master made them dissolve in the tearful giggling that was the climax of most of their performances.

Mrs. Lardner wrote plays for all the children of the neighborhood to perform, making costumes and settings and coaching the actors. Almost from the time he could talk Ring was involved in some kind of theatrical endeavor.

A horde of pet animals overran the house. At one time there were eighteen cats, and litters of kittens were deposited in bureau drawers and in the bottom of the tall clock that stood in the hallway. The traffic in halls and on stairs was heavy, with mother cats carrying their kittens around. It was not a matter of the feline population having got out of hand. Each cat was a pet and bore the name of a prominent Episcopal clergyman; there were bishops and canons as well as lesser clerics among them, named for the churchmen who came to visit Mrs. Lardner. There were also ten rabbits, which Ring took out of their cage every evening and placed on the living-room sofa. These were named after the children's friends. Ring loved cats all his life, as the whole family did; his own home was seldom without one or more.

His kindness to all animals was almost fanatical. When as a small boy he was taken out for walks along Bond Street, he noticed that at one house a dog was always shut out in the cold, howling in misery. Each time he passed, Ring boldly opened the door of the house and let the dog in. Mrs. Lardner, whose benevolence extended even beyond the human race, had the matter called to her attention; she is said to have reproached the owner of the dog, who thereafter was more considerate. Niles dogs did not bother Ring; but later in life he got what amounted to a phobia about the large dogs he encountered in Great Neck, Long Island. One of his neighbors there had a large black police dog, which Ring hated. He called it "The Plainclothesman."

Among the friends of the Lardners were the Jacks family, who had a paper mill in Niles. The three Jacks boys, near the Lardner children in age, spent much of their time at the Lardner house, and Arthur Jacks remained Ring's closest friend for many years. They were neighbors in Niles, then later in Chicago, and after that in Great Neck. Ring fell in love with the entire Jacks family, and at Christmas time when he was eight years old he bought them a set of seven pitchers graduated in size, one for each member of the family. He and Rex and Arthur had a passion for the railroad, and played around the Cincinnati, Wabash & Michigan track, across the street and down the hill from the house. They got acquainted with the train crews, and Ring made a special friend of a brakeman, who became another of his childhood heroes. He bought him a set of pipes and sent them to him; giving presents to people he liked was one of his lifelong habits. He decided to become a brakeman, and got so familiar with the trains that he said he could tell the number of the engine from the sound of the whistle.

The Jacks boys and other Niles children liked to play at the Lardners' because there was so much to do. Devout as she was, Mrs. Lardner placed no restrictions on Sunday activities, and there was generally a ball game in summer or tobogganing in winter. The boys whose families insisted on a strict observance of the Sabbath could only walk or ride in buggies past the Lardners' yard, enviously watching the sport.

The Lardners' greatest pleasure and talent was music, and all the children who showed any bent for it were extraordinarily well trained. Mrs. Lardner was a fine musician and an accomplished pianist. She had perfect pitch and could play literally anything by ear. Her eldest daughter Lena, also an excellent musician, was for many years organist and director of the choir at Trinity Church. The

18

Lardner home was constantly filled with music. Anyone who could sing or play a musical instrument was invited to perform, and most of Mrs. Lardner's entertainments were musical.

Ring inherited all of his mother's talent. He too had perfect pitch, just as he had a perfect ear for speech, one of his great gifts as a writer. The Lardner music room had a pipe organ, which Lena played, as well as a piano, which they all played. Ring liked to make two-piano arrangements for himself and Anna, and when one piano was not enough, Mrs. Lardner bought another; and Anna and Ring played the elaborate ragtime arrangements he devised. All the children sang in the choir, and their regular attendance at church was probably owing as much to their love of music as it was to piety. As a young man, Ring had a baritone voice, but he usually sang bass because nobody else could. Even on the bitterest of winter nights they followed the snowplow to church to sing. Ring's choir deportment, when he was not singing, was calculated to keep his fellows amused. He circulated notes which rocked the tenor section with laughter, while he sat solemn and dignified, and filled the chant books with drawings and witticisms.

Ring had a good background in classical music, but his real interest was in popular songs, and he professed to be bored by symphonies and appalled by opera. He might have developed a really professional talent if he had not used his gift merely for his pleasure; but he liked to improvise, transpose, and arrange at random and was never subjected to a very rigid discipline in his musical education, which came to him all too easily. Music remained his greatest delight all his life. He taught himself to play several instruments merely for the fun of it.

For the Lardner children learning of all kinds was so mingled with play and fantasy that their early education came to them almost painlessly. Ring didn't go to school until he was twelve years old. Mrs. Lardner began to teach him when he was five, and he learned reading and writing from her, while his sister Lena assisted with his musical training. Mrs. Lardner, who had been a schoolteacher, had her father's erudition and passion for educating, and there was always a flurry of intellectual activity around her. The home provided greater opportunities for learning than the elementary schools of Niles, and it had an extraordinarily good library.

Mrs. Lardner was a writer of varied skills. She wrote and published two books, miscellanies of verse and prose, *Sparks from the Yule Log* and *This Spray of Western Pine*. She often contributed

19

to the famous column in the Chicago *Tribune,* "A Line o' Type or Two," conducted by Bert Leston Taylor; and in addition she performed a great many of the writing tasks the community of Niles required: anyone could come to her for a valedictory address, class poem, holiday oration, obituary, or an occasional essay, and she would oblige.

Her own books are attractive reflections of her personality. They are excessively sentimental, and in this respect they follow the taste of the time. It was a popular taste: some of the prose pieces were originally written for the Chicago *Tribune, Lippincott's Magazine,* and *The Wide-Awake Magazine.* The tone is religious and inspirational and impeccably moral. She loved best verses about her children; she also wrote a number of religious poems, and although a staunch Episcopalian, composed an adulatory poem to Pope Leo XIII. She celebrated religious faith and homely virtues, but there is an endearing touch of worldliness in an essay on "The Beautiful Emily Marshall" of Boston. Emily is praised for her nobility of spirit, but much of the piece is devoted to describing Emily's gowns. The books are illustrated with pictures of the Lardner children, in outlandish costumes improvised at home, of her birthplace in Catskill, New York, and numerous allegorical figures of doubtful aesthetic value. But they have the charm of vitality, of overflowing sentiment, and the allusions indicate that Mrs. Lardner had read widely.

One story might very well have amused Ring. It tells of a rustic couple who come to a parsonage to be married. "The bride went through her part of the service easily and without mistake. The faltering bridegroom changed 'thee endow' to 'thee and thou,' 'holy ordinance' to 'holy audience' (at which the 'holy audience' found it difficult to keep from giggling), and 'troth' to 'trough.'" One is reminded of Ring's ball player who says "proudly" for "probably" and "probation" for "prohibition." In some ways Ring's literary ancestry can be traced right to his own home.

Her wide reading and her writing ability were not Mrs. Lardner's only advantages as a teacher for her children. In temperament they resembled her, and she had a perfect understanding of their tastes, talents, humor, and sensibility. She was not a stern disciplinarian; she believed that all children were angels, completely good and innocent, and never to be punished—a very dangerous assumption of which she had the good fortune not to be disabused. Such a theory is workable only with unusually responsive children. There were probably episodes that might have disproved it, but they have not gone down in family history. On the whole it worked, and there seem to have been no flaws in the understanding between Mrs. Lardner and her three youngest children, at least while they remained under her tutelage.

She gave them a good background in English composition and literature. They read English poetry and the great novelists, their favorites being the Brontës and Dickens. Mrs. Lardner had told them about the Brontës' lives, and they played being the Brontë children at Haworth Parsonage, a game which in the Lardner home must have been quite a feat of imagination. The only hint of severity in their regimen was that Mrs. Lardner insisted that they read everything without skipping, and *Bleak House* proved a trial to Ring at the age of eight. So the children read it all aloud to each other.

When the children were ready for more advanced studies, a tutor was called in. Harry Mansfield, who tutored two generations of Niles children, came to teach them Latin, mathematics, and geography when Ring was ten. He was surprised at Ring's acquaintance with literature and a little put off by his vast knowledge of baseball, which was a frequent distraction from schoolwork. Ring was then a plump, somewhat abstracted boy who absorbed his lessons without the slightest visible effort. This gave him time for music, baseball, and mischief. To the children their tutor seemed almost as funny as their dancing master. At nine each morning they stood at the schoolroom window to watch for him, hoping he would be late or not come at all. They referred to him as "Beady" because of his thin, birdlike face and small eyes, and Ring somehow managed to write that name on the ceiling of the schoolroom, where it remained, ineradicable, for years.

Ring recalled these lessons years later, writing in character and in a dialect that he never learned in a schoolroom. He could write classic English as well as anyone, but this dialect had become his trademark as a popular writer:

. . . us 3 youngest members of the family was too fragile to mingle with the tough eggs from the West Side and the Dickereel. We had a private tutor that come to the house every morning at 9 and stayed till noon and on acct. of it taking him 2 and a ½ hrs. to get us to stop giggling, why they was only a ½ hr. left for work and this was generally always spent on penmanship which was his passion.

The rules of penmanship at that time provided that you had to lean your head over to the left, wind up like they was nobody on second base, and when you finely touched pen to paper, your head followed through from left to right so that when you come to the end of the line, your right ear laid flat on the desk.

These lessons were enhanced for the children by their tutor's habit of wiping his pens in his hair.

Not all of their early education took place in the home. In the summer of 1893, when Ring was eight, his parents took them to the World's Fair in Chicago, where they rented an apartment for several weeks. Mr. and Mrs. Lardner were interested in the cultural aspect of the Exposition and hoped that the children would absorb some of it. But to Ring and Anna the apartment was the most fascinating thing, and while the rest of the family went to the Fair, he and Anna stayed home and played games of their own devising. However, they left Chicago with a vivid impression of the White City, the gondolas on the canals, and the bloody waxworks; and they also knew who Little Egypt was.

Mr. Mansfield never detected any writing ability in Ring, but he found all the children good pupils and was pleased with them until it was time for them to enter high school. Then they had to take entrance examinations. Rousseau's theories of education as practiced by Mrs. Lardner seemed to have been forever discredited. All the children flunked.

However, matters were arranged. Mrs. Lardner did not intend that her children should suffer any disadvantages. Although the superintendent of the schools disapproved of the children's having been privately educated, he agreed to let them enter on probation, placing Ring and Anna in the ninth grade and Rex in the tenth. It turned out that they knew a good deal more than the curriculum required, and they got through high school quite easily. Ring scarcely had to exert himself to come through with honors. After a moment of panic at having to take examinations he enjoyed high school and entered into the life of the town as if he had always known it. The uncanny result of a sheltered and exclusive upbringing was a boy who was devoid of any exclusiveness. He got along as well with the tough eggs from the West Side and Dickereel as he did with the children of more distinguished families, and he was popular with both. His occasional fights with the tough boys were only a normal part of a small-town childhood. His reputation as a humorist was quickly established, and schoolwork was not so taxing that he did not find time for conviviality, sports, and singing.

Most of we boys [he wrote later] done our studying at a 10 x 5 table with six pockets in it, but when we come yawning to recitation the next day they was no way for the teacher to know whether we had spent the night trying to get Coleridge or the 14 ball.

One of the boys or gals would get up and read the first few stanzas followed by questions in regards to same.

TEACHER: Mr. Brown, what is an ancient mariner?

MR. BROWN: Why, let's see. It's a it's a kind of a old sailor.

TEACHER: And what is meant when it says he stoppeth one of three?

MR. BROWN: Well well it means it means he stopped a man. They was three men, and he stopped one of them, one of the three.

TEACHER: Mr. Starkweather, what is a loon?

MR. STARKWEATHER: It means somebody that is kind of crazy. (*Aside.*) Like a lot of teachers. (*Laughter from admirers of Mr. Starkweather.*)

TEACHER: Let's have quiet. Now, Miss Millard, explain the line eftsoons his hand dropt he.

MISS MILLARD: It means that pretty soon right away he dropped his hand.

MR. STARKWEATHER (*aside*): He didn't even have a pair.

Ring and Rex formed a singing quartet with Ed Wurz, a young man from Dickereel, a neighborhood where families of German descent lived, and Ray Starkweather, the wag of the English class, and they spent many evenings serenading Niles girls. ". . . They was hardly an evening passed when some gal's father did not feel himself called on to poke his head out his Fourth Street window and tell these same boys to shut up and go home for the sake of a leading character in the Bible." Whenever a gang of boys was caught at a prank or a serenade, it was Ring alone who got the blame for it. He was over six feet tall now, and could be easily identified by his height even in the dark.

In his junior year Ring played tackle on the high-school football team. Apparently it did not have a very brilliant season, although Ring was a far better player than his self-deprecatory account of his brief athletic career indicates:

. . . All I learned was that a man is a sucker to play at Notre Dame without a steel headgear. We was playing Carroll Hall again and the ground was covered with wet snow. We had to punt and I started down the field hoping I would not get there first as their punt catcher was a man named Hogan. Well I did not get there first

23

*or last neither one as I decided to stop on the way and lay down a
wile. This decision was reached immediately after receiving a special message from admirers on the side lines in the form of a stone
carefully wrapped up in wet snow. The message was intended for
my ear and came to the right address. For the rest of that fall I was
what you might term stone deaf on that side and I thought maybe
that was the reason I never heard our quarterback call my signal.
But the quarterback said that was not the reason.*

The football team in Ring's senior year was more successful and
defeated all its traditional rivals from nearby towns. When the
games were in Niles, Mrs. Lardner often invited both the local team
and the visiting team to dinner, and such occasions must have taxed
even her hospitality.

Among Ring's studies was German, and he mastered enough of
it to be able to tell "Razzle, a gullible bartender, that Ich war ein
und zwanzig Jahre alt." But the bartender at the Pike House, Niles's
leading hotel (electric lights and steam heat), winked at the obvious youth of the Lardner boys and served them liquor when they
were still some years below the legal age. In "Symptoms of Being
35" Ring wrote:

*But I guess it ain't only the loss of a few ebony ringlets that makes
me look senile. It seems like I was over estimated long before I
began to molt. For inst. I can recall when I was 16 and had a thatch
on my dome like a virtuoso and I used to pal around with a boy
who we will call Geo. Dougan because that was his name and Geo.
was going on 21. Well this was in Niles, Mich., in the days when
they sold 6–⅔ beer in vases and for $.20 you could get enough to
patrol 4th St. serenading true music lovers of the opposing sex. In
them hellcyon days 1 of the few things that was vs. the law was
selling it to minors and 2 or 3 of the retail mchts. around town was
pretty strick and time and time again I and Geo. would be out shopping and go in a store and order 2 vats and Dave or Punk or whoever it happened to be would set one up for me to knock over and
then give Geo. a wise cracking smile and ask him would he like a
bottle of white pop.
. . . Well Geo. would say "Aw come on Dave I am older than
him." But you couldn't fool Dave and the result was that we would
half to take our custom down to Pigeon's where everybody that had
a dime was the same age and the only minors was the boys that
tried to start a charge acct.*

24

I must hand it to Geo. for one thing. No matter how sore it made him to get turned down he never told them the truth about me.

Of course, whether or not Ring realized it at the time, it would have been impossible for any bartender in Niles not to recognize him and to know that he was under twenty-one. The laws in Niles were not very strictly observed.

Sometimes Ring was refused a drink for other reasons. One night he gathered a number of friends together and took them down to Casey's, where beer was a nickel. He had $5.00. He went in and laid it on the bar and said to Casey, "One hundred beers."

"Lardner," said Casey severely, "you're drunk."

Ring and Anna graduated from Niles High School in 1901, Rex having got out a year before and gone to the University of Michigan. Ring wrote the class poem, one of his earliest verses, with appropriate salutes to his classmates. It was so bad that one can suspect Ring of satirical intentions even at the age of sixteen. He ranked high in his class and was offered a scholarship to Olivet College, but he turned it down without having any particular idea of what he was going to do.

Until the year of his graduation his life had been easy and ample. He had never known any insecurity or deprivation, and neither he nor Rex had occasion to worry about careers. But by 1901 the Lardner fortunes had collapsed. Henry Lardner's eldest son William had gone to Duluth, Minnesota, to become a partner in a bank in which his father invested heavily. Its assets were partly in Western land mortgages that proved to be worthless, and the bank failed. Mr. Lardner assumed his share of the loss and paid off his creditors one hundred per cent, at the sacrifice of nearly all his property. The rest of his money was invested in a mining venture on a Canadian island in the Lake Superior region; that too was a failure, and the family's resources were almost exhausted.

A loss such as Henry Lardner Sr.'s was not unusual at that time. A great many comfortable and seemingly secure fortunes in the Midwest, based on land holdings that had been easily acquired decades before, were doomed after 1900 because of expansion and speculation. Land had always been considered a safe investment. Mr. Lardner was a sound and conservative businessman and he met his obligations honorably. His standing in the community was not impaired by his business reverses; he had already served two terms as city treasurer and was elected to that office again in 1907. But such men as he could not withstand the economic trend that wiped

25

out so many small fortunes and portended the end of a way of life that was based on uninflated land values. The Lardners probably did not see the loss of their wealth as part of a great change in American life. They no doubt accepted it as personal bad luck, but their own world was not altered. Money was only a means whereby they lived in a manner to which they had been accustomed by training and tradition. They did not question that tradition.

Nevertheless, for Ring and many others of his generation, nothing was going to be the same again. He did not feel the full impact of his family's financial loss at once; for the time being it meant only a drastically reduced but not unbearable standard of living. The real change came slowly; it was a profound one, and it involved the whole society in which Ring had grown up.

By the age of sixteen Ring had grown from a merry small boy to a tall, solemn, and shy youth with an inordinate passion for baseball. Ed Reulbach, a player for Notre Dame and later a star pitcher for the Chicago Cubs, recalls his first meeting with Ring at about this time:

"In 1901 or 1902 the baseball varsity of the University of Notre Dame came on the field for practice before a game. A big kid approached the trainer, Tom Holland, and requested the job of water carrier. Tom informed him we had one. The kid was crestfallen. His eyes were as big as the tops of two water pails. He walked away and sat down at the corner of the grandstand. There he sat all during the game with his overalls and farmer's sun bonnet on.

"After the game some friends of mine from Niles, Michigan (about 12 miles north of Notre Dame), requested me to come to Niles the next day, Sunday, and pitch for the Niles team. I said yes. Before the game they gave me a pair of overalls, boots and a sun bonnet, same as the kid had the day before. I went to the bench and sat down. Suddenly a tin-cup full of water was offered me. I glanced at the individual and almost fell off the bench—there was the same kid I saw at the Saturday game when he asked to be water boy. He sat next to me on the bench and offered me a cup of water every few minutes, until I finally told him that I did not need a bath, just a cup of water every other inning."

It was some years later that Reulbach met Ring again, but he recognized him easily.

"About 1908 or '09 the Chicago Cubs were on the train leaving Chicago and we started our famous poker game, composed of Tinker, Chance, Fullerton, Veeck, Evers and myself. Suddenly I heard some one say to Tinker, 'I will get you a glass of water.' The voice haunted me and I looked up, lo and behold, there was the same water boy from Niles and Notre Dame. He smiled and said, 'Do you remember me?' I said 'Yes—but I do not need a bath.' Later on after a game I went over and sat down with him and he said he was writing for a Chicago paper and had been assigned to our team. I introduced him to the players, but there was never a smile on his face. Evers said 'What's the matter with him, got cramps, can't laugh?'

"So Ring started around the bases on his career as a baseball reporter.

"We often tried to make Ring break into a full laugh, but all we developed was a faint smile. Sometimes he would sit at the window of the train and stare out for a long time, if you sat down beside him he would greet you but never say another word, unless you forced him to answer a question.

"Ring was a kindly fellow, modest, intelligent on the fine points of the game, always careful about writing something that might hurt the feelings of a player, and we responded by tipping him off to some inside deal and he was always appreciative.

"We were all fond of Ring, but we were all at a loss as to why he never laughed . . . If he had any faults, we liked him too much to notice them, he was one of us."

The summer after his graduation from high school Ring went to Chicago, where his friends the Jacks family now lived. "I must mention Niles, Michigan, again," he wrote later, "and I cannot promise that this is the last time. I am not exaggerating when I say that my family was only one of a great many born and raised there. One of the others was named Jacks, and the Jacks boys were virtually inseparable from the younger Lardners, so that when the Jackses moved to Chicago, the Asmuses, Kaisers, Wolfords, and Mantkes, who were employed by the Michigan Central, had a good laugh at the sight of men ranging in age from twelve to twenty frankly shedding tears at parting. As matters turned out, the Jackses, particularly the Jacks parents, ought to have done all the crying, while the Lardners gave their tribal cheer, for on visits to Chicago during the next ten years the Lardners' hotel was the Jacks domicile, and the rates per day or per week, American plan, were nothing."

Ring "accepted an office boy's portfolio" with the McCormick Harvester Company at $5.00 a week, but was fired after two weeks. He loafed two weeks more before he got a job as "combination

27

office boy and telephone girl" with Peabody, Houghteling and Company. (Mr. Houghteling, a prominent Episcopal layman, was a friend of Mrs. Lardner; she once dedicated a poem to him.) Two more weeks proved him unqualified for this position, and he left the Jacks' family pension and returned to Niles. There he found employment as a freight hustler for the Michigan Central at $1.00 per day. His heart was not in his work, and he was fired "for putting a box of cheese in the through Jackson car, when common sense should have told me that it ought to go to Battle Creek."

His father's decision that he and Rex should study engineering was purely arbitrary, and perhaps a little desperate, since neither of the boys showed any bent toward a profession. In 1902 they entered Armour Institute in Chicago, sharing a small room which they used only for sleeping.

It was a career that was probably unique in the annuals of Armour or any other institution of higher learning. In the first place I entered during the second wk. in January which nobody else had thought of doing before. The regular time for entering was October or February, but they must of thought I had been there right along or didn't know I was there yet, anyway I got in without no objection. I had been told at home that I was to study mechanical engineering and I can't think of no walk in life for which I had more of a natural bent unless it would be hostess at a roller rink.

They had rhetoric class three times a wk. and as I was the only one in class that could speak English I did not even half to ever study to keep up with my mates and this give me plenty of time to practice on the cornet and I feel like I owe my success with that instrument to my rhetoric course and dear old Armour.

Along in February I recd. a valentine from the dean asking me to call on him on a certain evening at eight, but I didn't want to get into entanglements with a married man and also we had tickets for that night to see Williams and Walker in "The Sons of Ham."

Came spring and examination. I passed in rhetoric with one of the highest marks in the class and figured that this give me a perfect record as it was the only study I was taking. But came another valentine from the dean containing a few words of farewell and congratulating me on having finished at Armour in faster time than any other student in his memory.

Mr. Lardner also received a message from the dean, and Ring's formal education was over. He and Rex had divided their time between theaters and saloons. Ring's favorite star was Bert Williams;

28

he went to see his shows over and over again and they had a tremendous influence on Ring's later songs and theatrical sketches.

Ring flunked every subject but rhetoric, which he found easy. The notebook he kept for this course outlines "The Forms of Discourse" in a strict, old-fashioned way that seems to have disappeared from modern progressive education. "Discourse has been divided by rhetoricians into four forms: description, narration, exposition, and argumentation. Description is that form of discourse which has to do with the portrayal of persons and things. It does not always describe things as they appear to the senses, but as they really are." There follow analyses of these forms which break them down to basic elements and define their uses. It is all lucid, dull, and absolutely incontrovertible, and the principles Ring outlined apply to everything he ever wrote. Ring's notebook could serve as an elementary guide for any writer. Another part of the notebook is an analysis of the structure of Shakespeare's comedies and tragedies. The instructor gave Ring a B on the notebook; it is hard to see why he did not get an A, since it is letter-perfect.

On returning to Niles, Ring "rested" for a year; there seems to have been nothing else for him to do. Then he took Civil Service examinations, which qualified him to be a postal clerk and mail carrier, and for another year he got jobs at odd times as a substitute postman. At this time Ring was better known for conviviality and horseplay than for any consuming ambition. His upbringing had not been conducive to practical decisions, and while he had many talents, there was none that could be readily applied to the problem of earning a living in Niles.

In 1904 he got a job as "book keeper" for the Niles Gas Company at $5.00 a week. The manager who hired him later recalled that he was not very good at the job. He was too softhearted to collect bills from the poorer customers, and the gas company's affairs did not command his attention. But he stayed nearly a year and a half and was raised to $8.00 a week.

During the late autumn of 1905, the Niles, Michigan, Gas Company was paying me eight dollars a week to read meters, make out bills, keep books, try to collect bad debts—and I never heard of a good one—handle all moneys, get new customers and mop the office floor at least once daily.

The making out of bills and the keeping of books came under the head of hard labor. The mopping was a kind of game; I used to see whether I could do it today faster than I had done it yesterday.

29

Trying to collect bad debts and get new customers was a set up; I have always been a person who could take no for an answer. Reading meters was the rub, because meters are usually in dark cellars where my favorite animal, the rat, is wont to dwell. When I entered a cellar and saw a rat reading the meter ahead of me, I accepted his reading and went on to the next house.

At the gas company he learned a trick which was a minor social advantage to him. Trinity Church and the Presbyterian Church next door were lighted by gas. Ring found that by tampering with a valve and blowing on a gas pipe in the Episcopal Church he could reduce the gas pressure in the Presbyterian Church. Having made this discovery, he waited until the Presbyterians were holding a midnight service on Christmas Eve, and then extinguished their lights. This was thought by his fellow-churchmen to be a commendable sign of sectarian zeal.

Niles was then a town of something over four thousand people and, with its sports and theatricals, a lively place. Ring was having a good time. He was a member of the American Minstrels, a group of about thirty young men who put on minstrel shows in the Opera House, and an accomplished end man. Niles was used to professional minstrel shows, and to vaudeville, musical comedies, and the road companies of New York and Chicago plays; at home or in nearby South Bend the residents could see Mrs. Fiske, Sothern and Marlowe, and any number of traveling musical shows. In addition Niles had a small theatrical tradition of its own. Jeppe and Fanny Delano, a vaudeville team famous on the back circuits, came from there; so did the once-renowned Peak Family Bellringers, and the Warner Trio of trick cyclists. The original road show of *Uncle Tom's Cabin*, owned by John Stowe, a nephew of Harriet Beecher Stowe, had its winter quarters in Niles and opened its season there, and every local child had seen Eliza crossing the ice pursued by a familiar and not very frightening pack of bloodhounds. Rival Uncle Tom shows sometimes featured Two Uncle Toms and Two Little Evas. The amateur talent was good, and the American Minstrels were able to put on fairly sophisticated productions, in which Ring took part.

Their masterpiece was a program consisting of a minstrel show—The Grand Spectacular First Part—and a two-act musical comedy called *Zanzibar*. Ring wrote the music and lyrics for the whole show—except the interpolated numbers—and played a comedy role and sang. The minstrel act shows the influence of Bert Williams, Ring's

30

idol, and some of the songs were from Williams and Walker shows. Ring sang "I'm a Jonah Man," from the current Williams show *In Dahomey*, and "I Could Never Love Like That." Other numbers were "A Soldier of Love Am I," "The Poo-Bah of Blackville Town," and "In the Valley of Kentucky"—the standard fare of minstrelsy at the time; and the first part ended with operatic airs by the company. Rex sang in the chorus, and Anna played the piano. Ed Wurz, one of the serenading high-school quartet, and George Dougan, Ring's thwarted drinking companion, were featured singers. In fact almost all of Ring's friends were engaged somehow in the show.

Zanzibar was a comedy that owed a good deal to the then popular *Sultan of Sulu* as well as to Bert Williams. But it had original if somewhat parochial touches of its own, for it was a satire on the Niles town council. Its argument is no more preposterous than those of most modern musical comedies, and it offered obvious possibilities for high-spirited burlesque:

The story opens just after the death of the Sultan of Zanzibar. His son and successor, Seyyid Barghas, has been educated in foreign countries and is expected home to take the throne. Shylock and Padlock, whose former homes were in Buchanan, Mich., appear as valets to two young New Yorkers. [The comic effect of "Buchanan" in Niles was somewhat akin to that of "Flatbush" in New York.] Shylock is mistaken for the young Sultan. He at once assumes the throne, but being better acquainted with American government, he changes his title to Mayor, appoints Padlock City Clerk and the members of his court aldermen. In the second act the real Sultan appears and adds complications to the plot. Shylock explains that he was merely keeping the throne warm for the Sultan, and all ends happily.

Needless to say, the first line after the opening chorus is " 'Tis twenty years since the young Sultan left Zanzibar. No doubt he's changed . . ."

The book is credited to Harry Schmidt, a very talented young man, but some unmistakable Lardner touches found their way into it. The cast of characters (e.g. Uddu, Prime Minister, afterwards chef) has a resemblance to Ring's later nonsense plays, and the nearly unbearable puns are characteristic of his wilder flights. They were funny in direct proportion to their power to make the listener wince. The gags and wisecracks, which were designed for a Niles audience, were probably contributed by various members of the cast; in a group effort like this it is hard to sort out individual talents. The humor is the standard local product of the day. But the songs were definitely Ring's and, derivative as they are, they are quite professional and very pleasant:

> *Ujji, the moon is shining up in the skies,*
> *And stars are winkin' at me from above;*
> *Come, babe, and let me look into your eyes,*
> *Oh, Ujji, my Afcan love!*

> *Love is the chief of earthly joys,*
> *The cause of earthly ills,*
> *Two people in one armchair*
> *And a saving of gas bills.*

And a chorus called "Tale of the Cow":

> *Come back to me, my own sweet load of hay,*
> *Come back and let me eat you.*
> *I'll show you how I'll treat you.*
> *Sweetheart, O Timothy, don't run away,*
> *Be my own true load of hay.*

The songs were the important part of the show; there were thirteen of them in a book of only eight pages, which was meant only as a pretext for music. Ring played the leading role of Shylock and sang, in the manner of Bert Williams:

> *In the Isle of Zanzibar, oh my, how fine!*
> *Riding on my tall giraffe, up and down the line.*
> *Coons all stand and watch me puff my 15-cent cigar,*
> *And life is just like Paradise, in the Isle of Zanzibar.*

Some of the lines, puns on the names of Niles people, got a rousing laugh from the audience, and Ring, tall, gaunt, and big-eyed, was irresistibly funny. Although it was written for a special small-town audience, *Zanzibar* was a cleverly conceived and expertly produced show. First presented April 14, 1903, it was repeated by popular demand and the American Minstrels made a modest profit on it. Ring's professional debut in the theater was a complete success.

Niles was solidly behind the American Minstrels, and more than sixty local merchants and businessmen took paid advertisements in the program. This was excellently designed and printed and, except for the advertisements, which have an agreeable small-town air about them, it resembles the program of any metropolitan theater of the time. The list of advertisers is virtually a business register of Niles in 1903: "Niles City Bank, capital—$35,000"; "Hotel 52, Best $1.00 House in Town"; "George McOmber's Bus and Hack Line, Meets All Trains"; "H. E. Price, Undertaker and Embalmer, Dealer in Pictures, Frames, etc."; "The Owl Lunch Room, Open All Night"; "August Miller, Horseshoeing and General Blacksmithing"; and John Harrod, Proprietor and caterer, announced, "After the show the members of the company and the public will be banqueted at the Metropolitan Hotel. A fine menu has been prepared at 25 cents per plate. You are invited. Weddings, receptions, banquets and parties served up to date." The text of *Zanzibar* was published in pamphlet form and took its place in the annals of Niles. Only Ring's music is lost, but it is still remembered by his contemporaries as being tuneful and expertly arranged. Everything about the enterprise seems to have been amusing, and in good taste. Provincial as it might have been, Niles was very up to date.

Ring's childhood and youth seem to have been as happy as security, comfort, and maternal solicitude could make them. The Lardner family had its vicissitudes and frustrations and antagonisms the same as any other, but they bore them with a difference. The difference lay in Mrs. Lardner's character and personality. She wanted the atmosphere of the home to be amiable and unruffled, and so it was. Beside learning and sensibility she had a firm will, and she also had a way of closing her eyes to things that were disturbing. The less agreeable aspects of family and town life were minimized, and the three youngest children probably saw nothing of them. Whatever disappointment Mrs. Lardner might have suffered from her older children, whatever misgivings she might have felt from the threat of poverty or any other social embarrassment—none of these impinged much on Ring's early years.

Mrs. Lardner had high spirits, but she also had a profound sense of the sadness of life. It showed in her disposition and in her poems, which are full of a mournful piety. It was a matter of temperament, but it was also encouraged by an age of sentimentality in which the display of emotion was considered to be the sign of a good heart. The children were affectionate and tenderhearted, and their sensibilities were fully exercised. If they could suddenly go into hysterical giggles, they could just as readily melt into tears, and they were easily touched by the smallest emblems of sorrow. Their own childhood griefs were minor, but that did not prevent their weeping over the misfortunes, real or imaginary, of others. They cried over stories,

33

poems, and pictures. Ring could never endure the spectacle of pain; the sight of a suffering kitten upset him, and human suffering was more than he could bear. He developed a defense against this emotional susceptibility at an early age. By the time he was sixteen his demeanor was so solemn, his pose so dead-pan, that he actually appeared tragic to those who did not know him. The silence and reserve that marked all his adult life were in part a counterbalance to his extreme sensibility, and he covered his revulsion against unkindness, brutality, and violence with a mask of imperturbability.

He was predisposed to melancholy, and he also had a taste for the macabre. After a young woman who was a friend of the family committed suicide in the river, Ring and Anna often went to peer at the place where she was supposed to have drowned, imagining that they might see her. Near their home there lived a demented little girl who danced about her yard with curious gestures. Ring and Anna used to go to stare at her in fascination and dismay. Ring always had an affinity for odd, slightly cracked people.

The sheltered, exclusive childhood held some perils. After Ring had grown up, he felt that excessive maternal devotion had its dangers, inducing precocity in some respects, in others delaying maturity. He himself was precocious and he was praised for it. This often leads to later insecurity; after he left home Ring was never as self-assured as he appeared to be. Anyone accustomed to the admiration and approval of a loving family is apt to find himself at a disadvantage without them; and Ring had been indulged and encouraged more than most children. With his brother and sister the bonds of affection and understanding were so strong that they could never be duplicated in the outside world; it seemed impossible that anyone could ever be so dear to them as they were to each other.

But temperament and upbringing combined to produce in Ring an outward ease of manner, wit, social grace, and an interest in people that made him popular; and the early cultivation of generosity and a rigid sense of honor made him beloved. If the very seclusion of his early years increased a sense of his own singularity, it in no way inhibited a gregarious social life. In fact it may even have strengthened his wish to belong to a circle less restricted than his family.

While he was in his teens, a shy, awkward, romantic boy, he went with a Jewish girl from Chicago whose family spent summers at a lake near Niles. The young people were quite serious for a time, but their families disapproved of this on religious grounds. It was the subject of many poor jokes among the townspeople; it was outland-

34

ish that a gentile should fall in love with a Jewish girl; and no doubt the Jewish family took the same view. Ring and the girl never became engaged, although they always remained friends.

There is an undercurrent of melancholy in the life of many small towns, the sadness of Spoon River and Winesburg, that is difficult to escape because one lives at such close quarters with it. Niles was no different from any other small town in this respect; the stories of its failures, unrequited loves, suicides and murders, frustration and decay would make another *Spoon River Anthology*. Ring was susceptible to that feeling of sadness in a way that few city-bred people ever are. This susceptibility probably increased his desire to leave his small town and enjoy greater freedom. But while he lived in Niles, it still lay below the surface, and his life there was on the whole pleasant. His first romance did not blight his youth; he was soon to fall far more deeply in love. Neither class distinctions nor parental injunctions kept him from enjoying the freedom of the town, but he surely had a chance to sense the limitations that hedged a boy of his class in a place like Niles. He was never to escape some of the attitudes they ingrained in him.

Meanwhile he knew everybody and did very much as he pleased. It was from this contact with the town that he heard the language which formed his style, the speech of the average Midwesterner. Baseball provided the scenes and characters for his first stories, but the language he already knew. It was the way Niles boys talked, playing ball and singing and hanging around saloons; and no one had ever quite written it down before.

CHAPTER TWO

Ring never thought of the gas office as a career, but he was
not doing anything about getting out of it. Then in the fall
of 1905 he became a newspaper reporter by accident.

My brother Rex [he wrote] was reporter for the Niles Daily Sun
and Niles correspondent for the Kalamazoo Gazette *and South
Bend, Indiana,* Tribune. *He wrote so well that the editor of the
South Bend* Times, *Mr. Edgar Stoll, coveted him. Mr. Stoll came to
Niles and discovered that Rex was on his vacation. His employer did
not know where to reach him—or why Mr. Stoll wanted to reach
him—but was sure Mr. Stoll could get the desired information from
me. Mr. Stoll sought me out and stated his errand, also inquiring
whether my brother was tied up to a contract. I said yes, which was
the truth. I asked how much salary he was willing to offer. He said
twelve dollars a week. Why?*

"Oh," I said, "I thought I might tackle the job myself."

"Have you ever done any newspaper work?"

*"Yes, indeed," I said. "I often help my brother." This was far from
the truth, but I was thinking of those rats.*

*The upshot was that I promised to report for duty in South Bend
the following Monday morning—or was it Tuesday? Other members
of my family pointed out that while twelve dollars was four dollars
more than eight dollars, transportation on the inter-urban would
amount to $2.40 a week and I would have to pay for bad lunches in
cheap restaurants instead of getting good lunches at home, free. But
I had given my word.*

This was the beginning of the kind of success story that Ring later came to despise. Nevertheless he lived it. From this time on his progress was fairly steady, with only minor setbacks. None of the trimmings of the conventional success story was lacking. At Ring's death his former boss in the gas office said that he had always urged Ring to take up journalism, which was untrue, and the publisher of the *Times* recalled that Ring was the worst cub reporter he ever saw, but he couldn't bear to fire him because everyone liked him so much. Such dreary clichés accompanied every phase of Ring's success, and he satirized them in stories and articles. As a matter of fact, he became a very good reporter in South Bend, and the *Times* never had a better baseball writer. For $12 a week it had a genius.

On his first assignments Ring showed a characteristic independence. He was sent to cover the wedding of a scion of the Studebaker automobile family, any of whose activities were major social functions in South Bend. He came back with exactly five lines of news, which is probably just what he thought it was worth. He was not fired, but was assigned to cover a musical show that night, a task for which he was better qualified than for a society wedding. But his standards were too high for the *Times*. Already an old hand at theatricals, Ring thought the show was terrible and panned it thoroughly. The author happened to be the owner of the theater and an advertiser; he complained bitterly, and Ring was put to work covering the state league baseball games.

"Altogether I had a lovely time on that paper," Ring said later to a newspaper reporter. "In the morning I covered the police stations and courts. Then I would drop over to the Circuit Court to get the divorce news. In the afternoon I went to the ball park. The press box was a little sewing table right out on the field and I had a grand time ducking foul balls. When fouls were few the players would come up and abuse me for not praising them enough in my stories. In the evenings I covered shows. Then I would go to the office to write the day's events."

For a small Midwestern city the *Times* was a sophisticated paper. Its coverage of national and international events was thorough and detailed, and the local news was lively. It gave more than adequate attention to sensational murders and sex crimes, and unlike its successors, it followed every case, from the crime to the conviction or acquittal of the suspect, in the most gratifying way. The language of journalism at that time was stilted and fancy, but in treating a really lurid case the paper was surprisingly frank and specific. Its political reporting was lengthy and forthright and bordered on libel.

One of the paper's specialties—and this was common to all Mid-western journals of any style—was an elegant running chronicle of the doings of European royalty. Apparently the democratic West had an insatiable thirst for it. Ring did not fail to observe this; he later wrote some fine satirical columns on society and visiting royalty, recalling, no doubt, just such fashionable accounts as the South Bend paper printed.

The Niles column in the *Times* had more of a small-town air. Ring was not officially the Niles correspondent, but it is impossible not to suspect that he had a hand in supplying the South Bend paper with news from his home town. The social activities of the Lardners and their closest friends were reported fully, and more news about the private lives of Niles people reached the *Times* than ever got into the Niles *Daily Sun*. Divorces and adulteries were covered and uncovered, and corespondents named. Every drunk who was arrested got his name in the paper. Evidently Niles residents had a way of staggering onto the Michigan Central tracks and getting killed by trains; and, as if in revenge, other Niles residents wrecked the trains. A local bum who called himself Sampson the Zulu, whose profession was sword juggling, was periodically pinched for public intoxication, and also managed to cut up himself and members of his audience while performing. It was gleefully reported that a Niles man cheated a Hoosier in a horse trade. Then Sampson the Zulu Strong Man reappeared in the news, having redeemed himself by quelling a riot in a saloon. Life ran high in Niles, and someone was having a very good time with this column. Of all the local pranksters Ring is the most likely suspect.

The South Bend team belonged to the Central League, which numbered among its eight clubs such athletes as Rube Marquand, Donie Bush, Dan Howley, Jack Hendricks, John Ganzel, Goat Anderson and Slow Joe Doyle. The president of the league appointed Ring official scorer at $1.00 a game, largely because the new *Tribune* sports reporter was even greener than Ring. The minor-league hitters loved to get base hits; it impressed the big-league scouts, and the players always wanted Ring to score every fly and foul as a hit. Ring, however, was scrupulously correct and aroused the wrath of a Grand Rapids player who thought he was not getting his due. In revenge he began to persecute Ring by throwing the ball at him. Dan Howley intercepted two of them and saved Ring from being injured; and finally the chief of police, who was a regular spectator at the games, warned the player off.

The Grand Rapids team—"Jawn Ganzel's pretenders," Ring called them—were South Bend's chief rivals in the league. Ring pleased the local fans by taunting Ganzel's team mercilessly, but Grand Rapids won the league pennant in 1906. The next season, when South Bend defeated Grand Rapids, Ring crowed over the losers in verse:

> Wait till the gong rings, Jawnie,
>   Up in dear Grand Rapids town;
> We'll send you sliding, Jawnie,
>   Down, down, down,
>
> Bring on your pitchers, Jawnie,
>   They all look like pie,
> Wait till you're tied with Dayton,
>   Bye and bye.

Ring also was a scout for the South Bend club. Even before he went to work for the *Times*, he and Rex had gone to Springbrook Park to see a game between the Cleveland Spiders and Bryan, Ohio, in the expectation of seeing Cy Young pitch for Cleveland. Instead the pitcher was a newcomer named Owen J. (Donie) Bush. Ring persuaded the owners of the South Bend team to hire Bush as a shortstop. Ring, expanding his scouting activities, got in touch with Comiskey and urged him to buy Bush for the White Sox, but Comiskey declined. Ring next tried Murphy of the Cubs, and then Huff, scout for the Boston Red Sox; but nobody needed a shortstop. Bush went into the draft, and Detroit got him for $750. Ring had spent $9.30 on telegrams and phone calls to no avail. But he was right about Bush, who became a valuable player, and eventually landed with the White Sox as manager. The Central League was a good training ground; many of its players were sold to the major leagues, four from South Bend while Ring was there—Bush, Moffitt, Connors, and Anderson.

Although the *Times* was in many respects a metropolitan daily, its sports page was strictly small-town and it featured a kind of yokel humor which came naturally to Ring. The fans wanted morale builders for their own team. Ring was writing for a zealous home-town audience, and he tickled it by running down the rival teams of the league and egging on the local boys. The Evansville team, known as the "Evas," and Terre Haute, called the "Cheroots," were favorite targets, and South Bend gloated whenever they were defeated. Early in the season of 1906, Ring wrote an account of a South Bend victory over Evansville; there was no by-line, but it is not hard to tell when Ring started writing baseball for the *Times*:

Manager James E. Ryan of the Evansville base ball club was in Chicago Wednesday. Manager James did not make the trip to the Windy City for pleasure, nor was he called to the bedside of a sick relative. James Diogenes went to Chicago in search of a man; not an honest man, or he would have chosen some other destination, but just a plain man who can bat, run bases and play the infield. Ryan was unlucky in choosing this particular day for his journey, for there was an exhibition at Springbrook Park which he would not have missed for a .422 batting average. The aforesaid exhibition was given by a youth named Nye, who was stationed throughout most of the afternoon on the nigh side of second base. It is a fact, although he may deny it, that Nye is a descendant of Bill Nye, and the doctrine of heredity receives a big boost when it is known that the hero of this tale is a humorist of the first water.

The game at Springbrook Park resulted in a 6 to 4 victory for the locals, but this is a fact of small importance, as it could not have resulted in any other way. The hero attracted the attention of the fans in the first inning. After Fleming had been snuffed, William Anderson swung his stick against one of Wacker's tropical slants and the sphere whizzed through the air toward Nye. The Evansville wonder tried to check its mad career by kneeling on it and crushing it to the damp earth, but failed utterly, and William applied the brake at second base. J. B. Connors found a vacant spot in right field and dropped the ball there, William reaching third. Richardson hit Wacker's southwestern curve into Fremer's hands and Connors was doubled before he could get back. There was nothing marketable produced until Nye's half of the second scene, when Manager Grant ordered his trusties to give the visitors their handicap. Watson, appearing for the first time in the Evansville right field, was first up. He stayed until Moffitt hurled three missiles across the plate and then retired to the friendly bench. Lillian Sager elevated a fly to the right. R. V. Troutman glided to the south, balanced to the northeast and waited for the descent. When the ball finally reached the tall one's hands it had turned into a 16 pound shot and was too heavy for Richard to hold. Young Fremer biffed to the left, advancing Lillian to second. "Nig" Fuller, who was left in charge of the Evas during Ryan's absence, hammered a line to center, scoring Sager and sending Fremer to third. "Nig" sped to the halfway house on the first pitch and a pair of runs counted when Wacker's hit fell safe behind second. Nye was madly cheered when he advanced to the plate, and he fulfilled expectations by fouling out.

The jargon is that of the sports page, but the irony is Ring's own. This, one of Ring's earliest baseball stories, has in it the characteristics of his later great stories: instead of writing a stringy, inning-by-inning account he composed his story around a personality or a single dramatic play, and then put into it all the pace and color of a particular game; and he included a few good-humored digs at the players, who never seemed to mind. Although he plumped for the home team, they didn't escape his irony. At first he called them the "prides," then later the "delights," and he aimed a good deal of personal banter at them. Writing a story every day about a baseball game in a minor league could have been a tiresome task; some of the games were very dull, but Ring managed to bring something fresh to each one. "The league leaders had bagged a brace of tallies in the 2nd and 4th, and hits off Bliss were as few and far between as Sarah Bernhardt's appearances in Berrien Springs." (Ring often used Berrien Springs, a town north of Niles, as the symbol of the nadir of almost everything.)

Winter in the Central League was a baseball writer's despair; there was almost nothing to write about, but Ring managed to keep the league on the sports page nearly every day and in the spring of 1907 he took a swing around all the cities that had teams, as far as Wheeling, West Virginia, and wrote some heavily padded articles which had more personal reminiscence than baseball dope in them. He reported the off-season activities of the players, the sales and trades. When Buck Weaver, who played on the Terre Haute team, was sold to Little Rock, he wrote: "Since the cold weather set in Weaver has been keeping in shape by acting as a life-saving line at a Terre Haute skating rink. He is twenty-seven years old, 8 feet and 6 inches high, and weighs 25 pounds. By all those who have been up there to see it is said that his hair is light and curly. But it was not because his hair was curly that Smith was willing to let him go. The chief reason was that he is trying to build up a substantial ball team every member of which can be plainly seen with the naked eye." And when a new umpire was hired, he wrote:

"Ollie Chill is from Indianapolis and has had several brands of pickles named after him. He obtained his preliminary training throwing pianos into the second-story windows of flat buildings. He was lately occupied as a star in the pugilistic world and fought under the name of Jack Ryan. During his experience as an umpire, he has been known to pick small disgruntled ball players up by the Adam's apple and toss them to the roof of the grandstand. (Springfield papers please copy.)" When a player named Freese ran afoul of Umpire Chill, Ring worked the gag for all it was worth.

It was a kind of broad, hayseed humor that appealed to South Bend, and Ring, being of the locality, could supply it. But he had already begun to turn the clichés of sports writing to ironical purposes, to use the argot sardonically, and—especially when there was little to write about—to introduce pure nonsense into his stories. His writing for the *Times* was youthful, natural, and playful; he was not writing down to his readers, and he was certainly not consciously forging a style. He loved baseball with the same passion as the most enthusiastic of the fans, and he was having fun writing about it.

In the summer of 1907, Ring met Miss Ellis Abbott of Goshen, Indiana, whom he courted for four years and married in 1911. Ellis first saw Ring at a picnic in Niles, where she was visiting friends. He had stuck a cylinder of cardboard on his head like a stovepipe hat and looked utterly grotesque. She liked him at once and he liked her. She was exceptionally pretty, intelligent, and lively, and she appreciated Ring's wit. During the next four years while Ring was making his way as a sports writer, traveling with ball clubs or living in Chicago, and Ellis was finishing college and teaching school, they managed to meet often in Chicago, Niles, or Goshen, and when they were apart, they corresponded at great length, usually in verse. Ring seems to have been intent on marrying her almost from the time they met.

The autumn of 1907 Ring and Rex arranged their vacation so that they could go to Chicago for the World Series between the Cubs and the Detroit Tigers. They stayed with the Jacks family. Phil Jacks was a friend of Hugh Fullerton, who was one of Chicago's top sports writers. The year before, the Series between the Cubs and the White Sox had resulted in a complete upset. The Cubs had won 116 games out of 152; the Sox were known as the "Hitless Wonders," and nobody thought they had a chance, except Fullerton. Before the Series, Fullerton predicted the Sox victory, giving the order of the games and the scores. The incredulous editors of the *Tribune* refused to print the story. The Series came out exactly as Fullerton had foreseen, and the *Tribune* printed the story post-mortem with apologies. Nevertheless Fullerton quit and went to the *Examiner,* where he was working when Phil Jacks introduced Ring to him.

The hour was noon [Ring wrote], *the next day; the place, the Examiner office. Phil took me there, made the introduction and tact-*

fully left us, the great Hugh S. Fullerton and the—well, my name is signed to this memoir.

"There was a little chicken lived down on the farm." Thus Hughey opened on me.

I gazed at him in bewilderment.

"The next line," he went on, "is 'Do you think another drink would do us any harm?'"

I was going to be careful. "I can't have another, because I haven't had one."

"Don't you ever have one?" asked Hughey.

"No," I said.

"Phil," said Hughey sadly, "gave me to understand on the phone last night that you wanted to get a job in the sporting department of some paper here."

"I do," said I, "but I guess there isn't much chance."

"I'm afraid not," said Hughey. "There's one opening in town that might lead into a baseball job, but 'Do you think another drink would do us any harm?'"

My slow-motion Michigan mind began to function. "Is there any place we could get one—I mean in this neighborhood?"

"If there weren't, why would we have our office in this neighborhood?"

Though my favorite beverage was and is a bourbon highball, I wanted to show off on this occasion, and I took several big shots in small glasses, straight and neat. I do not recommend this as a regular diet—the intermissions are too brief—but I think it worked to my advantage in this crisis, for it did away with my innate reticence, and on the ride from the Examiner office to the White Sox park I discussed, intelligently and in regular baseball idiom, which is the same in a Class B league as in the majors, the merits and defects of the Central League's more promising athletes.

Fullerton introduced Ring to Charles Comiskey, who was by this time sorry that he had not snapped up Donie Bush when Ring had tipped him off. He commended Ring's perspicacity in spotting Bush.

Ring sat with Fullerton in the press box when the 1907 Series opened at the White Sox ball park at Thirty-ninth and Wentworth. Fullerton had already predicted the outcome of this series too, with his usual accuracy. When Ty Cobb came to bat, with Mordecai Brown pitching and runners on first and second, Ring and Fullerton watched carefully to see how the Cubs' star pitcher would treat the Tigers' star hitter. The press box expected Cobb to bunt on the first

44

pitch, but Ring said he wouldn't get a chance to. The pitch was high and out of Cobb's reach. Ring said to Fullerton that Brown was only trying to find out what the runners on base would do. They started out on the pitch, thereby tipping off Brown that Cobb had planned to bunt. "You're ready for this league," Fullerton told Ring. Ring followed the teams to Detroit and stuck close to Fullerton, who finally introduced him to Duke Hutchinson, sports editor of the Chicago *Inter-Ocean*, saying, "Here's your man. I give him to you."

"With reluctance?" Hutchinson asked.

"With more baseball sense than you've got," said Fullerton.

Ring was hired. "Have you figured out how you're going to live in Chicago on eighteen-fifty a week?" Hutchinson asked Ring.

"I can get on the wagon."

"You can get on the wagon," Duke said, "but nobody can work for us and stay there."

The South Bend *Times*, where Ring had been boy-of-all-work for fifteen dollars, was reluctant to see him go. So was the Lardner family; he had been away from home before, but this time it looked like a permanent departure. Mrs. Lardner arranged for Ring to live and board with a respectable Episcopalian lady of her acquaintance on the North Side, to be sure that he had three meals a day and that the fellow-lodgers were members in good standing of the Brotherhood of St. Andrew. This arrangement cost more than Ring was making and no doubt involved more surveillance than he wanted, and he found himself a room at the corner of North State Street and Goethe and ate in cheap restaurants. One of his more memorable meals was in the company of his boss, Duke Hutchinson, and Frank Gotch, the wrestling champion, whose phenomenal appetite nearly killed Ring's own.

Ring at twenty-two was six feet two inches tall, slightly stoop-shouldered, since he was very conscious of his height, with a swarthy complexion, black hair, and immense dark eyes that held a look of perpetual wonder. He was gaunt and solemn, and Fullerton said he looked like Rameses II with his wrappings off. Bud Fisher called him a wet owl, and the White Sox players later referred to him affectionately as "Old Owl Eyes." On his first assignment for the *Inter-Ocean*, a football game between Chicago and the Carlisle Indians, Ring was standing on the field with Glenn Warner, the Indians' coach, when he heard some girls talking behind him. One of them said, indicating Ring, "He must have some white blood in him."

After the football season was over, Ring was assigned to cover

45

indoor sports—swimming, basketball, wrestling and gymnastics—in which he never had much interest. He was particularly bored by track meets, which he had to cover in Chicago and out of town. One in Milwaukee he found particularly tiresome. "The outcome depended on the pole vault, and every time anybody got into the mood to vault, the pole broke, or the crossbar fell off, or the guy changed his mind. Meanwhile, of course, my sporting editor, Duke Hutchinson, or his assistant, Dick Tobin, would be murdering me via Morse code because the result was undecided and they were without a lead." On this occasion Ring wired back in exasperation, "Waiting for someone to pole vault."

As for wrestling, "Save when Frank Gotch was performing—and he was beaten once after a lot of rehearsals—the games generally went by service. I remember covering a match in Chicago one night, and after the first fall, I dropped in next door and had a drink with the referee. He asked me how I was betting, and I told him I had five dollars on the Turk. 'Hedge and get on the Pole if you can,' he advised. 'It's his turn.' So I hedged and got on the Pole, and the Pole won, though the Turk was one fall up."

Ring got his first by-line on the *Inter-Ocean*. The stories that carried it—on the West Side Y.M.C.A. basketball games, city bowling leagues, or off-season football stories on the Big Ten conference—were straight reporting, accurate and well written, but a long way from the untrammeled hilarity of his South Bend baseball stories. Ring was serving a modest apprenticeship and there was not much individuality in his writing at this time. He was getting his training in metropolitan journalism and at the same time he was making friends with such prominent sports writers as Fullerton, Charlie Dryden, Walter Eckersall, and Hugh E. Keogh, "Hek" of the *Tribune's* "In the Wake of the News." Dryden, the Mark Twain of baseball, according to Fullerton, was a great humorist and was popular with both fans and players. Ring literally sat at his feet; the Cub players called him "Charlie's hat" because he went everywhere with Dryden, who probably had a greater influence on his early career than any other writer. Dryden's baseball stories were comic masterpieces, and he was held in the same affection and respect by players and managers as Ring was to be later. Keogh had a wide and loyal following as a columnist and he created the style of the "Wake," which Ring later was to follow when he succeeded Keogh. Eckersall, whom Ring had admired as an athlete, became one of his closest friends. In spite of Ring's assumed air of sophistication, he was a

46

real tenderfoot, and Eckersall helped him over many of his beginner's difficulties.

Rex Lardner had followed Ring to South Bend the year before, and now he joined the staff of the *Inter-Ocean*. Ring and Rex were never separated for long; almost every time Ring moved, he found a job for Rex. Rex was easygoing, affable, and scholarly; he was less given to worry and responsibility than Ring. Ring took on the burden of worrying for everyone, and for all but a few years of his life Rex stayed close to him.

When Fullerton left the *Examiner* in 1908, he recommended Ring for a job there, and Ring started to work February 1 at twenty-five dollars a week. Ring was one of the domestics on the sports desk and had to wrestle with triangular five-line heads and take stories off the wire. One night when he first worked there, the entire sports staff went to Milwaukee to the Ketchel-Papke fight, leaving Ring alone to attend to the wire. Ring later wrote that the result was something like this:

The boys were called to the center of the ring and received instructions from William Hale Thompson, Ernest Byfield, Percy Hammond, Charles Richter, the Spring Valley thunderbolt tore in as if he had never heard another crowd made the trip as guests of William Lydon on his yacht the Lydonia Steve cut loose with a left uppercut that nearly makes certain another meeting between the Battling Nelson and Packy McFarland were also introduced. Steve slipped as he was about to. Seven special trains but the majority thought the round was even it was Papke's round.

In despair, Ring sought out Eckersall after he had left the office. Eckersall consoled him and they sat up and drank. ("I was the only person he knew who shared his horror of going to bed," Ring wrote. "Night after night, until it was almost the next night, we would sit and just talk; nearly always on one subject—football.") Eckie took Ring home and put him to bed; then he got Harvey Woodruff, sports editor of the *Tribune*, to assure Ring of a job in case Ring got fired from the *Examiner*. Ring was worried and restless and got up and took a taxi ride, although he had very little money with him. He rode around watching the fare on the meter increase. Finally he had the driver take him to the *Examiner*, where his boss paid the fare and forgave him.

Ring got a by-line on the *Examiner*, but it wasn't his own. His pseudonym was James Clarkson. A James Clarkson had been writing for the paper for years, and very few people knew that he was never the same man for more than a year at a time. In March, Ring was assigned to travel with the White Sox on their spring tour and to cover the season if he made good. Ring's idols that year were the Cubs. He had to switch his allegiance overnight from Frank Chance to Fielder Jones.

Ring paid his poker debts and set out on one of the rainiest spring seasons in baseball history, after sending his itinerary to Ellis, with copies to his family:

THE ROUTE OF RINGLETS
Published as a Guide for his genial Correspondents
(With Carbon Copies)

> *On March 18, young Lardner'll go*
> *Down to the city of N. O.*
> *New Orleans is the city's name,*
> *A city not unknown to fame.*
> *From March 19 to March 22,*
> *He'll tarry in New Orleans, Lou.*
> *And then, on March the 23,*
> *He'll sojourn in Montgomery.*
> *From this cute town in Alabam*
> *He'll travel up to Birmingham*
> *And there remain the 24th*
> *Before proceeding farther north*
> *To Nashville up in Tennessee,*
> *And there the next three days he'll be.*
> *On 28 and 29,*
> *In burg of Evansville so fine,*
> *On 30th and 31st*
> *In Terre Haute, of towns the worst.*
> *And on fair April's first two days,*
> *In Indianapolis he stays;*
> *In Cincinnati 4 and 5,*
> *And then, my goodness sakes alive,*
> *To old South Bend he'll go once more,*
> *Renew acquaintance made of yore,*
> *The sixth day of the month he'll spend*
> *Among the ruins of old South Bend.*
> *The next three days in cute Champaign,*
> *Eleventh, twelfth in cute Fort Wayne,*
> *And then back to Chicago go,*
> *To stay about ten days or so.*

48

And through this era, do not fail
As follows to address his mail:
"For Mr. Lardner, in the care
Of the White Sox," and b'lieve me, fair
Young correspondents, large and small,
I'm glad to hear from one and all.

Ring joined the White Sox in New Orleans, where he found Doc White, the left-handed pitcher, Ed Walsh, the spitball expert, and Jiggs Donahue sitting on a bed in White's room singing. At a table sat Frank Isbell, Billy Sullivan, Pat Dougherty, Nick Altrock and Frank Smith, playing a ten-cent-limit poker game. He felt at home.

Fielder Jones, the manager of the team, came in and put Ring through his initiation:

"I suppose," Fielder supposed, "you're just another pest. You'll probably ask a lot of childish questions."

"Undoubtedly," I said.

"Well, go ahead and shoot, and let's get it over. But first, where do you come from? I mean, where were you born?"

"Niles, Michigan."

"Have you been working in Chicago long?"

"Three and a half months."

"How old are you?"

"Twenty-three. White. Grandparents on both sides lived to be seventy."

"You're fresh, too, aren't you? What I'm trying to get at is, what qualifies you to write about baseball? You couldn't learn it in Niles. I've been through the place. There aren't enough men there to make up a ball club."

"We were shy one, so we used a woman in center field."

"Niles wit! But I'm serious. Why do metropolitan newspapers hire inexperienced kids like you to report big league baseball?"

"I think it's my turn to ask a childish question. Were you a manager the first year you broke into the big league?"

"All right, Niles. We'll get along if you don't pester me too much. The boys that drive me crazy are the ones who want to know who's going to pitch tomorrow. If I can't tell them and they guess wrong, they're sore."

"I promise never to bother you with a question like that. My paper will be satisfied if I guess right three-quarters of the time. So I'll just stick to Walsh."

Ring's autobiographical reminiscences are on the whole quite accurate when checked with the testimony of his contemporaries and intimates. But this particular case may be open to doubt, and it is possible that Ring was casting too fond a backward glance at the young man who was just breaking in as a big-league baseball reporter. Shy and reticent as he was, he probably did not beard the manager of the first team to which he was assigned with such breezy repartee as he set down here. Fielder Jones was not easily approachable; he was, according to Fullerton, withdrawn and given to worrying. Nevertheless he and Ring got on well from the start and became fast friends.

Jones had cause for worry that season. The Sox had trained on the West Coast and were in good shape when they left, but on the long ride to New Orleans they lost some of their condition. In New Orleans it rained two days out of three, one of their games was called, and another was played in a shower that ended in a deluge. The evening of the third day the team boarded a train for Montgomery, where two games were scheduled. But when they awoke at 7 A.M. the next day, they found themselves stalled in the gloomiest spot in Alabama, Bay Minette, drenched in a downpour of rain, with flood waters rising. The storm had washed out a trestle bridge ahead, and a freight train had plunged into the river. One member of its crew had survived to warn the train that carried the White Sox; otherwise it is doubtful that they would ever have got back to Chicago. Nick Altrock, after only a short time in Bay Minette, regretted the survival of the trainman who had saved their lives.

A diner was to have been attached to the train somewhere north of the washed-out bridge, but now famine descended on the players with agonizing pain, accustomed as they were to regular meals. The train was a mile from the town, at best an unlikely source of nourishment for hungry athletes. Ring wrote later:

. . . *A delegation, headed by Jacob Atz, donned raincoats, for it was still pouring, and set out for the village. A colored boy was sitting on the station's plaza. There was no roof, but he apparently enjoyed the novelty of having his clothes and body washed. "Oh, you pic," cried Mr. Atz, "where can we-all find something to eat?"*

The answer to this was just a broad grin.

"Is there a hotel here?" asked George Davis.

"Da," vouchsafed the pickaninny, and pointed to a shack a block

or so off that appeared to be on the point of floating away on the rapidly rising sea.

The athletes were too hungry to mind further drenching, so they set out. They preferred the sure ruination of their clothes and the possible catching of colds to the risk of death by starvation. Everybody's name was mud when the gang reached that "hotel." Just as the boys mounted the steps, the door fell in of its own accord, assuring them a welcome.

The combination clerk-proprietor-bell-hop-porter-baggageman-steward-headwaiter, reclining behind the stove in a chair that couldn't seem to do anything but recline, didn't seem at all surprised by the entrance, either of the door or the ball players. That there was a reason why he should be astonished was revealed when Doc White, looking at the register, found that the last previous guest had written his name two years before.

The "landlord" had a wife and a daughter. The family had eaten breakfast, so that meal was over. But, after half an hour's forceful argument, in which Messrs. Atz and Donahue were leading orators, the female part of the establishment was persuaded to cook everything in the house and to set the table. This took until 11 o'clock, because the ladies were nervous and kept dropping things until every plate, cup and saucer was demolished. When the near-meal was ready, those of the athletes whose wives were not on the trip consumed things ravenously. The faithful husbands put fried eggs, lettuce and bread into their pockets and started back to the car. Those wives were put on a liquid diet that day, for there wasn't a chance of keeping anything dry on the long journey from the "hotel" to the Pullman.

Everyone was back on the car by 1 o'clock and the conductor returned and announced that the bridge was almost ready. Jiggs Donahue found a pint of "medicine" among his belongings and thereupon became the most popular man on the team and remained so for about two minutes, when the bottle was empty.

In a corner all alone sat Fielder Jones. He was thinking about the lost hours of practice and the stiffening muscles of the men. Several players went up to speak to him, but his answers to all their overtures were of the unprintable kind. Two hours after the conductor's words of hope, a thing they called a test engine was sent over the repaired bridge. The engine went right on through the repairs into the creek and the Casey Jones and his fireman were killed instantly. News of this was brought back to the car and some real gratitude that our train hadn't done the testing was felt.

51

That uneasy, awkward last sentence seems shockingly callous; it was one of Ring's rare lapses of taste. But the feigned indifference to the death of the trainmen is significant; Ring was probably appalled.

The chief concern of the newspaper correspondents was to get some copy to the Chicago papers. They wrote their stories and went to the telegraph operator, who said he couldn't send collect messages from strangers and he couldn't send such long messages anyway. All the Chicago papers got identical telegrams saying, "Stalled at Bay Minette. See map. Bridge washed out. Everybody well. May be here week." In the Pullman car the spirits of the team hit bottom, and even when Doc White and Jake Atz, who was always merry, passed the whole night singing an improvised song about the glories of Washington, D.C., a city not favored by ball players, they failed to dispel the gloom. The following morning a train with a diner pulled up behind the immobilized White Sox, who rushed to it only to be told that they would have to wait until the second sitting. This delayed their train two hours more, and by the time the bridge was finally repaired and the team reached Montgomery it was too late to play the second scheduled game. "Jimmy Ryan [the manager], who had had time to get over his disappointment, came down to the station to laugh at us. The Sox stayed in their car and went through to the next stop, Birmingham."

The bad weather continued, and the Sox missed half their spring training dates. At best ball players had a lot of traveling time on their hands and were liable to get Pullman fever; on the 1908 trip the Sox got unusually restless and bored. Ring had become popular with the players at once. In spite of his shyness he soon entered into the rowdy fun with which the team passed its time. He was an invaluable morale builder for the team, with his dead-pan clowning, jokes, impromptu verses and parodies of songs. He and Doc White interrupted their game of pitch with outrageous minstrel routines which were so terrible that they kept the Sox in an uproar: "Can you tell me, Mister Lardner, why the young lady who waited on us at lunch resembles dark brown sugar?" "No, Mister White, I cannot tell you why the young lady who waited on us at lunch resembles dark brown sugar. Can you tell us, Mister White, why she resembles dark brown sugar?" "Because she is so sweet and unrefined."

The Sox's favorite pastime was poker. Ring seldom played, because he had found it possible to lose more than he could afford to even at the ten-cent limit imposed by Fielder Jones. But he was one of the most expert kibitzers the game ever knew. He liked to look on at the games, especially when Jake Atz and Frank Smith joined forces to fleece some innocent outsider who had the bad judgment to butt in.

After lunch the P.G. was started and among the participants were Nick Altrock, one of the champion hard-luck players, Jakey Atz and Frank Smith, who always managed to keep things livened up. Nick was losing as usual. After running second in a rather large pot, he jumped up, remarked that he was going to get a drink—of water— and left the table. A spectator, aged about 22, had been behind Nick's seat and as soon as the pitcher vacated, he took his place without an invitation and asked for some checks. Messrs. Atz and Smith glanced at each other understandingly and he was given a stack. Almost before the first deal, Nick returned but got the wink from Jake and Smithie and said nothing.

The two comedians were bound to get even with the "fresh guy" for taking Nick's seat. Smithie was at Jake's left and the stranger just ahead of Mr. Atz on the deal. What they did to the "recruit" was awful. If a pot wasn't opened when it came Mr. Atz's turn, he broke it whether he had 'em or not. And Mr. Smith promptly raised him. The others dropped out, except the buttinksy, and if he had something to draw to, he usually stayed. As soon as his checks were in, Atz raised it again and Smithie raised back. If the stranger still hung on, Jake came back with another tilt and so it went until the uninvited guest was driven out before the draw. Then, of course, the pair had it their own way.

Both of them usually stood pat. They bet a few times and then one of them said: "What have you got?" and the other said: "A straight." Then he would show his hand to his pal and to no one else, and the latter would say: "That beats me," and both hands would be thrown into the deck. Two or three times the stranger remarked that he would like to see the openers, but Jakey informed him the game had a special rule that made that unnecessary when there was a stayer. This special rule was made up in Jake's mind at the time and no one disputed it.

If the young man really did have something, it was quite the same. The others raised and raised until they frightened him out and finally he gave up in despair. Whereupon, Nick resumed his seat and did some more losing. After the combat, the proceeds were used to help pay for the evening meal in the dining car.

On that trip Ring fell in with a ball player who unwittingly had an influence on Ring's later writing career.

The Sox had a regular infielder named Jack Gibbs, his home was in Brooklyn and his wife's name was Myrtle. He had been graduated from college—cum laude—at the age of four, and everybody on the club knew that he could neither read nor write.

When I say that his name was Gibbs, his home was in Brooklyn, and that he was an infielder and his wife's name was Myrtle, I am not telling the truth. But when I say that he could neither read nor write, I don't mean maybe. Give him a sheet of paper with "Jack Gibbs" and "George Washington" written or printed thereon, and he could not tell one from the other. When a new contract needed his signature, he was Madame X.

He suspected that the other players and the veteran scribes were aware of his idiosyncrasy; nevertheless, he persisted in trying to convince them that they were wrong. He would buy a paper and go through it column by column, page by page. He would insist on seeing the bill of fare in hotels or diners, and after a long and careful study, order steak and baked potatoes, or ham and eggs or both.

Well, I don't claim to have brightened many a corner, but I certainly was a godsend to Jack Gibbs. Being new, I could not, he thought, have learned his secret. Therefore, I was the only one in the crowd who could be of real service to him. When we were traveling and he was tired of steak or ham and eggs, he would maneuver to sit with me in the dining car, knowing that I habitually read menus aloud from top to bottom. It was also my custom, he discovered, to turn to the baseball page in a paper and read that aloud just as I did the menu. So he breakfasted with me as often as he could. All this part of our relationship came after Nashville, where . . . my spare time job began. . . .

Anyway, my first order of business when I got to a town was to rent a typewriter, for portables had not been invented—had they?—in 1908. And so it happened that Jack Gibbs heard me clicking away in my room at Nashville, and was struck by a great idea.

"Hello, Eva," he said, entering without the formality of a rap at the door. "I was wondering if you would do me a favor. It ain't really a favor. It's a kind of joke."

To the rest of the ball players I was always Niles or Lard. But Jack Gibbs had christened me Eva, and perhaps that is what made me feel so close to him.

"You see," he went on, "I just got a letter from the old woman, the missus. I thought it would be a kind of joke if she got the answer back on a typewriter. She would think I wrote it and wouldn't know

54

what the hell. Would you mind writing me an answer on the type-writer, and I'll send it to her just like I wrote it myself."

"Sure, Jack," I agreed. "But you'll have to tell me what to say."

"Well, let's see. Well, I better read her letter over again first. Or suppose you read it, Eva. Then you'll know what she wants. And you may as well read it out loud."

My recollection is that the old woman's letter was short and busi-nesslike. It said, in effect: "How can you expect me to meet you in Chicago unless you send me some money? I don't intend to make the trip out there on a freight, and I don't want to get my feet all blisters walking."

Jack was no good at dictation. Neither am I—a failing I had for-gotten about.

"Well, I guess you better tell her where we are first. No. Start out this way: 'Dear Myrt.' Then tell her she knows damn well I don't get no pay till the last of April, and nothing then because I already drawed ahead. Tell her to borrow off Edith von Driska, and she can pay her back the first of May. Tell her I never felt better in my life and looks like I will have a great year, if they's nothing to worry me like worrying about money. Tell her the weather's been great, just like summer, only them two days it rained in Birmingham. It rained a couple of days in Montgomery and a week in New Orleans. My old souper feels great. Detroit is the club we got to beat—them and Cleveland and St. Louis, and maybe the New York club. Oh, you know what to tell her. You know what they like to hear."

Perhaps I didn't tell her all that they like to hear; perhaps my newborn loyalty to the South prevented my mentioning the rainy days in Montgomery, Birmingham and New Orleans. But I think I made her understand.

"Now, what's the address?" I inquired.

"Mrs. Jack Gibbs, 1235 Sterling Place, Brooklyn, New York," said my boss.

"Sterling with an e or an i?"

"Oh, that don't make no difference. But I'm much obliged, Eva. She'll be tickled to death."

I handed him the finished product, ready for stamping and mail-ing. He looked intently at the front of the envelope.

"Are you sure you put 'Brooklyn'?" he said.

It is generally believed that Jack Gibbs was really one of the Sox pitchers. Ring, of course, never had any such boring habit as reading menus or newspapers aloud; he did it as a special kindness to the ball player. Presumably, the pitcher's wife got regular news from her husband that season, thanks to Ring; and the pitcher ate well, although this new-found well-being wrought no improvement in his game. In 1907 he had won twenty-two games and lost seventeen; in 1908 he won sixteen and lost seventeen. But Ring got a glimpse into the domestic life of a ball player, one of several whose traits can be found in the character of Jack Keefe, of *You Know Me Al*.

Ring had a quiet way of inspiring confidence in the players he traveled with and wrote about. He was sympathetic, he listened, and he observed. The players read the newspaper accounts of the games the way an actor reads reviews, and they were eager for praise. Ring could deliver some fairly withering insults in his stories, but the players never seemed to mind. He knew what their real sensitive spots were, and he never hurt their feelings. They liked him and trusted him and talked to him. The uncanny accuracy of his eye and ear was only a part of his capacity for absorbing experience; another important part was the way he had of making people talk to him.

Ring spent the rest of the season traveling with the White Sox, a job that he liked, though it had the serious drawback of taking him away from Chicago frequently so that his chances of visiting Ellis in Goshen or Niles were few. He kept up a lively correspondence in verse, which, although it was playful, showed a persistent undercurrent of uncertainty on his part. He was really very serious about Ellis. When she returned from Smith for the summer vacation of 1908, he wrote:

> *What, Rabbits have come home to roost?*
> *Is this what you would tell us?*
> *A full-fledged senior now is she,*
> *But still heart-whole and fancy free,*
> *This girl entitled Ellis?*
>
> *Why no, she brought her trunk back home,*
> *Its each and every part,*
> *Then what was it she left behind?*
> *Her fertile brain, her brilliant mind?*
> *No, just her Goshen heart.*
>
> *Far East of here she left her heart;*
> *Is that what you would tell us?*
> *Ah, rather had she left her shoes,*
> *Her powder rag, the gum she chews,*
> *This most forgetful Ellis.*

> *What will she do without her heart?*
> *Why that no one can tell us,*
> *And least of all young Ringlets tall,*
> *Why, no, he cannot tell at all,*
> *So peeved is he and jealous.*
>
> *We've lived full twenty years and more*
> *And nothing e'er befell us*
> *That stung so much as this same news*
> *That she her Goshen heart did lose;*
> *Is't true? Come, tell us, Ellis.*

Later that summer he wrote from Detroit, where the White Sox were playing, a letter which indicates that he had received a rebuff, or pretended to have received one. It was a long and doleful piece in a mock-tragic vein, which began:

> *Dear Rabbit—*
>
> *Now seek I an explanation*
> *Of those words which closed your missive,*
> *Rather, almost closed your missive,*
> *For some sentences did follow*
> *Which were more intelligible.*
> *I would know what you did wish to*
> *Make me understand by saying*
> *That I might, to my cute drama,*
> *Write a sequel and might name it:*
> *"Hope Gonne." Did you wish to tell me*
> *In those words that Hope is really*
> *Lost to me? Or were you jesting? . . .*
>
> *Answer quickly, generously,*
> *That this fall may be a season*
> *Fraught with something else than sorrow,*
> *Something else than ghastly horror,*
> *Fraught with Hope, not Gonne, but present.*

Ellis's reply must have been reassuring; Ring wrote her again before she returned to school in the fall:

> *Dear Rabbit—*
>
> *Cheered in spirit by your missive cute and kind,*
> *And by the picture which accomp'nied it,*

I'll try my best to beat you, with this great piece of my mind,
In your race to see your mater, Mrs. Smit'.
But one thing now disturbs me, 'tis a most undoubted fact,
And it casts a cloud of sorrow o'er my joy;
It's farther from Chicago to Northampton than it is
From Goshen to Chicago, Illinois. . . .

I certainly was glad to get the picture you enclosed,
The next one you have taken, send it on,
I sit and gaze upon the little likenesses of you,
They're better far than nothing when you're gone.
Oh, usually, I hate to see the passing of the fall,
But now I long for Christmas and its toys.
It's farther from Chicago to Northampton than it is
From Goshen to Chicago, Illinois.

That fall there was an opening on the Chicago *Tribune;* Charlie Dryden left to retire to the South, and he recommended Ring for the job.

In October of that year Ring's sister Anna was married to Richard G. Tobin, Ring's colleague on the *Inter-Ocean,* with Ring as best man. The Tobins took an apartment on the South Side in Chicago, and Ring went to live with them. He reported the news to Ellis:

Dear Rabbit—

Here is a bunch of short ones:

GOING SOUTH
The winter blasts are coming on, and Ringlets is a'cold,
No more he stands them as he did before he grew so old.
To warmer climes he must depart, to sunny, sunny South,
Before icicles close his eyes and freeze up tight his mouth.
Next Monday, he will Southward fly, 'bout sixty blocks or more,
To stay at least until the winter's worstest chills are o'er.
Therefore, when you do write him next, his address it will be
At 468 West Forty-eighth Street, care of R.G.T.,
In care of Mr. R. G. Tobin, his young sister's spouse;
Oh, yes, please write him after this at Mr. Tobin's house.

THE TRIBUNE
And what is it, pray, this Chicago Tribune?
Which Ringlets is going to work on so soon?
'Tis a paper that's gen'rally rated the best
In North, or in South, or in East, or in West.

And better than best it is quite sure to be
When it has the services of Bright Young Me.
I can't just yet tell you what I am to write,
Whether checkers or football or racing or fight.
The chances are, Rabbit, I'll write not a thing
Till winter has yielded once more to the spring.
There'll be headlines, of course, and I'll send you a sheet
With each little task marked in pencil so neat;
I know this will please you, my innocent dove,
In return for which act, as a proof of your love
Devoted and grand, you must send out to me
Whatever that day's lesson happens to be,
And thus I can judge which is working the harder,
Miss Ellis, the Rabbit, or Ringlets, the Larder.

Now the Lardners, Rex, Ring and Anna, were together again in the Tobin apartment, and they amused themselves very much as they always had. Doc White, the Sox pitcher, came there, and he and Ring wrote a baseball song called "Ain't It A Wonderful Game?" and a "Southern Croon," called "Little Puff of Smoke, Goodnight." Arthur Jacks, who was now working in a bank in Chicago, organized a vocal quartet, and Ring wrote their arrangements for them. They all made frequent visits to the family in Niles, and during vacations Ring visited Goshen.

The Chicago *Tribune* was the largest paper in a city that had half a dozen or more dailies of wide circulation—the *News, Herald, American, Examiner, Inter-Ocean, Evening Post* and *Evening Mail.* Chicago's phenomenal growth as the railroad center, the grain and meat market of the nation, the merchandise center and clearing-house of the Midwest required an enormous press, and every paper tried to outdo its competitors in news coverage and features. A newspaperman could not have found a better time or place in which to sell his talents. The *Tribune* was far ahead of other papers in the number and variety of its special departments, and its sporting section was nearly as large as the *Inter-Ocean's.* During the time Ring worked for it—from 1908 to 1919 except for two and a half years with other papers—its staff comprised much of the best journalistic talent in the country, along with some of the best-known names. On the sport page Ring's by-line appeared along with those of Walter Eckersall, who had been Chicago's star quarterback; Jim Corbett, the heavyweight champion; and Battling Nelson, who covered boxing and wrestling.

The editor and manager was the formidable James Keeley, who had the reputation of being a martinet but who was friendly to Ring and appreciated his value. The city editor was Walter Howey, the prototype of the editor in Hecht and MacArthur's *Front Page,* with an unmatched flair for dramatizing news. The news staff included, at one time or another, Lucian Cary, later a writer of popular fiction; Marquis James, who became a historian; James O'Donnell Bennett, Floyd Gibbons, and Edward J. Doherty. The news coverage, local, national, and foreign, was extensive, and Chicago society got a flattering amount of space.

Its features, daily and Sunday, included the column "A Line o' Type or Two," conducted by Bert Leston Taylor, filled with contributions from readers as well as B.L.T.'s own rather arch and pedantic humor. It had a distinctly literary flavor and was deliberately highbrow if not downright snobbish. Burton Rascoe, who was a jack-of-all-trades on the *Tribune* before he became literary editor, wrote that B.L.T. often ran Latin verses in his column although he could not understand a word of them and had to have them translated to be sure they were not obscene. Ring took delight in making fun of the "Line." H. E. Keogh, "Hek," conducted "In the Wake of the News" on the sport page before Ring took it over; he had a large and devoted following.

Finley Peter Dunne wrote a Mr. Dooley article for the Sunday edition; Richard Henry Little, who had become famous as a foreign correspondent, contributed articles to its feature section; Percy Hammond was the local dramatic critic, and Burns Mantle contributed a weekly letter on the New York stage. Harriet Monroe, founder of *Poetry* magazine, wrote a column on art; in one piece she solemnly discussed the influence of the comic strips on American artists. The literary section, which until the advent of Burton Rascoe was edited by Robert Burns Peattie, dealt seriously with Harold Bell Wright, Eleanor H. Porter (*Pollyanna*), Gene Stratton Porter (*Freckles*), and Robert W. Chambers, ignoring both the younger writers who were making a spectacular appearance in the Midwest and the important European writers. Rascoe changed its policy when he became editor, roasted the best-sellers thoroughly, and, following the example of H. L. Mencken, brought to the attention of his readers new writers of genuine literary stature. Rascoe was one of Ring's early admirers. Nearly all of Ring's newspaper colleagues admired him, but not all of them foresaw his lasting importance.

Lillian Russell wrote beauty hints, and Laura Jean Libbey gave advice to the lovelorn. Joseph Medill Patterson, supervisor of the Sunday edition, had a genius for inventing popular features. He introduced such departments as "Bright Sayings of the Children," and "My Most Embarrassing Moment," which reached such a level of flatness that it could be suspected that they were written in the office with satirical intent. Patterson also transformed the funny papers into the comic strips. "Old Doc Yak," whose humor depended on the novelty of automobiles, was obviously doomed, and such strips as this gave way to "The Gumps," by Sid Smith, "Gasoline Alley," by Frank King, and "Little Orphan Annie," by Harold Gray, in which characters and story were emphasized, with Patterson directing the continuity. Of the topical cartoonists, John T. McCutcheon was already classic in Ring's day; and Ring's friend Clare Briggs drew cartoons for the sports pages.

Many of these features are stale and worn now, but in Ring's early days as a newspaperman they were fresh and original. The *Tribune* was a market for almost any kind of journalistic ability and, as it proved, a fertile ground for real literary talent. It provided Ring with exactly the opportunity he needed, first as a reporter, then as a humorist.

After a winter indoors on his new *Tribune* job Ring was assigned to travel with Frank Chance's Cubs on their spring tour. The Cubs were a great championship team, having won the Series of 1907 and 1908, and its personnel comprised some of the most colorful characters in baseball. Besides its famous double-play combination—Tinker, Evers, and Chance—there were Ed Reulbach, Mordecai ("Three-Finger") Brown, Jack Pfeister, and Orval Overall, pitchers; Harry Steinfeldt and Heinie Zimmerman, third basemen and bitter rivals; Frank Schulte, Jimmy Sheckard and Artie Hofman in the outfield. They were a salty, humorous, quarrelsome, opinionated, and loquacious bunch, and for two seasons they provided Ring with hilarious copy and high entertainment. Ring started out with them from Chicago in March.

This year the weather favored the ball teams and the Cubs played a full schedule. Ring organized a quartet composed of himself, James Crusinberry, a Chicago sports writer, Artie Hofman, and Jimmy Sheckard. They sang so well that a vaudeville agent, overhearing them in the back room of a saloon, wanted to sign them up. When Artie Hofman had a sore throat and could not sing, Ring gloomily reported it to the fans in a column of personal notes which he sent in with his regular stories. These were like the stories he had written in South Bend. "Incidentally, Jimmy Archer proved he had been slandered by those who said he did not have the head to make a major league catcher. Mr. Sybert, who pitched the last four innings for the Nashers, found this part of Jimmy's anatomy with a fast ball in the ninth inning. All doubts as to Archer's possession of a top piece were dispelled by the sound of collision between it and the ball." He liked to twit the players with a good-natured sarcasm, and Heinie Zimmerman, who always had a store of alibis, was one of his favorite subjects: "Zimmerman said the sun was shining in his eyes in left field and that was the cause of his misjudging two flies. It certainly was not shining anywhere else in Fort Wayne."

Like the White Sox, the Cubs passed much of their time in Pullmans playing poker. Their games were a good deal more serious than the Sox's, who were an easygoing gang compared to Frank Chance's high-strung team. The games started with a quarter limit, which soon soared to a dollar, until Chance brought it down again. Ring resisted the temptation to play poker by an act of will, as if he were going on the wagon. Early in the season he was broke, and he swore off. Tinker had had a streak of bad luck, and Johnny Evers had also gone sour on the game. The three of them signed a pledge, with reluctance and no doubt some mental reservations, and Ring kept it through the season, supported by Evers, who stood staunchly by the oath. Only Tinker was suspected of a lapse.

The Cubs played for high stakes and excitement, with Mordecai Brown and Orval Overall setting the pace. Chance played too, but only when there was money on the board instead of chips. Poker was a factor in Chance's judgment of his team; he was said to have formed an opinion of a new player's ability on the field only after he had played poker with him. If this is true, several promising recruits threw away their professional careers at cards. Heinie Zimmerman, however, was an exception. A terror on the field, the implacable scourge of umpires, he was a sadly reduced figure in a poker game, if he ever managed to get into one. The Cub sharks liked to play only with their peers; to avoid friction, Chance divided the poker players into seniors, juniors, sophomores, and freshmen. But Zimmerman once slipped into a game with the upperclassmen and pulled a boner which Ring made famous in the annals of poker:

As seldom happened, Frank Schulte was playing. Frank much preferred to sit and look out of the window, but he was coaxed in this day. He opened the pot on two small pairs, eights and fives, and Zimmerman raised him with a pat straight. The others dropped out and Frank saw the raise. Heinie refused to draw, of course, and Frank took one card. It was an eight spot. Knowing Zimmie would wager, he checked the bet to him.

Heinie bet half a dollar and Frank raised him a half. Back came Heinie with another raise, and Frank returned the compliment. Heinie then raised again and Schulte thought he must have something, so he called. Zimmie showed down his straight and Frank hauled in the money. Everybody jumped on poor Heinie and asked him what kind of betting he called that. He certainly did not improve his reputation a bit by answering:

"I thought he might have a flush or something."

Away from the poker table, Zimmerman was by no means so meek. He was jealous of his standing as a third baseman, and his particular rival was Harry Steinfeldt. Ring is said to have introduced Zimmerman to a friend as Harry Steinfeldt. "I'm glad to meet you, Mr. Steinfeldt," the friend said. "I think you're the greatest third baseman in the world," whereupon Zimmerman hauled off and hit him.

Frank Schulte was one of the Cubs' best hitters and outfielders and one of their most engaging personalities. He was a quiet and modest man, but a natural wit, coolheaded, intelligent, and independent. He had other interests besides baseball, and being occupied with them, he did not immediately join the Cubs for the spring tour of 1909. Chance wired him to join the team at Louisville, but he did not show up, and at Terre Haute he was still missing. Ring reported: "The train will pass through Jack Hendricks' town [Indianapolis] and Chance is hoping Frank Schulte at least will come down to the depot and wave at us as we go by." Schulte joined the team in his own good time. He did not take baseball too seriously. At the opening game of the season, when the Cubs were rained out, he said, in Frank Chance's hearing, "I hope it stays this way all season." Chance was so angry he nearly suspended him.

Schulte averaged ten or twelve home runs in a season, a champion performance in the days of the dead ball, and he was also a good outfielder. He was quite unassuming about his own ability and never claimed half the publicity he could have had; and he was mercilessly sarcastic about players who did. While he was sometimes aloof and preferred to sit by himself, he could also be very loquacious and outspoken. In his monologues he referred to himself in the third person, as "Frank" or "Schulte," and he named his dog Schulte. His nickname "Wildfire" he acquired from having named his favorite trotting horse "Wildfire" after Lillian Russell's famous play. Lillian Russell, who was to marry Alex Moore, a Pittsburgh sports writer, was a great admirer of Schulte, as he was of her. One time when both she and the Cubs were playing in Vicksburg, she gave a party at which Schulte, a natural comedian, shared the dramatic honors with her. Like Ring, Schulte was a dead-pan humorist and delivered his most telling thrusts without a smile. Like Ring, too, he hated any kind of bombast or pretense and could deflate it with stinging sarcasm. He and Ring liked each other, and he lent himself to Ring's friendly raillery with a droll air of feigned bitterness.

Schulte sometimes amused the Cubs with impersonations, the most notable being one of an auctioneer auctioning off horses in Skaneateles, with an upper New York State twang. But his specialty was monologues, some of which Ring wrote down with marvelous accuracy:

Never an ardent devotee of poker, never much of a reader of magazines nor novels and never a singer with enough confidence in himself to give the entire public the pleasure of hearing his voice, Frank M. Schulte, alias "Schlitz," alias "Bud," alias "Wildfire," alias "Schultz," is thrown on his own resources when the Chicago Cubs are journeying hither and thither. And they certainly are some resources. Mr. Schulte careth not whether he has an audience. When he is in the mood to talk, he will talk and talk loud, and he isn't particular whom he criticizes nor who is listening to his monologue. Mr. Schulte is at his best after the Cubs have lost a hard game. He likes to win, all right, but he doesn't see why defeats should be the cause of tears or post-mortems.

Aboard the sleeper after one of these defeats, for which two or three slips were responsible, there are gathered various little knots of athletes telling each other how it happened, how the beating could have been averted, and mourning and wailing over the unkindness of fate. In his seat all alone, or with a willing listener, sits Mr. Schulte.

"The boys seem to forget there'll be a game tomorrow to play. They act as if it was the last one they were ever going to get into. The pennant is lost now, and there isn't a chance for us to cop that World's Series money. Let's hope the White Sox don't finish first. A city series with them will net the boys enough to worry through the winter on. They didn't trim us today because they played better ball. Oh, no! There never was a day when any team played better

64

ball than these ten-time champion Cublets. Rigler called everything wrong and the luck was dead against us.

"You saw Jack Murray hit that one out of the ball yard. Well, that's no credit to Murray. He had his eyes shut or was talking to some one back in the grandstand when he let that one loose. He didn't meet the ball square. Oh, no! The ball hit his little fingernail and bounded over the fence. Besides, Edward (that's Reulbach) intended to get him to bite on his fall-away. No, Edward didn't want to get the ball over the plate. No, Edward was blinded by the dust and he pitched within Murray's reach when he really thought he was throwing to catch Doyle off second.

"Yes, and Schulte played that ball wrong, too. He ought to have left the park and stood on the approach to the elevated station. Then, you know there was a high wind blowing. Otherwise, that would have been a foul fly that Archer could have eaten up. But the pennant's gone now and we might as well arrange a barnstorming tour of some kind."

Then, if feeling particularly good, Mr. Schulte breaks into song so softly that he can't be heard more than two seats away.

"Kidney stew and fried pig's feet—

"That's the grub I love to eat.

"I guess there's no use of our going to Boston at all, the way luck's breaking against us and with all the umpires in the league ordered to give us the worst of it, we haven't a chance to take a game even from the Doves.

"Heard a lot of talk about the champagne wine,

"But a great big stein of beer for mine.

"Here, boy, bring up that pair of cobs. Born and bred in the Rockies, mealy nose and black points, sound as a dollar, catch him round the collar, hit him with a bootjack and—sold for 40 dollars to that gentleman right over there.

"Never mind, boys. There'll be another game tomorrow and Schulte will play right field and bat third. Three cheers for the national pastime!"

This is followed by a few moments of staring out the window into the dark night. Then, if he is in one of his rare poetic moods:

> "This baseball season soon will end,
>   Or else I am a liar;
> Then I'll go back to Syracuse
>   And drive my old Wildfire.

> Against the fastest horses there
> My old Wildfire will go
> And show his heels to all of them
> Upon the pure white snow.
> How glad I am the time is nigh
> When reins and whip I'll wield;
> 'Tis easier to drive a horse
> Than run around right field.

"I wish it would hurry up and be midnight, so I could go to bed."

Schulte was a natural rhymester and his habit of breaking into impromptu verse inspired Ring later to make him a "contributor" to his baseball reports. When the Cubs were rained out in St. Louis and there was nothing to write about, Ring published Schulte's masterpiece:

Frank Schulte hasn't had a chance to make any hits since Sunday and he said that he could hold back his masterpiece no longer. He explained that it was inspired by witnessing Robert Hilliard's production of "A Fool There Was" at Cincinnati the other night. Someone told Frank that Kipling's poem already had been parodied, but that didn't make any difference to him, as he figured that his effort would be superior to any that might have been made in the past. It is called "The Vumpire," and here it is:

> A fool there was and he had his say,
> Even as you and I.
> To a Klem, or a Kane, or a Hank O'Day,
> Or any other old judge of the play,
> And he said it all in a nasty way,
> Even as you and I.
>
> O, the howls we waste and the growls we waste—
> And the hit that inspired the howl
> Belongs to the umps who called it wrong,
> O, yes, I know that he called it wrong,
> For he said that the ball was foul.
>
> A fool there was and he got the can,
> Even as you and I.
> "You're out of the game," said the umpire man,
> And amid the jeers of each hostile fan,
> Down to the clubhouse the fool he ran
> Even as you and I.

66

But it isn't the shame of quitting the game
That makes it so hard to bear,
It's the thought of the hit that you'll never get,
The thought of the hit that you would have got
If the umpire had called it fair.

Schulte also appears as himself in one of Ring's early baseball short stories, "Sick 'Em," in which he is faithfully characterized as sardonic and wise:

Well, I went up to Schulte during battin' practice and ast him what was the matter with Fogarty.

"Nothin' at all," says Frank. "I don't figure they can be nothin' the matter with a guy that draws his pay for sittin' on the bench and lookin' beautiful. I wish I could get away with it."

"Don't he work none?" I ast.

"He pitches to the batters about oncet in two weeks," says Frank. "He does it when Hank can get his consent. And on the days when he pitches to us I manage to hide somewheres till the practice is over."

"Why?" I ast.

"'Cause," says Frank, "I figure that, barrin' accidents, I got many happy years before me. If he was to happen to put all his stuff on the ball oncet and hit me in the head, they wouldn't be nobody to drive the mules on my peach ranch in Georgia."

"He's got a lot of stuff, then?" I says.

"Yes," says Frank; "and he's savin' it up for somethin'—maybe to give it away for a birthday present. All he does now is sit and wait for everybody to look away from him, so's he can pull out his pocket mirror and enjoy himself."

Of course in the story Schulte's dope on the pitcher turns out to be correct. Between 1911 when he set down Schulte's Pullman monologue and 1914, when he wrote "Sick 'Em," Ring had begun to write ball players' dialogue exactly as they spoke it; in both pieces the picture of Schulte is authentic.

Ed Reulbach was often the butt of Schulte's sarcasm because he was given to antics of which Schulte, self-effacing as he was on the diamond, disapproved. Reulbach was always in impeccable physical condition, which was a reproach to the more convivial players. Schulte drank a good deal more beer than strict training rules allowed, and Chance was always having to tell him to stop.

After Schulte's days in the major league were over, he went to live on the West Coast. When he ran into hard times and ill-health, it was Ring who helped him out. Ring saw him in San Francisco years later and was reminded of an incident which showed that Schulte did not take baseball or his own batting average too seriously:

And here is another incident . . . it reflects on Frank Schulte's honor, but I am going to tell it without asking his permission. Mordecai Brown, who lots of us always thought was just as good a pitcher as Matty or anybody else, was finally sold down the river from Chicago to Cincinnati.

The Cubs went down there to play and Brownie pitched against them. As I recall it, he wasn't having a very good day, but that doesn't make any difference. What matters is that the pennant race was all settled. Well, Frank liked his base hits, but he also liked Brownie (as who didn't?).

Brownie got in the hole, three and two, on Frank and the next ball cut the heart of the plate.

"Gosh!" said Frank afterwards. "It was hard not to take a crack at that one!"

Schulte, Hofman, Sheckard, and Lew Richie were the high-spirited clowns of the team. Richie led them in playing kindergarten games; the ball players danced around singing "Happy Is the Miller When the Wheel Goes Round," "Ring-Around-a-Rosie," and "London Bridge Is Falling Down." Schulte and Sheckard appointed themselves guardians of the rookies and tried to teach them table manners. Schulte was an expert in conveying vast quantities of food from his plate to his mouth using only a knife. When he saw a young busher eating mashed potatoes with a knife, he said, "What are you doing, pal, learning to plaster?" Sheckard, familiarly known as the Squirrel, got hold of a chess set, and he and Ring, to fill in one of those endless voids that must have occurred frequently in Pullman travels, covered a board with chessmen and began to ponder over a lengthy and profoundly serious match. It seemed that hours passed before a move was attempted. Sheckard would cautiously hover over a piece, as if contemplating a move. Ring would exclaim, "Hah!" whereupon Sheckard would withdraw quickly to think it over for half an hour. The spectators, puzzled at first, began to break down in a slow, mounting access of laughter as it dawned on them that neither of the rapt, unsmiling players knew one thing about chess. Ring continued to play this kind of chess later with his newspaper friend in Chicago, Joe Farrell, who was a great comic

68

and played the game to the hilt. It reached its peak, and probably its end, in a five-hour match in the Press Club, during which neither Ring nor Farrell spoke a word except to say, "Hah!" whenever a move was attempted and remained quite oblivious to the dozen or so newspapermen who were nearly paralyzed with laughter.

Sheckard must have been very popular to have got away with the pranks he pulled on his teammates. He looked serious and innocent, but he was full of surprises. On one occasion, after three straight nights on sleepers and three defeats behind them, the Cubs went to bed worn out and dispirited. Sheckard, however, was fresh and wide awake. He retired reluctantly after the rest of the team had gone to sleep, but soon he emitted a groan which brought the trainer to his berth. Sheckard only wanted to ask him if he thought pork chops had any effect on the batting eye. After everyone had been roused and gone back to bed again, Sheckard got up and woke Reulbach, Schulte, Moran, and Overall in turn, asking each of them if he knew where Artie Hofman's berth was. Having located it, circumspectly avoiding Frank Chance's berth, he awoke Hofman and told him that the train had just passed a coal warehouse which he, Sheckard, owned, and it was too bad he had not found Hofman in time to point it out to him.

Ring never wanted to go to bed early, he was too tall to sleep comfortably in a Pullman berth, and it was probably on these trips that he first experienced the insomnia from which he was to suffer all his life. So he witnessed all of Sheckard's nocturnal antics. Joe Tinker once made the mistake, Ring reported, of giving Sheckard a stick of gum the night before a game in Philadelphia. The following day Sheckard got three hits, which his superstitious nature—greatly exaggerated for the amusement of his friends—attributed to the stick of gum. The next night he got another stick of gum from Tinker, and the next day got two hits. He was in his best form until Tinker ran out of gum, whereupon Sheckard took to waking him nightly to provide him with a lucky talisman, until the charm had lost its power and Tinker a lot of sleep. The Cubs either had a fairly primitive sense of humor or a great deal of tolerance, but in any case their travels were lively.

After everyone had gone to bed, Ring often sat up in the smoking room of the Pullman talking to the porter, who was always called George. George in a car full of ball players had an unenviable life. The men began bawling orders to him as soon as they boarded the train; some wanted their berths made up early, others wanted card tables, all wanted to be called at different times. When all the confused instructions had been carried out and the team was bedded down, George had twenty pairs of shoes to shine and his task lasted far into the early hours. Then in the morning he was greeted with twenty complaints before he finally collected twenty dimes or at best quarters for his labors. He always found in Ring a sympathetic listener.

Richie, Hofman, and Sheckard, inspired by Ring, spun out elaborate yarns about their mythical pasts, especially if there were any wide-eyed young players present. They would recall the days when they played in the Ark League, of which Noah was president and King Solomon the manager; or the Nile Valley League, where the games ran to over six hundred innings and Rameses climbed a pyramid to catch a high fly. A little of this usually sufficed to drive the listeners into a poker game, but Ring joined in and later wrote it down in his "Pullman Pastimes" columns. He was the best audience the Cubs ever had.

One of Ring's companions in his travels with ball clubs was Hugh Fullerton. On one trip Fullerton and Ring missed three trains and spent a day and a night in Buffalo following a gang of Great Lakes sailors from one saloon to another, listening to a song they were singing, an Erie Canal chanty that had captured Ring's alert ear. Ring and Fullerton recorded fifty verses of it before they wearily resumed their travels.

They often went to the telegraph office in the evening to file their stories. One night Fullerton took both their stories to the telegraph operator. Later he and Ring met him in a bar and asked him if the stories had been sent. The operator said that Fullerton's had gone off at once, but that it had taken him an hour to correct the spelling of Ring's. Ring had written his dispatch in the character of a semi-literate ball player, and it must have been singularly flat by the time it reached his paper. There are many instances of Ring's stories being corrected by overzealous operators and copyreaders, and they are probably all true. It still happens when Ring's stories are included in anthologies. On this occasion Fullerton lost no time in telling the team about it, and that evening's Pullman entertainment was a spelling bee held by the Cubs for Ring's edification.

In Chicago, Fullerton and Ring often drank together in Stillson's, a newspapermen's hangout near the *Tribune* office. One evening Ring asked Fullerton to stay with him and have dinner. Fullerton said he had promised his wife he would be home; they were expecting guests. Ring said that he would call Mrs. Fullerton and make excuses. Ring called and told Mrs. Fullerton that her husband was drunk. She said by all means to keep him there. Ring came back and told Fullerton that it was all right for him to stay. "What did you tell her?" Fullerton asked. When Ring confessed, Fullerton dashed for the train and went home.

Another close friend and traveling companion was James Crusinberry. They covered the White Sox training camp at Waco, Texas, in 1912. In training camp the correspondents did not live at such close quarters with the team as they did on tours, and Ring and Crusinberry found diversions outside the camp. Once after an evening of stiff drinking in a Waco saloon they hopped a ride on a cotton wagon and went to a tavern on the outskirts of town. Here Ring fell into conversation with a Texas rancher, who was farther gone in liquor than he. Ring was in a fairly satirical mood and although he intended no malice, his wit had a noticeable bite to it. Shafts aimed over the head can be irritating, perhaps especially in Texas, and the rancher was soon angry. Invoking the Code of the West, he challenged Ring to fight "till one of us is daid." Ring was no barroom brawler; the mere idea of a quarrel was repugnant to him. Still, he often got into such situations. He skillfully talked himself out of this one, and escaped mortal combat by getting to the piano where the rancher, charmed into quietude, joined him in singing.

Ring traveled every year with the Chicago ball clubs until 1913, when he took over the column "In the Wake of the News" for the *Tribune*. His own accounts of his trips are among the best of his early newspaper pieces, still alive with the freshness of his observation, the delight he took in his characters, the authority of his reporting, and the increasing sureness of his style. He was already an expert on the technical aspects of baseball, and his interest was turning to the personalities of the game and their humor. Not that he consciously set out to be a humorist; he was born one. And he certainly did not start with the intention of being a satirist. Although it is clear from his early pieces that he had quickly learned the foibles of his ball players, he wrote of them in a jocular and affectionate way because he really was amused by them, and he liked them, too. Even after he had been congratulated on having reduced the American ball player to a complete boob, he never renounced the fondness he had felt for him.

To the ball players he must have been somewhat baffling. He was friendly, modest, unaggressive, considerate, and very knowing without having any disquieting air of superior knowledge. Although he

71

contributed a good deal to their entertainment, he never laughed very much himself, and while he was always a good fellow among men, he was reticent, fastidious, and given to solitude and reflection, and a kind of privacy that is difficult to maintain in a Pullman car full of ball players unless one has their complete confidence and approval. He had won them; as Ed Reulbach said, "If he had any faults, we liked him too much to notice them—he was one of us."

Ring said farewell to his travels with some regret. When he took over the "Wake," he wrote: "The editor of this column gives up association with two Chicago baseball clubs more cheerfully owing to the release of S.T.J. Sheckard and R. Zeider, who provided at least 50% of the joy of traveling"; and he composed a set of answers to the standard questions asked of baseball reporters:

The following is aimed to save time and trouble for Messrs. Sanborn and Weller [Tribune sports staff reporters] and other baseball correspondents:

1. No. The ball clubs buy our railroad tickets and pay our hotel bills, and later collect from the paper.

2. Yes. We know Ed Walsh personally.

3. Some of them are very nice fellows and others not as nice. They're just like any other set of men.

4. No. He's of Irish descent.

5. Yes. We travel in the same cars and live in the same hotels, just as if we were members of the team.

6. Not at all. It gets mighty tiresome along about August.

7. We write it just as it appears in the paper and turn it over to the telegraph office which wires it, press rates.

8. No. The headliners are written in the office.

9. He isn't a crab off the field.

Ring returned to Chicago with the cubs in April 1909 for the opening game of the season. From the road he had written regularly to Ellis; now he wrote to her again in a tone of anxiety which was probably not entirely affected:

LETTERS
I've read sev'ral letters in my short career,
From Ladies and gents and from relatives, dear, (Note 1)
But the last from the Rabbit, I'm forced to admit,
Was the most soul disturbing I ever did git.
But perhaps I deserved all the bawling I got,
I think that I must have—I hope I did not.

I b'lieve my last missive was misunderstood,
Whatever I writ, my intentions was good.
Oh, please, young Rabbitsky, try not to be vexed
When you're getting ready to write to me next.

Note 1. *The word here has a double usage, as an adjective and as a salutation.*

REQUEST

Right here I'll be until May ten.
A letter I would like ere then;
On May eleventh, home stay's ceased,
I will have started for the east.

R.W.L.

For the rest of the season, Ring traveled with ball teams, usually the Cubs, but on several trips the White Sox. He felt at home with both. He went to Detroit and Cleveland with the Sox, then rejoined the Cubs—"*my* Cubs," he called them—for an Eastern trip. Early in May he wrote to Ellis:

Hotel Euclid
Cleveland, O.

Dear Rabbit—

Poesy was enjoyed thoroughly. We have been here since Monday and are to return Saturday night. On the way down, Monday night, I awoke, as usual, when we stopped at Goshen.

Next Sunday night, me and my Cubs depart for the East, stopping first at New York and then at Philadelphia. From Philadelphia we go to Boston, staying three days there and departing on Saturday evening, May twenty-two for Brooklyn. Sunday is likely to be an idle day, so, says I to myself, "Suppose I go not directly to Brooklyn, but stop off at Northampton, Mass., for a few hours on the Sabbath afternoon." So I procured a Boston and Maine time card and have been studying it ever since, but with small success. However, I will try to find a train which will get me out of Boston some time Sunday morning or afternoon and another which will start me on my way from Northampton to New York some time Sunday night or early Monday morning. There must be possible and plausible connections. In any event, I will call you up from Boston soon after I arrive there. In the meantime, write and inform me what time I might be sure to reach you by our O.F. the telephone.

I was given an awful scare a little while ago when I read in the Chicago American headlines that looked like this—

The man in the case certainly had a nice way of showing his affection, did he not?

POEM

1. *The Boston and Maine, the Boston and Maine,*
   A railroad which now and then runs out a train.
   Will I ever go riding upon it again?

2. *Oh, one day last summer, 'twas Sunday, it was, sir,*
   I wanted to swim because it was so hot, sir.
   So I boarded a train and rode up to East Gloucester.

3. *The Boston and Maine; that's the road that I tramped on,*
   But next time I'll see that East Gloucester's not stamped on
   My ticket; I'd greatly prefer your Northampton.

Ring found connections to Northampton and spent a Sunday with Ellis before he resumed his baseball trip. After he got back to Chicago he wrote a letter which, in comparison to previous ones, seems curiously subdued:

Dear Ellis—

Tried to write you from home this afternoon, but the ball yard is almost a day's journey from our hut, so I had to give up before I started—hence the green ink and the Chicago Daily Tribune—Editorial Rooms.

I enclose two songs appropriate for your or appropriate to your commencings. Also, on another page, I am giving you some hints on manners and deportment during the ordeal. I know about these things having beaten all records for smartness by going through Armour Institute in one year.

Niles is to [be] represented at the doings by Blanche Millard [a Niles classmate of Ring's]. I don't know whether you know her or not. The common council didn't know whether to send her or me—or she and I—but heard I had been at Northampton oncet this year. I'm still glad I was there oncet, but wisht I could be there twicet.

Please don't be too busy to write during your late bereavement.

COMMENCEMENT TIPS

1. *Don't commence too young.*
2. *Don't stay in the east too long after commencing. The west needs you.*

74

3. *If you feel in the humor to run around the table, do it, then tell them it is I. Very few of them know me, so your reputation wouldn't suffer. Then, when you feel out of the humor again, I will be the one to suffer and I won't mind it quite as much as I did when you refused to sign the contract, being more accustomed to suffering now. Ah yes, I have suffered.*

4. *Don't have anything to do with anyone from Amherst.*

5. *Don't forget or neglect to send me an account of the proceedings.*

6. *Don't hesitate to call on me if you want any suggestions regarding the proper gowns to wear.*

Also congratulations.

R.W.L.

This was one of the commencement songs Ring wrote for Ellis:

SAD (AIR—JEAN)

1. *June fifteen, with your sun so bright*
And your beautiful summer air,
Do you know that I'm through with this place tonight,
With this place where existence's a pure delight
And where trouble's as scarce as care?

2. *June fifteen, do you think it's right*
That I should be exiled from here,
Where the maniacs cry like ghosts in flight
And the freshmen study the livelong night,
While the seniors watch and sneer?

3. *June fifteenth, when the blizzards roar*
On some wintery Goshen day,
'Tis then I will wish I were here once more,
Warm inside Mrs. Washburn's door,
And that you were years away.

Ring evidently felt further misgivings about his suit of Ellis after his visit to Northampton. Ellis had not yet consented to marry him, and he seems to have thought that he had a rival. This was caused more by his oversensitivity and impatience than to indifference on Ellis's part. In reality, he never had any serious competition. It was merely that Ellis was not ready to think of marriage in the near future.

He saw her during the summer, between trips with the Cubs and White Sox, and when he went away to cover the World Series between the Pittsburgh Pirates and the Detroit Tigers, he kept her advised of his address:

POME

My father wrote to me and asked:
"Why don't you tell your ma
"Just where you're going?" And I said:
"I'm going to Pittsburgh, Pa."

I had a friend named Callahan,
Said, "Where you going, Pal?"
I answered him as quick as that:
"To San Francisco, Cal."

I had a friend named Moses, and
He asked: "Where will you go?"
I hesitated not at all,
But said: "St. Louis, Mo."

I had a friend named Michael,
He said: "Hello, old fish,
"Where do you go from Pittsburgh?" And
I answered: "Detroit, Mich."

We will be at the Ponchartrain in Detroit Sunday, Monday and Tuesday. Please write. Excuse errors.

Ringlets.

Some time before Ring wrote stories in dialect he was writing letters in it.

Chicago, Ill.
Thursday [December 16, 1909]

Friend Ellis,—
Well, Ellis, I was glad to hear from you. How have you been?
I have been so busy making Xmas presents that I haven't had time to write to you before now. Well, Ellis, you know how it is. I don't have much time to get out, let alone write letters any time of the year, but of course this time of the year, just before the holidays is the busiest time of the year for me, as I suppose it is the busiest time of the year for you, in fact for all.
Say Ellis, I must insist that you come to Niles before Jan. 6. I know Ellis you must be busy at this time of year, so near the holidays but say Ellis you certunly will have one evening to spare before then. Why, Ellis, I intended to show you a good time some evening before then; we could go to South Bend to some show. I

76

don't suppose we could see anything there as fine as we seen in Chicago.

Ellis, I wish you lived in Chicago. Sometimes on my nights off I could take you out and we could have great times. I don't know many people here, that is girls, none that I care anything about and of course you can't really enjoy yourself with some one who you don't care for, at least I can't. I never was one of those pretenders. I always show my feelings and I can't pretend to not care for anyone when I don't. I don't suppose it's a very good way to be, but Ellis, you know it's my nature and I can't help that, can I? If people don't like me for what I am they don't half to like me, that's all.

Well, Ellis, I suppose I am tiring you with all this talk about myself. But, Ellis, you have knew me a long time and if you hadn't of liked me you would of told me so a long time ago. You see I know you got a frank disposition, to.

My married sister and myself are going home to Niles next Friday morning that is a week from tomorrow (Friday) morning. My sister isn't going to stay but till the following Wednesday morning. So you see you must come over to Niles before then.

I hope you'll anser real soon, dear, (you don't mind if I call you dear, do you dear?)

Yours with love
Ringgold Lardner

P.S., I don't think none of us can come to your party. My married sister and her husband will be back from Niles and so will Rex.

In January, Ring went to Goshen, which was rather like a town in a Booth Tarkington novel, where the Abbotts lived in a large, imposing house with a mansard roof. It was spacious, but there were five very attractive Abbott daughters and only three parlors. When Ring arrived, he found them all in use. So he hired a sleigh from a livery stable, took Ellis for a ride, and asked her to marry him. She agreed, but they did not set a date because Ring was still a traveling reporter and he was not making enough money to marry. Moreover the obstacles to his marriage were for Ring rather formidable. Ellis's father, Frank Abbott, was a well-to-do lumber manufacturer, who accumulated a solid fortune and was able to leave a modest annuity to each of his nine children. Ellis had been brought up in comfort. Ring's family had lost their money, and his immediate prospect of making more money was not very encouraging. But he was very much in love and he knew what he wanted. For so modest and unaggressive a man he had tremendous ambition;

and he had already begun to plan for his marriage. He wanted to make his engagement official, and so he wrote formally to Mr. Abbott to ask his consent:

Chicago, July fifth [1910]

Dear Mr. Abbott,

I'm sorry not to have been able to meet you this afternoon, for I know that it would have been more satisfactory than writing. I intended leaving here last night, seeing you this morning and returning in time to attend the ball game here. The paper is very much opposed to allowing us to skip a regular game. There is some rule about not taking the signature off a baseball story during the championship season. Tonight we are going east again, and when we come back, about the first of August, I will manage to get over and see you for a few hours anyway.

Of course you have guessed by this time that I care a great deal for Ellis. I can't help it, although I realize that no one is really worthy of such a girl and do not flatter myself that I am. That she cares for me in return is my only excuse for this letter, which is a request for your consent to our marriage. I know the life she has been used to and know I am not "well off." But I do believe I can take care of her. She told me she would like to wait awhile, and, although I want her just as soon as possible, I know it will be better to wait until I have done some more saving.

My present work takes me from home too often to suit me and I intend to have another arrangement after this season ends. I can tell you more about it after this trip. I know how a father must feel about such things and all I can do is give the assurance that I can take care of her now, and know that I will do better as time goes along.

I realize how much I am asking of you and Mrs. Abbott and Ellis' sisters and brothers. But I care so much for her I can't help asking and hoping that you will give her to me whenever she is ready.

We are going to stop for one day—tomorrow—at Cleveland, and from there will go to New York to stay from Thursday night until next Tuesday. I would like to hear from you and will be at the Somerset Hotel.

Sincerely,
Ring W. Lardner

Ring was not merely observing an outmoded courtesy in writing such a painfully earnest and humble letter; he really felt that way. It must have been tormenting not to receive an answer. When he got back from the East he went to Goshen to see Mr. Abbott, who greeted him cordially and raised no objections whatever to the marriage. After they had talked, Mrs. Abbott came in and asked, "Is Mr. Lardner going to stay for dinner?" "Dinner!" Mr. Abbott said. "He's going to stay all night!"

Back in Chicago, Ring told his friend Jack Brady, a sports writer, about his trip to Goshen.

"Who are you marrying?" Brady asked.

"Banker's daughter," Ring said.

"Did he smell your breath?" Brady wanted to know.

"He asked me if I drank, and I told him and asked him for a drink," Ring said. He got the drink.

Ring got on very good terms with the Abbott family. Even after they became engaged, Ellis was never as enthusiastic a letter writer as Ring, so he frequently wrote to her sister Ruby for news of her.

Chicago, August 4, 1910

Dear Ruby:

You have a peculiar sister entitled Ellis Abbott. I write letters to her occasionally and I don't believe she reads them. At least, she pays no attention to anything in them. There's something I'd really like to know—namely, on what day in September is she coming to Chicago and about how long can she stay? You know I want to try to arrange my schedule accordingly. If you could find out from her and tell me, I'd do almost anything in your behalf.

Also, I ask you personally if you know a song by Robert Louis Stevenson and Mr. Homer called Requiem? Please don't let Ellis Abbott know I have communicated with you.

As a partial reward for your trouble, I send you a picture of myself called "Complete Bewilderment."

And please don't show that to her either.

I haven't much to do this afternoon so I think I'll go to the ball game.

Please remember me to Dorothy, Florence, and Jeannette.

Your affectionate aunt,
Ringgold

Aldine Hotel, Philadelphia
August 22, 1910
Sunday Eve

Dear Rubina C.:

You are not overpaid at all, on the contrary, you are very worthy of your hire.

I was going to delay writing you until I had saved up or borrowed money enough to buy some stationery, but I have more time now than I'm likely to have again for a week, so please forgive it.

I want your peculiar sister to be in Chicago on the eleventh day of the coming September. If she is not there on that date and if she doesn't stay more than a week, I will seek death by strangulation and you will be held as accessory before the fact. And please don't think that is meant as a threat. It is merely a friendly warning. I am rather fond of your p.s., in fact, I care more for her than I do for my work, or the great game of baseball, or anything to eat. And it is rather unpleasant not to be able to see her for weeks and months at a stretch—therefore, when there is a chance, I want her as long as I can have her, whether she likes it or not.

Gladly will I deliver your message to my sister and nephew or niece, or whatever it is, when I see them. But I'm afraid it will not be much impressed, as it has failed to show much interest in my conversation so far. There must be something wrong with it.

I can't begin to pay you for all your services, but I stand ready to obey your commands.

Please keep this letter a dark secret from P.S. also.

> *Yours in absolute sanity,*
> *Ringgold Wilmer*

Ellis visited Chicago as often as possible, staying either with friends or with the Tobins, where Ring and Rex were living. None of them had very much money, but they had a good time. They were a close group who liked each other's company and had the same tastes. Ring and Rex got free passes to shows, and they all went to musicals and vaudeville.

Ellis returned to teach school in Culver, Indiana, where Ring went to visit her. He found Ellis busily entertaining the children of the family with whom she stayed. He wrote to Ruby:

Dear Ruby:

You didn't owe me any thanks for delivering your purse, because it was a bone play to keep it, but you did owe me a letter and I'm glad you paid up.

If you know where Ellis Abbott is going to spend Saturday and Sunday you have something on me. She is the most mysterious and secretive girl I ever was engaged to, and that's saying a lot.

There isn't a great deal of news to tell you. They are putting a new pavement on Fifty-first street and the Tribune is going to press half an hour earlier than usual. I didn't learn anything new in Cul-

ver about children's marches except what I saw at Mrs. Crandall's. Perhaps that would help a little. You need a girl about Ellis's size, shape and weight to be used as the dance floor. Then you want five children, all of them cross-eyed and generally homely, and three of them boys. They must range in age from three to twelve. The dance floor sits in a chair. The youngest child sits in her lap and the next oldest stands on her feet. The other three assume careless poses on her head and neck and shoulders. At a given signal, all the children start a screaming contest, at the same time kicking the dance floor all over with their heels. The floor sits quietly smiling until the children are tired out. Then she says: "Aren't they just too sweet to live?" They certainly are. I think you will find this very effective and inspiring.

I'm very grateful for your invitation and I'll come again as soon as I can.

Yours with my happiest respects,
Ring

Friday afternoon.

Now you're in debt again.

Ring, who was to become an almost insufferably proud father, had not yet learned to appreciate children, especially when it was Ellis whom he had come to see.

He was looking for a job that paid more money than he was making and did not require him to travel. He found one as managing editor of the *Sporting News* in St. Louis, and in December he resigned from the *Tribune* with regret and left Chicago.

It was on the *Tribune* from 1908 to 1910 that Ring developed a unique style in reporting baseball games. It grew naturally out of the kind of reporting he had done for the South Bend *Times*, and he retained that small-town familiarity that made his stories vivid and actual. His turns of phrase became sharper, his style more fluent, and his reports were colorful, dramatic, and funny. In this respect he was not an innovator. Two generations of Chicago sports writers before him had won for themselves a greater freedom than other journalists of the time enjoyed. Leonard Washburn, writing for the *Herald* and the *Inter-Ocean* in the 1880's, and Finley Peter Dunne, Charlie Seymour, and Tom Foley all wrote baseball stories in their own way; and they were more concerned with being entertaining than with being technically knowledgeable about the game. After them came Dryden, Fullerton and Keogh, who were still writing when Ring came to Chicago. The high level of sports writing today owes a great deal to the talents of the early Chicago sports reporters and the latitude their papers allowed them. Ring made an original contribution to sports writing, but the field was already wide open for him.

Ring knew the technical aspects of the game thoroughly, and his reports day after day are accurate and complete; not a single play escaped him. Besides he had the knack of conveying the atmosphere of each game, on the field and in the stands. The White Sox and the Cubs provided him with more dramatic and colorful material than the Central League had done, but when they were dull, Ring said so. He could sum up the whole character of a game succinctly, conveying the mood that hung over it. Covering a White Sox game in New York in 1909, he wrote:

Ed Walsh came back today after a month's illness and, after a sad start, steadied and pitched as if nearly back in the old form, beating the Yankees 4 to 3.

The game was about as interesting as watching eighteen street sweepers trying to pretend to cook, and except for one of the freakiest hits ever made, was without feature. It lasted two and one-quarter hours, during a great part of which time the spectators looked over the back of the stands at a balloon flight over the Hudson, then the score board of the Cubs-Giant game, and finally a beautiful sunset.

He could be very rough with his own team. "Bill Burns," he wrote of a Sox-Tigers game, "pitched four joke innings before he was ejected. He was about as effective as brown pop." The players never seemed to mind this kind of slur; Ring was still welcome to sit on the bench with them.

The well-worn jargon of baseball became fresh when Ring used it; he ironically twisted the old clichés to his own purpose, he got the pace of the game into his stories, and dramatized each game by building his story around its outstanding incident. His account of a game between the Tigers and the White Sox on August 1, 1910, is typical. The Tigers had won the first three games of this series, and they won the last. 6 to 5.

THE LONGEST WAY 'ROUND ISN'T THE BEST WAY HOME
by R. W. Lardner

In the extreme left hand corner of Mr. Comiskey's new ball park stands a gate, whose pickets are far enough apart to allow a regulation baseball, weighing not less than five nor more than five and a

82

quarter ounces avoirdupois, and measuring not less than nine nor more than nine and one-quarter inches in circumference, to roll between any twain of them and into the great beyond.

Citizens who had gone sight seeing around the park were aware of the presence of this gate, but none but the contractors and workmen who had constructed it knew just how far were those pickets apart. Lee Tannehill learned their approximate distance from each other yesterday afternoon by driving a regulation baseball between two of them. It looked like a most fortunate discovery for the White Sox at the time, for there were three other Chicago ball players on bases when Lee made it and the four runs that resulted left the score of the ball game between the Sox and Detroit even, at five runs apiece.

But Lee forgot that there was a certain person playing center field for the Detroit baseball team possessed of a pair of good eyes and a dead conscience, a person who would stoop to spy and would take advantage of the knowledge gained by such spying. Ty Cobb saw Tannehill hit that ball between the pickets of that gate and said to himself: "Why can't I?" Then he answered himself: "I can." This was the right answer, for Ty can do anything that anyone else can do in a baseball way. Fearing he would forget the exact location of that convenient gate if he waited over long, he got busy, as users of slang say, in the very next inning, and out-Lee'd Lee. Tannie's home run had tied the score. Ty's homer to the same spot beat us. Reliable witnesses say his drive went through the Tannehill groove. That is interesting but not essential. It went through some groove and into the great beyond and the Tigers came a bit nearer that fourth straight pennant.

Cobb's wallop was made off Edward Walsh in the fifth inning. Therefore Tannie's came in the round just before it. This round made the south side of Chicago happier than it had been for weeks before. The White Sox actually entered it five runs to the bad, lit into Bill Donovan as if he had been the biggest joke on the Fort Atkinson, Wis., Y.M.C.A. pitching staff, and scored just enough runs to tie.

Rollie Zeider gave a hint of what was to come by opening the inning with a hard fly to Davy, not Casey Jones. Red Kelly was cracked in the trunk by a pitched ball. Then they started. Pat Dougherty pulled a single to right and John Collins slapped one to center. With the bases thus filled up, Purtell poled a base hit over Lathers' bean and Kelly counted. The bases were still full and Tannie strode forth. Two strikes and two balls was the count on him when he did the deed. His drive was a fierce one. It beat Jones in a warm foot race to the left field gate, struck bottom between David and the boundary, and hopped between the pickets. The crowd of 20,000 forgot completely that it was Sunday, forgot everything except that Tannehill had tied up the game with the first home run drive on the new grounds at Thirty-fifth and Wentworth.

As Lee Ford crossed the plate and turned to stroll to the bench he was handed something and the word ovation does not describe it. And when he reached the resting place every teammate grabbed his meat hand and expressed rough and warm appreciation. The rest of the inning was much to the anticlimax. Freddie Payne struck thrice in vain and Frank Smith he did just the same, which is not meant for poetry. Smith did his striking out in place of Young Cy Young, whom Manager Duffy decided to extract.

There was another outburst of joy from the 20,000 assembled when it realized that Ed Walsh was going to the front to stop the hungry Tigers. The outburst continued while Edward was throwing out Charley O'Leary, and the crowd defied Mr. Cobb to hit the main hope of the White Sox race.

But Ty paid no heed. He was gazing at that gate and those pickets. To carry out his fell design it was first necessary to connect with the regulation baseball. Ty did it. He lifted it far into left. The crack of the bat was not as convincing as had been the sound of the collision between Tannie's and the sphere but the result was the same. For a brief moment it was hoped that Dougherty would catch the ball. But there was a wind to contend with that had been keeping occupants of the stand cool and blowing the flags right in the direction of the same pickets. Losing hope of getting it on the fly, Pat pursued with top speed with the idea of spreading his frame in front of the gate before the ball arrived. He was too late. He made a despairing effort to intercept the thing with his foot, but failed again and the defeat of the Sox had been accomplished.

Walsh was not present with us for long after that. He finished the inning and started the sixth. With the count two and two on Bush he pitched what he thought was a third strike. Bull Perrine called it a third ball. Bush hit the deciding one to the left for a single. As Bull went out to take his position behind Edward, the latter turned out conversation not approved of by Emerson, Ruskin and others. Perrine was among the others and Edward went to the bench. Then appeared Jim Scott, who had done so well against the champions on Saturday. He did every bit as well this time. In the remaining four innings he was not touched and it remained for his backers to get to Mr. Donovan again. But the Sox had done enough hitting for one

Sabbath afternoon. Only two of them got on after their mad dissipation, and neither of the two got past second base.

As for the early doings that made the fourth inning rally so joyous a thing, they may be told in a few words. Frederick Olmstead was our first pitcher. Detroit couldn't hit him at all because he didn't get anything close enough to the plate. The Tigers scored thrice in the first inning without the aid of a base knock. Olmie passed Davy Jones and O'Leary sacrificed. There followed passes to Cobb and Crawford. The U. of M. shaving stick came up with the bases full and hit one at Cap Zeider which went right on through. When it came back to the infield, David and Ty had scored, Samuel was on third and Lathers on first. Exit Olmie. Enter Young.

Lathers and Crawford started a double steal but Payne pegged the Wolverine at second and Crawford was held at third. Bush walked and the double steal with Sam was worked because Young intercepted the ball enough to gum things up. Tom Jones flied to Zeider for the last out.

The runs that increased the Detroit lead to five came in the fourth. One down Dougherty missed Tom Jones' fly and Schmidt sent Tom to third with a single to the right. Donovan hit safely to center, scoring Jones and sending Schmidt to third. Schmidt came home while Davy Jones was forcing Wild Bill at second.

The Sox hit a couple of balls hard off Donovan before the fourth, but couldn't find a safe spot for them. Davy Jones and Cobb made nice catches off Purtell and Parent before the big show opened.

Ring seemed to cover a game from all over the ball park—from the press box, from the stands, the bench, the plate, the pitcher's box, the umpire's position, the infield and the outfield. His stories were rounded, detailed, and graphic, and in addition they are marked by an irony that is all Ring's own. H. E. Keogh, besides conducting the "Wake" column, covered some of the Chicago teams' trips, and his writing was easy, genial, and humorous; Cy Sanborn was lively and accurate; but Ring's stories, in their sardonic humor and a kind of controlled excitement, excel all his contemporaries'.

Ring also spent a good many seasons covering football; it did not offer the possibilities for color and humor that baseball did, but he remained interested in it as a game long after his enthusiasm for baseball had waned. In football he was an expert's expert; he was always getting letters from coaches commending him on the accuracy and completeness of his coverage. As with baseball managers who allowed him to sit on the bench, he had the respect and confidence of coaches. Alonzo Stagg said of him, "Lardner comes to the training quarters after the game with the other reporters. He doesn't ask any questions. But he listens to the others' questions while those big eyes of his are roaming around. Then he goes to his office and writes a story that contains more real football information than any of the others have gathered."

In the fall of 1914 Ring went to Ann Arbor to accompany the Michigan team to Cambridge for the Harvard game. At the training quarters he found Germany Schulz, the assistant coach, told him who he was, and asked to watch the team's secret practice. Schulz thought only a madman would make such a preposterous request before a big game and was about to throw him out when Fielding Yost, Michigan's athletic director, arrived. He and Ring were already good friends, and he let Ring, alone of all reporters, watch the secret practice.

In St. Louis, Ring missed Ellis and anxiously awaited their wedding, which had been set for June. He wrote to Ruby:

> [*St. Louis, January 20, 1911*]
> *Thursday night*

Dear Miss Abbott—

After long and careful deliberation, I've decided not to kill you, because (1) you are too nice; (2) we would have to get another bridesmaid; (3) your family might not like it; (4) we might not get any napkins. As for forgiving you, I will do so under the following conditions: that I receive a good picture of Ellis before the first day of February, and that you send me at once the proofs of those she had taken at home, which I had, and which I bone-headedly returned. And if you don't comply with these conditions I will never speak to any one of the Abbotts except Ellis, Mr. and Mrs., Florence, Dorothy, Jeannette, William, John and Frank.

Ellis certainly has one record—no one in the world ever had so many awful pictures taken.

Will you explain something to me? Ellis says she doesn't see how she will find time to "get ready." What does that mean? I've been "ready" for a great deal over a year (except financially) and I haven't exerted myself a bit. But if she really does want time, why does she stay at Culver?

Thanking you in advance for answering these queries in the next issue of your valuable paper, I am

> *Yours Respectfully,*
> *A Bug*

86

January 30, 1911

Dear Ruby,—

You needn't expect those proofs back, because I never make the same mistake twice except sometimes. Three of them I like very much. I won't tell you which three because I want all of them. But I must have them the minute they are done.

I got a letter from Ellis last month and in it she said nothing about weddings, so honestly I don't know whether or not there's going to be one. If there is, you'll have to be the maid of honor because I used your name in bribing my best man (Arthur Jacks). When he was sixteen (he's twenty-nine now) he was desperately in love with a girl named Ruby who was not half as many carats fine as you. He is fond of the name so he has consented to act as my second. If he knew you, he'd like you if your name were Bethia, but he's just depending on my promises now.

And you know it isn't absolutely necessary for the groom and the maid of honor to be on speaking terms. I may not speak to you but I'm going to kiss you. Please don't back out on that account, for it will be all over in a minute. Part of my reason for contemplating an alliance with Ellis is the privilege it will give me to kiss her sisters and mother.

I'll thank you when the pictures come. Also now.

H-pp—st R-sp-cts,
Peer Gynt

You owe me.

Ring stayed in St. Louis only three months. Besides his editorial duties he also wrote baseball features, including the series called "Pullman Pastimes," about his travels with the Chicago clubs, with brilliant portraits of the players he knew best. But he did not find his job congenial. Hugh Fullerton later wrote, ". . . I tried to keep Lardner from going to the *Sporting News*, because I knew him so well and because I knew and loved Charley Spink so well. I was certain those two never would understand each other, and they didn't. So when I was offered a job in Boston and had to refuse, I suggested Ring for the place and he wired me to get it for him."

Ring was given an order of which he did not approve, and he left the *Sporting News* abruptly. Shortly after, he became sports editor of the Boston *American* and he hired his own staff. He sent for his brother Rex and another Chicago newspaperman, Frank Smith.

In June he took his vacation and went to Goshen for his wedding.

CHAPTER THREE

Ring and Ellis were married June 28, 1911, and the Niles *Daily Star* reported the event in detail:

At eight o'clock last evening at the home of the bride's parents, Mr. and Mrs. Frank P. Abbott of Goshen, Ind., occurred the wedding of Miss Ellis Abbott and Mr. Ringgold Lardner, youngest son of Mr. and Mrs. Henry Lardner of this city. The ceremony was performed by Rev. Mr. Van Nuys, pastor of the Presbyterian church.

The bride was given away by her father and was attended by her sister, Miss Ruby Abbott. Mr. Arthur H. Jacks of Chicago was best man. The ribbon bearers were Miss Wilma Johnson of this city, Miss Helen Gibson of Boston, Miss Julia Dole of Evanston, Miss Margaret Meyer of South Bend, Miss Ruth McGee of Toledo, and Miss Florence Abbott, another sister of the bride.

The wedding march was played by Noble Kryder, a young musical prodigy of Goshen, which was of his own composition.

The bride was gowned in Japanese hand-embroidered silk, trimmed with real lace, with tulle veil caught with orange blossoms. She carried a boquet of bride's roses and lilies of the valley, and wore a cameo in antique setting, the gift of the groom.

The bridesmaid wore pink marquisette over pink satin and carried pink roses.

The ceremony which was witnessed by 175 guests, was performed in front of a beautiful screen of elderberry blossoms. Roses and hydrangeas were also used effectively.

89

The color scheme in the dining room was pink and green, where a three-course collation was served by caterers from Toledo.

Beautiful gowns were worn by the guests and the affair was one of the most elaborate ever given in Goshen.

The gifts were numberless and very beautiful, among them being a solid silver vegetable dish from "Doc" White, the noted Soxs pitcher, who is a particular friend of the groom; from the Cubs, a 200-piece Haviland set of dishes; from Ban Johnson, Pres. of the American League, a cut glass dish; Chicago Tribune, of which the groom was formerly sporting editor, electric lamp; from Jimmie Callahan, another celebrated base ball man, set of glass-cut tumblers and pitcher.

Mr. and Mrs. Lardner left last night for Boston, where they will go to housekeeping at once, the groom having the home all ready. Mr. Lardner is now sporting editor of a Boston paper. The young man's many friends in Niles, where he was born and reared, extend best wishes, and offer hearty congratulations to the bride, who has also many friends here, having visited in Niles a number of times.

Ring and Ellis were handsome, brilliant, and very much in love. They had strong family ties and deep bonds of friendship which were to last all their lives. Arthur Jacks met Helen Gibson, a classmate of Ellis, at the wedding, and the following year they were married, with Ring as best man and Ellis attending the bride. Arthur Jacks was also Rex's best man when he married Miss Dora McCarley of Nashville. Not long after that, Ring and Ellis, Rex and his wife, and Richard and Anna Tobin all lived within a block of each other on the South Side in Chicago, and the Jackses also lived nearby. The Jackses went to New York in 1918; shortly after that Rex moved there to work for the New York *Post*. Ring went to New York in 1919, and by the early twenties the two Lardner families and the Jackses were neighbors again in Great Neck. They were a close-knit group with common interests and affections, and they were intensely loyal.

From Boston, Ring wrote almost at once to Ellis's mother:

The Fourth of July

Dear Mother II,—

My wife and I are having a quarrel. She says I must show her this letter and I say I mustn't. I suppose she will win the argument. People who said she didn't know much about keeping house and cooking were trying to deceive me. Last night's supper and this

90

morning's breakfast—our first meals at home—were absolutely the best I ever tasted.

I wish I could make some sort of return to you for giving her to me, but I know I can't, so I'll just have to be grateful to you all the rest of my life.

You must come to us the first minute you can get away. I want you to, for my own sake as well as Ellis'. And you must stay a long time when you do come.

I'm having the best time of my life now. The next best times were spent at your house and I'm thankful to you for them, too.

It's desperately hot here now, but it can't last long. I hope it won't, anyway, for I don't want Ellis to be utterly discouraged right at the start.

Give my love to yourself and the girls and tell Mr. Abbott I'm grateful to him, too, for my everlasting happiness.

                                                                              Ring

Ring was full of happiness, gratitude, and humility; at the same time he was deeply concerned with the responsibilities he had assumed. He said later that, from a practical point of view, he had chosen a bad time to be married—he was not earning enough money, his family in Niles was having a hard time, and he wanted to help them much more than he was able to do. But just now his immediate preoccupation was his marriage. He kept writing to Mrs. Abbott as if to reassure her that everything was going well.

                                                              Sunday night
Dear Mother II,—
Your small daughter fell asleep while I was reading to her, so I am stealing a little time to write to you. I'm not allowed to do anything but read and try to play the piano while she is awake and I am at home.

I suppose you've heard that Mr. and Mrs. Lardner are to chaperone a houseparty at Helen Gibson's the latter part of this week. It will be a novel experience but if it's half as nice as all the other novel experiences I've been having, I won't object a bit.

A new arrangement at "my" office requires me to work late every Saturday night. To make up for it, I don't have anything to do until Tuesday morning, and you may be sure I enjoy the Sunday–Monday vacation at home.

I think Ellis has been a little homesick once or twice, although she wouldn't admit it. It's a cinch she'll be glad to see Ruby and Frank and John—and any other members of the family who can be enticed away from home—when they come. It would be wonderfully nice if you, yourself, could come to see us.

We went to Andover a couple of Sundays ago to call on "Cousin Mary" [a relative of the Abbotts] and she proved to be quite the nicest person of her age I ever met. I'd like to go back there once a week, but my wife has a fiendishly jealous disposition, as was evidenced this instant. She awoke and asked me what I was doing and when I informed her I was writing to a girl, she went right back to sleep again.

All but two people have quit writing to me. The two are Mrs. Henry Lardner and Mrs. Abbott, and I hope they won't give up the practice.

Love to everybody, including yourself.

Ring

The summer and fall were happy for Ring and Ellis, even though his income was not large nor his job very promising. If they ever needed company, Rex was there, Helen Gibson lived nearby, and Ring always had friends everywhere he went. Ruby Abbott paid them a visit. Ring generously urged Ellis and her to go out on the afternoon of his day off, while he got dinner. They returned and found no trace of dinner or of Ring. He was discovered in the kitchen reading the newspaper and drinking beer. Dinner was ready; it consisted of lamb chops, potato salad, and pie, all fresh from the delicatessen. Ring was inordinately proud of this achievement and boasted of it years later.

His job required him to travel very little, but he went to Philadelphia in the middle of October to cover the World Series between the Athletics and the New York Giants. On his return he found that his brother Rex and Frank Smith had been dismissed in his absence. The baseball season being over, the paper was cutting down its staff. Ring had hired them and he objected to their being fired, and so he walked out. He had no money saved, and Ellis was pregnant. He was fully aware of his responsibilities, but this was a matter of principle and of loyalty to Rex. He borrowed money from the owners of the Boston teams, the Braves and the Red Sox, and he and Ellis and Rex went back to Chicago.

They stayed for a short time with the Tobins, and Ring got a job as copyreader on the Chicago *American*. Since he had already been a sports writer and editor, this work was hardly the kind he wanted, but it served to support him until in February 1912 he went back to the *Examiner* as a reporter and was assigned again to the White

Sox. Rex got a job with the Associated Press and lived with the Tobins, while Ring and Ellis found a small apartment. Ring was still close to his family; something of the atmosphere of the Lardner home in Niles still existed in Chicago. On Monday nights Ring and Ellis went to vaudeville shows on passes. Other nights they stayed at home and Ring read aloud or played the piano, or the other musical instruments he enjoyed practicing. Ellis began giving him a new instrument each year at Christmas, and eventually he taught himself to play the accordion, cornet, violin, clarinet, saxophone, and French horn. He did not play with any group, but only for his own pleasure, which was not shared by the neighbors, who wrote anonymous letters of protest.

That winter Ring accompanied the White Sox to their training camp at Waco, Texas, leaving Ellis at home, not without anxiety since she was expecting their first baby. He was back in Chicago in April, and his first son, John Abbott Lardner, was born May 4, 1912. Ring paced the floor of the small apartment in agony during the long labor and vowed that this would be their only child; he could not endure to see Ellis suffer. His joys and anxieties as a young husband and father were typical except in their intensity. He took everything harder than other men did; it was one of the penalties of his abnormal sensibility.

Ring was no longer "James Clarkson" on the *Examiner;* he had his own by-line and he could write very much as he wished. He wrote a series of verses called the "Cub Primer" and ran them under Frank Schulte's name. For years Schulte was to be a favorite "contributor" to Ring's columns. The first of the alphabetical Cub series was:

> *A is for Archer, whose first name is Jim.*
> *An A No. 1 first-class catcher is him;*
> *As first baseman also this gent has made good;*
> *He's strong with the bat, which they build out of wood.*
> *When bases are empty, he stands there so calm*
> *You'd never suspect the full strength of his alm;*
> *But wait for the time when the foe gets a man on;*
> *Stand out of the way, sir, the boy has a cannon.*

His Sunday poems were parodies of popular songs, and during the 1912 World Series, he wrote another primer about the leading players. Sometimes he wrote his advance stories in outrageous doggerel:

93

Dear Reader: Here we are once more, in Boston by the ocean's shore, in Massachusetts' famous town where fish is fresh and bread is brown, and where it is such a royal treat to eat and eat and eat and eat.

Three men are missing from the fold, the rest are lonesome, young and old. Ed Walsh, he stopped in Meridian to see his two kids once again. He'll be here in the morning mail to beat the RED SOX without fail. Jack Collins went to Pittsfield, Mass., to call upon his fair lass—at least that's what the boys all said; when we asked Jack he turned real red.

Well, there's one other absentee, the holder of the captaincy. Way up amid the pines of Maine to see his family again went our smart captain Harry Lord, for virtue is its own reward. He's going to remain up there till we have had the first affair with Boston's Red Sox, then return, his well known salary to earn. . . .

Ring was ingenious at solving what must always be a problem for a baseball reporter: to be entertaining between games when not very much is happening. He merely followed a natural bent; he had been an irrepressible versifier for years, at first a rather crude one; but he eventually became a very polished one. He was becoming more and more a columnist.

On his last traveling season with the *Examiner*, in the winter of 1913, Ellis accompanied him to California, where the White Sox were training, leaving John with the Abbotts in Goshen.

When Ring returned to Chicago that spring, the *Tribune* offered him the job of conducting the daily column "In the Wake of the News." Hugh E. Keogh, who had run it for many years, was a popular sports writer with a flair for epigrams and light verse. He made the "Wake" the most brilliant feature of the *Tribune's* sport section, and when he died in 1913 he was hard to replace. For a while Hugh Fullerton tried his hand at the column, but although he was a fine sports reporter, he had no particular talent for humorous writing and no liking for it. He recommended Ring for the "Wake"; Ring always seemed to be stepping into Fullerton's jobs. But he had other partisans on the *Tribune*. James Keeley, the managing editor, who was notoriously unenthusiastic about most of his staff, wrote to Ring: "I am very glad indeed to know that you are coming back to us and I hope the reunion will take place just as soon as possible. I feel absolutely sure that you will make good. If I didn't, I would not have been so insistent on telling Woody [Harvey Woodruff] to get you." Ring was hired on three months' trial, and began the column June 3, 1913; he continued it for six years.

Ring was not at all confident that he would make good. Keogh had a large and devoted personal following; his column had been unique, and a merely fair imitation of it would not do. At first Ring felt, because of some unenthusiastic letters he received, that he was a complete failure, and he was extraordinarily sensitive about it. One day when delivering his copy to the desk he overheard someone say, "Does he think he's as good as Keogh?" For weeks he never went near the copy desk, but sent his column up by messenger.

Actually Ring was successful from the start. He followed the forms and devices that Keogh had used—poems, epigrams, portraits of sports figures, letters and verses from contributors—and he invented new features, contests, serials, parodies of all kinds. He also burlesqued the high-brow "A Line o' Type or Two," conducted by Bert Leston Taylor on the editorial page. In the "Wake" he experimented with almost every form and style he used in his later work, columns, short stories, plays, and verse. He put his own stamp on the "Wake" from the very first; some of his finest humor appeared in it, and it exhibited the whole range of his talent.

Ring set his own standard, and it was a hard one to live up to. The column did not pour out spontaneously; he labored all day over his brief stint. It was not hard to be funny when an idea struck him, but to write a variety column seven days a week takes a lot of ideas, and sometimes he paced the floor of the office, or looked in on his colleagues to ask them for suggestions. He was offered a great many, but he did not often use them; somehow they started off a train of thought and in a few hours he would have enough items to fill his space. His column required concentrated effort, but it did not show the strain of it. He was a meticulous and anxious worker; he wrote slowly and thoughtfully, always knowing exactly what effect he was aiming for. When a column was finished, it was the best he could possibly do. On one occasion, after a long, hard afternoon at his typewriter, he finished his column and then wrote a letter. He went downstairs to file his copy well ahead of his deadline, and on his way he was stopped by one of the guards of the building who sold insurance as a side line. Ring was a good prospect; he had an obsession about taking out life insurance; it was the only way he could save money. He listened to the sales talk, then, distracted by it, went on and filed his "Wake" copy in the mail chute. When he found himself handing his letter to a copy boy, he was panic-stricken. He got someone to phone the post office and had the whole postal system of the *Tribune* turned upside down until the copy was retrieved. Then he turned it in and went over to Stillson's to calm himself with a drink. Anyone else, having just written a column, might easily have gone back to the typewriter and written an approximation of it, but not Ring. He had labored to put down every word of it exactly as he wanted it to be, and it could never be done again.

The "Wake" appeared every day including Sunday. It is impossible for anyone to be consistently funny seven days a week, and Ring thought that he managed it only once a week. Actually his average was better than that. The "Wake" was seldom dull, it was full of variety, and at its best it contained some of Ring's masterpieces. He quickly learned how to fill the space allotted to him. When his column ran a little short the first day, he wrote: "We are advised by our family physician not to do too much the first day. The boss might expect too much the second." He solicited contributions from the beginning, inviting contributors to the "Line" to send rejected contributions to him: "We offer encouragement and hope to those sorrowful ones who have failed to make the Line. You have found it impossible to butt in there. You will find it next to impossible not to do so here." When there were no suitable contributions, he wrote them himself and ascribed them to imaginary writers or to his friends. He found that writing a full column on Sunday for Monday's paper gave him no day off at all, so he wrote only a brief verse for Monday.

A friend of mine who reads the Wake (a friend he sure must be)
  Had me to dine a week ago last Sunday,
And after we had dined a while, the friend inquired of me:
  "Why is the Wake so very short on Monday?"

I told him, and I'll tell you too—'twas thus my boss did speak:
  "Each week, to rest your brain, we'll give you one day,
We really can't expect a man to keep a Wake all week,
  So just send in a verse or two for Monday."

And, yielding to the boss, which is the proper thing to do,
  I set aside each Sunday as a fun day,
And Tuesday, Wednesday, Thursday, Friday—all the whole week
    through—
  I wonder wotinel to write for Monday.

Most of his Monday verses were devoted to describing his infant son John, and later he wrote many other columns about his children. When a reader wrote in complaining that the Monday column did not deal with sports, Ring replied in verse: "If kids aren't sport, what is?" Ring was a proud and affectionate father, and his poems about his children are tender and unabashedly sentimental:

TASTE

I can't understand why you pass up the toys
That Santa considered just right for small boys.
I can't understand why you turn up your nose
At dogs, hobby-horses, and treasures like those.
And play a whole hour, sometimes longer than that,
With a thing as prosaic as daddy's old hat.

The tables and shelves have been loaded for you
With volumes of pictures—they're pretty ones, too—
Of birds, beasts, and fishes, and old Mother Goose
Repines in a corner and feels like the deuce,
While you, on the floor, quite contentedly look
At page after page of the telephone book.

BLASPHEMY

When my son John gets good and sore,
Which is, I'm glad to say,
No oftener than three or four
Or seven times a day,
He kicks at chairs and other things,
His countenance grows dark,
And in an awful voice he springs
His swear-word, "Garfield Park!"

It's almost more than I can stand
To hear my youngster curse,
The habit's bad in grownups, and
In little ones, much worse.
It is a practice frowned upon
In Matthew, Luke and Mark;
So, I beseech thee, my son John,
Eschew that "Garfield Park!"

THE FIRST REAL HAIRCUT

Yes, I said that your curls look too much like a girl's;
That on you they seemed quite out of place.
And my argument won—you are rid of them, son,
You are saved from their crowning disgrace.

97

You're a regular boy, and no less of a joy
   And a pride to your dad, I vow,
But how sadly I miss that sweet go-to-bed kiss,
   Which I wouldn't dare ask for now.

A number of Ring's poems about his children were collected in a volume called *Bib Ballads*, illustrated by Fontaine Fox, who originated "Toonerville Trolley." The verses were an enormously popular feature of the "Wake," whose readers, the rest of the week, got accustomed to some fairly biting satire.

For half the year baseball was Ring's main topic, and he provided an endless variety of angles and insights and comments. The busher language for which he became famous made an early appearance in the "Wake," when Ring reported a game in the character of a disgruntled player:

THE FIRST GAME
(By a Athlete)*
*Unassisted

We ought to of trimmed 'em. When Egan, the big shot, said I was out at second he musta been full o' hops, the big boob. I like t' known where he was at las' night, the big bum. Some o' them umps oughta be on the chain gang, the big boobs.

Matty pitched wrong to Collins. That little bum couldn't hit a curve ball with a mattress. Matty's been pitchin' long enough to know how to pitch, but sometimes he pitches like a damfool. I wisht he'd let me tell him somethin'. But d'ya think he'd listen to me? He knows it all. He oughta knew he didn't have speed enough no more to get one past that guy.

Wisht Mac had let me wallop when I had the big Indian three and nothin' that time. 'Member? Merkle was on third base. I looked 'round and Mac gives me the sign to take one. That's rotten baseball, I think. I took one that I could of hit out o' the park. Then the big Indian hooks one on me and I missed. Then I'm lookin' for another hook and he comes with a fast one. And the Catfish calls me out. If I'd a known he was goin' to call it on me, I'd a hit that one out o' the park. The big rum.

Then there was that third innin' decision when Egan calls me out at second, the big slob. Barry missed me that far. I wouldn't lie about it. He missed me that far. If I'd a been out, I'd never opened my clam. But Barry missed me that far. The big slob. He was lookin' out in right fiel' somewheres. Barry missed me that far. Bet if you was to go to Barry now and ast him, he'd come through and say he missed me that far. The big rummy. I'm glad we don't have them umpires in our league. No wonder Milan steals bases. He's probably out all the time, but the umps is lookin' out the window. Why Barry missed me that far.

I ain't no pitcher, but I bet I know as much about pitchin' as some o' them pitchers. Ja see what Matty handed Collins? He slips him a fast one right over the heart when all he had to do was hook one and Collins would a fell dead. Matty's been pitchin' fifty years and he don't know no more'n a baby. McGraw oughta tell some of them guys somethin'. But no, he sits on the bench and don't say nothin' till the innin's over. And then it's too late.

. . . Bender pulled a boner at that. He oughta walked me and took a chance on Larry. But he got away with it, the big lucky slob. But he never woulda got away with it if it hadn't been for Mac and then Klem callin' that third strike on me.

An' didja see what Egan done to me? Where'd they get them umpires. They oughta be peddlin' eggs, the big boobs. Barry missed me that far.

We'll get 'em tomorrow. Big Rube'll make 'em quit like dogs, the big lucky rums. They was ready to quit today, only Egan and Klem wouldn't give 'em no chancet.

Watch me tomorrow. Plank's pie for me. I'm liable to knock a couple men dead in them bleachers. We'll fix 'em, the big lucky slobs. Rube'll make 'em look sick.

Ja see that doll in the box back o' our bench? She couldn't keep her eye off o' me.

We'll get 'em tomorrow, the yellow, quittin' dogs.

This churlish character is a long way from the genial boys in the Pullman cars, but he has something in common with the ball players of Ring's later stories: boastfulness, vanity, and a store of alibis. His language is neither so funny nor so graphic as Jack Keefe's was to be only a few months after; but he is the prototype of many of Ring's characters, the kind of ball player who hates umpires, blames everyone else for his mistakes, and maintains a consistent bad humor. He had his counterparts among the spectators too: Ring often sat in the bleachers and listened to the fans:

IN THE BLEACHERS
(A Cubs-Philly game, with comments from the bugs.)
I had long wondered what manner of manager and man this

Evers was. I learned in the sixth, after Bob Emslie had canned the Trojan for kicking at a decision at second base.

"That's right, Bob. Send the crab to the clubhouse. It'll strengthen the team."

"Robber! Robber! If you can't beat us fair, you'll do it by puttin' our best man out of the game."

"Best man, eh? If he's the best man, it's a heluva team."

"It'd been a heluva team if he wasn't manager. You'll notice he's got 'em up there fightin'."

"Yes, and when there's a chance to win he breaks up the team by gettin' put out."

"Accordin' to your dope, the team's better when he's out. You got your wires crossed."

"Oh, go on and get your hat cleaned."

This brilliant dialogue was renewed when the teams changed places between innings and Emslie came over to his regular position near first base.

"Give 'em the game, you big boob."

"Whaddya talkin' about give 'em the game? Ain't they ahead?"

"That ain't Eason's fault."

"Eason? That's Emslie."

"Eason or Emslie, what's the difference, they're all rotten."

"They ain't no rottener than Evers."

"You're from Philadelphia."

"No, I'm not from Philadelphia, either."

"Then why don't you go back there?"

"Why don't you shut your trap?"

Ring had a low opinion of the "bugs," and he was always sympathetic to umpires. "Fans outside of Philadelphia," he wrote, "are probably peeved at not witnessing Al Artle's nasty fall. If there is one thing a baseball crowd dearly loves, it is the sight of an umpire getting hurt. Some day one of them will be killed by a foul ball and the bugs will laugh themselves sick."

"In the Bleachers" was a regular feature of the "Wake," and perhaps some of the more thoughtful fans could detect in it a note of scorn for the followers of the national pastime:

It was the first game of the first double-header with the Athletics. I picked out a seat that gave me a better view of Mr. Bodie than of the ball game; or, perhaps, I should say the rest of the ball game.

100

On my right sat a gent who knew something and he soon gave evidence of the fact. Morris [sic] Rath opened the Sox attack with a safe bunt. He was nailed at second when Lord missed his swing on a hit and run.

"Stealing second with nobody out," remarked the g. who ks. "And the papers call him a brainy ball player. If he had good sense, he'd trade all his brains for a little bit of ability."

The Sox took the field for the first half of the second. I had purchased a "program" for a certain reason. Mr. Rath's critic, observing that I was armed with the official document, asked:

"Is that Scott pitching?"

"No," I replied politely, "that's See-cott," giving the name its proper pronunciation.

"You mean Sy-cott," said my neighbor.

"Yes, that's what I mean," I responded rather crossly.

Two young men came in and took places next to me on the left. One of them looked enough like "Sy-cott" to be mistaken for him. Eddie's twin brother had hardly settled himself when he caught sight of Bodie.

"There's the new guy," he said.

"Chappell?" inquired his comrade.

"Yes, that's the new guy. Clean cut fellow, too. Looks a little like Bodie, but slimmer."

"Why, that is Bodie."

"No, it isn't. Bodie's fatter."

"Why, it is Bodie. Just look at him."

"Gosh, I believe you're right. Well, then, that's the new guy," and he pointed to where Mattick was stationed.

"Yes, that must be him."

Every few minutes the guy on my left was giving fresh evidence of the fact that he had a strong imagination. He was positive that Chappell was playing, although, for all I know, Chappell may have been dining on dust in Yuma, Ariz. My neighbor also knew that Schang was catching and was disturbed when he referred to his program in the Philly half of the fifth and found that the number on the board corresponded to the name "Lapp" in the booklet.

"Lapp," he said wonderingly. "L-a-double p. How do you pronounce it?"

"Lapp," his friend told him, and all I could do was wonder how else one could pronounce it.

101

The party who was so positive that Chappell was playing ought to have wised up when with Mattick at bat in the Sox fifth, the score board flashed "68."

" '68'," he said. "Why, that's Mattick. Who's he batting for?"

"Must be batting for Chappell," suggested his companion.

"Chappell must be a swell hitter, then," he rejoined.

Ring, after eight years as a baseball reporter, still had a passion for the game, but he had no illusions about the character or intelligence of the average athlete, and he was equally skeptical about the fans. Of course the fans were his readers, and his job was to entertain them. They liked to see him disparage their idols; and as for themselves, they thought that he was mocking other baseball fans. In any case, he disarmed them by writing in character, or in verse, and by being sentimental about children. The irony was there, but it was all innocent merriment, and most of his columns were a kind of broad raillery, as in the verses he wrote on the occasion of the New York Giants trading Otis Crandall for Larry McLean of St. Louis:

GOTHAM GETS READY

There's an air of busy bustling
Along the Gay White Way,
The barkeeps are a-hustling
As ne'er before today.
Do they expect a visit
From sportive royalty?
O, what occasion is it,
That such a stir should be?

Pat Keefe has got 'em ready—
The ice, the lime, the gin—
It just remains for Eddie
To shoot the seltzer in.
They say that Con O'Farrell's
Engaged the whole supply—
Some forty thousand barrels
Of Kelly's Aged Rye.

They're planning to deliver
The town from debt's dark spell
By trading Hudson River
For something they can sell.

Can talk of graft and scandal;
Attend to business first—
McGraw has traded Crandall
For Larry and a Thirst.

We won't vouch for the truth of the report that six places in St. Louis voluntarily relinquished their licences when the Crandall-McLean trade was announced yesterday.

He ran prize contests, inviting contributions on "The Best Play I Ever Saw," offering one dollar for each item used. This cost him nothing, since he wrote them himself:

Ward Miller on a summer's day
Was ordered to left field to play.
And with his bat this gloomy geek
Broke up the Giants' winning streak.

This contest soon degenerated into a free-for-all: "Chicago, Ill.—(Baseball editor of the Wake.) The best play I ever saw was 'Hedda Gabler' with Mrs. Fiske doing the Gabling. R.W.L. The R.W.L. is ourself and we will therefore keep the dollar." To restore order, he held a contest for "The Worst Bonehead Play I Ever Saw," which elicited the following: "Bonehead Editor of the Wake—The worst bonehead play I ever saw was Bill Shakespeare's Hamlet. 'Alas, poor Yorick.'"

He kept serials running in the form of letters, epic poems, and detective stories, and he ran one complete novel, a baseball thriller called *The Pennant Pursuit:*

CHAPTER I
As Verne Dalton strod passed the jymnaseium one day in April, bound for the college ofice, where he was going to make arrangmunts for entring the college next fall, the ball nine composed of 20 (twenty) or more members came out on its way to the atheletic feild. O said Verne I wonder if Ill ever have a posichion on that team and fight for the glory of my ama mather, but he did not have much hope because his parents had said he must devoat all his time to study.

CHAPTER II
(Synopsis—Verne Dalton strode past the college gymnasium and saw the baseball squad. Now go on with the story.)
A year past. Verne Dalton was now a full fleged student at the

college. . . . Very happy Verne Dalton saught the coche of the ball nine for he had pitched lots of times against the boy teams at home.

CHAPTER III

It was the 17th (seventeenth) of June, commencement day and the Yale nine was on hand to play our nine for the college championship. Everything depended on our hero Verne Dalton. . . . When the rivle nines took the feild the grand stand was filled with enthustic college men and fair co-eds bueying the crimson and the blue glancing up in the stand just before taking his place in the box Verne Dalton caught the eye of Lillian Hazelton the daughter of a New York millionair. Verne who had loved her at first sight felt his heart leep as he saw her smile o he said to himself if I can only win today maybe I can win a bride as well.

CHAPTER IV

Sixteen innings past neither side had been able to score. . . . Using his famous upshoot and indrop he rapidly strick the next three batters out and it was the crimsons turn to cheer. There was two men out in the last half of the seventeenth and it was Verne Dalton's turn to bat so he said if I could just conect now he swung with all his might and the ball sailed over the fence for a home run. . . . As he strod off the feild a young girl made her way through the throng of admirers and rushing up to him throwed her arms around his neck and kissed him it was Lillian Hazelton.

CHAPTER V

That evening at the commencement ball Lillian Hazelton and Verne Dalton became each other's fiancee, but in the midst of Dalton's joy his loved one made a remark that filled him with dispair she said my father will not alow me to wed he whose fortune does not amount to $100,000 (one hundred thousand and no hundredths dollars) Verne Dalton's parrents were poor farmers and he was hopless when he thought of the amount of money involved. Little did he know that George Hoff the scout for the New York Giants had been hiding behind the stand that afternoon and threw a crack in the boards had watched Verne Dalton's performance. . . .

CHAPTER VI

Verne Dalton and Lillian Hazelton were sadly parting at the depo I am afraid our dream of love is ore said Verne Dalton for where am I ever going to get $100,000 if you really love me replide Lillian you will get it somewhere just then a messenger boy came running up to them. Are either one of you Verne Dalton he asked I am he said Dalton and tore open the telegram which the messenger handed him. It read will give you $75,000 a year to pitch for the New York Giants signed John J. McGraw manager Verne Dalton almost busted with delight and showd the telegram to his sweatheart That makes everything all O.K. he said $75,000 is not $100,000 but maybe we will play in the worlds serious and then I can marry you this fall with that they parted.

CHAPTER VII

Four months past threw the wonderful work of Verne Dalton the Giants had won the pennant and the worlds series was to begin on the morrow with the atheletics as the Giants oponents Manager McGraw called Verne Dalton to his room in the hotel where they was stopping. We are depending on you for to win for us the highest honors in baseball if you do what I expect of you instead of giving you a share in the recipes which will not amount to more than $4000 or $5000 per player I will give you a check for $25,000. Make it $25,100 said Verne Dalton for he wanted a totle of $100,000 in his bankbook to show to Lillian Hazelton's father and he alreddy had squanderd $100 of his $75,000 salary. All right said McGraw who is a jenerous man now go to bed and remember to pitch nothing but your famous snake twist to Baker.

CHAPTER VIII

Before a crowd of 60,000 exited fans who swormed around the playing feild and made ground rules nessary the Giants and Atheletics had battled 18 innings in the first game of the serious without ether team being abul to score in the nineteenth inning with no giants on bases Verne Dalton our hero broke down the Indin pitchers with a home run the longest hit ever made at the grounds. . . . The crowd carried Dalton off the feild on there shoulder. Only three more to win and the $25,100 is yours shouted McGraw.

CHAPTER IX

See CHAPTER VIII.

CHAPTER X

They all went downtown to supper, driving in Mister Hazelton's foreign limoseen south on eight avenue to the park, threw the park to fifth avenue, south on fifth avenue to 39 st and west on 39 st to Bustanybodys.

(THE END)

Note—"The Pennant Pursuit" will be out in book form the day St. Louis (A.L. or N.L.) goes into first place.

Ring's features in the "Wake" were interspersed with shorter paragraphs and comments on sports; later on he extended his observations to politics, Prohibition, and the war, but sport remained the backbone of it. He carried on playful little campaigns in which prize fighters and wrestlers came off rather badly, but he was most deadly about automobile racing, which he really despised.

HAPPY THOUGHT

O, to be a race fan,
And near the speedway stand
And see somebody drive himself
Into the Promised Land!

"The Del Rey motordrome at Los Angeles," he wrote, "burned to the ground with a great saving of life."

He pretended to a staunch chauvinism in regard to American supremacy in sports, and ridiculed all foreign claims. In one of his regular features, "On the Bench," he wrote a rather laborious account of an Australian reporter covering a baseball game under the impression that it was cricket, and giving Chicago a score of 96. "What in the world will we do," he wrote archly, "if they bar boxing in Belgium?" And when France presumed to have a boxing champion, he inquired, "Champion of what?" He wrote scathing paragraphs on a Jack Johnson bout: " 'Tell my friends,' says Jack, 'that I am not fool enough to risk my title in a bout where I am not prepared.' We'd be glad to do it, Jack, but they're both out of town." The "Wake" was a good-humored column and athletes had long been accustomed to taking a ribbing from sports writers, but occasionally there was a touch of venom in it.

Ring had hardly even touched the possibilities of Frank Schulte as a poet, and he quickly engaged him as a contributor. He began his career in the "Wake" with a series called *Life:*

You people here in Chi have been
Complaining of the heat,
But down in Cinncinnatti, that
Is where we had the heat.
Up here it probably was hot—
It very well might be;
But down in Cinncinnatti there
Was not a bit of breeze.
(To be prolonged)

> *It's better not to eat much meat*
> *In these hot days of summer.*
> *If you must eat, then why not eat*
> *An egg or an cucumber?*
> *The life of a ball player's not*
> *What many people seem.*
> *I play right field and I bat third*
> *On Johnny Evers' team.*

After four of these stanzas a controversy arose:

> *In recent interviews, Luke McGluke, owner of the Dublin club*
> *in the Japanese League, has made vicious attacks on the Wake and*
> *particularly on one of its feature writers, Frank M. Schulte, asserting*
> *that the Wake was trying to deceive the public by signing Schulte's*
> *name to stuff he did not write and charging that the Schulte poems,*
> *than which there is none other, were direct and uncalled for knocks*
> *at the Dublin club.*

And Schulte's reply:

> *Editor Wake of the News—Dear Sir: In answer to the vicious*
> *charge made by President McGluke, I will say that, to all intents*
> *and purposes, I write the verses over which my name appears. By*
> *this I mean that I read them the day after they are written, or rotten.*
> *In the off season, when I am not too busy during the evening, figur-*
> *ing out ways in which to hit 'em farther away and not so high, I*
> *nearly write them; that is, I sit near the person who do. I will admit*
> *that Red Corriden writes some of them, but I give him the inspira-*
> *tion and always approve what is rotten before it appears in print.*
> *Hoping that I have convinced you that I write what I write, I am,*
> *etc.*
>
> > *Frank M Schulte*
> > *Right Field, Chicago*

> *Mr. Schulte's gentlemanly note convinces the Wake that in regard*
> *to this here now controversy, to which there is nothing to it. Mr.*
> *Schulte does not draw his enormous salary from the Wake for the*
> *mere use of his name. We will leave it to the army of our readers to*
> *decide whether or not the verses are printed with intent to deceive.*

Schulte resumed:

> *We leave tonight to go due east,*
> *Where many games we'll play;*

We may not lose as many as
We did when it was May.
I'll write you from the different towns
In whom for games we're booked in:
From Boston, Philadelphia,
From New York and from Brooklyn.
(All right.)

I've often been in New York town
And certainly do love
A town in whom the subway is
Below and not above.

At this point Schulte was displaced as the "Wake" laureate by Heinie Zimmerman himself. Zimmerman was constantly being put out of the game for swearing at umpires. An anonymous fan summoned him, produced a hundred-dollar bill, tore it in two, and gave him one half of it, promising him the other half if he could refrain from insulting an umpire for two weeks. Ring reported Heinie's ordeal of restraint in the "Wake," and after the ninth day estimated that the third baseman's equity in the prize was $64.2857, provided he could resist his native temper, his avarice, and his desire to win the money to spend on smart togs and to offset his frequent fines. Heinie, as torn as Hamlet, made this soliloquy:

The C or not the C, that is the question—
Whether 'tis nobler for the dough to suffer
Mistakes and errors of outrageous umpires,
Or to cut loose against a band of robbers,
And, by protesting, lose it? To kick—to beef—
To beef! Perchance to scream—
Yes, I'll keep still. . . .
Thus money does make cowards of us all;
And thus the native Bronix disposition
Is stifled by a bunch of filthy luc;
And ravings of my own fantastic sort
Are all unheard, tho my long silence does
Disgrace the name of Heinie.

Ring invoked Tennyson to describe Heinie's plight:

Half a C, half a C,
Half a C, sundered,

Cut from the other half,
Half a big hundred.
Forward the Cub Brigade!
"Charge at the umps," they said,
But Zim in silence stood.
O you big hundred!

Zimmerman stayed on the field for two weeks and got the hundred dollars. After it was awarded, the *Tribune* acknowledged having put up the money. It provided the "Wake" with a feature full of suspense.

But Schulte wrote sourly:

For two hole weeks I've wrote this poem;
  But not a cent for mine,
'Though Heinie got a hundred bucks
  For not saying nothing the same length of time.

Then he began another serial poem called "A Epick," a success story of a baseball player, which stumbled to a halt when Schulte paused to boast:

I'll break in on this tale a bit,
  If you are perfectly willing
And call attention to the way
  I'm hitting 'em in Philly.
And now I will resume the thread
  Of what's appeared above,
The story of a youth who wins
  In Athaletics and love.
                    (All Aboard)

At this point, the "Wake" rebelled:

Frank Milton Schulte was last night severely reprimanded and indefinitely suspended. I have been convinced that he was not trying. I have been in the game long enough to know that he is one of the greatest poets of modern times, but I must say that his work (recently) has been awful.

It is said that Schulte has been dissatisfied with his berth on the Wake and wants to be traded to Breakfast Food or Day Dreams. But the Wake manager has no intention of letting go of a man who is capable of filling so much space.

Ring next tried some pinch-hitters:

TRYOUT
by Art Phelan*
I've often wondered which would be
The greatest pain and torture—
To have bunions, like Tom Needham,
Or busted fingers like Jimmy Archer.

*Phelan batted for Schulte

TRYOUT
by Red Corriden*
I'll challenge Weaver of the Sox
And bet him all my tin
That I can make more errors in
An afternoon than him.

*Batted for Schulte

But the Wake could not get along without Schulte: "It was formally announced at Wake headquarters last night that the differences
between Frank Marvellous Schulte and the management have been
patched up. Schulte has promised to work harder and expects to
regain his old stride in a new series called 'Different Cities.' "

Of all the big league cities, one
Is easy to get lost in.
I hardly need to tell you that
The one I mean is Boston.
A man may think he knows his way,
But suddenly he'll lose it
In Boston, the metropolis
Of Mister Massachusetts.

After nearly a month of the city series, in which Schulte seemed
to get stuck frequently in Boston and Philadelphia, he got tired of
it and switched to another called "Romance, Love and Hate," which
began with:

I sympathize with Harry Thaw,
The poor unlucky man;
He's got to live in Canadaw
Or else in Matteawan,

and ran on far into the fall before Ring dismissed his poet at the
end of the season.

Ring invented a great variety of features for the "Wake," one of

110

the best of which was the letters of Bill to Steve. These ran in the
"Wake" at the same time the first "Busher's Letters" were appearing
in *The Saturday Evening Post;* both derive from his early experiments with baseball players' language. Bill's adventures appeared
intermittently in the column for more than two years, and they were
more amusing for their characterization of a typical ball player than
for their continuity:

*Steve: Well, Steve, I guess I told you that Schulte promised to
interduce me to the swell society girls from N. Y. down to Atlantic
City last Sunday, but he did not do no such a thing and when we
got down there, I asked him where was all them N. Y. .400 hitters
that you promised to interduce me to and he says I guess they must
of all slumped because I dont see none of them so how could he
interduce me. At that they was a lot of pretty girls down there in
batheing but most of them had guys a long with them but of coarse
I could of busted some of them guys in the nose and tooken there
girls a way from them but why should I start a hole lot of trouble
over a girl when I got a girl in Chi that is plum nuts over me and got
enough money to buy the hole town of Atlanta City but why should
any body want to buy it because they is not nothing there only the
ocean and some hotels and dago frute stores and they have not even
got cement walks but a old bord walk like this on Oak st down
home. We hung a round down there all day and I had a fare time
but if I had knew that we was not going to meet no girls I would
not of broughten no new out fit of shirts and collars because I might
as well of wore a swetter for all the good the new togs done me but
we went in batheing and I noticed they was a lot of girls give me
the onct over like they done up to Revere and if Schulte had not of
been a long probably I could of coped 1 of them. We came back to
Phila Sunday night and road back to the hotel on the st car and
Schulte says you better pay the st car fair so as you can tell the boys
you spent some money and then he says No I will pay the st car fair
so as you wont brake your record and I dont know what he was
talking about but he is a funny fellow and says a hole lot of things
that I can't make head or tale of them.*

Letters to Congress, letters from lovelorn stenographers to matinee idols, plays and dialogues, the Wake Matrimonial Bureau,
parodies of grand opera, fairy tales and bedtime stories, letters to
Ring's boss explaining why he is out of town—the "Wake" brought
endless surprises to its readers, who were a far vaster audience than
baseball fans. Everybody read the Wake; it was by far the best and

111

most popular column of its day in Chicago. People quoted it, and Ernest Hemingway and James T. Farrell, who were then in their teens, imitated the Lardner dialect in their high-school papers. It had considerable power, as Ring later pointed out:

> . . . I was doing a sport column on the Chicago Tribune. My readers had never learned to write, so I was entirely without contributions, and therefore hard up for material. On Thanksgiving morning I printed a dream story of a Michigan-Chicago game that was supposed to take place that afternoon. I wrote an introduction and followed it with a probable line-up, naming players who had been stars ten or twenty years in the past.
>
> Now, there had been no hint of a resumption of athletic relations between Chicago and Michigan. Moreover, Thanksgiving games had been ruled out of the Middle West long, long before, because they interfered with church or turkey or something. Nevertheless, believe it or not, a crowd of more than five hundred people—this is Mr. Stagg's estimate—went to the University of Chicago's football field that day and stood around for hours, waiting for the gates or the ticket windows to open. At length they returned home mad, and many of them telephoned indignant messages to my boss.
>
> That much goes to show that I had Chicago pretty well under my thumb when I sold it to the Sicilians. Also that the typewriter is pretty near as mighty as the rod.

Now that Ring was securely established on the *Tribune* staff, the Lardners were settled in Chicago for an indefinite period, and Ellis was expecting a second baby. The small apartment on Prairie Avenue was inadequate, and they bought property in Riverside, a suburb west of the city, and built a house, with money which Ellis had inherited at her father's death in 1912. Ring no longer had to travel for any length of time and he took a great deal of pleasure in his family and his new home.

The Lardners' second son, James Phillips, was born May 18, 1914. Ring wrote for Ellis to the Abbotts:

Dear Family:—
This here baby I've got now is probably the best looking baby that ever happened. He weighed 7-¾. While he is good looking, he also is mad looking. His expression is one of permanent anger. I don't know why. He cries very little, but thinks a whole lot. All the nurses say he is the prettiest baby they ever saw.
The alarm sounded about five o'clock Monday morning. I immedi-

112

ately told Ring to call up Dr. Courtright. Ring did so (he always does his duty) and also got me a taxi at some expense. The doctor was mad, as usual. He hurried with his shaving and cut himself twice. Then he had a quarrel with the hospital about the condition of the room, etc. Ring was mad because the taxi didn't come soon enough and the nurses were mad because the doctor bawled them all out. James Phillips was therefore born in an atmosphere of rage and he shows it.

I expect to be in the hospital (Washington Park) two more weeks. Then I will move to Riverside, where James Phillips and I will be glad to see each and every one of you.

Ellis

Ring's salary was less than three thousand dollars a year, and with a growing family he needed more money. He had written some baseball stories and submitted them to Chicago newspaper editors without success. Then early in 1914 he sold one to *The Saturday Evening Post,* which immediately asked for more; and after it was published he received offers from several national magazines. His income was substantially increased, and it kept growing steadily for many years. Even so he did not feel any financial security; he wanted much more for his wife and children than he had been able to provide, and he also wanted to help his family in Niles. His father had never recovered his losses, and his health was failing. Now Ring wrote to him urging him to install a new heating system in the Niles house and to hire a man to look after the yard and the garden. Ring was now able to pay for them. From that time on Ring gave away a considerable part of the money he earned; and at the height of his success he virtually kept a payroll of relatives and friends, broken-down baseball players, or Niles boys who were in difficulties; not even Ellis knew the extent of his secret charities.

There are several conflicting stories about how Ring sold the first "Busher's Letters": that they were rejected everywhere else before the *Post* bought them; that they were sent first to the *Post* and immediately accepted; that a scout for the *Post* virtually dug them out of obscurity. Actually Ring had some difficulty in selling them, but it was not a desperate struggle. While he was covering a World Series, he invented the character of a left-handed pitcher who gave an account of the games in the language with which Ring had long been familiar—the ordinary speech of the uneducated Midwesterner, peppered with baseball terms. It was very popular, especially among Ring's colleagues who recognized the authenticity of it and encour-

113

aged him to write more in that vein. He used it several times in the
"Wake," in a relatively unpolished form. Guy Lee, the Sunday
editor of the *Tribune*, offered Ring fifty dollars for any story he
could use in the feature section, and Ring wrote the first "Busher's
Letters." Lee turned them down, saying that his readers would
never accept the slang; and other Chicago editors refused them for
the same reason. Lee bet Ring a suit of clothes that no one would
take them. He sent them unsolicited to *The Saturday Evening Post;*
they came back so fast that Ring was convinced that the *Post* had
some sort of interceptor in Cleveland—they couldn't have got to
Philadelphia and back in so short a time. But in January 1914,
Charles Van Loan, who had been a sports reporter for the New
York *World* and was now a writer and a scout for *The Saturday
Evening Post,* came to Chicago, and Hugh Fullerton introduced
Ring to him.

Ring showed the rejected manuscript to Van Loan, who was convinced that George Horace Lorimer, editor of the *Post,* would publish it if he read it himself. He advised Ring to send it to Lorimer's
home address, while he wrote to Lorimer about it. A check came
back almost as fast as the manuscript had come back the first time,
and Lorimer asked for more. Ring received $250 for the first story,
the price for subsequent stories increasing at intervals by $250 until
it had reached $1250, which was Lorimer's top price at the time.

The "Busher's Letters" appeared frequently in the *Post* for the
next four years. Most of them were collected in book form, in three
volumes, of which the first, *You Know Me Al,* is still the most widely
known of Ring's works. It is in the form of letters written by Jack
Keefe, a pitcher from the Central League who is bought by the
White Sox, to his friend Al back in his home town. Jack is a true
yokel with a combination of innocence and arrogance, vain and
boastful of his athletic prowess. He fancies himself a lady-killer, a
shrewd tactician, a hail-fellow-well-met; he flaunts his successes, and
has a ready alibi for his failures, if he admits them at all. He is a
champion liar and fourflusher who deceives nobody but himself. He
thinks he is tough, but he is only thick-skinned; none of his igno-
minious defeats leaves a dent in his self-esteem. He is mean, petty,
and penurious; gluttonous, self-indulgent, and self-pitying. Yet he is
curiously sympathetic and not unlikable. He is not very much worse
than anyone else; he is real. He is not quite like yourself, but he
bears a fatal resemblance to your friends.

From the start everyone knocks him down to size, but he is un-
dismayed:

114

Dear Friend Al: Well I will be home in a couple of days now but I wanted to write you and let you know how I come out with Co-miskey. I signed my contract yesterday afternoon. He is a great old fellow Al and no wonder everybody likes him. He says Young man will you have a drink? But I was to smart and wouldn't take noth-ing. He says You was with Terre Haute? I says Yes I was. He says Doyle tells me you were pretty wild. I says Oh no I got good con-trol. He says Well do you want to sign. I says Yes if I get my figure. He asks What is my figure and I says three thousand dollars per annum. He says Don't you want the office furniture too? Then he says I thought you was a young ball player and I didn't know you wanted to buy my park.

We kidded each other back and forth like that a while and then he says You better go out and get the air and come back when you feel better. I says I feel O.K. now and I want to sign a contract be-cause I have to get back to Bedford. Then he calls the secretary and tells him to make out by contract. He give it to me and it calls for two hundred and fifty a month. He says You know we always have a city serious here in the fall where a fellow picks up a good bunch of money. I hadn't thought of that so I signed up. My yearly salary will be fifteen hundred dollars besides what the city serious brings me. And that is only for the first year. I will demand three thousand or four thousand dollars next year.

I would of started home on the evening train but I ordered a suit of cloths from a tailor over on Cottage Grove and it won't be done till tomorrow.

Jack runs afoul of the manager, makes a poor showing his first season, and is quickly hauled out:

After Veach had hit one in the eight Callahan calls me to the bench and says You're through for the day. I says It's about time you found out my arm was sore. He says I ain't worrying about your arm but I'm afraid some of our outfielders will run their legs off and some of them poor infielders will get killed. He says The reporters just sent me a message saying they had run out of paper. Then he says I wish some of the other clubs had pitchers like you so we could hit once in a while. He says Go in the clubhouse and get your arm rubbed off. That's the only way I can get Jennings sore he says.

Well Al that's about all there was to it. It will take two or three stamps to send this but I want you to know the truth about it. The way my arm was I ought never to of went in there.

Jack is sold to San Francisco, but before the end of the season he is back with the White Sox, and he stays with them in spite of incessant quarrels and threats to jump to the Federal League. In San Francisco he becomes engaged to Hazel—"and she is some queen, Al—a great big stropping girl that must weigh one hundred and sixty lbs. She is out to every game and she got stuck on me from watching me work." When he gets back East, she writes to ask him for a hundred dollars so she can come to Chicago to marry him. He sends her thirty dollars and asks Al to rent a house in Bedford for him. Then:

But Al I have got bigger news than that for you and I am the happyest man in the world. I told you I had not heard from Hazel for a long time. To-night when I got back to my room they was a letter waiting for me from her.

Al she is married. Maybe you don't know why that makes me happy but I will tell you. She is married to Kid Levy the middle weight. I guess my thirty dollars is gone because in her letter she called me a cheap skate and she inclosed one one-cent stamp and two twos and said she was paying for the glass of beer I once bought her. I bought her more than that Al but I won't make no holler. She all so said not for me to never come near her or her husband would bust my jaw. I ain't afraid of him or no one else Al but they ain't no danger of me ever bothering them. She was no good and I was sorry the minute I agreed to marry her.

Jack marries his roommate's sister-in-law Florrie and begins a domestic life of endless bickering. Jack is always broke, and borrows money from Al. Florrie is too extravagant. They move in with their in-laws, and out again; then the in-laws move in with them. Finally they separate, and Jack is going to "sew her for a bill of divorce." But they are reunited before their baby is born. Jack manages to economize even on naming the child:

Friend Al: Al I beat the Athletics 2 to 1 to-day but I am writing you to give you the surprise of your life. Old pal I got a baby and he is a boy and we are going to name him Allen which Florrie thinks is after his uncle and aunt Allen but which is after you old pal. And she can call him Allen but I will call him Al because I don't never go back on my old pals.

At the end of the season and several quarrels later Jack decides to take Florrie and little Al to Bedford to stay with Al. He writes

116

him the time of their arrival, and adds: "I wish you would ask **Ben Smith** will he have a hack down to the deepo to meet us but I won't pay no more than $.25 and I should think he should ought to be glad to take us from the deepo to your house for nothing." But two days later he suddenly decides to accompany the White Sox and Giants on a world tour and writes again to cancel the plans for returning home:

All so I remember I told you to fix it so as a hack would be down to the deepo to meet us to-night and you wont get this letter in time to tell them not to send no hack so I supose the hack will be there but may be they will be somebody else that gets off of the train that will want the hack and then every thing will be all O.K. but if they is not nobody else that wants the hack I will pay them ½ of what they was going to charge me if I had of came and road in the hack though I dont have to pay them nothing because I am not going to ride in the hack but I want to do the right thing and besides I will want a hack at the deepo when I do come so they will get a peace of money out of me any way so I dont see where they got no kick comeing even if I dont give them a nichol now.

After a great deal of wavering Jack does embark on the world tour; and in a moment of self-pity, for fear the ship will sink, he writes Al to say good-by:

Here is the things I want to ask you to try and do Al and I am not asking you to do nothing if we get threw the trip all right but if some thing happens and I should be drowned here is what I am asking you to do for me and that is to see that the insurance co. dont skin Florrie out of that $1000.00 policy and see that she all so gets that other $250 out of the bank and find her some place down in Bedford to live if she is willing to live down there because she can live there a hole lot cheaper then she can live in Chi and besides I know Bertha would treat her right and help her out all she could. All so I want you and Bertha to help take care of little Al untill he grows up big enough to take care of himself and if he looks like as if he was going to be lefthanded dont let him Al but make him use the right hand for everything. Well All they is 1 good thing and that is if I get drowned Florrie wont have to buy a lot in no cemetary and hire no herse.

Well Al old pal you all ways been a good friend of mine and I all ways tried to be a good friend of yours and if they was ever any thing I done to you that was not O.K. remember by gones is by

*gones. I want you to all ways think of me as your best old pal. Good
by old pal.*

Your old pal,
Jack

*P.S. Al if they should not nothing happen and if we was to get acrost
the Ocean all O.K. I am going to ask Mcgraw to let me work the
1st game against the White Sox in Japan because I should certainly
ought to be right after giveing my arm a rest and not doing nothing
at all on the trip acrost and I bet if Mcgraw lets me work Crawford
and Speaker will wisht the boat had of sank. You know me Al.*

Ring soon found himself with an audience of millions. It is not
hard to see why the "Busher's Letters" had such immediate and
immense popularity. Baseball was then as much the national pastime
as it is now; in fact it was far more ingenuous, much less organized
as an industry, and its great figures had something of the stature of
Paul Bunyan. In the character of Jack Keefe, Ring reduced the baseball hero to purely human dimensions. It may be that people take
an unaccountable pleasure in seeing their idols diminished; it brings
them closer. But it is probable that most people liked the Keefe
stories simply because they were funny. Nevertheless to discerning
readers they were a great deal more than that; they exploded the
myth of the baseball hero, although they did him no visible damage,
to judge by his continued popularity. And Jack Keefe is not merely
a baseball player; he is an average American, and there are millions
of him outside ball parks.

Ring had no illusions about the intelligence of ball players, but
he did not set out to debunk them with any missionary zeal. He
wrote about them as they looked to him. The quality of his vision
turned out to be satirical, but the stories are strict realism in their
language and their conception of character, even though the plots
are contrived according to the conventions of magazine fiction, and
the legitimate device of exaggeration is used for comic effect. The
important thing about Jack Keefe is that he is real and familiar,
he speaks the language one hears every day, his personal difficulties
and his reactions to them are much like any other dullard's.

Once Ring had been generally recognized as a satirist, it seemed
that everybody had known all along that the "Busher's Letters" were
a spoof on baseball and that Jack Keefe was the archetype of the
dumb athlete. This is true enough, but it begs the essential point.
Ring's influence on American prose has been so pervasive that it
is easily taken for granted; and Jack Keefe has been around for so

118

long that it is easy to label him as an eccentric type. It is instructive to observe how he appears to someone who knew and cared nothing about baseball or its players and would hardly have known whether or not they were being satirized. Virginia Woolf wrote an essay on "American Fiction," in which she discussed the merits of Sherwood Anderson, Sinclair Lewis, and Ring Lardner. This was in 1925, long after Jack Keefe had been discovered and tagged by American readers; but *You Know Me Al* was new to her. She had been impressed by Lewis but felt that his portraits were caricatures and that in some way he was apologetic for his American types.

. . . Look at Americans as an American, see Mrs. Opal Emerson Mudge as she is herself, not as a type and symbol of America displayed for the amusement of the condescending Britisher, and then, we dimly suspect, Mrs. Mudge is no type, no scarecrow, no abstraction. Mrs. Mudge is—but it is not for an English writer to say what. He can only peep and peer between the chinks of the barrier and hazard the opinion that Mrs. Mudge and the Americans generally are, somehow, human beings into the bargain.

That suspicion suddenly becomes a certainty as we read the first pages of Mr. Ring Lardner's You Know Me, Al, *and the change is bewildering. Hitherto we have been kept at arm's length, reminded constantly of our superiority, of our inferiority, of the fact, anyhow, that we are alien blood and bone. But Mr. Lardner is not merely unaware that we differ; he is unaware that we exist. When a crack player is in the middle of an exciting game of baseball he does not stop to wonder whether the audience likes the color of his hair. [The creator of Jack Keefe might not have agreed with this statement.] All his mind is on the game. So Mr. Lardner does not waste a moment when he writes in thinking whether he is using American slang or Shakespeare's English; whether he is remembering Fielding or forgetting Fielding; whether he is proud of being American or ashamed of not being Japanese; all his mind is on the story. Hence, incidentally, he writes the best prose that has come our way. Hence we feel at last freely admitted to the society of our fellows.*

That this should be true of You Know Me, Al, *a story about baseball, a game which is not played in England, a story written often in a language which is not English, gives us pause. To what does he owe his success? Besides his unconsciousness and the additional power which he is thus free to devote to his art, Mr. Lardner has talents of a remarkable order. With extraordinary ease and aptitude, with the quickest strokes, the surest touch, the sharpest insight, he*

119

lets Jack Keefe the baseball player cut out his own outline, fill in his own depths, until the figure of the foolish, boastful, innocent athlete lives before us. As he babbles out his mind on paper there rise up friends, sweethearts, the scenery, town, and country—all surround him and make him up in his completeness. We gaze into the depths of a society which goes its ways intent on its own concerns. There, perhaps, is one of the elements of Mr. Lardner's success. He is not merely himself intent on his own game, but his characters are equally intent on theirs. It is no coincidence that the best of Mr. Lardner's stories are about games, for one may guess that Mr. Lardner's interest in games has solved one of the most difficult problems of the American writer; it has given him a clue, a centre, a meeting place for the divers activities of people whom a vast continent isolates, whom no tradition controls. Games give him what society gives his English brother. Whatever the precise reason, Mr. Lardner at any rate provides something unique in its kind, something indigenous to the soil, which the traveller may carry off as a trophy to prove to the incredulous that he has actually been to America and found it a foreign land.

. . . But in America there is baseball instead of society, instead of the old landscape which has moved men to emotion for endless summers and springs, a new land, its tin cans, its prairies, its cornfields flung disorderly about like a mosaic of incongruous pieces waiting order at the artist's hands; while the people are equally diversified into fragments of many nationalities. . . . To describe, to unify, to make order out of all these severed parts, a new art is needed and the control of a new tradition. That both are in process of birth the language itself gives us proof. For the Americans are doing what the Elizabethans did—they are coining new words. They are instinctively making the language adapt itself to their needs. . . . It is significant that when we want to freshen our speech we borrow from America—poppycock, rambunctious, flipflop, booster, good-mixer—all the expressive ugly vigorous slang which creeps into use among us first in talk, later in writing, comes from across the Atlantic.

It is not Mrs. Woolf's views on the disparity between English and American culture that matter here. It is the fact that to her Jack Keefe was a real and fully rounded character in a masterfully written book. With no preconceptions about baseball players or even about Americans, she found him a fellow human being. Her essay is full of admirable perceptions. For American readers the mere mention of a ball game suggests the whole feeling and color of the ball park, and Jack Keefe's letters back home call up a familiar picture of small-town life; it is a proof of Ring's power that even for an English reader, who had in mind no such images and memories, his prose evoked Jack Keefe's whole world. This happens in all of Ring's stories. He was sparing of adjectives and wrote very little description, yet even when he is writing in character, and usually an inarticulate character with a limited vocabulary, his language has an extraordinary power of evocation.

Mrs. Woolf was absolutely right about the vigor and objectivity which Ring gained through his complete unself-consciousness, by keeping his mind firmly on his character. It is the source of the directness and immediacy of his stories; and these are the qualities of his fiction which have had the greatest influence on younger American writers.

It was Ring's great linguistic gift that made the "Busher's Letters" unique. He was not the first to use the language of uneducated people. Mark Twain had done it in *Huckleberry Finn*. Nor was he the first to use slang; George Ade had written *Fables in Slang*, "the slang consisting," Ring once wrote, "in every other word being spelt with a capital"; and Charles Van Loan, who wrote stories about sports, was using a kind of dialect at the time when he discovered Ring for *The Saturday Evening Post*. There was nothing new either about stories in letter form. The medium and the devices were commonplace enough; all Ring brought to them was genius. His style cannot be explained entirely as slang, dialect, or baseball argot, although it contains all of them. Much of the slang is no longer current in speech, but it is still perfectly expressive in the context of the stories. People no longer say, "You know me Al," as millions once did, but the phrase is no less valuable as a tag for Jack Keefe's foolish boasts. Some of the baseball argot is dated, but no one needs to know much about baseball terms to understand what Jack Keefe is talking about. And if dialect is a language spoken and understood only by the inhabitants of a certain region, then Ring's style, although it is based on Midwestern speech, is not merely dialect; it is understood all over America and in England too.

Ring's style, comprising these different elements, was his own creation, and it bears the stamp of his own genius; no imitator ever matched it. He achieved it by scrupulous observation and painstaking work; he suited it exactly to the characters he was writing about. He reproduced not only the vocabulary of his ball players but the

121

rhythm of their speech; their hesitations and outbursts of fluency suggest the workings of their minds. He also solved the difficult technical problem of writing dialect and still keeping it readable. His style is a perfect instrument. H. L. Mencken, who was one of the first to recognize Ring as a stylist and a philologist, found no flaw in all Ring's works. He expressed some misgivings as to whether people would understand Ring's characters' language in fifty years' time, but he need not have worried. More people talk like Lardner characters now than ever before.

It is easy to speak English badly, but very hard to make a literary style out of bad English. The idea that Ring wrote as he did because it was simple is false. He was very aware of the subtleties of common speech. An article he wrote for the *Bookman* in 1921 shows the fine accuracy of his observation. It was a review of *In American*, by John V. A. Weaver:

The faintest praise with which I can d—n the book is to say that it's a d—n good b—k of mostly verse, readable and buyable because the poems have story interest and are written in the language we, this means you, speak. Pure American, nearly. The few impurities are a lifesaver for the critic. We can't hope to land the old K.O. on the writer's jaw, but we can fret him a little with a few pokes to the ear.

For the most part this organ has served Mr. Weaver well. But I think that on occasion it consciously or unconsciously plays him false. It has told him, for example, that we say everythin' and anythin'. We don't. We say somethin' and nothin', but we say anything and everything. There appears to be somethin' about the y near the middle of both these words that impels us to acknowledge the g on the end of them. Mr. Weaver's ear has also give or gave (not gi'n) him a bum hunch on thing itself. It has told him to make it thin'. But it's a real effort to drop the g off this little word and, as a rule, our language is not looking for trouble. His ear has gone wrong on the American for fellow, kind of, and sort of. Only on the stage or in "comic strips" do we use feller, kinder and sorter. Kinda and sorta are what us common fellas say.

And how about the lines, "Now that I'm sure he never won't come back" and "You don't know how to dream and never won't"? Never will and won't never are American. Never won't ain't. Other lines I challenge are "I crope up on him" and "You should of hearn the row there was." I don't say crope and hearn are impossible. I do say crep' and heard are a great deal more common.

The line, "Look what I done for you and him and me," is good American, but better American, I believe, would be, "Look what I done for him and you and I." This, however, brings up a subject to which one ought to be able to devote a whole article, but one ain't goin' to. One is only goin' to state that mysterious rules govern the cases of personal pronouns in our language and one hasn't had time to solve the mysteries even since prohibition. We say, "He come up to me in the club," but we also say, "He come up to I and Charley in the club." Charley's presence in the club seems, for "some reason another," to alter my case. The other night I was reading a play script by one of this country's foremost dramatists; and recurring in it was the stage direction, "A look passes between he and So-and-So." But this playwright wouldn't think of saying or writing, "She passed he a look."

My theory on this particular point is that when the common American citizen, whom we will call Joe, was in his last year in school (the sixth grade), the teacher asked him how many boys there were in his family. He replied: "Just Frank and me." "Just Frank and I," corrected the teacher. And the correction got Joe all balled up.

Ring rewrote his first busher story several times, but after he had mastered the language, he did not need to revise. He wrote all his stories slowly and carefully in a single draft; then he changed nothing and stubbornly refused to allow any editorial intervention. He knew exactly what he was doing. When the *Post* set up the first story, a copy editor questioned what he thought to be an inconsistency in spelling: common, simple words were misspelled, but long and unfamiliar words and place names were correctly spelled. Ring pointed out that an uneducated ball player would assume that he knew how to spell such ordinary words as "series" and "schedule," and so he would write them as he pronounced them, "serious" and "skedule." But he would write "Philadelphia" correctly because he could see it on hotel stationery; and if he had any doubt about an uncommon word, he would look it up or ask someone how to spell it. Ring had seen enough actual letters from ball players to know how they were written.

Readers and baseball fans liked to speculate about who was the original of Jack Keefe. Ring's colleagues saw in him something of the braggadocio of Ping Bodie, the White Sox outfielder, and Frank Smith, the pitcher; his alibis reminded them of Ed Walsh. In addition, Fullerton saw in him the traits of Artie Hofman, Jimmy Sheck-

123

ard, Frank Schulte and Lew Richie of the Cubs. All of which indicates that there was no single original of Jack Keefe. He has the traits of many ball players in him, but he is a created character and now he is also a type. People did not know that he was an American type before they read Ring Lardner, any more than it had occurred to them that Huckleberry Finn and Tom Sawyer were types of American boys until Mark Twain had created them. After that everyone recognized them. Ring's ball player became so familiar that Heywood Broun could write, "Dizzy Dean wasn't born; Ring Lardner invented him."

In the preface to the 1925 edition of *You Know Me Al*, Ring wrote:

The writer has been asked frequently, or perhaps not very often at all, two vital questions regarding the letters published in this book: (1) Are they actual letters or copies of actual letters? and (2) Who is the original of Jack Keefe?

The first question seemed highly complimentary until you thought it over and realized that no one with good sense could have asked it. Some of the letters run as long as a thousand words and there is only one person in the world who writes letters of that length. She is a sister-in-law of mine living in Indianapolis, and when she sits down to write a letter, she holds nothing back. But she is a Phi Beta and incapable of the mistakes in spelling and grammar that unfortunately have crept into this volume.

As to the other question, I have heretofore declined to reply to it, as a reply would have stopped the boys and girls from guessing, and their guesses have given me many a thrill. But now there are no ball players left whom they haven't guessed, from Noah to Bucky Harris, and I may as well give the correct answer. The original of Jack Keefe is not a ball player at all, but Jane Addams of Hull House, a former Follies girl.

The publication of the first "Busher Letters" marks the beginning of Ring's career as a popular artist. Jack Keefe found a secure place among the characters of American fiction, and "You Know Me Al" became part of the American language.

CHAPTER FOUR

Even with a home of his own, the "Wake" column, and the unexpected success of his first published story Ring did not feel settled or secure. He was extremely ambitious and restless, and he was also determined. When he finally left Chicago for New York, it was not a sudden stroke of luck. He had been thinking about it for a long time and had planned it that way. After the publication of "A Busher's Letters Home" he wrote to Franklin P. Adams, who had already moved on to New York:

Chicago, March 12 [1914]

Dear Mr. Adams: I'm glad you liked the Post stuff and also glad that you took the trouble to write to me. It may not sound reasonable, but sometimes I almost prefer appreciation (from real guys) to dough. However, it's dough and the prospect of it that would tempt me to tackle the New York game. I think a gent in this business would be foolish not to go to New York if he had a good chance. From all I can learn, that's where the real money is. I'm not grabbing such a salary from the Trib. that I have any trouble carrying it home. But I do make a little on the side owing to my acquaintance with people hereabouts who want special stunts done—such as vaudeville acts, ads and alleged lyrics for stage songs. (Of course one might expect to get some of that work in New York after a reasonable length of time.) Moreover, I've just finished building a little house in Riverside, the suburb Briggs lived in until he heard I was coming. I suppose I could sell it or rent it, and I mention it merely as a thing I have to consider. I could be torn away from here

125

—and Riverside—for $8,000, and that's probably more than I'm worth. But you see how things are. It's not that I'm swelled on myself as much as some of our well-known diamond heroes, but that I'd have to get something like that to make the change pay. However, I suppose the sooner a person lands in New York, the sooner he feels as if he had a permanent residence. This letter, I'm afraid, is unintelligible in spots. I hope you may be able to make some sense of it. It might have been clearer if Ted Sullivan hadn't come in to see me twice during its composition.

Sincerely,
Ring W. Lardner

Happiest respects, as Jimmy Sheckard says, to Briggs and Rice.

What attracted Ring most about New York, aside from the prospect of making more money, was the theater. Chicago had always been a good show town, but everything originated in New York. But he had had no particular success in the theater and did not feel sure enough of himself to risk his present security.

One of the "stunts" on which Ring collaborated was a souvenir booklet called *The Homecoming of Charles A. Comiskey, James J. Callahan and John J. McGraw,* which he compiled with Edward G. Heeman to celebrate the return of the White Sox and Giants from their world tour on March 6, 1914. It was a collection of jokes, pictures, songs, and cartoons, with a foreword by Ring which seems perfectly solemn but must have been written tongue in cheek. The home-coming was a pretentious affair, marked by gala luncheons at the Biltmore in New York and the Congress Hotel in Chicago; the menus, including celery and olives, are reproduced complete, along with pictures of the hotels and fulsome descriptions of them; and a picture of the Sox's special train, which looks very much like any other railroad train. There are a few dreadful poems, and a song by Ring and Aubrey Stauffer, "He's a Good Old Scout," in praise of the three entrepreneurs; Joe Farrell contributed a song and Rube Goldberg a cartoon. It is a memorial to a milestone in international sport and good will and it is impossible to believe that Ring was not highly amused by his chore. Regarded as a serious production, it was a good deal below the intellectual sophistication of Niles, Michigan.

The Sox-Giants world tour also inspired Ring to write "The Busher Abroad," which appeared in four parts in *The Saturday Evening Post* the following year. Jack Keefe was still a fresh character, and his travels in the Orient and in Europe offered innumerable possibilities for him to display his mindlessness. His popularity seemed undiminished, but these stories somehow lack the reality and brilliance of the first series. Ring was writing of backgrounds he did not know, of situations that had to be contrived, and while his character and his style were consistent, Jack Keefe, away from his native surroundings, seems far less sure-footed in his stupidity and brashness than he was on the home grounds.

Ring's friend Joe Farrell—Joseph Chesterfield Farrell, to give him his full and stylish appellation—Ring's adversary in the famous silent marathon chess games, covered the Sox-Giants tour for the *Tribune*. In London, King George V attended a game, and Farrell was delegated to sit in the royal box and explain the fine points of American baseball to him.

"I started out," Farrell said later, "trying to be very factual about everything and refrain from using baseball expressions that were common to us. The King seemed to be an interested listener and he asked some questions. Most of the time he just watched and said nothing.

"There came a time in the game when the score was tied at 2 to 2 and the White Sox got a runner on third base, with two out. I volunteered that that was a crucial point in the game, and explained that if the White Sox got that run in, the way Jim Scott was pitching, it might decide the ball game. I explained in detail all the ways the run might come in, such as on a hit, an error, a wild pitch, a passed ball. The man on third, I said, could even steal home, though I remarked this would be unusual.

"The King just looked at me politely, nodded now and then, and finally turned to the field. Just then the batter hit up a dinky foul that the third baseman caught, retiring the side. The King turned around to me and said: 'A most useful catch, wasn't it?'"

In his dispatch to the *Tribune*, Farrell reported that he had shaken the hand of His Majesty. On the following day Ring wrote in the "Wake":

> *I wonder, will Farrell be just as of old*
> *And treat us as equals and chums?*
> *Or will he be distant and offish and cold*
> *And snobbish and mean to us bums.*
> *Will it be presumption to buy him a drink*
> *Since Farrell, Joe Farrell, shook hands with the Kink?*
>
> *He used to be so democratic and nice,*
> *The pal of us poor common folks.*

O, will he now freeze us with glances of ice?
Regard us as pests and as jokes?
I never will feel quite at home with the gink
Since Farrell, Joe Farrell, shook hands with the Kink.

Ring called Farrell the greatest natural comic he ever knew, and the two of them contrived some informal entertainments that are still classic in the memory of their contemporaries. Farrell suffered from none of Ring's shyness; he could and did talk enough for both of them, and he was noted for his oratory.

Ring was incapable of making a speech in public; in fact he talked only in the presence of close friends. Farrell was a fluent and willing orator. When Ring was offered $200 to make a speech at a banquet in Cleveland, he shuddered at the idea, and consulted Farrell, who agreed to go with him to lend him moral support. On his feet before an audience Ring dried up completely; so he and Farrell devised a way of carrying off the speech. Farrell announced that Ring had lost his voice and that he would speak for him. They stood side by side, and Ring pretended to whisper to Farrell, who then said: "Mr. Lardner says . . ." and improvised something relevant to the occasion. This went on until Farrell had delivered a suitable speech, which was quite successful. He and Ring split the fee.

Ring was once asked to make a speech at the Advertising Association of Chicago, without the assistance of Farrell. In desperation he bought a book on "How to Make a Speech," and when the time came he arose and without any preliminary remarks began to read Chapter I aloud in his usual dead-pan manner. The audience was slow to arouse, but when he came to "(Pause here for laughter)" he paused, and the laughter broke out uncontrollably.

On one of the few occasions when Ring actually attempted to make a speech, he tripped himself up badly. He had recently been elected a member of the Chicago Athletic Association, whose members were more businessmen than athletes. A banquet was given for an executive who apparently was retiring honorably from an exalted position. Ring was asked to speak, and he began by saying solemnly that it was too bad that Mr. —— had been fired. This unfortunately was exactly what had happened, and Ring found himself before a silent audience. It was his last speech at the Athletic Association.

At the Chicago Press Club, however, with Farrell as straight man, Ring had a great reputation as an informal entertainer. Ring, who never told funny stories and hated even worse to hear anyone else tell them, told one about two little girls named Pat and Mike and their Lithuanian nurse. It was long, involved, pointless, and as un-funny as anything could be. At intervals Joe Farrell would burst into uproarious laughter. Ring would proceed gravely, and again Farrell would explode. In the presence of two famous wits their listeners hesitantly joined in the laughter as the story went solemnly on, punctuated by Farrell's outbursts. It ended with the house burn-ing down with the two little girls and their nurse, and the entire Press Club reduced to tears.

A parody of a funny story was the closest Ring ever came to tell-ing one. As for listening to them, if anyone said to him, "Stop me if you've heard this one," Ring would promptly reply, "Stop." It never seemed to offend anyone, and his friends quickly learned that this was not Ring's kind of humor. When he was asked why he detested funny stories, he said, "Because most of them are so old, and most of them aren't funny anyway, and most people are such rotten storytellers."

Not all Ring's friends deferred to his aversion to storytelling. Irvin Cobb, whom Ring liked personally, was a professional raconteur, and his conversation as well as much of his writing consisted of one "funny" anecdote after another. One time they met in Chicago, where they had been covering a convention. Cobb had reserved a drawing room back to New York and invited Ring to share it. Ring appreciated the kindness but found himself trapped. All the way to New York he sat in silence while Cobb told joke after joke from his inexhaustible treasury. It may be that Cobb was just as impervious to Ring's spoken humor; in all his autobiography there is only one reference to Ring: he was present at a small gathering in Chicago where Cobb seems to have done all the talking. And when Ring once wrote, "Mr. Cobb is never so happy as when he is amongst his books of which he has a complete set," Cobb did not find it amus-ing.

Even worse than funny anecdotes, Ring hated off-color jokes. In fact he was almost pathologically squeamish about them, and when-ever he felt his sensibilities menaced by a story, he did his best to interrupt it or else left the company. Ring was quite used to fairly hearty companionship, in Niles and on his travels with ball clubs, and he did not mind hearing colorful language. But a pointedly lewd joke was highly offensive to him. It was only one symptom of his puritanical streak, and it was more than a superficial eccen-tricity. It was directly related to a rigid moral code and to an uneasy sexual repression which made any conversation about sex taboo. It was an attitude which became marked later in his life, when he criticized obscenity on the stage and waged a lone crusade against pornography in popular songs; but it is sufficiently evident even earlier in his life. It accounts for the total lack of any sexuality in his own writing, and his consistent abhorrence of sexual laxity. Even in the case of serious writers—Dreiser, Hemingway, and Anderson, for example, whom in some respects he admired—he did not really approve of the freedom with which they treated sex in their books. His prudishness—he admitted being a prude—was quite outmoded in the time and milieu in which he lived, but he clung to it stubbornly. Oddly, it did not seem to alienate people who had freer habits of mind; indeed most of them had a kind of respect for it. The persistence with which he upheld his standards of taste and morality raised them above mere naïveté—although there is something a little innocent about his objecting, as he is said to have done, to the relatively harmless performance of a quasi-strip-tease dancer at a Chicago Press Club stag smoker.

Most of the standards of conduct to which Ring had been brought up were being overthrown. The revolution in sexual morality hit its full stride just after the war, but even in the years preceding it Ring's own generation had cast aside a good many of the old rules, and he was going to find himself less comfortable in the world. He never accommodated his views to the new freedom. They were based on positive concepts of honor and decency and also of chivalry, because in this respect Ring was romantic; his rules were fixed and he had to observe them.

However, Ring's personal morality and his solemn air never dampened his companions' spirits. He was notably convivial, fond of idle pastimes and horseplay, in dread of being bored, and always eager for good company. In sporting and newspaper circles the company was often to be found in saloons. Ring had been a formidable drinker since early youth, and he had a creditable capacity. His mind stayed clear, he relaxed his usual habit of silence, and he could talk sensibly for hours. He never lost track of where he was, he remained aware of engagements, and he kept all his commitments. Since he produced a column for the *Tribune* every day and wrote a number of short stories and articles beside, it is hardly possible that his drinking was on such a heroic scale as the legend has made it out to be. The exact nature of his drinking exploits, too, is understandably obscured by the condition of the eyewitnesses. Of the dozens of anecdotes told of Ring when he was drinking only a few can be corroborated by reliable testimony.

Ring's early drinking was purely sociable, and it was limited by a shortage of money and by the necessity of working hard and regularly. One of the most familiar legends about writers who drink is that they sometimes write their most brilliant pieces when inspired by alcohol. Ring was a meticulous craftsman and writing was hard, slow work for him; it is just possible that he wrote an occasional column, or a story on a game or a fight, when drinking; it is not likely that it happened very often. He never missed a deadline, and he never let anyone else write a column for him. In his Chicago days, at least, his drinking was confined largely to those brief periods when he could finish a column or two ahead of the deadlines, to short trips or to weekends. After his marriage he had stopped drinking for a while; he had regular hours and spent a good deal of time at home. But like the rest of the *Tribune* staff, he frequently drank at Stillson's tavern, from which many legends emanated.

One of his companions at Stillson's was Ben Kendall, who worked on the *Tribune* city desk. He was a short, dark, slender, thin-faced man from Alabama, who was something of an oddity even in the motley newspaper world of Chicago, and an even odder companion for Ring, with whom he did not have much in common. But Ring always liked eccentric people, and Kendall was one of his confidants. Ring was already remarkably successful as a columnist and short-story writer, but he had spells of depression and needed reassurance. He and Kendall talked over drinks, Ring asking him if Kendall thought him as good a writer as Finley Peter Dunne, George Ade, or Harry Leon Wilson, or finally, as Mark Twain; and Kendall would tell him that he was the greatest of humorists. They sometimes drank together evenings; Kendall is said to have sent Ring telegrams signed "George Horace Lorimer" to lure him downtown on the pretext of talking over a story with his editor.

He drank enough to develop an obsessive sense of guilt about it and a dread of what it might do to him and his work. He sometimes called Burton Rascoe to his office in the *Tribune* building and unburdened himself of his misgivings. Ring believed that the manufacture of alcohol should be entirely prohibited; for medicinal or industrial uses a substitute could be found. As for himself, he said he couldn't write a paragraph if he'd had a drink. This may have been intended partly as friendly advice to a younger man, but he was perfectly serious, and he clearly showed the anxiety he felt about drinking. Even discounting his feeling of guilt about it, his own testimony is still more significant than anyone else's opinion; later, when he was writing a weekly column, he never drank unless

131

he had written it for some weeks ahead. He said that Prohibition would never work because people would manage to get alcohol as long as it was made. When Prohibition actually went into force, Ring had a momentary hope that perhaps he would get along without liquor, but his earlier guess had been right, and he went on drinking.

If at first he had drunk because he liked it, he kept on because he needed to. It deadened the shocks and dulled the pain of a discomforting clarity of vision and an extreme sensibility. As long as his health could stand it and he could work when he had to, it was an effective means of escape, and not an unreasonable one. He carried liquor well; it seemed to bring about no change in his personality, except to make him more talkative and demonstrative. He could drink and talk all night and still make complete sense; he did not become maudlin, aggressive, tiresome, or somnolent. Later, drinking seemed to increase his melancholy and bring on even deeper silences than were customary with him, but while he was a young man, it was no social disadvantage to him. But Ring was immoderate in everything: when he worked, he overworked; when he sought diversion, his pursuit of it was almost hectic; his habits, such as smoking, were excessive; when he worried, there was hardly anything he did not feel anxiety about; and like everything else, his drinking eventually became compulsive, and although he was a strong-willed man, will power alone did not suffice to overcome it entirely.

Ring's apparently contradictory qualities are really the signs of a remarkable consistency of character. He was an idealist and a perfectionist, and he was given to worry and self-doubt because he was always aiming at perfection; since he never thought that he came close to it, he never felt very sure of himself. His reticence and outward imperturbability concealed all kinds of misgivings; they also became a shield for his acute sensitivity. He remained silent much of the time because he did not talk unless he had something to say. It was not an unfriendly or forbidding silence. His poise and his grave courtesy were unaffected; he was genuinely kind, generous, sympathetic, and without pretense. He was strict without being censorious, and he showed a fine tact and consideration to everyone with whom he came in contact. He was universally liked.

He inspired both affection and awe, more affection than he ever could really accept, and probably more awe than he wished to inspire. Yet no one seems to have found him uneasy company. No one claimed to understand him, he seemed to live in the middle of a

132

solitude, but everyone accepted him and loved him. He could have sudden bursts of loquacity in the presence of the few people to whom he gave his confidence, and talk seriously and at length, first fixing his listener with a glance, then expounding an idea with his chin up and his eyes roving about the room, sometimes pointing with his middle finger for emphasis. Or he could spend a whole evening in company without saying anything, and then by one apposite remark—which no one could ever quote exactly afterward —give the impression of having been hilarious the whole time. His appearance—his awkward height, slenderness, and his large, dark, and rather mournful eyes—added to his singularity.

Ring's family was growing. His third son was born August 19, 1915 and named Ringgold Wilmer Lardner, Jr., and Ring wrote in the "Wake":

> *When you are nicknamed Ringworm by the humorists and wits;*
> *When people put about you till they drive you into fits;*
> *When funny folk say, "Ring, ring off," until they make you ill,*
> *Remember that your poor old dad tried hard to name you Bill.*

Ring, Jr. was known in the family as Bill.

By 1916, Ring's income was more than he had anticipated two years before, when he thought he was probably not worth $8000 a year; but his *Tribune* salary was still about $5000. James Keeley had fallen out with the *Tribune* and left with some rancor to become editor of the *Record-Herald*, financed by Illinois liquor interests which wanted an organ to counteract the rising propaganda of the Prohibitionists, who were gaining ground at an alarming rate. Although Chicago papers had a gentleman's agreement not to plunder each other's staffs, Keeley raided nearly every paper in town to get the men he wanted. Ring, whom he had encouraged the *Tribune* to hire, was one of them. Keeley offered him a substantial but not staggering increase in salary to come to the new paper, and Ring considered it seriously, since, in spite of increasing magazine sales, he was still preoccupied with raising his income. Keeley wanted Ring to resign from the *Tribune* at once without allowing his employer, Joseph Patterson, an opportunity to better Keeley's offer. However, Keeley's designs on local newspaper staffs could hardly have been a secret; Patterson countered Ring's resignation by offering to increase his salary from $75 a week to $200, on a three-year contract. Ring had made no binding commitment to Keeley and naturally accepted Patterson's offer. Keeley was indignant and accused Ring of a breach of faith, although there had been none. Nevertheless Ring worried about it, talked it over exhaustively with his newspaper friends, fearing that he had seemed unscrupulous. Ring had always felt that newspapermen were underpaid; no one could afford to be sentimental when such increases of salary were concerned; still Ring tormented himself over the fine ethical point of whether or not it was Keeley's offer that had pried a raise out of Patterson. He need not have concerned himself; Patterson had a shrewd idea of what Ring was worth to the *Tribune,* and he was under no obligation to Keeley. His offer settled Ring's dilemma. But Ring was so punctilious about all his undertakings that he was troubled by the idea that he had taken advantage of anyone.

Ring's standard of living was substantially increased by his new *Tribune* contract as well as by the sales of short stories and articles. The *Post* continued to publish Jack Keefe's letters and other baseball stories, and in addition he was selling to *Redbook, McClure's, American,* and *Metropolitan,* receiving about $750 for each piece. He had a workroom in the basement of his house in Riverside, and later took a room in the Great Northern Hotel when he needed complete solitude for work, a habit he continued for many years.

Sport was not his only subject. For *Redbook* he wrote a series of four stories later collected under the title *Own Your Own Home,* about Fred Gross, a Chicago detective who builds a house in a suburb of Chicago. Ring could draw on his own experience as a suburban householder for the situation, and the character is a relative of Jack Keefe; he speaks the same language, and has some temperamental resemblances. Gross writes letters to his brother Charley, telling him at first enthusiastically about the new home he is building, then with mounting irritation of the builders' mistakes and delays, the unexpected costs, the troubles with the plumbing, followed by a touch for a loan to cover it all. Then come the social climbing, the pointless efforts to outdo the neighbors in appearances, the Grosses' attempts to crash the best society of the suburb, all ending in sordid quarrels. Gross lets the air out of his neighbor's tires; the neighbor sends him a comic valentine; Gross puts a smallpox sign on the neighbor's house when he is about to give a party; they are all small and vindictive people who live in perpetual exasperation, anxious to create false impressions, justifying themselves by petty revenge, and relaxing in complacency when they think they have gained a momentary advantage over a rival social climber.

These are the first of the suburban figures who were also to appear in Ring's later stories; the ambitious new middle class which was to flourish in the twenties was already portrayed clearly in Ring's prewar stories of people who owned their own homes, bought pianos they couldn't play, cars they didn't know how to drive; who cheated at cards and complained continually about losing; whose values were not only material but of the very cheapest material; and whose relationships, between husbands and wives as well as among friends and neighbors, were based squarely on antagonism and jealousy.

But the stories are funny. You laugh at Gross's ignorance and despise his meanness, but his problems are like everyone else's, the vicissitudes of daily life, the endless chore of merely existing; however ruthlessly Ring might expose the idiocy and meanness of such people, he had the knack of hitting a vein of common experience which made them interesting and sympathetic.

The traits of the Grosses show up again in the series of stories first published in the *Post* in 1916 and later collected as *Gullible's Travels;* but there is a difference. Jack Keefe and Fred Gross are allowed to present themselves, but the narrator of the Gullible stories is a sardonic and wise type who comments on the other characters and on the action of the stories. He is an average American who speaks ungrammatically and spells as he pronounces, but he is no fool. If he is gullible, it is because he is indulgent and easygoing rather than stupid; and he pricks the pretenses of his wife and his friends with a sharp sarcasm. He is an indefatigable wisecracker, but he is sensible and practical; and he is continually showing up the brainlessness and fatuity of his fellows. He is a character with whom an unwary reader might identify himself. In the title story he allows his wife to persuade him to take an expensive trip to Florida in the hope of hobnobbing with society people; she is thoroughly snubbed when she is mistaken for a chambermaid, and returns home cured of her pretensions. Two other stories concern the wife's sister Bessie and her undesirable suitor, whom the husband gets rid of by subjecting him to a rough lake voyage. The narrator so far seems the embodiment of good plain common sense. When his wife aspires to become a member of a bridge club, he tolerantly goes along with her but ruins their chances by bidding ineptly. The polite gathering turns into a brawl, when his partner blows up:

"I won't play it!" she hollers. "I won't be made a fool of! The poor idiot deliberately told me he had spades stopped, and look at his hand!"

135

"You're mistaken, Mrs. Garrett," I says. "I didn't say nothin' about spades."

"Shut your mouth!" she says. "That's what you ought to done all evenin'."

"I might as well of," I says, "for all the good it done to keep it open at dinner."

This is social life among the urban middle classes. One shares the husband's contempt for it. And when his wife insists on his putting on evening clothes and going to see *Carmen,* and he does so under protest, the reader is on his side up to a point:

Carmen *ain't no regular musical show where a couple o' Yids comes out and pulls a few lines o' dialogue and then a girl and a he-flirt sings a song that ain't got nothin' to do with it.* Carmen's *a regular play, only instead o' them sayin' the lines, they sing them, and in for'n languages so's the actors can pick up some loose change offen the sale o' the liberettos. The music was wrote by George S. Busy, and it must of kept him that way about two months. . . . The first act opens up somewheres in Spain, about the corner o' Chicago Avenue and Wells. On one side o' the stage they's a pill mill where the employees is all girls, or was girls a few years ago. . . .*

The Hatches, their card-playing friends who have accompanied them to the opera, do not care for it, and Mr. Hatch spends most of the time in the bar. Gullible and his wife feel superior to them. When they discover in the next morning's paper that people who sit in boxes get their names in print, they decide to go again to the opera the following week and sit in a box. Gullible himself, the scorner of affectations, has succumbed to snobbery and found a new joy.

In some respects the narrator of these stories is a sketch for a character who appears in later stories. While he is a little crude and not immune to the foibles he delights in mocking in others, he is basically a man of rough common sense, salty humor, and an engaging turn of phrase. Ring used him in a play which he based partly on *Gullible's Travels* and partly on *The Big Town,* and he describes him there as "A wise boob; hails from a small town; migrated to Chicago; is convinced that it is the greatest town in the world. A thirty-five dollar a week man with a real sense of humor, reads all the newspapers, The Saturday Evening Post, The American Magazine, the Sunday supplements and an occasional popular novel. Has a faculty for crystallizing any subject he discusses into

136

a few lines, expressed in a manner characteristic of a certain type of American. Never had much use for rhetoric and proves it in his speech. A regular honest-to-god he man. Leads a regular life; has regular friends and is perfectly content to wade through life in a regular way." This is an idealization of Gullible, who probably reads nothing and errs a little bit on the side of the boob. But Gullible is a Lardner type who is central to much of Ring's fiction; and he is particularly important because he is essentially the "character" of Ring's most famous newspaper columns.

Although by 1917 Ring had written more than a score of short stories, his reputation was that of a humorist who used the short-story form. In an interview in the New York *Times* magazine section, one that is a curious mixture of sly humor and seriousness, he indicated that he was tired of baseball stories in dialect and wanted to write short stories in the third person. When he was asked who was the greatest living humorist, he promptly replied, "Elinor Glyn," and explained that her peculiar charm lay in the fact that her humor, like that of Conan Doyle and Harold Bell Wright, was unconscious. But he appeared to be quite serious in his views on American humorists:

Mr. Lardner is not one of those who pay unstinted homage to the memory of Mark Twain. To a question as to the name of the greatest humorist that America had produced, he said:

"Well, I wouldn't consider Mark Twain our greatest humorist. I guess that George Ade is. Certainly he appeals to us more than Mark Twain does because he belongs to our own time. He writes of the life we are living, and Mark Twain's books deal with the life which we know only by hearsay. I suppose my forebears would say that Mark Twain was a much greater humorist than George Ade.

"But I never saw one of Mark Twain's characters, while I feel that I know every one about whom George Ade writes. You see, I didn't travel along the Mississippi in Mark Twain's youth, so I don't know his people. Harry Leon Wilson is a great humorist, and Finley Peter Dunne is another. But I'll bet Finley Peter Dunne is sick of writing in Irish dialect."

"But as to Mark Twain," said the reporter, "you admire his 'Huckleberry Finn,' don't you?"

"Yes," said Mr. Lardner, "but I like Booth Tarkington's 'Penrod' stories better. I've known Booth Tarkington's boys and I've not known those of Mark Twain. Mark Twain's boys are tough and poverty-stricken and they belong to a period very different from

137

that of our own boys. But we all know Penrod and his friends.

"No, I certainly don't believe that Mark Twain is our greatest American humorist. Some of his fun is spontaneous, but a great deal of it is not."

An extemporaneous interview does not necessarily reflect a considered opinion, and Ring was often misquoted. Nevertheless he seemed quite sure that Ade and Tarkington, Wilson and Dunne were greater humorists than Mark Twain, although the reasons he gave have no objective validity. When Ring was eighteen, *Tom Sawyer* and *Huckleberry Finn* were his favorite books, and no doubt he still liked them even though he did not think them very humorous. He was always more interested in contemporary writing than in classics, and these writers also had more influence on him.

The many similarities between Ring's work and Mark Twain's do not inevitably imply a direct influence, but it is hard to doubt that Mark Twain had some influence on Ring. But the writers who influenced him most immediately were those who were currently popular and those he had known personally: Charlie Dryden, Charles Van Loan, Fullerton, Hugh Keogh, Wilson, William McGeehan, and possibly Dunne. They all wrote about the contemporary scene and used to some extent language as it was actually spoken. There is a great deal more resemblance between Mark Twain's and Ring's use of dialect than between Ring's and that of any of the writers he was reading when he first began to write; but the latter gave Ring a more direct stimulus. They were not so much specific influences as examples. They were all sports writers or popular-magazine writers; their medium allowed them considerable freedom to develop a personal manner. Ring, following them, had the same latitude in which to perfect an individual form of expression. All of them had in common an ear for everyday language; Ring's use of it, as well as the cast of his humor, was entirely his own. As with any authentic genius, influences were secondary and circumstantial. He was an original.

In this interview the *Times* reporter seems to have composed his questions after having heard Ring's answers:

"Most successful writers seem to want to do a sort of work different from that with which their names are associated. They seem to grow tired of the sort of writing that brings them fame. How is it with you? Do you still enjoy writing about baseball players?"

Mr. Lardner gave a melancholy smile.

"No," he said. "I'm tired of this sort of writing. I'd give anything

138

*to be able to stop writing dialect stories. And I'm tired of writing in
the first person. I'd like to write in the third person."*

*"Do you think," the reporter asked, "that it is good for a fiction
writer to have regular employment, such as your newspaper
work? . . ."*

*"Writers ought not to do anything but write," said Mr. Lardner.
"The necessity of working for a living at something besides writing
inevitably robs a writer of much of his energy, and causes his work
to deteriorate. . . . I'd like to do nothing but write fiction, and fiction of an entirely different sort from that which I write now."*

He went on to say that short stories would be better if authors
were to limit themselves to three stories a year and magazines to
pay as much for three stories as for twelve; the fact that the demand exceeded the supply led to the publication of inferior work.
He thought that Henry Sydnor Harrison (who was also a sports
writer) was our best story writer; he did not write too much and
he took pains with his work. He enjoyed the stories of W. L. George
and some of H. G. Wells's, and the books of St. John Ervine. Of
all humorists he liked best Edward Lear and Lewis Carroll.

In the years that followed Ring wrote many stories in the third
person; he also continued to write baseball stories in dialect, and,
like other popular writers, he had to write more than he wanted to
in order to make a living, and he inevitably published some second-
rate stories. He also went on being a newspaperman for a decade,
and he never got over the newspaperman's habit of mind, of regarding each day's work as finished and forgotten when the deadline
was met.

At the time when Ring was paying tribute to the established
popular writers of an older generation, he was living in the midst
of a flourishing literary renaissance, but he was no more aware of it
than the other young Chicago writers who contributed to it. Even
when in retrospect these writers were seen to have constituted a
more or less cohesive school, Ring never seemed to belong to it, although he grew to literary maturity at the same time and place,
and under the same circumstances as the rest of them. Some of
them he knew, at least casually, as fellow newspapermen, and since
he read widely and was generally aware of what went on around
him, he was acquainted with some of their individual works. But
he was quite unconscious of them as a literary movement, and none
of the principal figures of that movement had any direct influence
on him.

Chicago had long been the acknowledged cultural center of the Midwest. The region had never been devoid of culture. Willa Cather came from Nebraska with an intellectual heritage that was admired in Boston; families like the Lardners who came from the East to settle the land were highly educated. But as the area of economic development grew more vast and energies were consumed in the building of transportation and industrial centers and the exploitation of land, culture was spread rather thin until it found its focal point in Chicago in the 1890's. The Columbian Exposition of 1893 gave it a new impetus, official sanction, and money. If the fine arts came off rather badly there, at least they were recognized. Presently Chicago had its Library, Art Institute, Field Museum, a symphony orchestra, an opera house, and the University of Chicago. By the turn of the century it had become a center for a generation of alert, vigorous, and talented young men and women who in their Midwestern towns had been isolated from cultural advantages.

The writers came mostly from small towns; few of them were natives of Chicago. Among the earliest Theodore Dreiser came from downstate Indiana; later Carl Sandburg came from Galesburg, Illinois, Vachel Lindsay from Springfield; Sherwood Anderson from Ohio, Edgar Lee Masters from Kansas, Floyd Dell from Iowa, Ben Hecht from Racine, Wisconsin. These and many others came to the city for various personal reasons, not to found a movement, and not always driven by purely artistic ambitions. The literary circles which the writers frequented were not highly organized. A young writer coming to Chicago early in the century would find some circles rich, fashionable, and conservative; others poor, bohemian, and radical; but mostly he would not find circles at all, but a number of individuals working independently in an atmosphere that was supercharged with vitality. Many of the writers were working newspapermen and produced their stories, novels, plays, and poems in their spare time.

Others had more conscious and dedicated literary aims, such as the group that surrounded Harriet Monroe when she founded *Poetry: a Magazine of Verse* in 1912, and began to publish Yeats, Ezra Pound, and the imagists, and new American poets like Lindsay, Sandburg, Masters, Alfred Kreymborg, Maxwell Bodenheim, Edna St. Vincent Millay, Eunice Tietjens, and others. Margaret Anderson founded the *Little Review* and published the works of James Joyce and other European writers. The *Friday Literary Review,* a supplement to the *Evening Post,* became an outstanding literary paper under the editorship of Francis Hackett; and when Burton Rascoe became literary editor of the *Tribune,* he filled its columns with reviews of the new American writers and also of established European writers.

By the time the Chicago writers were recognized as a school, most of them had moved on to New York. They had become a vital and conspicuous force in American letters in the years just before the First World War and had brought about the eclipse of the genteel tradition of the late nineteenth century. In spite of some differences in age and background and talent they had common motives and aims: they were in revolt against the narrowness of small-town life, against the traditional form and style of the conservative Eastern writers. They were realists and iconoclasts; in politics many of them were radical; they had been exposed to Debs and Ingersoll, but they were motivated by a spirit of egalitarianism and individualism rather than by ideology. They all wanted personal and artistic freedom.

There was no social cleavage between the literary and journalistic worlds in Chicago in Ring's time. Burton Rascoe and Harry Hansen moved freely in both, Ben Hecht and Charles MacArthur were in and out of many a newspaper office and just as many literary gatherings, and a good many writers, from those who turned out to be giants like Sandburg down to the feckless aesthetes and bohemians, did workaday jobs on Chicago papers. Yet Ring never knew many of them personally. As a writer he was proceeding quite independently, and his personal life revolved around a conventional suburban home and family. His only public acknowledgment of the existence of a high-brow literary world was an occasional parody of an imagist or "cubist" poem in the "Wake"; and for the most part the literary world was unaware of him except as an amusing columnist; neither suspected that they would be mentioned in the same pages of future literary histories.

There are resemblances between Ring and the Chicago writers with whom he is often identified. Like most of them, he left his small town for the city, but he was moved by ambition, and a fancy for brighter lights and better baseball teams rather than by a spirit of revolt against a narrow kind of life. Niles was too small for him, but he never showed any positive distaste for it. He had not felt alienated from the fountainheads of culture or isolated on the prairie. If in the end he became a greater iconoclast than any of the self-conscious rebels of his generation, it was not the images of Niles, home, family, or childhood that he shattered. He remained faithful all his life to the values of his early environment; it was the world he found outside it that was to repel him. He was not seeking self-expression or personal freedom through writing. It was a professional matter with him. It was only later, and then rarely, that he became self-conscious about being a writer. Literary life, as such, did not attract him, although in New York he would see a good deal of it; it was only certain people who drew him, and they could be anywhere.

Ring often went back to Niles, where he had many friends, and took an interest in local activities. It was still a good town for sports and gambling. Some of its leading citizens enthusiastically promoted prize fights and backed the baseball team, the Niles Blues, with heavy bets. Like many other bush-league teams, the Blues tried to get big-league players for Sunday games, and Ring sometimes was able to induce his ball-player friends to participate. It was against league rules and the player was liable to a fine. The Blues overcame this small obstacle by paying the fine, plus a fee, sometimes as much as $250. The Blues had an important game scheduled with Benton Harbor and wanted Ring to get them a pitcher. Ring did, the pitcher pitched a shutout game and also hit a home run, and $25,000 in bets is said to have changed hands that day. The pitcher was Guy Morton of the Cleveland Indians.

Ring's social life, like any newspaperman's, was lived all over town, but it centered in his home and family. Ellis, like Ring, had brothers and sisters of whom they saw a great deal; their combined family circles were a considerable throng, and a merry one. He was on close terms with his fellow workers on the *Tribune*, not only sports writers, but all the staff. Two young women society reporters, India Gillespie and Kate Weber, were especially fond of Ring, and he was friendly, attentive, and helpful to them. Miss Gillespie had come from the South at the age of nineteen, tremendously impressed with Chicago and eager to acquire an urban sophistication, and Ring took great pleasure in contributing to her education. He and Ellis invited the girls to their home, and Ring often took them to the sports events he covered, and had dinner with them when he stayed downtown in the evening. The girls had a taste for night clubs, boxing matches, and restaurants which were supposed to be frequented by gangsters, and Ring was a very knowledgeable guide. He took them to Big Jim Colisimo's, where Dale Winter, a protégée of Big Jim's, sang. Ring had a sentimental crush on her and liked to admire her from a distance. It was a large, inelegant restaurant with a raffish clientele. A party of men and women sat at a table next to

142

Ring's, ordered drinks, and got very boisterous. Suddenly one of the men leaned across the table and delivered his girl a blow on the jaw. She fell over in a faint, while two husky bouncers removed the ungentlemanly character. The girl came to and said in a loud, clear voice, "Thank God, now I know he loves me."

The young ladies were properly thrilled by this coarse episode; it was just what two well-bred Southern girls would find exciting in Chicago. Ring, too, seemed quite gratified by it. When the girls thought it over, however, it seemed a little too pat to them. They never got over the suspicion that Ring had arranged the scene as a treat for them; and it is quite possible that he did.

In the course of their education in city ways Miss Gillespie and Miss Weber wanted to see what was then called a "black-and-tan" night club, and Ring and a friend from the city desk took them to one. Miss Gillespie, however, was not quite so steeled to the experience as she thought she would be, and when the entertainment became too risqué for her taste, she faintly asked Ring if they could leave. Ring chivalrously took her away, somewhat amused but probably just as willing to leave as she.

In their turn the girls asked Ring to go with them to the opera, which they were taking in along with the other cultural advantages of city life. Ring always went, under protest, never admitting that he enjoyed it. His views on opera were roughly the same as the man's in *Gullible's Travels*. Still, he did go, and there is hardly a case on record where Ring was dragged anywhere against his will; and so he must at least have enjoyed the company. When they asked him to go to the opera especially to meet some visiting friends from Little Rock to whom they wished to exhibit him with pride, Ring obliged but never said a word all evening. The girls' friends were a little piqued and asked why they had brought an undertaker.

The three of them dined at Freiberg's or the Louisiane, and the girls tried to make Ring eat. He had very little appetite and had to be coaxed. He repaid their solicitude with favors, of which they asked many—he called them the "Gimme Girls" because he said they always wanted something. In their company he was talkative and amusing. He was susceptible to youth and charm and he had a great capacity for friendship with women, and he enjoyed their company as much as that of men. He had none of the locker-room chauvinism of the average male; he liked wit, intelligence, and beauty in themselves, and found them especially attractive in women. He treated them with an unself-conscious gallantry and an equitable confidence and friendliness which made him very much loved by his women friends; and they found in him a kind of sensibility which is generally thought to be characteristically feminine.

He idealized women, and when he wrote of those who fell short of his ideal, the portraits were harsh and bitter. There are very few admirable women in all his stories; there are very few admirable men, either, but when women were coarse, egotistical, or pretentious, they were much worse because he had expected them to be so much better. The women of his stories, ambitious, mercenary, jealous, and domineering, are the obverse of his sentimental ideal.

In the spring of 1917, Ring and Ellis sold their Riverside house. America's entry into the war unsettled their lives as it did everyone else's, and Ring had no definite plans for the future, although the idea of going to New York eventually was in the back of his mind. It was an advantageous time to dispose of the property, which tied him to Chicago, even though the uncertainties of wartime precluded his making a drastic change at the time. Ellis and the children went to St. Joseph, Michigan, for the summer, and in the fall Ring rented a house in Evanston. He was exempt from the draft because he was "thirty-two years old, with a dependable wife and three unreliable children," but in August 1917 he went to France as a correspondent.

From the outbreak of the war in Europe in 1914 the *Tribune* had taken a neutralist position and as pressure on the side of intervention increased it became more outspoken; and it represented the prevailing opinion of the Midwest at the time. But in the East and locally interventionist propaganda increased; after Wilson's re-election in 1916 on the slogan "He kept us out of war" most of the American press became overwhelmingly interventionist, and the fortunes of the Allies made American participation in the war inevitable.

Ring's writing before America entered the war, and after, showed no political character whatever. In fact, it was anti-political. The issue affected the daily lives of everyone, including the sports world, and the "Wake" carried reverberations of it. In May 1916, at the opening of the presidential campaign, Ring ran a semiliterate poem expressing a mild bias in favor of Wilson:

THE PRESIDENT HAS A FRIEND
The 1916 campaign is on,
Each candidate's in line
To take a chance at skill and fate,
As they have other times.

We cannot say we have a choice,
Since we're somewhat a floater,
For well you know if this was so,
The Bunch would have no voters.

Of those that fate's decreed to run,
The chances seem the wider
For him that's famed so far and near
By hunting moose and tiger.
W.H.T. one time the thrown held down,
They call him Bill for short.
I spose he's groomed to run again.
I no he likes the sport.

And Billy B. is on the job,
He's always there in line,
So with our pleasure we may vote
For him at any time.
For some of us already know
The champion we'll vote for.
He is the guy with matchless brains
That's kept us out of war.

Since this is written in character, it is hardly a rousing declaration for Wilson.

After America's entry into the war Ring wrote dryly in the "Wake":

PLAN VIGOROUS WARFARE

Washington, D.C. (Special to the Wake)—The president and his cabinet, after a protracted session this afternoon, announced a policy of vigorous warfare against Germany, to be in effect the instant that nation does something to us it shouldn't ought.

The reporters were given the plans by Secretary Daniels, who read them from his portfolio. Briefly, this country intends to

1. Stop the sale of frankfurters by amusement parks, baseball clubs and circi.

2. Hiss ball players like Felsch, the Wagner, Knabe, Hoblitzel, Heilmann, Schneider, Shultz, Schulte, Zimmerman and Myers.

3. Drop the word "Gesundheit."

4. Suppress Skat.

5. Be shaved only by allied barbers.

6. Drink none but Jim M's beer.

7. Patrol the Des Plaines River with a leaky canoe.

8. *Change the names of the Chicago streets, Goethe and Schiller,
to Chambers and Glyn.*

9. *Eschew sour kraut.*

And in the same vein he wrote:

WASHINGTON CORRESPONDENCE

*Washington, Aug. 3 (Delayed)—There being no other business
before the Senate save trifling legislation pertaining to some unim-
portant war we are said to be engaged in with Germany, it was
decided to dispose of a bill having to do with the preservation of
certain migratory birds. The Canadian government, it seems, opined
that these birds ought not to be shot and suggested to our government that both Canada and the U.S. act to that effect.*

*The preliminary red tape had been disposed of and all that re-
mained was for the Senate to take its final vote, provided there was
no objection.*

Senator Reed of Missouri objected.

*"We have no evidence here that the Canadian government has
acted," said he. "The Canadian government proposed this legislation and now you are trying to make us pass it before we know
whether or not Canada has done anything about it."*

*The sponsor for the U.S. end of the bill arose and said he had
read in a Canadian newspaper that parliament had already passed
the law.*

*"Yes," said Senator Reed, "but we have not been officially notified.
There is not one Senator here who can get up and guarantee that
Canada has acted."*

(He said this often.)

*"If you gentlemen keep on doing business this way," said Senator
Reed, "the time will come when you and this country will regret it.
We have no evidence that the Canadian government has acted on
this law."*

(He said this seven times.). . . .

*When Senator Reed began his hair-raising speech, four-fifths of
the statesmen present had gone out to smoke. But they were back in
time to vote on his motion (to table the bill). The vote was forty-
three Noes to six Ayes. Elapsed time: one hour and fifty minutes. . . .*

Ring was unmoved by any wartime enthusiasm, but like many
other newspapermen, he wanted to go overseas because it looked as
though the war were the biggest assignment. *Collier's* engaged him

for a series of articles, and he continued to write the "Wake." The trip seemed to be disappointing from the start. "General Pershing has just shut down on having correspondents travel with troop ships," he wrote to his mother from New York, "so I guess I can't be in soldiers' company on the way over . . . I enclose a sheet from the [Ziegfeld] Follies program. Contrary to my previous information, the song Bert Williams is singing is one to which I wrote both words and music. He has been sick and didn't do very well with it the night we heard him. It was the only song he sang. He expects to put it on a record this fall."

On shipboard he found himself among a group of oddly assorted civilians, some of whom appeared to have very little business going to France at all. When he landed at Bordeaux, he was held up by the immigration authorities, a practical joke arranged by some shipboard acquaintances, and not very funny. He got to Paris in a leisurely way and applied for permission to visit the British front. While waiting for the formalities to be observed he looked around Paris and the American camps and wrote his column. His cables to the *Tribune* were headed "In the Wake of the War," and if the title is feeble, it is at any rate literal. Ring never got to the front, and did not try to get very close to it, since he was not sent to cover military action. He wrote about the backwash of the war, the camps, officers' headquarters, life in Paris, the inconsequence of military bureaucracy; and he was not amused by any of it. His first dispatch to the *Tribune* was an account of a baseball game between American and Canadian soldiers. "At the end of the fourth, the score was 5 to 5 and I left on account of illness." His next, one of a series, was a lesson in French: "The French for Dog is Rover, the French for Taxicab is Murderer, the French for Waiter is Jesse James, etc." Lesson Two continued: "Comme du like Paris? We suis crazy about him. Au comme long are vous restez here? Till I get enough money to leave." Although the humorous limitations of this vein were obvious, Ring continued the feature in a sort of Busher French until it got tiresome. There was not much else to write about.

After some tedious attempts to cut military red tape he visited an American camp where he found that the censorship far exceeded the available news. The officers were bored, the men were bored, the proverbial French rain fell incessantly, the muddy roads were nearly impassable, and getting back to Paris was as hard as getting out of it.

He met Floyd Gibbons, the *Tribune's* regular correspondent, in Paris and borrowed a spare uniform for a trip to the British front.

147

"You look as if you had been poured into it," Gibbons remarked; but Ring felt as though he hadn't said "When" soon enough. On the way to visitors' headquarters by train Ring and Gibbons conversed with Australian soldiers about baseball, and stopped to see a Chinese labor camp, where Ring pretended to learn to speak Chinese in a few minutes. His struggles with languages provided him with a good deal of his copy.

The American visitors' headquarters behind the British lines was the château of Radinghem, near St. Pol, and well staffed with French servants, stocked with food and wine, run like a caricature of a British officers' mess, and presided over by a major who afflicted Ring with a paralyzing boredom. The rest of the officers were no more interesting, the atmosphere was distinctly behind-the-lines, and there was no wartime anxiety visible. Ring and Gibbons had met Hal O'Flaherty of the New York *Sun* on the way; they had stopped for drinks and all arrived at the château in high spirits, which wore off in the course of a long, formal dinner, during which an orderly stood behind each chair and Ring spoke his newly acquired Chinese with a Harvard professor. While Gibbons and O'Flaherty visited a Canadian trench the following day, Ring was stuck at the château with the major, who kept telling him jokes of which he—the major—had failed to grasp the point. Ring needled him in every possible way without penetrating his imperturbable blankness. The major called his attention to the dining-room mural, a ghastly barnyard chromo, depicting a milkmaid and a cow and an ox with his tongue in a tin can labeled "Ox Tongue." The major thought it was pretty good. After lunch Ring went to his room, got a length of string and a bent pin, and tried to fish in the moat from his window. He hooked a swan, which caused a slight flurry until the servants disentangled it from the line.

The next day the correspondents visited a training camp and watched a squad of underage ineligibles drilling, and the day after, with the Harvard professor and an American philanthropist whose presence was unexplained, made an expedition to a point from which the British trenches could be seen through strong field glasses. There was some desultory sniping going on, but no organized action. Then Ring returned to Paris and after an unconscionable amount of red tape managed to clear himself to go to London.

In France everything had been frustrating, drab, and pointless, but in London Ring enjoyed himself with O'Flaherty and Webb Miller, a war correspondent who came from Dowagiac, Michigan, a few miles from Niles. They went to shows nearly every night; one of them, *Chu Chin Chow*, he liked so much for its music that he saw it over and over again when it came to America after its London run. He also made the rounds of the night clubs and, inspired by the plenitude of good whiskey, he made friends with the orchestras and singers, and at his most exuberant introduced the American song, "I'm a Little Prairie Flower, Growing Wilder Every Hour," which enjoyed a brief but intense popularity in the West End because of Ring.

Aside from the pleasant interlude in London, everything about the trip abroad seemed dismal. Ring appeared to be ill at ease, and he did not have his heart in the assignment of covering the war from a humorous angle. The articles "A Reporter's Diary," which appeared in *Collier's* in November and December of 1917 after Ring got back from Europe, are written in a low key of understatement and disparagement; they have little enthusiasm or wit. A few casual conversations with soldiers are in his best vein; but he did not see many enlisted men, and he was trapped in an unreal world behind the lines where the issues of war and the tragedy of it seemed to have no importance. Being a humorist there was a distinct disadvantage. He knew that he couldn't kid a war, and so he limited himself to a straight report on what he saw, with some sardonic and skeptical comments.

The articles were published the following year in book form under the title *My Four Weeks in France;* the first chapter title, "Dodging Submarines to Cover the Biggest Game of All," indicates how miscast Ring was in the role of war correspondent. The humor of the book derives from continual frustration, from the stupidity of military people, the meaninglessness of bureaucratic procedure, the irrationality of the French language and of foreigners in general; the apparent silliness of a war of which all he saw were Chinese laborers in pens, brass hats in châteaux, squads drilling in mud, traffic jams in Paris, and complacent supernumeraries everywhere. He seems to have felt that he didn't have much business being there himself. He was reduced to making easy fun of foreigners and fiddling with lame jokes about languages, like a literate Jack Keefe venting his xenophobia. He did not, in fact, have much feeling for Europe, and his attitude toward the oddities of alien ways was a little provincial.

After Ring got back from Europe, he wrote another series of Jack Keefe letters for the *Post*. Although Ring displayed no wartime zeal, Jack Keefe assumed a glowing patriotism. In 1917, Ring wrote a Jack Keefe letter in support of the Liberty Loan drive, without a trace of irony. Then Jack is called to the colors. In his first brush with his draft board Jack tries hard to dodge the call; that story is significantly omitted from the book composed of Keefe's experiences in training camp: it shows Jack as a very willing slacker. But once in the Army, Jack is out to lick the Germans singlehanded; he is still boastful and vain, the butt of the practical jokes of his Army buddies, and as a soldier his fans found him brimming with a noble resolve.

My Cher Ami: I suppose you will think I have gone crazy when you read the way I started this letter out and you will wonder if I have gone crazy. Well Al that is the French word for my dear friend in English so you see I have not gone crazy after all. . . .

Well Al we had some lessons in trench takeing today and I feel like I had been in a football game or something. We would climb up out of the trenchs that was supposed to be the U.S. trenchs and run across Nobody's Land and take the trenchs that was supposed to be the German trenchs. . . .

Well Al this may be the last time you will ever hear from me or at least for a long time and maybe never. I'm going over there old pal and something tells me I won't never come back . . . Well Al it's a big honor to be 1 of the men picked and it means they have got a lot of confidence in me and you can bet they are not sending no riff and raff over there but just picked men and I will show them they didn't make no mistake in choosing me.

Jack's training-camp experiences were collected in *Treat 'Em Rough*, and Ring continued to write about his adventures overseas in six more *Post* stories. In France, Jack takes command of the war, and his buddies encourage him to become a master spy. When he finally discovers that he has been tricked, his companions "was all set to give me the Mary ha ha but I beat them to it. 'Well, Alcock,' I says when I come in, 'you are some joke Smith but you wouldn't think you was so funny if I punched your jaw.'" Eventually Jack gets beaten up by the "spy" he is trailing. "But," he concludes, "they better remember that they's plenty of time for the laugh to be on the other foot before this war is over." Jack flirts with French girls, writes Pershing letters of advice on "stragety," and is finally ignominiously wounded in a tussle with a "bosh" who turns out to be one of the pranksters of his own company; his single military engagement is just another practical joke. Ring let Jack follow his bumbling nose through a series of incredibly contrived plots, and the stories became very strained. The miracle was that he had created a kind of folk figure so indestructible that he remained tolerable and amusing in any situation, however ludicrous; and when the thread of the plot becomes unbearably tenuous, there is always the inexhaustible fascination of the busher's epistolary style to carry it off. But the wartime stories deteriorate into caricature; the reality and conviction of *You Know Me Al* are not there. Jack remains a consistent enough character, and Ring managed him with great skill through some perilous moments, as in this passage where Jack utters some sentiments about the soldiers who went over the top and did not return:

Well it don't make a man feel any happier to think about them poor boys and god only knows what happened to them if they are prisoners or dead and some of them was pals of mine to but the worst part of it is that the word will be sent home that they are missing in actions and their wifes won't know what become of them if they got any and I can't help from thinking I might of been with them only for not wanting to crowd somebody out. . . .

Jack's pious, mindless clichés cut dangerously close to the most sacrosanct sentiments of his readers; for an instant one is afraid he is going to say something about the war, but as usual it is only his own hide he is talking about. But in these stories he becomes a simple buffoon, stupid beyond belief; we no longer recognize him as a fellow human being. The same thing happened to him in his wartime background as had happened to him in "The Busher Abroad"; when Ring took him out of the surroundings and situations he himself knew, Jack Keefe became a mere stereotype.

Ring's wartime writing was skeptical and noncommittal. He neither protested against the war nor joined in the flag-waving. He kept on writing about people as they behaved, and they were still the same people. When he took Jack Keefe into the Army and overseas, it only showed that Jack was no brighter, braver, more honest or modest in uniform than he had been on the baseball diamond. His personal report on his trip to France deflated the idea that there was any glory to war at all. He saw only boredom, incompetence, frivolity, indifference, and irresponsibility. In that report there is no note of tragedy or even of sentiment and no indication that beyond the lines he never crossed there was anything serious going on. Ring cannot have been unaware of or insensitive to the tragedy of war. It seems rather that it belonged with those matters that were too serious for him to be funny about; he decided to say as little as possible about it, and made the best of an unfortunate

151

assignment. At least, if he said nothing about it, he avoided regarding it as a spectacle that would give play to his talents; he did not try to put himself in the place of a combatant, and he did not write from "inside" anywhere.

There was something prophetic about Ring's skepticism. The returning soldiers brought back the news that a great deal of war *was* boredom, mud, red tape, and what a later generation called snafu. And when the postwar disillusionment set in, when the futility of the war and the subsequent peace conferences began to afflict thoughtful people with an anguished sense of having been betrayed, Ring at least was not surprised.

Perhaps the best of Ring's wartime writing appeared unobtrusively in the "Wake." "The Epistles of Edna," letters of a lovelorn stenographer, anticipated Ring's fine short story, "Some Like Them Cold." "The Diary of a Siren" introduced Clara Meyers, who set down her "inwardmost thoughts," which were all about her beauty and her social graces—"I believe that's what gives me the advantage over other girls because some girls seems to think that because they're pretty they don't have to say nothing but I don't rest on my looks but it's the combination of my looks and the things I say that gives me the advantage and Joe Klein that's the staff lyric writer down to the office says they ain't nothing freshs him up so after he's wrote a song and is all fagged out mently as looking at me and listening to me talk. . . ."

Clara's letter to her friend Belle on the occasion of the false news of an armistice is a chilling little masterpiece:

> *Home*
> *November 8 [1918]*
>
> Dear Girlie:
>
> *Well girlie you sure did miss something not being in old Chi yesterday and talk about your New Years Eve well we made it look pretty sick and I sure wish you could of been along.*
>
> *Well I guess it was about 7 minutes to 12 and the whistles begun blowing and I said to Jean Doran it must be 12 o'clock but she looked at her watch and said no only 7 minutes to and just then old Craig came down the aisle and you know what an undertaker he is, well this time he was grinning all over the place and he said "Well girls its all over." Well I knew in a minute he meant the war and I just let out a scream and if he hadn't been too quick for me I sure would of kissed him.*

152

Well the minute he had beat it Jean and I got our things and beat it down on State and you ought to of seen the mob. Well girlie it was some mob and they was a crowd of men yelling like Indians and I ran up to them and knocked two of their hats off and they tried to catch me but I got away from them and we started up toward Madison and it was sure some chore getting anywhere in that crowd but I guess Jean and I between the both of us must of knocked about 100 men's hats off and only 3 of them got back at us and finally when we got up to Madison they was a wagon load of girls and men going over towards Michigan and I ran up to them and asked them to take us along but somebody said they wasn't no more room but I said I have got a soldier boy in France and you better make room for me. So then one of the men grabbed me and pulled me up on the wagon and tried to kiss me but I told him not to get fresh so I knocked his hat off and sat down in his lap, but it was too slow riding, so I jumped off before we got to Wabash and started back towards State to find Jean but of course I couldn't find her but I bet I knocked 1,000 men's hats off in less than a block.

Well everybody was walking all over the st. and it was raining and mud up to your knees but who cared and I started over towards Dearborn with the crowd and a man come along with a drum and I knocked his hat off and took his drum away from him but pretty soon a man tried to kiss me so I threw the drum in his face and everybody give him the laugh.

Well pretty soon a boy in khaki come along and we were pushed right together in the crowd so I said to him "Well old boy you are a soldier but I have got a soldier in France." So he said give us a kiss then so I knocked his hat off and then a big truck come along and they pulled me up on it in the drivers seat and they was already 5 there but I sat in somebody's lap but it was too slow riding so I jumped off at the corner of Clark and the crossing policeman tried to hold me back but I knocked his cap off and then a man in the crowd said "What's the matter with all you people the story isn't true." So I ran up to him and I says "Oh it isn't true isn't it? Then you're a German." And I slapped his face and knocked his hat off.

Well that's the way it went and I didn't get home till 9 o'clock and I didn't go downtown today as I wasn't feeling the best and besides my hat and shoes and suit are a wreck but I certainly wish you could of been along to enjoy it with us. I notice the paper this morning says it wasn't true and the report was all wrong but they can tell that to the fish and as far as I am concerned the war is over and Jim

153

will be home in about 2 weeks at the outside. So you know how I feel girlie and can you blame me.

Clara

In 1918, Ring's mother died in Niles, after many years of poor health, and her death affected him deeply. He was devoted to her and often talked of her to his friends, although he seldom spoke of his father. The last child of her middle age, he had inherited her temperament and talent and many of her qualities: wit, personal charm, an unreasonable generosity, a painful sensitivity to the misfortunes of others, and an emotional susceptibility which she displayed and which Ring concealed under a mask of skepticism and ironic indifference. She had encouraged him and indulged him and taken pride in his success. She was the dominating influence of his early life.

Ring felt some misgivings about the dangers of excessive feminine influence on men, loyal as he was to his mother, his sisters, his wife, and his women friends. It is reflected in the plight of the husbands in his stories: almost all of them are henpecked, resigned, and submissive to their assertive wives. Ring himself was not in the least submissive, but he recognized the perils of matriarchal authority. He had a rather significant admiration for a novel of 1916, *In Cotton Wool* by W. B. Maxwell, the story of a man who is smothered with love by his mother, sisters, and wife, who shield him from experience until he is left without any will or character of his own.

Ring himself, while remaining close to his family, had become quite independent; the bonds of affection were as deep as ever, but he was not easily swayed by anyone else's will. But his mother's death grieved him; he remarked that he was reaching the time of life when he would begin to lose a great deal that he had loved.

His father had died in 1914. Ring had been devoted to him, too, although he was never so close to him as to his mother. Mr. Lardner was taciturn and reserved, a man with few close friends; he had been a very indulgent husband and father, kindly, honorable, and responsible, but he had not left the mark of his personality behind him so vividly as Mrs. Lardner had done. Ring's letters to him were respectful and solicitous, but not intimate.

Ellis and the three boys spent the summer of 1918 in St. Joseph and in the fall the Lardners moved to an apartment on Buena Avenue in Chicago. Ring had definitely decided to move to New York, but delayed it until after the birth of his fourth son, who was

154

born March 11, 1919. The problem of naming him was submitted to the readers of the "Wake":

STILL ANONYMOUS

Nearly a week has elapsed since announcement was made of our great prize contest, by the provisions of which the person first suggesting an acceptable first name for a two months old male child will be given a box seat at his christening—and still the child is Nonnie. Suggestions have come from many well known persons, among them I, Mary MacLane, who offers "Wake," but of the number received so far only one—Tom—has the slightest chance. Others on file are: Earring, Herring, Timothy Ringlets, Leif, Lafayette, Niles.

The contest will run another week, and if no suitable handle is offered in that time, we'll call him what we want to.

The child was named David, without the help of Ring's readers.

The year 1919 was one of general disorder. Freed from the restraint and uncertainty of wartime, everyone was poised on the verge of some new enterprise. There was restlessness and ferment everywhere; the victory was supposed to herald an upsurge of universal prosperity. People who had found new ways of making money during the war wanted to make more; men returning from overseas wanted better jobs and more pay. Labor had won the eight-hour day and vastly increased wages, but its gains were offset by those of capital, which had come about through higher interest rates, cost-plus contracts, and war profiteering, and there were strikes and civil violence all over the country. Civil liberties had taken a beating; the Attorney General raided every suspected "Red" meeting in America. The crusade for democracy had filled the country with optimism and arrogance, but the crusade for the domination of business only filled it with hysteria. The peace conferences in Europe resulted in the betrayal of democratic idealism, although this was not yet apparent, but the world was made safe for bigger business and wider markets, and the American middle classes with their new recruits from a rootless working class got set for the long free ride to prosperity.

As a concession to public virtue, the country piously submitted to Prohibition, a perverse error in which it stubbornly persisted for fourteen years. The triumph of democracy had produced a bloom of self-righteousness; and to make money and not to drink, at least not publicly, seemed to fulfill the requirements for ideal citizenship.

People migrated from farms and small towns to the cities, and

155

from the smaller cities to the larger ones, and everybody wanted to go to New York. The literary Bohemia of Chicago moved on to Greenwich Village in New York; many of the Chicago newspapermen went too. Ring had decided some time before this that New York would be his destination. It was not because everyone else was going; he probably did not notice the breaking up of the Chicago literary circles. The fact that many of his newspaper friends—Franklin P. Adams, Percy Hammond, Clare Briggs, and Rube Goldberg among them—were already living in New York surely made it more attractive to him. He went from Chicago to New York for the same reason he had come to Chicago from Niles. There was more going on, and he was drawn by the fact that it was the center of the theater and journalism. He could have stayed on with the *Tribune,* written short stories and made a comfortable living, but he liked New York, and after he got there he never wanted to stay away from it for very long.

Early in 1919 he made an agreement with John N. Wheeler, a former baseball reporter who had established a syndicate for selling newspaper features, to write a weekly column, after his contract with the *Tribune* had expired. Wheeler's Bell Syndicate had been highly successful in selling such writers as Richard Harding Davis, Theodore Roosevelt, George Ade, William Jennings Bryan, Billy Sunday and Rupert Hughes; and the cartoonists Bud Fisher and Fontaine Fox. Ring now had a national reputation, gained largely through *The Saturday Evening Post;* he was quite aware of the kind of prestige that the *Post* had brought him, and he knew too that he could make more money writing for a syndicate that served hundreds of papers than for a single paper, even a large one.

Ring went to New York and discussed the deal with Wheeler and agreed to work for the syndicate after the *Tribune* contract had terminated. Then he returned to Chicago. Some weeks later Wheeler heard that a rival syndicate had made Ring a large offer for a newspaper column. He wired Ring that he would come to Chicago with a contract to confirm their agreement. Ring wired back:

BEFORE FIVE WITNESSES TWO OF WHOM WERE SOBER I MADE A CONTRACT WITH YOU IN THE WALDORF BAR, SO WHY ARE YOU BOTHERING ABOUT A CONTRACT NOW?

This was the only contract Wheeler had with Ring, and it worked out to their satisfaction. Ring's income from the syndicate was contingent on the number of newspapers that bought his column. Eventually it brought him about $30,000 a year.

Of the unrest, expectancy, and staggering disorder of that year Ring took no notice in his writing. The "Busher" returned to the big league, and the "Wake" continued to comment on sports and daily life with its usual familiar and domestic tone. Minor repercussions of the war sometimes reached its columns, such as this:

IN A SMOKING COMPARTMENT

(The Navy and the Journalist are discussing cigarettes when the Stranger enters.)

STRANGER (addressing the Navy): Well, boys, we licked 'em, didn't we?

FIRST ENSIGN (breathes heavily)

STRANGER—Did you boys get over there?

SECOND ENSIGN—Yes, sir.

STRANGER—Well, if the war'd went on just a little w'ile longer, I'd of got over there, too.

FIRST ENSIGN (breathes heavily)

STRANGER—I'm forty-three years old and got a wife and a couple of kids, but you can bet I wasn't going to claim exemptions.

THE CHIEF (sighs)

STRANGER—Where I made my first mistake was not getting in when she first started. But the wife wasn't very well, and it would of just about killed her for me to of went in. But afterwards, she says, "Charley"—that's my name: Charley—"Charley," she says, "if you want to get in so bad, I'm not going to stand in your way." But then it was too late.

FIRST ENSIGN (breathes heavily)

STRANGER—At that, they wasn't hardly a day passed when it wasn't all I could do to keep from killing a German. You know we got a whole lot of the damn bums out in my town. I live in Chicago. Well, I'd run into some of them every day or so, and it was all as I could do to keep from taking a wallop at them. If they'd of ever opened their heads to me, it would of been good-night.

SECOND ENSIGN—Yes, sir.

STRANGER—And that's one thing the wife was a scared of. She used to say, "Charley, if you don't learn to keep yourself in hand, you'll get in trouble."

FIRST ENSIGN (breathes heavily)

STRANGER—But what she was most a scared of was that the war would go along long enough so as I couldn't stand it no longer and go in. I tell you boys whenever I seen one of you in uniform, I used

157

to say to myself, "Charley, you was born about twenty years too soon."

SECOND ENSIGN—Yes, sir.

STRANGER—But I did manage to get into the Spanish war. I——

JOURNALIST (falls asleep).

He kept a sharp eye on Congress, though, and occasionally offered a political comment:

TO CONGRESS

Chi, April 8. Dear Cong.: You know the name of my column means behind the news and once in a while I get way behind it and have a tough time catching up and it wasn't till yesterday that I found out that you had plastered a tax onto sporting goods and if I had known it before I would of congratulated you all the sooner.

It's a great move, Cong., and a step in the right direction as it will put a stop to a lot of brats playing ball in the park and trampling down the grass and it will keep them at home where they belong out of the open air. Children of all kinds is getting too much encouragement, Cong., and having too good a time and by slapping a tax onto baseball bats and gloves and etc. and make them too dear for the boys to buy them you have certainly gone a long way towards checking such evils like outdoor exercise.

Ring went on to recommend a tax on schoolbooks to relieve overcrowding in schools.

It was the year of the Dempsey-Willard fight and the Black Sox scandal. Ring wrote his last "Wake" column for the *Tribune* June 20 and a few days later went to Toledo to cover the fight for the Bell Syndicate. Prohibition had already come into force in Ohio; some old companions in sport—Ring, "Tad" Dorgan, Jimmy Isaminger, Tiny Maxwell, H. C. Witwer, Rube Goldberg, and Grantland Rice—got together for some illegal drinking. Ring composed a lament for the occasion which they sang over and over:

I guess I've got those there Toledo Blues,
About this fight I simply can't enthuse.
I do not care if Dempsey win or lose,
Owing to the fact I've got
Toledo Blues.

Ring was one of a foursome who played golf before the fight, with caddies carrying golf clubs and bottles of liquor around the course;

158

they never got beyond the tenth hole, and Ring disappeared completely.

It was a foregone conclusion that Willard would win; Dempsey looked too small and inexperienced to have a chance. Ring wrote the day before the fight: "Probably some of you will say to yourself what does this bird know about the manly art of self-defense. Well I don't know nothing and don't expect to learn, but I can point with a whole lot of pride to some of my pickings in the past. For instance I thought all along that the Allies would win the war especially after America got into it. I chose Jack Johnson to lick Jeffries though I didn't tell nobody for fear of affecting the betting odds." He had bet $500 on Willard, and when Dempsey knocked him out in the third round, Ring felt no immediate enthusiasm for the new champion. The day after the fight he wrote: "Well, gents, it was just a kind of practical joke on my part and to make it all the stronger I went and bet a little money on him, so pretty nearly everybody thought I was really in earnest."

As far as bets went it was a bad year for Ring. He often had poor luck with prize fights, but he was an expert in foreseeing baseball results. He went along with the rest of the experts on the World Series that year in favoring the White Sox over the Cincinnati Reds; the odds were five to one at the start. The Cincinnati team was good, but the Sox were considered phenomenal. Public interest ran so high that the Series was extended to a possible nine games instead of the usual seven, and a record attendance was expected. Ring wrote some advance stories on the Series and bet his extra earnings on the White Sox.

Even before the first game the odds dropped to even money. There was something suspicious about this, but it was thought impossible to throw a series, and to honest sportsmen it was unbelievable. When the flagrant evidence piled up, the very crudeness and transparency of it made it all the harder to believe. But after the first game it was apparent that something was irregular; Cicotte, supposed to be almost an invincible pitcher, allowed Cincinnati hit after hit for a final score of 9 to 1. He was later quoted as saying that it was easy to throw a ball game, and "you can make it look so good." He did not make it look very good to his manager, Kid Gleason, or to Charles Comiskey, the owner of the White Sox. They were both suspicious, but, lacking any conclusive evidence, they failed to get any support from high baseball authorities. Among the sports writers Ring and Hugh Fullerton were the first to suspect a fix. Ring later told his friend Arthur Jacks that he had asked Eddie

159

Cicotte to his hotel room after the game and said to him, "What was wrong? I was betting on you today." Cicotte made excuses and assured Ring that everything would be all right. But after the White Sox lost the second game, a quartet composed of Ring, Nick Flatley, Tiny Maxwell, and James Crusinberry, who gathered in a tavern in Bellevue, Kentucky, across the river from Cincinnati, was singing:

I'm forever throwing ball games,
Pretty ball games in the air.
I come from Chi.
I hardly try,
Just go to bat and fade and die.
Fortune's coming my way,
That's why I don't care,
I'm forever throwing ball games,
And the gamblers treat us fair.

Ring's story on the second game, in the Chicago *Tribune*, was headed: "IT'S A BIG SCANDAL! Ring Discovers Cause of Defeat," and began: "The biggest scandal of a big year of baseball scandals was perpetrated down here this p.m. when the American league turned against itself and beat the White Sox out of the second game of the present horror." But Ring was writing in character, and his joke could not be called an accusation. When the Sox won the third game, Ring said it was only because he hadn't bet on them.

Cincinnati won the series, 5 to 3; Chicago won the third, sixth and seventh games, which kept up the hopes of White Sox fans and gave the gamblers an additional advantage. At the end there was little doubt in any reasonably enlightened mind that a conspiracy of gamblers and White Sox players had thrown the series. The eight players who were suspected—Gandil, Cicotte, Jackson, Felsch, Risberg, Williams, McMullin and Weaver—were treated as outcasts by some of their teammates. Comiskey hired private detectives to find evidence against them, but none was found. With the exception of Gandil they had all signed for the 1920 season, and it was not until September of that year that the scandal broke.

By that time Ring's suspicions had already been confirmed. He was in New York that summer when James Crusinberry called him and asked him to join him at Dinty Moore's. There Kid Gleason had run to earth Abe Attell, a former featherweight boxing champion, who had long been suspected of having a part in the fix. Attell, aggrieved at not having received his full share of the spoils, was revealing the plot. He implicated Arnold Rothstein, then the top gambler of the country, although there was no conclusive evidence that Rothstein actually participated in buying off the Black Sox players. Shortly after that Billy Maharg, a disgruntled gambler from Philadelphia, told everything, and the scandal became public. Cicotte was summoned before a Chicago grand jury, along with Jackson, Williams and Felsch. They signed confessions—which later disappeared—and Comiskey disbanded his team, even though it stood a chance of winning the pennant. Out of the hearings came two lines that Ring might well have invented: Shoeless Joe Jackson on leaving the courthouse was approached by a tearful newsboy who pleaded, "Say it ain't so, Joe"; and Eddie Cicotte said (three times) that he "did it for the wife and kiddies." The players were indicted, but the case against them was dismissed because the Cook County court found it had no jurisdiction; but all eight men were thrown out of baseball forever.

The Black Sox affair was only the first scandal in a decade of scandals, but it administered a profound moral shock to the public, and to a dedicated baseball fan it must have seemed very close to a personal betrayal. The corruption in public affairs which was to characterize the twenties—the Teapot Dome scandal, gangsterism and vice, stock-market manipulation—was not without precedent, but baseball, not yet highly organized as an industry, embodied a code of honor and sportsmanship that was almost sacred to America's view of its character and way of life. That the squalid bungling of the cheapest kind of gamblers could very nearly destroy it came as a blow to its devotees. Baseball recovered by employing a high commissioner to supervise it and by multiplying the rules and regulations to preclude any possible lapse, and the lively ball and a vast publicity campaign brought back its prestige as the national pastime. But for many of its old-time fans it never was the same again. The scandal itself could have been forgotten; it was exposed, the guilty were reprimanded, and the plot was never repeated. But by that time all the old rules had been revised, the old standards were gone, and baseball, along with almost every other enterprise in America, had become big business, a mass spectacle that still held millions in thrall and produced superheroes for the fans but had lost a good deal of the intimate appeal that had inspired the enthusiasm of the South Bend fans back in the Central League.

For Ring baseball was not the same after 1919. He blamed the decline of his interest in the game on the rabbit ball, which made home runs easier to hit and caused the home-run king to replace

161

the all-round natural baseball player as the hero of the sport; but his disillusionment had set in long before the fast ball was introduced. The busher stories of 1914 are considerably less genial and affectionate than the "Pullman Pastimes" of 1911; and there is an increasingly sardonic tone in his coverage of baseball games from 1909 to 1919. The Black Sox episode surely added to his growing disenchantment.

He had been passionately absorbed in the game and at one time he could never see enough of it. Even if a long association with ball players had diminished the luster of his boyhood heroes, even after he had discovered that many of them were as stupid, vain, and lacking in moral refinement as Jack Keefe, the whole world of baseball still had a certain magic. Jack Keefe, as foolish as he was, could never have thrown a ball game; even the merest suggestion of it, and he could not have survived a single issue of *The Saturday Evening Post*. It is an ironic coincidence that Jack Keefe left the White Sox, in fact disappeared for good, just in time to avoid the stain of the 1919 scandal. In a story written before the Series of that year and published in the *Post* only a week after, Jack leaves the White Sox for Cincinnati: he has been deteriorating for some time, he is more given to drinking and quarrels with his manager and teammates, but he leaves without any official blight on his character, after—presumably as a mark of his stupidity—predicting that the White Sox are going to lose the Series that year.

Whatever Ring thought of Jack Keefe's intelligence, he never expected anything so grossly shameful as the Black Sox scandal. The White Sox were one of his favorite teams, and many of the players were his friends, including some who were thought to be the prototypes of Jack Keefe. None of the players involved in the fix was close to Ring personally, but he had a particular admiration for Eddie Cicotte as a pitcher. In 1915 he had written an article for the *American* magazine, naming his ideal ball team composed of players from both major leagues, and he said of Cicotte: "There's one bird that I got the figures on, and they show that it's harder to score off of him than anybody else, that is, the last figures I seen. But a fella doesn't have to chase up the figures to know he's a whale. They ain't a smarter pitcher in baseball and they's nobody that's a better all-round ball player, no pitcher, I mean." Cicotte had won twenty-nine games out of forty in the 1919 championship season; his performance in the Series was a profound disappointment to Ring. In spite of his knowing that ball players were as corruptible as anyone else, the whole episode was bitterly shocking and too close to him to be passed off philosophically. But he assumed a cynical attitude about it, as if he had not been surprised by it at all. It was part of his defensive mask.

Baseball, on which his whole career and reputation had been founded, had lost its enchantment. And so had a great many other things. It was not in baseball alone that the old rules were being changed and the old standards crumbling away.

It was in many ways a year of crucial changes in Ring's life, as in everyone else's. Singular, aloof, and detached as he was by temperament, he was deeply involved in the life of his time and the American middle class; and his material fortunes increased with theirs. He was also aware of the profound changes in the moral climate of American life that accompanied the upheavals of the postwar years. The progress of his career was running according to the timetable of the century; but he followed it with an increasing sense of withdrawal and alienation.

CHAPTER FIVE

In midsummer of 1919, Ring and Ellis had gone to New York and rented a house in Greenwich, Connecticut, and in the autumn they moved their family there. The bare facts of this move are recorded almost faithfully in one of Ring's funniest stories, "The Young Immigrunts," of which the dramatis personae are Ring, Ellis, John, Jimmy, Ring, Jr., David, and Miss Feldmann, who had joined the household at the time of David's birth. A registered, trained nurse, she came home from the hospital with Ellis, and remained with the family for twelve years as nurse and governess to the children. Actually the story, which appeared in the *Post* under the authorship of Ring Lardner, Jr., "with a preface by the Father," was a parody of *The Young Visiters* by Daisy Ashford, which had recently been published, and it would hardly serve as an accurate biographical guide to the Lardner family.

The Young Visiters purported to be the work of a twelve-year-old girl, as indeed it was; although, since Sir James Barrie wrote an introduction to it, he was widely suspected of having launched a highly amusing spoof. It was written, with the kind of misspellings in which Ring himself delighted, in the high-flown language of a Victorian novel as understood by a rather original and precocious child, and it turned out to be a gorgeous unconscious burlesque. Ring, skeptical of the authenticity of the book, achieved a brilliant parody of it, adapting its lordly style to his own uses. But "The Young Immigrunts" is much more than a parody of Daisy Ashford's classic; it is a wonderful burlesque of ordinary domestic life based

165

on the hilariously trivial details of an auto trip from Goshen to "Grenitch."

The narrator is four-year-old Ring, Jr., who travels with his parents in their "costly moter" to Greenwich, while the nurse takes the other three boys on the train. (Actually it was John who accompanied his parents, but Ring, Jr., was substituted in the story because of his name.) The account is highly circumstantial, and the young author comments on the ways of grownups with something less than childlike innocence.

Well said my mother simperingly I suppose we can start east now.

We will start east when we get good and ready said my father with a lordly sneeze. . . .

Soon my father had payed the check and gave the waiter a lordly bribe and once more we sprang into the machine and was on our way. The lease said about the results of my fathers grate idear the soonest mended in a word it turned out to be a holycost of the first water as after we had covered miles and miles of ribald roads we suddenly come to a abrupt conclusion vs the side of a stagnant freight train that was stone deef to honks. My father set there for nerly ½ a hour reciteing the 4 Horses of the Apoplex in a under tone but finely my mother mustard up her curage and said affectedly why dont we turn around and go back somewheres. I cant spell what my father replid. . . .

. . . In some way ether I or he got balled up on the grand concorpse and next thing you know we was thretning to swoop down on Pittsfield.

Are you lost daddy I arsked tenderly.

Shut up he explained.

On the boat from Detroit to Buffalo the author observes this scene of married life:

A little latter who should come out on the porch and set themselfs ner us but the bride and glum.

Oh I said to myself I hope they will talk so as I can hear them as I have always wandered what newlyweds talk about on their way to Niagara Falls and soon my wishs was realized.

Some night said the young glum are you warm enough.

I am perfectly comfertible replid the fare bride tho her looks belid her words what time do we arive in Buffalo.

9 oclock said the lordly glum are you warm enough.

*I am perfectly comfertible replid the fare bride what time do we
arive in Buffalo.*

*9 oclock said the lordly glum I am afrade it is too cold for you out
here.*

*Well maybe it is replid the fare bride and without farther adieu
they went into the spacius parlers.*

*I wander will he be arsking her 8 years from now is she warm
enough said my mother with a faint grimace.*

The weather may change before then replid my father.

Are you warm enough said my father after a slite pause.

No was my mothers catchy reply.

Settled in Greenwich, Ring began to write the syndicated weekly
letter which made its first appearance November 2, 1919, and continued for seven and a half years. The first letter was about nothing
at all, except that he had been visiting his in-laws in Goshen and
had moved East with his family. It began:

To the editor:

*No doubt your subscribers is wondering what has became of me
and the last time I was in your city the genial editor of this paper
whom this letter is addressed made the remark that it was to bad
that a man like I whose friends was legions (according to the editor) did not keep in touch with their old friends in the different
citys and correspond with their friends in all the different citys.*

*So I says maybe some people has enough spare time to write to
all their friends but personally time means money to a man like
myself and if I was to even take time to drop a card once in a while
to all my old pals why they would not be time for me to do nothing
else, wile the wife a kiddies went out in the forest and gathered
Herbs and wild hurtleberrys for the evening meal.*

*The editor laughed heartily at the way I put it, but after he had
recovered made the remark that this paper reached all my old
friends as well as people that takes an interest in a man like I and
feel like they know me though we have never met and if I cared to
keep my old friends posted on my movements and etc. why he
would feel highly honored would I write in a letter once in a while
that he would publish it in this paper containing news of my family
and I as well as items of interest occurring in the big world which
I have the privilege of comeing in contact with them more so than
you dear people of this old town beautifull though it is.*

*I have expected the kindly editor's genial offer and wile I do not
claim merit as a literary man the editor says that does not matter*

and if I will just write in my own breezy style (the way I talk as he expressed it) he and his readers will be more than satisfied.

I will do my best which as I often say is as much as any man can do and I will half to crave your indulgents if a word or 2 of up to date slang drops into these cols. once in a wile as I am only trying to be natural which is where a man is at their best after all.

Many of my friends all ready knows that I am going to move east from dear old Chi where I been located on and off for the past 10 yrs. but perhaps a few of you is curies as to how I come to make this decision.

Well they was a show name Chu Chin Chow that come to Chi last winter and the bird that owned it was name Mr. Gest and 1 night we become acquainted and he asked me why didn't I write him a play.

So I says I haven't never wrote 1 and don't know if I can or no, and wile I was makeing the experiment the wife and kiddies would half to live on memorys so when he got through laughing at the quaint way I put it he says yes but suppose I was to give you enough jack to keep them in fruit and cereal wile you are writeing the play so I says O.K. and he set down and wrote out a check and come to find out it was good. . . . Well I found out that he makes his home in N. Y. so I says we would move down there. . . .

This first column is far from Ring's best; he seems to have been floundering for an introductory subject, and he often had trouble finding something to say. But the column is significant because it presents so clearly the character in which Ring became known to his widest audience and the kind of material he used. The material, as in the case of stories like "The Young Immigrunts," came from the minutiae of daily experience and from his observation of familiar and trivial matters. A great many of his columns dealt with "items of interest occurring in the big world"—a convention, a prize fight, or a World Series; but even then he regarded them in a highly personal way. He was not reporting an event; he was projecting the reactions of a character to an event or a situation.

The character in which he wrote most of his columns over seven years became the image of him that stuck in the popular mind. He did not invent a person, like Abe Martin or Mr. Dooley; rather he used the vernacular as a comic device to present his own personality. Roughly, the character in which he expressed himself was the "wise boob," the average man of common sense, cynical, humorous, a conceited wiseacre, but genial and likable. He has a certain inno-

168

cence which often appears to border on stupidity, and tastes that are so commonplace that they are pleasantly vulgar. But the apparent innocence points up a native shrewdness, and his vulgarity, the very ordinariness of his predilections, endear him to the average man. He is natural and unpretentious, as astute and clear-sighted as any wise boob likes to think himself. In this he has much in common with the traditional characters of American humor from the Yankee peddler to Mr. Dooley. In his broader outlines he appears to be the kind of man with whom the average reader can identify himself, in his innocence, shrewdness, and disregard for the niceties of discourse. But the character is deceptive. It is really a burlesque of all wise boobs, of all humorists and commentators; it is a burlesque of Ring himself.

Thus Ring's newspaper audience, which came to number millions, thought of him generally as the wise boob whose language and whose views were so reassuringly familiar. The language became his trademark; actually the variations in it and in the character are wide. Sometimes Ring wrote in a loose and rambling style, as in his first column, than which nothing could be more disarmingly genial; at other times his prose was taut and disciplined and highly sophisticated and delivered a satirical punch that no boob, however wise, could have mustered. Before he stopped writing the weekly letter, he had abandoned the vernacular completely and was writing either straight commentary or in a character vastly different from the one which had made him famous. But even in the poorest of the columns and articles he wrote in character he had the faculty of making his readers take "an interest in a man like I and feel like they know me though we have never met."

Writing in character is an ancient comic device and particularly honored in American humor. One thinks of *The Biglow Papers*, Artemus Ward, and Josh Billings; one might also think, mistakenly, of Will Rogers, but he was another matter entirely. He really was an Oklahoma cowboy and the language he spoke was his own. With Ring writing in character was in a way a mask. It came to him easily enough, since he had a perfect ear and a gift for language; but it also served a purpose. For one thing, it was almost surefire in its comic effect. It also permitted him to say to the widest possible audience a great many things that would have sounded downright ill-tempered in straight prose. A case in point is a column about baseball. Ring had made his reputation as a baseball writer and was still best known as one. He was one of the game's most sardonic commentators, but nevertheless one of its best press agents. But, as he told several million baseball fans in his weekly column for July 17, 1921, his enthusiasm for the game had turned to something like contempt:

I got a letter the other day asking why didn't I write about base-ball no more as I usen't to write about nothing else, you might say. Well, friends, I may as well admit that I have kind of lost interest in the old game, or rather it ain't the old game which I have lost interest in it, but it is the game which the magnates has fixed up to please the public with their usual good judgment.

A couple yrs. ago a ball player named Baby Ruth that was a pitcher by birth was made into an outfielder on acct. of how he could bust them and he begins breaking records for long distance hits and etc. and he become a big drawing card and the master minds that controls baseball says to themselfs that if it is home runs that the public wants to see, why leave us give them home runs, so they fixed up a ball that if you don't miss it entirely it will clear the fence, and the result is that ball players which use to specialize in hump back liners to the pitcher is now amongst our leading sluggers when by rights they couldn't take a ball in their hands and knock it past the base umpire.

Another result is that I stay home and read a book.

But statistics shows that about 7 people out of every 100 is ½ cuckoo so they's still some that is still interested in the national pastime so for their benefit I will write a little about it as long as I don't half to set through a game of it to get the material.

This is neither funny nor satirical; it is just what Ring thought. But it sounds less bitter and antagonistic in the vernacular than it does in straight prose. The same year, Ring wrote an essay on "Sport and Play" for the symposium *Civilization in the United States,* edited by Harold Stearns. That book, containing articles by thirty prominent writers in all fields, reflected the postwar disillusionment of the intellectuals in its view that American civilization was washed up. Ring became a contributor to it, not because he wished to join the company of the intellectuals in proclaiming the catastrophe, but for the simple reason that his friend Burton Rascoe asked him to write an article for the symposium. Harold Stearns in his autobiography reveals how at least one intellectual of that time regarded Ring as a writer:

No Harvard pride or vestigial Boston correctness prevented me from going after Ring Lardner hammer and tongs for the essay on sport and play—he was the man I wanted, and I wanted him badly. He could write in his "Americanese," if he wanted to? Why not? That was his natural style of writing anyway; he would be self-conscious had he tried to do anything else. Even to this day I don't exactly know what Ring thought of being in such "high-brow" company, but I do know how he felt—that he was doing us an honor, not we him. Anyway, I managed to persuade him finally, although I had to see him several times.

Stearns had about ten years to correct his misapprehension about Ring before writing his autobiography, but in spite of his Boston broad-mindedness he and no doubt a great many others less well informed continued to think of Ring as a "natural" who could write nothing but vernacular. However, the essay he got says in straight prose very much what Ring, writing in character in his newspaper column, had often hinted at. The essay is a total indictment of sport in America, brief, pointed, and unqualified.

Bartlett does not tell us who pulled the one about all work and no play, but it probably was the man who said that the longest way round was the shortest way home. There is as much sense in one remark as in the other. . . .

If it were your ambition to spend an evening with a dull boy, whom would you choose, H. G. Wells, whose output indicates that he doesn't even take time off to sleep, or the man that closes his desk at two o'clock every afternoon and goes to the ball game? . . .

No, brothers, the bright minds of this or any other country are owned by the men who leave off work only to eat or go to bed. The doodles are the boys who divide their time fifty-fifty between work and play, or who play all the time and don't even pretend to work. Proper exercise undoubtedly promotes good health, but the theory that good health and an active brain are inseparable can be shot full of holes by the mention of two names—Stanislaus Zbyzsk and Robert Louis Stevenson.

It is silly, then, to propound that sport is of mental benefit. . . .

Ring goes on to say that the only reason for sport is to promote health and increase longevity, but that in America people do not participate in sport any more; they only watch it.

We don't play because (1) we lack imagination, and because (2) we are a nation of hero-worshippers . . . But hero-worship is the national disease that does most to keep the grandstands full and the playgrounds empty. To hell with those four extra years of life

171

if they are going to cut in on our afternoon at the Polo Grounds,
where, in blissful asininity, we may feast our eyes on the swarthy
champion of swat, shouting now and then in an excess of anile
idolatry, "Come on you Babe, Come on, you Baby Doll."

Ring had come a long way from the boy in Niles who thought he
could never see enough baseball; and he was far removed here from
the genial character who wrote "Americanese" for the Sunday
papers. This essay was written for a book of limited circulation; it
would hardly have appealed to Ring's newspaper audience.

The masterpiece among Ring's baseball reports is his coverage of
the world series of 1922, between the Yankees and the Giants. Ring
had picked the Yankees to win, but the Giants beat them, 4–0, with
one game tied. Ring wrote:

ADVANCE NOTICE

Sept. 30—All though they have been world serious practically
every yr. for the last 20 yrs. this next world serious which is sup-
posed to open up Wed. p.m. at the Polo grounds is the most impor-
tant world serious in history as far as I and my family are conserned
and even more important to us than the famous world serious of
1919 which was win by the Cincinnati Reds greatly to their surprise.

Maybe I would better exclaim myself before going any further.
Well, a few days previous to the serious of 1919 I was approached
by a young lady who I soon recognized as my wife, and any way
this woman says would I buy her a fur coat as the winter was come-
ing on and we was going to spend it in Connecticut which is not
genally considered one of the tropics.

"But don't do it," she says, "unless you have got the money to
spare because of course I can get along without it. In fact," she
added bursting into teers, "I am so used to getting along without
this, that, and the other thing that maybe it would be best for you
not to buy me that coat after all as the sight of a luxury of any kind
might prove my undoing."

"Listen," was my reply, "as far as I am conserned you don't half
to prove your undoing. But listen you are in a position to know that
I can't spare the money to buy you one stoat leave alone enough
of the little codgers skins to make a coat for a growed up girl like
you. But if I can get a hold of any body that is sucker enough to bet
on Cincinnati in this world serious, why I will borrow enough from
some good pal and cover their bet and will try and make the bet
big enough so as the winnings will buy you the handsomest mule-
skin coat in New England."

Well friends I found the sucker and got a hold of enough money to cover his bet and not only that but give him odds of 6 to 5 and that is why we did not go out much in Greenwich that winter and not for lack of invitations as certain smart Alex has let fall.

. . . the fur coat situation in my family is practically the same like it was in 1919 only as I hinted in the opening paragraph of this intimate article, it is a d-a-m sight worse.

Because this year they won't be no chance for the little woman to offset the paucity of outdoor raps by spending the winter in the house. She is going to need furs even there.

Therefore as I say this comeing serious is the most important of all as far as we are conserned for Mother ain't the same gal when she is cold and after all is said and done what is home with mother in her tantrums?

The Giants won the first game of the series, although there is no mention of the game in Ring's article on it:

Well friends you can imagine my surprise and horror when I found out last night that the impression had got around someway another that as soon as this serious was over I was planning to buy a expensive fur coat for my Mrs. and put a lot of money into same and buy a coat that would probably run up into hundreds and hundreds of dollars.

Well I did not mean to give no such kind of a impression and I certainly hope that my little article was not read that way by everybody a specially around my little home because in the first place I am not a sucker enough to invest hundreds and hundreds of dollars in a garment which the chances are that the Mrs. will not wear it more than a couple times all winter as the way it looks we are libel to have the most openest winter in history . . . and any way I believe a couple can have a whole lot better time in winter staying home and reading a good book or maybe have a few friends in to play bridge. . . .

The second game of the series was called after the tenth inning because of darkness, although it was still broad daylight, and the teams were tied 3–3. The fans booed the decision so loudly that Commissioner Landis ordered the day's receipts, $120,000, turned over to charity, although the outcries of the spectators indicated that they would rather have had their money back. This decision did not impede the headlong fall of the Yankees.

Oct. 6—No doubt my readers has been tipped off by this time that the 2nd game of the big serious was called on acct. of darkness but a great many of them may not know that the umpires and club owners was called a lot of different names which I will not repeat here but suffice it to say that none of them was honey, dearie, and etc.

The boys that had paid $5.50 and up to see a ball game did not seem to think it was dark enough for the umps to step in and stop it. Personly I will not express no opinion as some of my best friends is umpires, but will merely state that I started out of the press box the instant it was over and by the aid of a powerful candle which I genally always carry to world serious games when Shawkey and Barnes is scheduled to pitch, why I was able to find my way down to the field where I run plum into A.D. Lasker who had forgot to light his headlights. Will further state that nobody who I passed on the way out of 8th avenue had yet put on their pajamas or made any other preparations that would indicate the fall of night and even when I got down to park's row, pretty near a hr. after the game's untimely end, I was still able to grope my way to the office by feeling along the sides of buildings and was seated right here at my typewriter writing this article before the hoot owls and nightingales begun to emit their nocturnal squawk.

Anyway it means we are going to have a extra ball game to play over and some of we boys who predicted a short serious is being made to look like a monkey. Personly I was never so ashamed of myself since I picked Willard.

The general opinion amongst the writing boys tonight was that the game being a tie is a big help to one of the two teams but I forget which. It certainly ain't no help to me and the only thing I liked about the day was the weather, which it would make a person sick to even talk about a fur coat in such weather, and it goes to show what a sucker a man would be to squander thousands and thousands of dollars in a costly fur garment and then may be have a whole winter of just such days like yesterday.

Personly I seen a girlie on the street last night wearing a linen duster and you have no idear how good they look on some people and keep you plenty warm too if you move a round and don't stand still.

. . . Jess Barnes pitched better than Bob at the start and not so good at the finish. The way Jess pitched to Ruth did not seem to rouse unanimous enthusiasm amongst the bugs in the grandstand. Slow balls is what Jess feeds the Babe and the reason for same is

because Babe dont hit slow balls out of the ball park. If Jess did not feed the Babe slow balls when he knows he cant hit slow balls so good, why that would make Jess a ½ wit and when he does feed the Babe slow balls, why it shows he is thinking. That is why the crowd hoots him for pitching slow balls, because the average base-ball bug hates to see anybody think. It makes them jealous.

Oct. 7—Among the inmates of our heavily mortgaged home in Great Neck is 3 members of what is sometimes referred to as the feline tribe born the 11th day of last April and christened respect-fully Barney, Blackie, and Ringer.

These 3 little ones is motherless, as the lady cat who bore them, aptly named Robin Hood, took sick one June day and was give away by Fred to a friend to whom he kindly refrained from mentioning her illness.

These 3 little members of the feline tribe is the cutest and best behaved kitties in all catdom, their conduct having always been above reproaches outside of a tendency on the part of Ringer to bite strangers knuckles. Nowhere on Long Island is a more loveable trio of grimalkins and how it pierces my old heart to think that some day next week these 3 little fellows must be shot down like a dog so as their fur can be fashioned into a warm winter coat for she who their antics has so often caused to screek with laughter. Yes boys the 3 little kittens is practically doomed you might say and all be-cause today's game at the polo grounds was not called on account of darkness long before it started though they was no time during the afternoon when the Yanks could see.

I probably never would of heard of a cat skin coat was it not for an accidental introduction last night to a man who has did nothing all his life but sell and wear fur coats and who told me that no finer or more warmer garment can be fashioned than is made from the skin of a milk fed kitty.

"Listen," was the way he put it. "You would be a even worse sucker than you are if you was to squander thousands and thousands of dollars on the fur of a muskrat or a mule when you have right in your own asylum the makings of the most satisfactory and hand-some coat that money can buy."

"Yes," was my reply, "but the fur of 3 kittens would make a mighty small coat."

"Small coats is the rage," was his reply, "and I personally seen some of the best dressed women in New York strolling up and down

175

10th avenue during the last cold snap with cat skin garments no bigger than a guest towel."

So while I said a few paragraphs ago that the result of this ball game spelled the doom of our little kitties, why as a matter of fact I have just about made up my mind to not buy no costly furs even if the Yankees does come through and bring me out on the right side of the public ledger. Whatever I win in bets on this series I will freely give to charity.

I would try and describe the game to you in intimate detail was it not played in such darkness that I was only able to see a few incidence. . . .

At the end of the series, Ring complained that traffic regulations had not been handled properly; the Yankees needed traffic policemen stationed between home and first base, and first base and second, to tell them which way to run. As for the fur coat, it was decided "to not doom the little members of the finny tribe to death." By means of a chain letter he hoped to accumulate enough covers off plush-bound albums to make the little woman a fur coat. Ring did not cover very many series after this one; as far as his copy goes, it is the classic one of his career. After that he steadily lost interest in them.

The characters of Ring's weekly letter increased in popularity until the feature appeared in one hundred fifty-seven newspapers including the Tokyo *Japan Advertiser,* the Niles *Daily Star,* and several British newspapers; and it brought Ring about $30,000 a year. The reason for its success was not that it delivered homespun wisdom, although it did from time to time; not that it was satirical, although it was frequently; it was simply a spirit of broad burlesque that ran through it. Ring was not funny every week; out of more than three hundred fifty of the weekly columns, there are perhaps less than fifty which represent Ring at the very top of his form, and there are a good many that are weary and strained. Ring was at his best in these letters when he reduced the extravagant and the outlandish to the trivial and familiar and brought common sense to play upon it; when, in the desperate weekly search for something to write about, he tried to inflate the commonplace, the result could be rasping and laborious.

A few years after he had begun this feature, he took on another task for the Bell Syndicate—a comic strip called "You Know Me Al," based on the character of Jack Keefe. Ring wrote the continuity and the drawings were by Dick Dorgan, brother of "Tad"

176

Dorgan, the newspaper cartoonist and Ring's great friend. This appeared from October 1923 to September 1925 in more than a hundred newspapers, but Ring gave up writing the continuity in the fall of 1924, even though he sacrificed about $20,000 a year. It was a daily grind, and he hated it. The comic strip was not his medium, he felt that what he was doing was flat and insipid, and he could not find enough ideas for a daily strip. After Ring gave it up, Dick Dorgan continued it for almost another year.

Ring was unfortunately right about the strip. It was lame and forced, and Jack Keefe is a very dim figure in it. A typical situation is that of the unmarried sister-in-law for whom Jack and his wife are trying to find a husband. This was used in the stories of *Gullible's Travels* and was to appear again in *The Big Town*—Ring was never very fertile in plot situations and made the same ones serve over and over. The first panel of the strip usually was a letter from Jack Keefe to Al, such as: "Friend Al: Well Al Edna is trying to make a match between her sister and a picture director name Brown who she says he must be getting $10,000 a yr. at lease. Will I dont know if he gets that much but whatever he gets he has still got it. He was to our house for supper 4 nights last wk. and never even brought the gals a cake of milk chocolate and I aint never seen him yet when he has not left his cigarettes in his other suit. Well one thing we been haveing a whole lot better meals since he begin bording with us as women figures that the way to make a man like them is to feed him good though for some reason another they dont seem to think that includes husbands." This left three panels for the gag, which was never very telling. Ring was draining a limited store of ideas for the strip; nothing was really left but the busher's language, and it was not enough to sustain it. Ring gave it up with relief.

During his first year in New York Ring wrote the five stories which were collected in book form as *The Big Town*. They are about a family who comes from Niles and South Bend to New York, but they have no autobiographical reference whatever, as Ring pointed out in a preface to a later edition. He was always having to do this even when he wrote in character, fiction or nonfiction. The superficial events of some stories bore enough resemblance to his own life to tempt readers into making an identification that was never intended.

The Big Town is derived somewhat from the characters and situations of *Gullible's Travels*. The narrator, Finch, is again the wise boob for whom Ring had an admiration and sympathy: that shrewd,

177

pungent, middle-class American with a good-natured cynicism and a gift for phrasemaking. He is much more refined than Gullible, who occasionally is guilty of the follies that he mocks, and his observations are sharp social satire. Unlike Gullible, who is a naturalized urban type, Finch is a hick and his home town is good enough for him. But he must take his wife and his sister-in-law Kate to New York to find Kate a husband. The Finches are *nouveaux riches*—a class that was growing in the early twenties and that Ring had spotted and defined a good deal more quickly than most of the writers who were to deal with it—and the tainted source of their wealth is significant: the girls have inherited seventy-five thousand dollars apiece from their father, who made it in war profiteering in a smelly hide factory in Niles, Michigan. (Finch himself would have nothing to do with the hide factory.) In the Lardnerian vernacular Finch tells of their adventures in New York, of the Big Town phonies, snobs, and grifters whom Kate tries to snare. The first one, a Wall Street clerk posing as a broker, gets beaten up by Finch, an upright family man, however fatuous he thinks his sister-in-law; a second turns out to be a chauffeur with a wife and children. The third candidate is an aviator who is killed testing the new invention which was to have made him rich. After this Finch says:

"Wile I and Ella was getting ready for supper I made the remark that I s'posed we'd live in a vale of tears for the next few days.

" 'No,' said Ella. 'Sis is taking it pretty calm. She's sensible. She says that if that could have happened, why the invention couldn't of been no good after all. And the Williamses wouldn't of give him a plugged dime for it.' " Kate is one of the earliest of the calculating and unromantic women of Ring's fiction; she is also one of the most stupid, and it is she who is finally caught in a matrimonial trap.

In search of a rich man the Finches have taken up residence in a fashionable Long Island hotel:

Was you ever out there? Well, I s'pose it's what you might call a family hotel, and a good many of the guests belongs to the cay-nine family. A few of the couples that can't afford dogs has got children, and you're always tripping over one or the other. They's a dining room for the grown-ups and another for the kids, wile the dogs and their nurses eats in the grill-room a la carte. One part of the joint is bachelor quarters. It's located right next to the dogs' dormitories, and they's a good deal of rivalry between the dogs and the souses to see who can make the most noise nights. They's also a ballroom

*and a couple card rooms and a kind of a summer parlor where the
folks sets round in the evening and listen to a three-piece orchestra
that don't know they's been any music wrote since Poets and Peas-
ants. The men get up about eight o'clock and go down to New
York to Business. They don't never go to work. About nine the
women begins limping downstairs and either goes to call on their
dogs or take them for a walk in the front yard. This is a great big
yard with a whole lot of benches strewed around it, but you can't
set on them in the daytime because the women or the nurses uses
them for a place to read to the dogs or kids, and in the evenings you
would have to share them with the waitresses, which you have already had enough of them during the day.*

*When the women has prepared themselves for the long day's
grind with a four-course breakfast, they set round on the front porch
and discuss the big questions of the hour, like for instance the last
trunk murder or whether an Airedale is more loving than a Golden
Bantam. Once in a wile one of them cracks that it looks like they
was bound to be a panic pretty soon and a big drop in prices, and
so forth. This shows they're broad-minded and are giving a good
deal of thought to up-to-date topics. Every so often one of them'll
say: "The present situation can't keep up." The hell it can't!*

*Saturday nights everybody puts on their evening clothes like
something was going to happen. But it don't. Sunday mornings the
husbands and bachelors gets up earlier than usual to go to their real
business, which is golf. The womenfolks are in full possession of the
hotel till Sunday night supper and wives and husbands don't see
one another all day long, but it don't seem as long as if they did.
Most of them's approaching their golden-wedding jubilee and
haven't nothing more to say to each other that you could call a
novelty. . . .*

*The hotel's got all the modern conveniences like artificial light
and a stopper in the bathtubs. They even got a barber and a valet,
but you can't get a shave wile he's pressing your clothes, so it's
pretty near impossible for a man to look their best at the same time.*

The last sentence is one of Ring's most dazzling. Lacking any
grammatical sanction, it is nevertheless of a matchless clarity and
succinctness.

The fourth candidate for Kate's spouse eludes her after some
scenes at Belmont race track; hesitating between a jockey and a
stable owner, Kate loses both. But she meets her fate in a loud,
boastful Ziegfeld comic, a theatrical faker who had "given Bert

Williams the notion of playing coon parts, and learnt Sarah Bernhardt to talk French." After he has got some of Kate's money from her to produce one of the most dreadful plays in fiction, if not in actuality, he marries her for the rest, and Finch returns gratefully to South Bend. "So here we are, really enjoying ourselfs for the first time in pretty near two years. And Katie's in New York, enjoying herself, too, I suppose. She ought to be, married to a comic. It must be such fun to just set and listen to him talk."

In this book Ring observed a certain kind of uprooted middle-class life: people on trains, living in hotels, going to race tracks, seeking the most boring pastimes, incapable of real enjoyment. Even without roots and without homes they are in a hopeless rut from which they lack the imagination and the desire to escape. And it is particularly among these drifting people that the bores, the poseurs, and the phonies flourish; as if the upheaval of a secure, well-founded prewar world had set loose upon society a horde of predatory migrants in search of easy success; to whom all human relationships are a confidence game, and every triumph a prop to a petty ego that is bent on presenting a featureless, invulnerable false image to its fellow men. Lacking any fixed place in society, they also lack any code of conduct. They are another symptom of the breaking up of American life that took place in the twenties.

The Big Town comes as close to being a novel as anything that Ring ever wrote, although he did not plan it that way: he probably did not have the last episode in mind when he wrote the first. After he had written two of the stories, he moved from Greenwich to a hotel in Garden City, Long Island, which immediately suggested the background for the third story. Ring assimilated material quickly; he did not have to store it up in his mind for long. The book was written chapter by chapter over a period of more than a year; but it has a single theme and its narrator is a consistent character as well as a cool and unsentimental observer. For the breadth of its social observation *The Big Town* was the most important work of fiction that Ring had written thus far.

Ring and his family had lived a year in Greenwich, and after that for several months at the Garden City Hotel. Early in the spring of 1921 they moved into a large house on East Shore Road in Great Neck, Long Island, which Ring had bought and remodeled. His brother Rex, who had come to New York before him, lived in Great Neck; and Arthur and Helen Jacks also became their neighbors. Franklin P. Adams, who conducted "The Conning Tower" on the

180

World, lived nearby and saw much of Ring. "Lay late," he wrote in "The Diary of Our Own Samuel Pepys," "and R. Lardner and his brother Rex and I played tunes all morning, I on the harmonicka, and they on the piano, the saxophone, and the accordion, and I tried to play the accordion too, and mastered it easily enough." In his "Diary," Adams often recorded his meetings with Ring and Ellis. "To the circus with Neysa (McMein) and Lardners, where she and Ellis rode upon the elephants, and looked more royal than any queens I ever saw." "With Mistress Mildred Bowen to Princeton, and met so many persons on the train I could not find a moment to read in 'The Age of Innocence,' which I brought for that purpose, and Mistress Ellis Lardner and Marjorie Trumbull gave me of their sandwiches and chicken, very good, too . . . the train did not leave until after 7 o'clock, and got to New York at near 9, but so pleasant, what with M., and my flute-playing and R. Lardner's and Edith Fox's singing, I would as lief the train had been four hours longer on the journey."

In Great Neck or near it lived many of Ring's friends, and for a few years he lived a social life so active that it seriously crowded his working schedule and he often had to retreat to a New York hotel room for peace and quiet. His next-door neighbor was Herbert Bayard Swope, executive editor of the New York *World,* who gave many large parties. They often overflowed to the Lardners' house, and the Lardners' guests sometimes joined the Swopes'. All of Great Neck seemed to be a continuous party.

Long Island society was somewhat stratified, but in the twenties social barriers were breaking down. There were the old rich who belonged to the Social Register and entertained in a decorous atmosphere of intellectual conversation and croquet-by-gaslight; there were the new rich who did nothing but drink and play bridge and golf; there were people of talent who worked hard and made a lot of money but were not rich—theatrical people, writers and journalists, composers and artists. There were probably a few hosts like Fitzgerald's Gatsby, but mysterious bootleggers were not typical of Long Island society. But the stratifications were not rigid. The Swopes entertained everybody, although not all at the same time, having some principles of segregation which Ring did not observe. They gave parties for celebrities, and also for high society. It was the former at which Ring was a frequent guest, not because he craved celebrities as such, but because he liked to be entertained. He was of course a celebrity himself, and he went and was welcome everywhere. But in the main his friends were professional people of talent, and he was particularly fond of theatrical people and musicians. He once gave a party for J. Rosamond Johnson, the Negro composer of "Under the Bamboo Tree," whose songs Ring had loved for many years. It was not customary in Great Neck to entertain Negroes, but Ring thought that Johnson was so much more talented than most of the people he knew that he did not care what Great Neck thought. A great many of the invited guests did not come; those who did had a wonderful time, and so did Ring, singing his favorite songs and listening to his guests.

There were people who drank, and there were the really heavy drinkers. Ring and Scott Fitzgerald belonged to the latter, although membership in that club was not very limited at that time and place. Occasionally an anxious hostess who liked to keep things formal would quail at their appearance, but there was nothing at all distinctive about drinking in any circle. The society of that time was dependent on talent, success, and alcohol; in that respect it epitomized upper-middle-class life in America; but it was easily the most sophisticated and fashionable sector of society in the country, and the reason was that so many of its members were genuinely talented. Their names were not merely in gossip columns: they were on books, magazines, newspaper columns, theaters, billboards, music, and records. They lived fairly untrammeled personal lives and drank as they pleased, which made for a certain irregularity; but they also had solid-looking, expensive homes, children, and servants, and they belonged to the best clubs.

Ring qualified in every way to belong to such a circle, or rather, a cluster of overlapping circles. He was famous and prosperous, an acknowledged genius; he had a large and attractive home and entertained a great deal; he played golf and bridge, he was sociable and amusing, and he belonged to half a dozen clubs. He knew everyone worth knowing, though he often wished he didn't, and many people who weren't. But although he entered into fashionable suburban life in all its aspects, he remained unique, detached, and critical; and in spite of the fact that he was a familiar figure at Long Island parties, no one felt he knew him very well, not even those people who went often to Ring's own house. It was always filled with brilliant and amusing people. These entertainments were so continual and so large that being a guest at the Lardners', or at many other open houses, was no guarantee of intimacy with the host. Ring's closest friends remained the Jackses, the Grantland Rices, the Adamses, the Goldbergs, and for a time Scott and Zelda Fitzgerald.

Fitzgerald had written *This Side of Paradise* and a great many popular short stories and was enjoying a rush of renown and prosperity. He and Zelda were young and handsome; they looked a little like children dressed up for parts too old for them, their behavior was sometimes infantile, but they were beautiful and exuberant. "Scott is a novelist and Zelda is a novelty," Ring wrote of them. He was fascinated by Zelda's beauty and her oddness—Ring was always attracted by eccentricity, even madness, and perhaps he had some deep intuition of her fragility and her precarious emotional balance. Ring was solemn and morose and eleven years older than the loquacious and excitable Fitzgerald. Fitzgerald had a romantic admiration for rich and fashionable people by whom Ring was not taken in at all; he struck intellectual poses at which Ring could only feel a tolerant amusement. Some of the Fitzgeralds' rowdy capers must have been an embarrassment to Ring; but strict as he was in his own conduct, he was never openly censorious about his friends and he even enjoyed the spectacle of other people's lack of inhibition. In spite of vast disparities of temperament and behavior Ring and Fitzgerald had a deep and solid friendship which lasted through years of separation. To no one else outside his family did Ring write such affectionate, trusting, and revealing letters.

During the year and a half that Fitzgerald lived as Ring's neighbor in Great Neck, from 1922 to 1924, they were almost constant companions. They sat up many nights at each other's house, drinking and talking, alone or with a few other friends, about writing, about people, about events; Fitzgerald enthusiastic, inflated with youthful ideas, often talking off the top of his mind; Ring cynical, deflating, and unimpressed. Sometimes Ring, if he had drunk enough, solemnly told uproarious nonsense stories; at other times, long after Fitzgerald and some of the guests had been overcome with drink, Ring went on talking without the slightest impediment of speech or thought, making perfect sense. They read and discussed the same books; Ring, like Fitzgerald, read *avant-garde* magazines, although he pretended to scorn them. Fitzgerald got Ring to read *Three Lives*, by Gertrude Stein, and Ring liked it; and Ring no doubt filled in some of the gaps in Fitzgerald's literary background. Fitzgerald was given to extravagant and sometimes fuzzy opinions; Ring was precise, accurate, and well-informed.

Edmund Wilson recalls an occasion in mid-April 1924, just before the Fitzgeralds went to Europe: "Fitz said he was going abroad because his reputation was diminishing in America, and he wanted to stay away until he had accomplished something important, and then come back and have people give him dinners. There was great talk on Lardner's part of going to the Red Lion or some other road-house, but when we did leave—all the liquor now gone—we simply went to Lardner's, where we drank Grand Marnier—he insisted on presenting us each with a little bottle—and more Scotch. Fitz's attempt to deliver himself of a great self-revelation—egoism, *The Egotist*. Lardner said, 'No, you haven't got that right.'

"'Well, *Egoist*, then—don't interrupt me just for a little thing like that.'

"Lardner thought it was a good book, didn't agree with him. "'Where he sees the professor . . .'

"'Oh, yes: he was the mother of the girl.'" Loud laughter.

"Zelda had gone to sleep in an armchair and covered herself with a shawl—she was bored by Scott's chart of the Middle Ages and had made herself very disagreeable about it. Scott was sore, because we had crabbed his revelation. 'You mispronounce a lot of words,' Lardner had said."

Ring, a purist in language, always corrected people's errors if he knew them well enough; otherwise he had to endure them, although they irked him.

"Lardner read the golf rules aloud. (This was a little book put out by the local golf club. Lardner read these rules at length with a saturnine deadpan scorn that was funny yet really communicated his disgust with his successful suburban life.)—Then we went back to the Fitzgeralds'. Lardner and I started talking about the Oil Scandal, and Fitz fell asleep in his chair. Lardner and I went on talking about baseball, Heywood Broun, Lardner's writing, the Americanized *Carmen*, the Rascoes, etc. Deep blue patches appeared at the windows. I couldn't think at first what they were—then I realized it was the dawn. The birds tuned up one at a time. It grew light. It was seven o'clock. Scott asked what we had been talking about. Lardner said we had been talking about him.

"'I suppose you analyzed me ruthlessly.'

"Zelda was sick and had the doctor and apologized profoundly for her 'rudeness.'

"When we were talking about his own work, Lardner said that the trouble was he couldn't write straight English. I asked him what he meant, and he said: 'I can't write a sentence like "We were sitting in the Fitzgeralds' house and the fire was burning brightly."' (This was before he had written his few short stories in straight English.)"

184

On another occasion when Edmund Wilson was at the Fitzgeralds', Ring told one of his characteristic burlesques of the kind of "funny story" he hated: "Ring Lardner, far gone in liquor, insisted upon silence from the entire company and then told a story: Once there were two foxes in the bathtub together, Pat and Mike. They took turns sponging each other off. Finally, one said to the other, 'Here,' he said, 'here, you've been sponging off me long enough!'—so he kicked out the stopper. And, what do you think, the next morning they woke up in the same street. —He also told about a woman who was a Lorna. The thing about a Lorna is that they can't prune trees. That was how they found out that this woman was a Lorna—they took her out by a tree and she couldn't prune it—and so they knew she was a Lorna.

"I remember on one occasion his saying that he had just seen a 'queel' looking in through the window and then later—or on some other occasion—when he was leaving the Fitzgeralds' brushing some queels off his own coat."

Ring's sardonic attitude about life in Great Neck—he mocked it, reading the golf-club rules, telling laborious "funny" stories, correcting Fitzgerald's errors—appealed to Fitzgerald, who knew that Ring was serious and troubled. After such evenings Ring would rise and say: "Well, I guess the children have left for school by this time—I might as well go home." He slept very little now and sometimes needed a sedative to sleep at all. Yet he was carrying a heavy load of work at this time—two syndicate features, magazine articles, and his persistent efforts to write something for the theater. It was a day-to-day grind, and Fitzgerald thought Ring was wasting himself on it. He had tremendous admiration for Ring as an artist, for his ability to find out about different kinds of people, and would ask him how he managed it. Ring would tell him just to enter into conversation with anybody that he happened to be sitting next to on the Long Island railroad. Fitzgerald was incapable of this: his way of trying to document himself was to ask ill-mannered leading questions that would shut up anybody like a clam: "How much money did your family have?" "Do you still sleep with your wife?" etc. It seemed to him a miracle that Ring could understand enough about such people as the couple in "The Golden Honeymoon" to write a story about them.

At the same time Fitzgerald was afraid that Ring had begun to let go, to confine his talent to trivial forms, and to suppress his real genius. It seemed to him that Ring's excessive preoccupation with other people's troubles was an evasion of his own.

185

*The woes of many people haunted him—for example the doctor's
death sentence pronounced upon Tad [Dorgan], the cartoonist
(who, in fact, nearly outlived Ring)—it was as if he believed he
could and ought to do something about it. And as he struggled to
fulfill his contracts, one of which, a comic strip based on the character of "the busher," was a terror indeed, it was obvious that he
felt his work to be directionless, merely "copy." So he was inclined
to turn his cosmic sense of responsibility into the channel of solving
other people's problems—finding someone an introduction to a manager, placing a friend in a job, maneuvering a man into a golf club.
The effort made was often out of proportion to the situation; the
truth back of it was that Ring was getting off—he was a faithful and
conscientious workman to the end, but he had stopped finding any
fun in his work. . . .*

Fitzgerald was not entirely right about Ring's worries over other
people. They were simply part of his nature. Long before he had
ever had to face any personal or artistic problems, Ring concerned
himself with the welfare of his friends; even as a child he went to
great lengths to do favors for people he liked, and he was congeni-
tally incapable of resisting the appeal of a friend in trouble. Years
before, he had virtually kept a vigil at Walter Eckersall's bedside
when Eckersall had pneumonia; he worried constantly about everyone, nothing was too much trouble if he could be helpful, and this
did not necessarily mean that he was abandoning his own fate to
watch over others, although certainly it was related to his sense of
the tragedy of life and his need to alleviate it wherever he could.
But his work at this particular time had become mechanical—a
weekly column, some rather perfunctory burlesques for magazines,
and his constantly thwarted efforts to write something that could be
produced on the stage. Some of his best short stories were yet to
come, but he was to find them difficult to write, and he would have
preferred to concentrate on songs and plays. His daily writing tasks
had never been a pleasure; the arduousness of labor was nothing
new. It was not that work had become so much harder; but the re-
wards were bringing a diminishing satisfaction. He did not care for
fame, he required money for the security of his family—and he
needed a wide margin, anxiety-ridden as he was—but not for pleasure; and the whole idea of success had lost its luster. He had a sense
of personal failure, he had misgivings about his health and his compulsion to drink, but above all a deep and ineradicable pessimism

186

had set in and he was inclined to doubt the value of his very existence.

Fitzgerald modeled a character in *Tender Is the Night* on Ring —Abe North, the musician who has had one brilliant success but cannot seem to develop his talent any further and who wastes himself skulking idly about Europe drinking, finally getting killed in a drunken brawl in New York. North has Ring's lovable and awe-inspiring qualities, and Fitzgerald uses in describing him some of the same phrases he applied to Ring: proud, shy, solemn, shrewd, polite, kind, merciful, honorable. He has a sad mien, Indian cheekbones, a "face like a cathedral," "like the wreck of a galleon, dominating with his presence his own weakness and self-indulgence, his narrowness and bitterness. All of them were conscious of the solemn dignity that flowed from him, of his achievement, fragmentary, suggestive and surpassed. But they were frightened by his survivant will, once a will to live, now become a will to die."

"Why does he drink?" Nicole asks. "So many smart men go to pieces nowadays."

"And when haven't they?" Dick Diver says. "Smart men play close to the line because they have to—some of them can't stand it, so they quit."

Abe North is a fictional character, but there is no doubt that he embodies what Fitzgerald saw in Ring at the time he knew him in 1924, when he was "getting off." This was a despair that inhibited his creative faculty and led to slow self-destruction. Abe North did not think it was worth the trouble to go any farther; and he haunts the novel like an unburied ghost, likable, aimless, helpful, but utterly finished. Ring was far from finished; the problem which Fitzgerald foresaw—for Ring, for himself, for any creative artist— was only suggested by Ring's attitudes, and it is magnified in Abe North. But it is indicative of Fitzgerald's fears for Ring.

So Fitzgerald urged Ring to "organize" his work. It was a futile suggestion. In the first place Ring was not susceptible to any suggestions on how to work or live, and he did not think of his "work" as an entity that was capable of being organized. He was a journalist meeting a deadline, even when he was writing a short story. What Fitzgerald meant was that Ring should write something deeply personal, that he should tap his inward self for his material, that he should undertake a big project, with enough time to do it. But Ring's limitations were twofold: he was a master of the observed, phenomenal world, and the essence of his talent was his clear, objective view of the visible, within a small compass. There

187

is no indication that he had any eye for a large canvas, nor for the mysterious realm of rarefied, undefined emotions. His own description of how he worked would seem to preclude the idea of a large, ambitious work such as Fitzgerald suggested. "I don't worry much about plots. I just start writing about somebody I think I know something about. I try to get him down cold. The other characters seem to walk into the story naturally enough. I seldom write a story of more than five thousand words—my mind seems geared to that length. I write three thousand words about nothing; that is a terrible struggle. Then I come to, and say to myself, 'I must get a punch in this.' I stop and figure out the punch, and then sail through to the finish." This alibi is as transparent as some of Jack Keefe's, but the limitation was real enough. There was also—as Fitzgerald saw—a limitation of temperament. Ring had already decided "to speak only a small portion of his mind"; to withhold what was most deeply personal. To him whole areas of human behavior were taboo. There was never any possibility that he could do otherwise. He had erected certain defenses between the world and his own sensibilities, and they stood. He felt vulnerable enough without self-revelation.

But at least Fitzgerald persuaded him to collect his short stories and was instrumental in getting Scribner's to publish them, and to reissue Ring's earlier books; and this was a considerable service. It is possible that they would have been neglected for years; Ring himself did not have the vanity to suppose that his stories were worth preserving. He had not even saved copies of them, and they had to be photographed from back numbers of magazines in the public library. Scribner's had to be pressed somewhat; they regarded Ring as a newspaper humorist; it is said that the enthusiasm of Sir James Barrie was a decisive factor in their undertaking to publish Ring's work, but certainly Fitzgerald's insistence played a part. It was he who suggested the title *How to Write Short Stories*, a remarkably poor one if he hoped to establish a literary reputation for Ring. Ring submitted to this treatment graciously enough, though with no great enthusiasm; but after the book came out and was an enormous success with critics, and even exceeded Ring's expectations in sales, he was genuinely pleased, and took a great deal of satisfaction from the reviews. It is even likely that its success gave him some stimulus to write his fine short stories in straight English. He had wanted seven years earlier to abandon dialect and the first person, and within two years after the success of his book he wrote his best third-person stories.

Of Ring's personal devotion to Fitzgerald and Zelda there is no doubt; his letters are the best evidence of it. The Fitzgeralds charmed and amused him, but beyond that he had a deep affection for them and a real respect for Fitzgerald as a writer. There was an understanding between them; on Fitzgerald's part it is clear that in contemplating Ring's fate as a writer he was projecting his own fears for himself; he knew what Ring was up against. As for Ring, he knew that Fitzgerald, although he seemed to personify a whole generation that had revolted against the moral code to which Ring still clung, was at heart a romantic and a moralist like himself. Fitzgerald was young and he was still to find glamour in a kind of life which Ring had seen through, and he had dreams of success which Ring had abandoned; but nevertheless they were both disabused in the same way, they had lost their beliefs, and their judgments on their times were basically the same.

Ring admired *The Great Gatsby,* with some reservations. It was written in Europe, beyond Ring's immediate influence, if indeed Ring had any influence on Fitzgerald's writing. It is tempting to suppose that contact with a precise and disciplined mind like Ring's would benefit a young writer, but there is no concrete evidence of a specific influence. Ring read the page proofs and suggested a few minor corrections, some of which were made. He wrote:

I read Mr. F.'s book (in page proofs) at one sitting and liked it enormously, particularly the description of Gatsby's home and his party, and the party in the apartment in New York. It sounds as if Mr. F. must have attended a party or two during his metropolitan career. The plot held my interest, too, and I found no tedious moments. Altogether I think it's the best thing you've done since Paradise.

On the other hand, I acted as volunteer proof reader and gave Max [Perkins, editor of Scribner's] a brief list of what I thought were errata. On page 31 and 46 you spoke of the newsstand on the lower level, and the cold waiting room on the lower level of the Pennsylvania station. There ain't any lower level on that station and I suggested substitute terms for same. On page 82 you had the guy driving his car under the elevated at Astoria, which isn't Astoria, but Long Island City. On page 118 you had a tide in Lake Superior and on page 209 you had the Chicago, Milwaukee and St. Paul running out of the LaSalle Street Station. These things are trivial, but some of the critics pick on trivial errors for lack of anything else to pick on.

189

After the book had come out, Ring wrote to H. L. Mencken, with whom he held so many views in common: "Your stuff about Scott in the Sunday World was, it seemed to me, close to perfection in criticism. And you have the right dope on the pains he took with Gatsby. He rewrote the whole book four or five times and had Scribner's crazy at the finish with revisions by cable."

Mencken's review of *The Great Gatsby* was not unqualified praise. In fact he called it a glorified anecdote and objected to the improbability of the plot and the falseness of all the characters except Gatsby. But he praised the charm and beauty of the writing and commended Fitzgerald for having taken pains with his style. And as a social historian, he gave him a rousing accolade, with a thunderous condemnation of the corrupt Long Island society that Fitzgerald depicted so vividly in the book. As a moralist, Mencken found Fitzgerald's picture of it rich and satisfying. "We are in an atmosphere grown increasingly levantine. The Paris of the Second Empire pales to a sort of snobbish chautauqua; the New York of Ward McAllister becomes the scene of a convention of Gold Star Mothers. To find a parallel for the grossness and debauchery of New York one must go back to the Constantinople of Basil I." Whether or not he saw any humor in this portentous pronouncement, Ring endorsed it. The realism of the party scenes and the morality implied in Fitzgerald's view of Long Island society had his approval.

He had also liked other stories of Fitzgerald's. The year before, he had written to Mencken, "I liked Scott's 'Absolution' in the current Mercury (my favorite magazine) though parts of it were over my head." This last was, of course, deliberately disingenuous; Ring sometimes pretended that he did not understand stories about sex. But he understood Fitzgerald very well.

After a year and a half in Great Neck the Fitzgeralds discovered that they were spending $36,000 a year and running a roadhouse, which was very much what Ring was doing. They went to France, and although they wrote to each other frequently and the Lardners paid them a short visit, they never saw much of each other again. Ring wrote a poem of farewell to Zelda:

> So dearie when your tender heart
> Of all his coarseness tires
> Just cable me and I will start
> Immediately for Hyères.
> To hell with Scott Fitzgerald then!

190

To hell with Scott his daughter!
It's you and I back home again
To Great Neck where the men are men
And booze is ¾ water.

They left Ring in charge of renting their house, and his first letters to them are largely concerned with frozen water pipes, plumber's bills, and a broken oven door. Ring deposited the rent check in Fitzgerald's bank account; later, when Fitzgerald overdrew, Arthur Jacks, manager of the bank at Great Neck, told Ring, and Ring covered the overdraft.

The Fitzgeralds were gone but the parties continued. "The peace and quiet of Great Neck is a delusion and a snare, I can assure you," Ring said in an interview. "There is a continuous round of parties in progress here, covering pretty nearly twenty-four hours a day. It is almost impossible to work at times and still more difficult to sleep. Mr. Swope of the *World* lives across the way and he conducts an almost continuous house-party. A number of other neighbors do the same; there are guests in large numbers roaming these woods all the time. Apparently they become confused occasionally and forget at whose house they are really stopping, for they wander in at all hours demanding refreshment and entertainment at the place that happens to be nearest at the moment. The telephone is going almost continuously. Of course wives are useful to answer telephones. Scott Fitzgerald ran away to Europe, to escape the parties and other interruptions, hoping to be able to get some work done over there."

The traffic at Swopes' was heavy. In a weekly letter Ring wrote a burlesque description of his own house and said, "Right behind the fence is a large floral tribute consisting of my name and the wife's maiden name planted in toadstools. This was put there for use as well as beauty as the whole family was sick and tired of having moderate price motors stop out in front and ask if the Swopes lived there." Ring himself roamed the woods. Sometimes he appeared on Saturday nights, having reached a certain decorous stage of inebriation which he contrived to maintain for the entire evening without becoming incoherent. He amazed people by his capacity for conducting himself graciously with a heavy load of liquor. At such times he was inclined to perform, and if the way was clear he generally headed for the piano, where he would improvise operas. One of the best had the recurrent love-motif, "Gretchen, I'm retchin' for you." Unfortunately they were not all funny and sometimes the solemn, calculated repetition that was part of Ring's humor did not

191

amuse everyone. But no matter how much he drank, he was never argumentative or ill-tempered; at the worst he was only harmlessly persistent, and in Great Neck in that era he was a model of gentlemanly conduct. He was not aggressive but his mere presence was commanding; it often made him seem more self-assertive than he really was.

Ring's satire was not confined to his writing. At parties he took a special delight in kidding people who did not know they were being kidded. It was fun for everyone including the victim, and Ring did it so delicately that he never hurt anyone's feelings. It was done without malice; he was often sardonic at the expense of people of whom he was very fond. Occasionally his humor misfired. When he was introduced to Jane Cowl, then at the height of her fame, she asked him what he did. He told her he was a writer, then solemnly asked, "And what business are you in?" She was affronted. This trivial episode bothered Ring; he was quite upset to think he had unwittingly offended anyone.

Ring's loquacious moods came over him when he was in informal and familiar surroundings; at other times he could keep silent for a whole evening, or sit through a dinner without saying a single word. Or he might make just one remark so well timed that he seemed to be the funniest man there. Ring's casual remarks are largely lost; they pertained to a single instant, in circumstances that would never occur again, and—since few people can ever quote correctly from memory—they have not survived the moments they were intended for. On the other hand, countless remarks which Ring made without the intention of being funny were hailed as great witticisms. He had acquired the reputation of being a humorist and people expected everything he said to be funny. He was particularly bored by this, and he detested adulation. It is possible that a good many of his long silences on social occasions were simply a refusal to perform as a humorist. He did not talk when he had nothing to say, and there was nothing antisocial or unfriendly about this taciturnity. He was nearly unique in this respect; most people, even very intelligent ones, feel it necessary to talk in company. Those forced and perfunctory conversations constitute a large percentage of everything that is said in the world; Ring's stories reproduce them with a deadly accuracy which makes one think that he found nearly everyone a bore.

But with people with whom he was on easy and confidential terms he could be very talkative, and his keen observation and dry wit made even the most commonplace things lively and funny. He loved

192

gossip because he always wanted to know what was going on. His letters to the Fitzgeralds are good conversation, full of literary and theatrical chatter—Fitzgerald, too, had a flair for gossip—and they also give a vivid picture of Ring's social life in Great Neck and New York. Even his account of Fitzgerald's financial affairs in connection with the renting of his house is amusing:

Why and the hell don't you state your address, or haven't you any? I'm going to send this registered to plain Hyères, with a prayer.

First the financial news, which I am afraid is bad, but I am enclosing plenty of documentary evidence to support it.

The day after you left, Miss Robinson called up to say that she had rented the house to Mr. and Mrs. S—— for $1600. "But listen, Miss Robinson," I remonstrated; "Mr. Fitzgerald told me that if you rented it right away, the rent was to be $2000." "But listen, Mr. Lardner," said Miss Robinson; "Mr. Fitzgerald called me up just before he left and said I was to rent it as soon as possible for $1600 as he had given up ideas of making a profit and just wanted it off his mind." Well, she seemed honest so I said all right and I hope it was. Now then, it seems that William and Sally had kind of let things get dirty in out of the way places and Miss Robinson said that both the house and the yard needed a thorough renovating, which ought to be at the expense of the last tenants. Not knowing the ethics, I asked Ellis and she said this was according to custom. So I said go ahead and renovate, and all you were soaked for that was $50. Then there was the matter of the oven door, mentioned in one of the enclosures. . . . Then along came a water bill for $22.06 which I paid because if I hadn't, the company would have shut off the water and the S——s would have had to join the Kensington Association in order to use the pool. S—— is a French name and they ought to get along without baths, but they are kind of Ritzy. . . .

John Golden wants me to write a play based on "The Golden Honeymoon," but I don't see how it could be done without introducing a pair of young lovers or something.

Personally I am now reading "The Beautiful and Damned."

We have a parrot which talks, laughs and whistles.

We are going to Cleveland Sunday night for the Republican Convention.

Victor Herbert dropped dead a week or so ago. The papers said he spent the forenoon with his daughter, then had lunch with Silvio Hein and died soon after lunch, but Gene [Buck] says he was with him virtually all day up to the time he died. How he missed being with him when he died or put him in the death business is a mystery to me. Anyway he was the leading pall bearer. I didn't find out whether or not your stunt was going into the Follies because all we could talk about was Victor's death which came like a bolt from the blue.

Ellis says she will write as soon as she is through with the dentist. Personally I have written a thousand words. Love to one of you.

Gene Buck, to whom Ring referred in connection with Victor Herbert, was a song writer, producer, playwright, and manager for Ziegfeld, and lived near Ring in an oversized house on Nassau Drive. Ring called his living room the Yale Bowl and was vastly amused by the scale of grandeur on which the Bucks lived. He and Ring collaborated on a musical for Ziegfeld, which was never produced. His professional vicissitudes were also of epic proportions, and Ring recounted them in detail in his letters. Both he and Fitzgerald were fascinated by them:

But I know you are in a fever to hear the latest Buckshot, which is the title I have just thought of for my column of news about the Bucks. Well, Gene, after threatening, for several years, to go into the producing end of the "game," finally bought a play by J. C. Nugent, called "Gunpowder." The thesis was that when an elderly man marries a young girl, she may some day become a mother at the hands of somebody her own age. The play opened in Washington and ran a week, a record-breaking week. The house for opening night was $300 and for the Saturday night, $8.00. Gene decided something was the matter with the show and took it off to have it rewritten by (you'll never guess) Brandon Tynan, who was also engaged to play the elderly husband's part, replacing Nugent. Well, they opened here in New York on Thursday night and we all got dressed up and went and I wish you could have been there. The audience, trying its best to be decent, laughed hysterically and uproariously at the saddest parts and when the girl finally announced she was in a two-family way, there was almost a panic. Two tickets were sold for Saturday night and then Gene took it off.

Late in July, 1924, Ring wrote:

Now for the bad news:

She whom I married and I are going to leave for France on the Paris, September tenth; will stay in Paris a week or so, and then go to the south of France, where I have a first cousin, aged about 60, in Montpelier, and we may possibly drop in at San Raphael, but if we

194

*do, we're going to stop at a hotel, because we have agreed we don't
like the service in private homes. We'll try to find the Villa Marie,
and if we do, don't let me forget to tell you the many peculiar things
that have happened in Great Neck. Most of them have happened to
nobody but me, but I always like to talk in the first person.*

Give my fondest regards to her whom you so generously married.

*If we do come, I'll wire you from Paris or Montpelier the approxi-
mate time of our arrival. Could you go to Biarritz or Spain with us?
I want to see a bullfight.*

Before sailing Ring wrote again: "We leave here September 10
and will stay a week in Paris before going south. I hope you and
Thelma or whatever her name is can be ready to go with us to
Biarritz for a day or two." Ring and Ellis landed at Le Havre and
took the ferry to Deauville, "on account of a cousin of mine living near there"—Ring's idea of the geography of France seems to
have been a little hazy. They found that the season was over in
Deauville; even the casino was dull, and they went on to Paris.
There they hardly heard French spoken. It was full of Americans
and they stuck close to the tourist route—the Eiffel Tower (Ring
wrote that he didn't know what it was for), the Folies Bergère, and
Montmartre, where Ring was shocked only by the size of the check.
He also went to Harry's New York Bar, where all American newspapermen went. There Ring got into a crap game, deeply absorbed
and observing his customary silence. A noisy drunk at the bar was
making a disturbance. One of the dice players looked up and said,
"Ah, shut up!"

"Well spoken," Ring said.

After a visit to Montpellier, which Ring finally located, the Lardners went on to St. Raphaël, where the Fitzgeralds met them. They
had a hair-raising ride in Fitzgerald's car over the Grande Corniche
to Monte Carlo, where Ring played the roulette wheel, losing four
thousand francs the first night but winning five thousand the second.
Ring liked roulette; he was not a heavy gambler, but he was fascinated by the mathematical possibilities of the wheel and the mystery
of why they never worked out. For him it was pure chance; he had
no faith in systems.

They made another brief visit to Paris, and then went on to London, where they met several American friends. Ring made the
rounds of the night clubs and made friends with musicians. The
Lardners decided they had had enough of Europe and came home on
the *Mauretania.* Ring wrote a series of five articles for *Liberty* called

"The Other Side." He said in a letter to Fitzgerald: "Instead of working on the ship coming home, as I intended, I did nothing but lap them up. But as soon as I was home and on the wagon, I wrote the five European articles in nine days."

Perhaps this haste accounts for the thinness of these pieces, but it seems more likely that Ring really had very little feeling at all for Europe. His early wartime book, *My Four Weeks in France*, although written in different circumstances, was also a perfunctory effort. There is not very much about Europe in either of them, and it is hard to escape the impression that Ring was indifferent to it. Of course he limited himself by writing in character; and the reactions of the wise boob abroad are fairly predictable. He observes a few details which lend themselves readily to the facile humor of disparagement; he is typically unimpressed by history or culture. But what is really lacking is the wonderful evocative power which shows in even the slightest pieces Ring wrote about America, and the character's gift for pungent phrases. Here there is no background, no color. The details of American life which Ring reported are significant and characteristic; the minutiae of European life which he observed are isolated and meaningless, set down without affection or interest. He was burlesquing the innocent abroad, but he had none of Mark Twain's eagerness or curiosity.

Back in Great Neck, Ring wrote to the Fitzgeralds:

Friday, January 9, 1925

Dear Wops:—

You would get a lot more mail from me if you had a decent and permanent address. I hate to write letters and think all the time that they'll never get anywhere.

I have talked with Max Perkins several times since he received Scott's novel. He is very enthusiastic about it, saying it's much the best thing Scott has done since "Paradise," that parts of it are inspired, and etc. He wasn't crazy to have anybody use it serially on account of the delay it meant in getting out the book, but he told me today that "College Humor" had made a good offer which he thought you might accept. "College Humor" seems to be l---y with money and careless of how it spends it—not knocking Mr. Fitzgerald. My brother [Rex, fiction editor of Liberty] was strong for the book and wanted "Liberty" to run it, but some of the other readers thought it was better as a book than it would be as a serial, meaning that it couldn't be arranged so that the reader would be left in suspense at the end of each installment.

I have been on the wagon since Armistice Day and Ellis and I have seen a lot of shows. Laurence Stallings' play is a bear, even with a few of the words left out. I see no reason why it shouldn't beat a record or come near it. Dorothy Parker's "Close Harmony" got great notices and was, we thought, a dandy play, but it flopped in three weeks. Dorothy, Beatrice Kaufman and Peggy Leech gave a party at the Algonquin six or seven weeks ago. I was enjoying an intellectual conversation with Mary Hay when Peggy tore me away to talk to a lady who seemed kind of lonely . . . and I'd have been with her yet if June Walker hadn't come in with a bun and rescued me.

We got back from the other side [Europe] in time to see the Yale-Princeton game. Art Samuels was host to a huge party of us— Swopes, Brouns, etc.—at lunch at the Cottage Club. The Princeton team, which had made a sucker of Harvard the Saturday before, acted on this occasion as if football was a complete surprise and novelty. We stood up all the way home and I swore it would be my last trip to old Nassau.

I have quit the strip and Dick Dorgan is doing it, with help from Tad.

. . . Rube and Irma [Goldberg] gave a New Year's Eve party to which 150 people were invited and 500 came. Rube said he never saw so many strangers in his life. Billy Seeman had a lot of the Follies people there to help entertain, but the affair was such a riot that little attention was paid to the entertainment. Ellis and I missed this party. . . . I was in the hospital having my antrum cut open. I'm nearly all right again now, I think, though if I get up suddenly or stoop over a regular Niagara of blood pours forth from my shapely nostrils.

I took "Vanity Fair" (Thackeray's, not Crowninshield's) to the hospital with me and one day the nurse asked me what I was reading and I told her and she said, "I haven't read it yet. I've been busy making Christmas presents."

Ellis is at present in Danville, Illinois, where her last brother is being married tomorrow to a gal named Bredehoft. I was kept at home by my nose. We are leaving next Tuesday, with the Grant Rices, for Miami and then Nassau, to be gone till nearly the first of March. Our address at Nassau will be New Colonial Hotel. I think I'll take up golf again, but won't stick to it if I don't like it.

And I think you've staid away long enough.

Mrs. Nell

Ring's running chronicle of life in New York and Great Neck continued:

Michael Arlen, who is here to watch the staging of The Green Hat, said he thought How to Write Short Stories was a great title for my book and when I told him it was your title, he said he had heard a great deal about you and was sorry to miss you. He also said he had heard that Mrs. Fitzgerald was very attractive, but I told him he must be thinking of somebody else. Mike is being entertained high and low. He was guest of honor at a luncheon given by Ray Long. Irv Cobb and George Doran sat on either side of him and told one dirty story after another. Last Sunday night he was at a party at Conde Nast's, but who wasn't? I was looking forward to a miserable evening, but had the luck to draw Ina Claire for a dinner and evening companion and was perfectly happy, though I regretted being on the wagon. The last previous time I saw her was at the Press Club in Chicago about eight years ago and she says I was much more companionable on that occasion. George Nathan said he heard you were coming home soon. George, they say, is quitting the associate editorship of the Mercury but will continue to write theater for it.

So far as I know, Zelda, Mary Hay and Richard [Barthelmess] are still together; they were when I met them.

We had a dinner party at our little nest about two weeks ago; the guests were the Ray Longs, the Grantland Rices, June Walker, and Frank Crowninshield. As place cards for Ray, Crownie and Grant, we had, respectively, covers of Cosmopolitan, Vanity Fair and The American Golfer, but this didn't seem to make any impression on June and right after the soup she began knocking Conde Nast in general and his alleged snobbishness in particular. Finally Crownie butted in to defend him and June said, "What do you know about him?" "I live with him," said Crownie. "What for?" said June. "Well," said Crownie, "I happen to be editor of one of his magazines, Vanity Fair." "Oh!" said June. "That's my favorite magazine! And I hate most magazines! For instance, I wouldn't be seen with a Cosmopolitan." After the loud laughter had subsided, I explained to her that Ray was editor of Cosmopolitan. "I'm always making breaks," she said, "and I guess this is one of my unlucky evenings. I suppose that if I said what I think of William R. Hearst, I'd find that even he has a friend here or something." [Grantland Rice wrote for the Hearst papers.]

198

The annual Dutch Treat show comes off this week. I have a sketch in it which is a born flop.

I met Gene on the train the other day and he said, "Come over and play bridge with us tonight," and I said I couldn't because Arthur Jacks was coming to our house. When I got home, I called up Arthur to inform him of this and he said it was tough luck, but it just happened that he had been invited, several days before, to dine at Gene's that very night.

Thanks for the idea, which I think I can use. I wrote to you yesterday, but don't mind doing it again as I left out one piece of news which may be of interest, namely that George Jean Nathan and Lillian Gish are often seen together these days. And a handsome pair they make.

Looked up Capri in the encyclopedia and learned that the water supply for drinking was unsatisfactory. Hope to God this is not ruining your stay. . . .

Visited Mr. Perkins yesterday, had myself sketched by a lady named Anderson, and saw the wrap of your book, which looks good. Then dined at the Princeton club with Art Samuels and attended a Dutch Treat rehearsal, after which I went backstage at the Follies and turned down three offers of drinks, one from a lady, or at least a female.

Must close now and nibble on a carrot. Love to the little woman.

Ring went on the wagon for months at a time; it did not keep him from going out a great deal, although generally, after a period of intense social activity, he liked to stay at home for long stretches, rarely going to New York. When he got tired and sick and lost weight, he could give up both drinking and smoking and force himself to eat, even foods he did not like, such as oatmeal, until he had gained ten or twenty pounds. Giving up smoking was an ordeal he dreaded. Once, before coming home from a trip, he warned Ellis by telegram, "I DONT SMOKE," but when he arrived he had a cigarette in his hand. He explained that his nights on the train had been so sleepless that he had to get up and smoke. Sometimes he put dozens of sticks of gum around his typewriter so that when he reached for a cigarette he would get gum instead.

For two or three months Ring often stayed close to home, but when an occasion for conviviality arose, he would go off the wagon. He wrote to Fitzgerald, after he had stayed on for six months:

199

I might consider visiting Paris if you will guarantee me an introduction to Miss LeGallienne who is my favorite actress and with whom I have been secretly in love since Liliom.

Gene [Buck] told Dorothy Parker in my presence one night that the new house had been bought as a memorial to the kiddies.

Dorothy visited the Lardners for a week at my invitation. . . . for some reason or other, I thought a visit to us would cheer her up. I got into this sympathetic mood on the seventh of May and it lasted till the tenth of July; during the two months I was constantly cockeyed, drinking all night and sleeping all day and never working. Fortunately, I was eight weeks ahead in syndicates before the spree started.

One night during Dorothy's visit, Herman Mankiewicz called up from Petrova's and said he would come and see us if we'd come after him. We did and I took them, Mank and Dorothy, to Durand's, Ellis (very sensibly) refusing to go. The place was full of Durand's big, husky Irish clients. After a few drinks, Mank remembered that he had been in the Marines and ought to prove it by licking all the inmates of the joint. I (as usual) acted as pacifist and felt next day as if I'd been in a football game against Notre Dame. We finally got Mank home (our house) and put him to bed and he arose next day at ten and said he had to go right to town and do some work for the Sunday Times. Ellis gave him a few highballs to brace him up and he finally left at five in the afternoon. . . .

Mrs. Lardner and I will be highly honored by the dedication of your book [All the Sad Young Men] *to us. I hope "The Great Gatsby" is going better. It certainly deserves a big sale. I think it probable that the reason it got no notice from Frank Adams was that he was on vacation and getting married about the time it came out. Max Perkins said he thought the size of the book was against it (in the eyes of the buyers). This is a great commentary on American life and letters. What is your new novel going to be about? . . .*

On the Fourth of July, Ed Wynn gave a fireworks party at his new estate in the Grenwolde division. After the children had been sent home, everybody got pie-eyed and I never enjoyed a night so much. All the Great Neck professionals did their stuff, the former chorus girls sang, Blanche Ring kissed me and sang, etc. The party lasted through the next day and wound up next evening at Tom Meighan's, where the principal entertainment was provided by Lila Lee and another dame who did some very funny imitations (really funny) in the moonlight on the tennis court. We would ask them to imitate Houdini, Leon Errol, or Will Rogers, or Elsie Janis; the imitations

200

were all the same, consisting of an aesthetic dance which ended with
an unaesthetic fall onto the tennis court.

Charley Chaplin's new picture "The Gold Rush," opens here next
week and we are going to a party in his honor at Nast's.

We do miss you and Zelda a great deal. Write again and tell her
to write, too. And I might add that I have a little money to lend at
the proverbial six per cent, if worst comes to worst.

Tom Meighan, the movie actor, was a close friend of Ring and a neighbor in Great Neck, where their escapades were famous. They put away a great deal of liquor in their best days and designated themselves as "two-bottle" men to distinguish them from drinkers of lesser capacity.

Ring's insomnia and restlessness led him to wander about at night. One of his favorite haunts was René Durand's restaurant at Manhasset, where a great many Long Islanders ate and drank. Sometimes he would pick up Arthur Jacks and say, "We'll go over to Durand's for a drink," not "Let's go over to Durand's"; when Ring had made up his mind to go, he went, and whoever was with him went along. He always drove slowly and carefully; at Durand's he would drink until he was ready to come home, and he always got back safely.

Sometimes he drove over to visit a friend late at night. One of the many stories told of him is of a night visit to Clarence Budington Kelland, a *Saturday Evening Post* writer, who lived in nearby Port Washington. One morning about 2 or 3 o'clock Kelland was awakened by pebbles thrown against the window of his bedroom. He looked out and saw Ring, a silent and lonely figure, standing before the door. Kelland put on his bathrobe, went downstairs, and invited Ring to come in. Ring did so and took a chair by the fireplace. Kelland brought him a drink and sat down and asked Ring if there was anything he could do for him. Ring said nothing. When he had finished his drink Kelland got him another, and gave up all attempts at conversation. Finally Kelland fell asleep in his chair and was awakened some time later by Ring tapping him on the knee and saying, "I don't want to seem rude, but aren't you *ever* going home?"

CHAPTER SIX

How to Write Short Stories was published in the spring of
1924 and immediately attained a success far beyond Ring's
expectations. He had not taken his literary debut very seriously. The
title of the book, the irrelevant nonsense prefaces to each story, and
the introduction all disclaimed any literary pretensions; and while
they irritated the critics somewhat, they did not alienate the public
to whom Ring's pose as an ordinary hack was familiar and amusing.

Ring did not even write a new introduction to the book; he used
one of his old columns, only slightly revised; and he prefaced each
story with a rather strained joke which deprecated the idea that his
writing had any merit at all:

*. . . But a little group of our deeper drinkers has suggested that
maybe boys and gals who wants to take up writing as their life work
would be benefited if some person like I was to give them a few
hints in regards to the technic of the short story, how to go about
planning it and writing it, when and where to plant the love interest
and climax, and finally how to market the finished product without
leaving no bad taste in the mouth.*

*The first thing I generally always do is try and get hold of a catchy
title, like for instance, "Basil Hargrave's Vermifuge," or "Fun at the
Incinerating Plant." Then I set down to a desk or flat table of any
kind and lay out 3 or 4 sheets of paper with as many different colored pencils and look at them cockeyed a few moments before making a selection.*

How to begin—or, as we professionals would say, how to com-mence—is the next question. It must be admitted that the method of approach ("l'approchement") differs even among first class fiction-ists. For example, Blasco Ibanez usually starts his stories with a Spanish word, Jack Dempsey with an "I" and Charley Peterson with a couple of simple declarative sentences about his leading char-acter, such as "Hazel Gooftree had just gone mah jong. She felt faint."

Personally it has been my observation that the reading public prefers short dialogue to any other kind of writing and I always aim to open my tale with two or three lines of conversation between characters—or, as I call them, my puppets—who are to play im-portant roles.

"Where was you?" asked Edith Quaver.

"To the taxidermist's," replied Dorothy Abbott.

The two girls were spending the heated term at a famous water-ing trough. They had just been bathing and were now engaged in sorting dental floss.

"I am getting sick in tired of this place," went on Miss Quaver.

"It is mutual," said Miss Abbott, shying a cucumber at a passing paper-hanger.

There was a rap at their door and the maid's voice announced that company was awaiting them downstairs. The two girls went down and entered the music room. Garnett Whaledriver was at the piano and the girls tiptoed to the lounge.

The big Nordic, oblivious of their presence, allowed his fingers to form weird, fantastic minors before they strayed unconsciously into the first tones of Chopin's 121st Fugue for the Bass Drum.

From this beginning a skilled writer could go most anywheres, it would be my tendency to drop these three characters and take up the life of a mule in the Grand Canyon. The mule watches the trains come in from the east, he watches the trains come in from the west, and keeps wondering who is going to ride him. But he never finds out. . . .

Stories ("yarns") of mind which have appeared in various publi-cations—one of them having been accepted and published by the first editor that got it—are reprinted in the following pages and will illustrate in a half-hearted way what I am trying to get at.

Ring Lardner

"The Mange"
Great Neck, Long Island, 1924

The collection contained ten stories written over a period of ten years. Taken chronologically they show no consistent development. The earliest, "My Roomy" (1914), written at the same time as the earliest "Busher's Letters," is an excellent story; while "A Frame-Up" (1921) is inferior. But in general the best stories were the latest, and two of them, "Some Like Them Cold" and "The Golden Honeymoon," are among Ring's masterpieces. Ring wrote almost constantly and sometimes under pressure, and he turned out a great many potboilers; some of these were good stories, and some of his more labored efforts were not. Between 1914 and 1926 he tended toward a greater strictness of form and a more pointed satirical intention; but his progress in this direction was not steady, even if it was to some extent premeditated. His first fiction pieces, the "Busher's Letters," were, within their limits, perfectly achieved, while many later ones suffered from formlessness, repetition, and thinness of ideas. Ring had a just idea of which stories were his best; they were those to which he gave his most thoughtful efforts. Some of his stories do seem to have been written in the way he described— he wrote three thousand words about nothing, then thought of a punch; but the best are very cannily constructed.

Six of the stories here are about sports, naturally enough, since that was the background of Ring's earliest writing experience. Fitzgerald deplored this as a fatally limiting influence on Ring's work:

> During those years, when most men of promise achieve an adult education, if only in the school of war, Ring moved in the company of a few dozen illiterates playing a boy's game. A boy's game, with no more possibilities in it than a boy could master, a game bounded by walls which kept out novelty or danger, change or adventure. This material, the observation of it under such circumstances, was the text of Ring's schooling during the most formative period of the mind. A writer can spin on about his adventures after thirty, after forty, after fifty, but the criteria by which these adventures are weighed and valued are irrevocably settled at the age of twenty-five. However deeply Ring might cut into it, his cake had the diameter of Frank Chance's diamond.

Actually sport provided Ring with a serviceable framework within which he could examine quite a range of human behavior. In Ring's fiction baseball is an ordered world with definite rules of conduct; it demands skill and integrity and it has a code of honor; it also has a hierarchy—at the top, umpires and managers, authority and intelligence, always sympathetically portrayed; at the bottom, the idolatrous fans, the shifting rabble whom Ring distrusted. (The rabble as such does not figure much in Ring's fiction.) In between there is a variety of characters, good ball players and bad, intelligent and stupid, amiable and otherwise. Baseball implied an ethical ideal; and in Ring's work there is always an implied ethical ideal whether he is writing about sports or not. His affinity for games which embodied a code of behavior was not merely accidental. Ring's mind and his values were fairly well formed before he became a baseball reporter; they had been formed by his home and by Niles, Michigan; he applied his own values to sport, and they had not been conditioned by association with illiterate boys. His preoccupation with sport reflected a longing for an ideal world where the rules, if observed, guaranteed the triumph of merit; it also reflected his acute sense of the disparity between the way people were supposed to behave and the way they did. Sport provided Ring with a useful and significant scale for measuring his characters. Moreover the criteria of sport were especially valuable because everyone knew exactly what they were.

There are four baseball stories in this collection, three of them "yarns" which do not probe any emotional depths or raise weighty ethical questions. They all take place in the sportsman's world of prescribed behavior, from which the principals do not deviate very far. They all have ingenious ideas, spun out a little too long, possibly to accommodate the magazines for which they were intended; and they are in the busher dialect. "Horseshoes" is about a young ball player who is called by that nickname because all his best plays appear to be pure luck, whereas his rival, who has nothing but luck, is credited with being a good ball player. Their rivalry comes to a climax over a girl, and the hero wins her by neither luck nor skill, but just by punching his rival in the face. As a character, he is not especially memorable except for an excess of temperament; and the story is only a well-turned anecdote. "Alibi Ike" is the famous story of a ball player who has an excuse for everything he does even when it is good, and is noted chiefly for having contributed a phrase to the language. "Harmony" is something a little closer to Ring's heart, the story of an outfielder who really cared more for singing than for baseball. This engaging figure gets his club to sign up a semi-pro, whom he has never seen in action, just because he is such a good singer. The new player turns out to be as brilliant on the diamond as he is in the quartet and costs the outfielder his own position on the team; but he has no regrets. You would have to look far for any satiric barb in this story; these were ball players as Ring liked them.

The fourth baseball story, "My Roomy," is a very different matter; unique among Ring's stories, it is a full portrait of a man who is really insane. The story is told by the roommate of Elliott, a busher from Michigan "who is a whale of a hitter and fast as Cobb, but he don't know nothin' about his fieldin'." Elliott arrives without baggage, wearing a filthy collar, and is put in the outfield, where he makes no attempt to catch anything; but at bat he is phenomenal. In the hotel he insists on running the water in the bathtub all night long because it reminds him of a dam near his home; and he gets up in the middle of the night to shave, wielding his razor ominously over successive roommates. He talks continually about his fiancée, whose distinction is that she can sing as loud as he can, which is loud enough to get the whole team evicted from hotels. Although he tears up her letters without reading them, because they are all alike, he is stuck on her and his only reason for staying with the club is to get enough money to marry her. Evenings he goes to movies; he likes especially the ones where people kill each other. He goes berserk in the hotel elevator, running it up and down ten times while the lady passengers faint. Finally in desperation the club sells him to Atlanta, and he disappears after smashing a mirror with his fist and wiping blood on his roommate's face.

His roommate worries about him—he seems to be an infantile giant whose behavior is unaccountable—and persuades the manager to send him a share of the team's bonus money won in a city series. The last news of him comes in two letters:

Dear Sir: They have got poor Elliott locked up and they are goin' to take him to the asylum at Kalamazoo. He thanks you for the check, and we will use the money to see that he is made comftable.

When the poor boy come back here he found that his girl was married to Joe Bishop who runs a soda fountain. She had wrote to him about it, but he did not read her letters. The news drove him crazy—poor boy—and he went to the place where they was livin' with a baseball bat and very nearly killed 'em both. Then he marched down the street singin' "Silver Threads Among the Gold" at the top of his voice. They was goin' to send him to prison for assault with intent to kill, but the jury decided he was crazy.

He wants to thank you again for the money.

Yours truly,
Jim ———

207

And from Elliott:

Old Roomy: I was at bat twice and made two hits; but I guess I did not meet 'em square. They tell me they are both alive yet, which I did not mean 'em to be. I hope they got good curve-ball pitchers where I am goin'. I sure can bust them curves—can't I, sport?
                                                            Yours,
                                                        B. Elliott
P.S. The B stands for Buster.

Elliott is an intolerable character in every way, yet throughout the story he is entirely sympathetic. The story is funny all the way through—Elliott is just another eccentric busher—until the macabre finish, when he becomes a towering grotesque. There is nothing "psychological" about the story; Elliott is seen only from the outside. Everything he does is exasperating and abominable, yet he is never outside the range of Ring's compassion; Ring feels for him none of the savage disgust he has for the merely stupid; he has for him the same sympathy he has for the idiot boy who shoots and kills the practical joker in "Haircut." Real madness seemed to elicit a certain tenderness from Ring. The story is one of his earliest and it has some technical crudities; yet Elliott's wild idiosyncrasies are so skillfully underplayed that his violence at the end comes as a breathtaking climax; he is a convincing and memorable character.

"Champion" (1916), a famous anthology piece, was the first short story that Ring wrote in the third person and in straight English. It tells of the rise of Midge Kelly, a brutal fourflusher, to the welterweight championship by means of beating his crippled brother, deserting his wife and child, cheating his managers, throwing fights, or simply slugging anyone outside the ring who gets in his way. Ring's indignation at violence and the corruption of professional sport was never fiercer than in this early story; and it is not only on the fighter that he vents his fury; he despises, too, the cynicism of newspapermen and the gullibility of the public. Midge Kelly is built up by the press as a lovable family man and an ideal sports hero, although the reporters know that he is a heel. "Suppose you can prove it," the sports editor says. "It wouldn't get us anything but abuse to print it. The people don't want to see him knocked. He's champion." Ring's disillusionment with professional sport was not the result of a gradual enlightenment; he had seen through the vast hoax at the start of his career. "Champion" is an impressive and memorable story, but it is far too melodramatic to be entirely believable, and its irony is a little heavy-handed. Its excessive brutality is an indication of Ring's hatred of violence.

The boxer in "A Frame-Up" is a simple-minded farmer boy from Michigan who has to be enraged before he hits very hard; and his managers, in order to make him win a fight, have to perpetrate an elaborate hoax involving a mythical girl whom the boy sets his heart on. The hoax is more convincing to the boxer than to the reader; but the story is a good example of Ring's virtuosity in handling the cheap, wisecracking dialogue of prize-fight circles. It is not a particularly good story, and neither is "The Facts" (1917), which was also included for some reason. This one, however, has a special interest, because the characters in it are prototypes of those who appear in an unfinished play which Ring was working on at the time of his death, and they have a particular significance there. The story, which has a plot which might have beguiled O. Henry, concerns a young man named Billy Bowen, an easygoing, heavy-drinking Chicagoan, who meets a girl at a football game and thinks he has fallen in love with her. He meets her family, prosperous middle-class people, hymn-singing, bridge-playing, hypocritically high-minded and humorless bores. At Christmas time Billy gets drunk and leaves his shopping to an equally drunk friend, who manages to send the girl and her family the most insultingly inappropriate gifts possible, thereby—mercifully—ending the engagement. The characterization of the family of drab, conventional, loveless people whose human relationships are meager and stunted is sharp and skillful; they have a significant place in the fictional world Ring created.

Ring wrote "The Golden Honeymoon," one of his finest stories and his own favorite, on a trip to Florida in 1922. He and Ellis were staying at Belleair with the Rices; Ring made a short trip to St. Petersburg, the background of the story, then rejoined the party and wrote the story on the train back to New York. He sent it to the *Post;* it was rejected by George Horace Lorimer, who felt the story was too far from Ring's usual line to be suitable. It is also possible that he thought Ring had not been exactly respectful in his handling of the old people who are the central characters. Ring liked the story and was irked by Lorimer's refusal; he did not publish again in the *Post* for nearly ten years. Ray Long of *Cosmopolitan,* who had been trying to lure Ring away from the *Post* for some time, accepted it at once, writing, "I see what the Post meant. That story isn't the usual Ring Lardner story. All it is is a fine piece of sympathetic human interest writing. I should be glad to trade you a check for $1500 for it and I shall be very proud to publish it. If those terms are satisfactory to you, give me the high-sign." Even before the story appeared in July, Long was importuning Ring for more stories about the old couple.

The story is a monologue by an elderly man who has brought his wife to St. Petersburg to celebrate their golden wedding. A ready talker, he recites the entire timetable of the journey and all the irrelevant details that are the stock topics of the empty-minded; repeats his own flat jokes with relish and "Mother's" with admiration. They meet Mother's suitor of fifty years past and his wife; the two couples become friendly, until they fall out over cards, horseshoes, and checkers. The old man's jealousy, dead fifty years, revives and he and Mother indulge in the petty bickering that presumably has marked half a century of married life. Then they cheerfully make up the quarrel. "So I put my arm around her shoulder and she stroked my hand and I guess we got kind of spoony."

The old man's innocent recital is set down with complete detachment; the author never intrudes upon it, the language and the stuff of the garrulous monologue are of a miraculous fidelity. This is exactly how old people of that class and time and place actually do talk; it is how they feel. The conviction of the story is absolute. It is something one has overheard from real life, without the intervention of a writer.

"The Golden Honeymoon" aroused varying reactions. Ray Long's was one; a canny editor, he saw it as a sympathetic human-interest story and was so sure of its success that he wanted more stories like it. Gilbert Seldes wrote that the character of the old man was created "with loving kindness and power." On the other hand, Clifton Fadiman wrote: "Lardner's subtlest story is without doubt The Golden Honeymoon. When this was first published most readers thought it very touching, even a trifle sentimental—this account of an old couple's wedding-anniversary trip to Florida, their little quarrels, their small-town complacencies, their petty satisfactions. Actually it is one of the most smashing indictments of a 'happy marriage' ever written, composed with a fury so gelid as to hide completely the bitter passion seething beneath every line. Under the level of homey sentiment lies a terrific contempt for this quarrelsome, vain, literal old couple who for fifty years have disliked life and each other without ever having had the courage or the imagination to face the reality of their own meanness." And William Bolitho went even further when he wrote: ". . . Lardner's story of that golden wedding in Florida seems to me one of the deepest manifestations of sheer world despair since 'The City of Dreadful Night.' "

Be that as it may, such people as the old man and Mother must remain blissfully unaware of what they have contributed to the pessimism of mankind, because, whatever gelid fury and bitter passion Ring concealed so successfully, the old folks have quite a good time at horseshoes, watching the timetable, haggling over prices at restaurants, and enjoying a resurgence of youthful jealousy that has survived half a century of marital drabness. Their complacency is harmless, their irritability is only standard human equipment, their sentimentality is normal for their age, there is no sign that they have disliked life or each other at all, and they have the kind of "happy marriage" which smashing indictments don't smash. If Ring had meant anything other than this, he would have contrived to get it into the story. By this time he knew pretty well what he was doing. The old couple are rather amiable bores; compared to other married couples in Ring's stories, they are utterly blessed.

The boy and girl in "Some Like Them Cold" (1921) will probably never be so lucky. Chas. F. Lewis, a young song writer on his way to New York, strikes up a casual acquaintance in a Chicago railway station with Mabelle Gillespie, who is there to meet a train, and they exchange addresses. To her surprise, but not beyond her hopes, he writes to her:

Dear Miss Gillespie: How about our bet now as you bet me I would forget all about you the minute I hit the big town and would never write you a letter. Well girlie it looks like you lose so pay me. Seriously we will call all bets off as I am not the kind that bet on a sure thing and it sure was a sure thing that I would not forget a girlie like you and all that is worrying me is whether it may not be the other way round and you are wondering who this fresh guy is that is writeing you this letter. I bet you are so will try and refreshen your memory.

Well girlie I am the handsome young man that was wondering round the Lasalle st. station Monday and "happened" to sit down beside of a mighty pretty girlie who was waiting to meet her sister from Toledo and the train was late and I am glad of it because if it had not of been that little girlie and I would never of met. . . .

Well girlie you asked me to tell you all about my trip. Well I remember you saying that you would give anything to be makeing it yourself but as far as the trip itself was conserned you ought to be thankfull you did not have to make it as you would of sweat your

*head off. I know I did specially wile going through Ind. Monday
P.M. but Monday night was the worst of all trying to sleep and
finely I give it up and just layed there with the prespiration rolling
off of me though I was laying on top of the covers and nothing on
but my underwear.*

*. . . Tomorrow I expect to commence fighting "the battle of
Broadway" and will let you know how I come out that is if you answer this letter. In the mean wile girlie au reservoir and don't do
nothing I would not do.*

Your new friend(?)
Chas. F. Lewis

Miss Gillespie, undaunted by the intimacy of Mr. Lewis's account
of a hot night in the Pullman, replies:

*My Dear Mr. Lewis: Well, that certainly was a "surprise party"
getting your letter and you are certainly a "wonder man" to keep
your word as I am afraid most men of your sex are gay deceivers
but maybe you are "different."*

*. . . Suppose you will think me a "case" to make a bet and then
forget what it was, but you must remember, Mr. Man, that I had
just met you and was "dazzled." Joking aside I was rather "fussed"
and will tell you why. Well, Mr. Lewis, I suppose you see lots of
girls like the one you told me about that you saw on the train who
tried to get "acquainted" but I want to assure you that I am not one
of those kind and sincerely hope you will believe me when I tell you
that you was the first man I ever spoke to meeting them like that
and my friends and the people who know me would simply faint if
they knew I ever spoke to a man without a "proper introduction."*

Miss Gillespie blushingly goes on to hint at her popularity and
her talents as a homemaker, and soon the correspondents are addressing each other as "Dear Girlie" and "Dear Mr. Man." Lewis
meets a lyric writer and they collaborate on a song:

> *Some like them hot, some like them cold.*
> *Some like them when they're not too darn old.*
> *Some like them fat, some like them lean.*
> *Some like them only at sweet sixteen.*
> *Some like them dark, some like them light.*
> *Some like them in the park, late at night.*
> *Some like them fickle, some like them true,*
> *But the time I like them is when they're like you.*

212

He expects to make $25,000 from it. He indicates that he is a quiet, home-loving man who is avoiding the New York girls who pursue him. Miss Gillespie enlarges upon her peaceful, domestic nature: "Well, it is true that I had rather stay home with a good book than go to some crazy old picture and the last two nights I have been reading myself to sleep with Robert W. Service's poems. Don't you love Service or don't you care for 'highbrow' writings?" Lewis's letters grow increasingly indifferent, Miss Gillespie is worried for fear she has said something rash, and finally Lewis writes to tell her of his engagement to the song writer's sister, whom he has depicted as a very cold type indeed. Mabelle Gillespie ends the correspondence:

My Dear Mr. Lewis: Thanks for your advice and also thank your fiance for her generosity in allowing you to continue your correspondence with her "rivals," but personly I have no desire to take advantage of that generosity as I have something better to do than read letters from a man like you, a specially as I have a man friend who is not so generous as Miss Sears and would strongly object to my continuing a correspondence with another man. It is at his request that I am writing this note to tell you not to expect to hear from me again.

Allow me to congratulate you on your engagement to Miss Sears and I am sure she is to be congratulated too, though if I met the lady I would be tempted to ask her to tell me her secret, namely how she is going to "run wild" on $60.

Sincerely,
Mabelle Gillespie

These characters reveal themselves in every turn of phrase with the utmost clarity; there is nothing more to be said about them; their whole history from the first spark of mutual attraction to the time when it is stifled by their pitifully small ambitions is contained in these few letters. It is a masterpiece, the purest possible use of language as a medium. It is his most artful story, but its art is totally unobtrusive; no technique or device is visible. But Ring's compassion for the shallowness and ineptitude of these characters is evident; there is no scorn or hatred here.

"A Caddy Diary" (1922) is a devastating revelation of the pettiness and dishonesty of a group of golf players at a fashionable club; it also contains a low-keyed commentary on the futility of such a revelation. The writer of the diary begins:

I am 16 of age and am a caddy at the Pleasant View Golf Club but only temporary as I expect to soon land a job somewheres as asst pro as my game is good enough now to be a pro but to young looking. My pal Joe Bean also says I have not got enough swell head to make a good pro but suppose that will come in time, Joe is a wisecracker.

The caddy is already full of an evil wisdom about the ways of his elders and betters. He knows how they cheat on their scores, how the rich men tip little or nothing unless they win; what really poor golf players they are; and how much they prefer an agreeable and complacent caddy to one who seems to know too much.

How ever on the days when theys ladies on the course I dont get a chance to caddy with Joe because for some reason another the women folks dont like Joe to caddy for them wile on the other had they are always after me tho I am no Othello for looks or do I seek their flavors, in fact it is just the opp and I try to keep in the back ground when the fair sex appears on the seen as cadding for ladies means you will get just so much money and no more as theys no chance of them loosning up. As Joe says the rule against tipping is the only rule the woman folks keeps.

The members of the club are penurious, envious and spiteful, and fiercely competitive. They will do anything to win.

Miss Rennie is a good looker and young and they say she is engaged to Chas Crane, he is one of our members and is the best player in the club and dont cheat hardly at all and he has got a job in the bank where Mr Thomas is vice president. Well I have cadded for Miss Rennie when she was playing alone or with another lady and I often think if Mr Crane could hear her talk when he was not around he would not be so stuck on her. You would be surprised at some of the words that falls from those fare lips.

Mrs. Thomas cheats Miss Rennie out of a quarter, and Miss Rennie takes it out on the caddy by not tipping him. Mr. Thomas is no better; with the connivance of the caddy he cheats on his score in order to win a prize of nine golf balls instead of six.

The big news of the season comes when Crane absconds from the bank with $8000 and a stenographer, and the members piously lament the fact that he has sold his soul.

Joe I said what do these people mean when they talk about Crane selling his soul?

214

Why you know what they mean said Joe, they mean that a person that does something dishonest for a bunch of money or a gal or any kind of a reward why the person that does it is selling his soul.

All right I said and it don't make no differents does it if the reward is big or little?

Why no said Joe only the bigger it is the less of a sucker the person is that goes after it.

Well I said here is Mr Thomas who is vice president of a big bank and worth a bbl of money and it is just a few days ago when he lied about his golf score in order so as he would win 9 golf balls instead of ½ a dozen.

Sure said Joe.

And how about his wife Mrs Thomas I said, who plays for 2 bits a hole and when her ball dont lie good why she picks it up and pretends to look at it to see if it is hers and then puts it back in a good lie where she can sock it.

And how about my friend Mrs Doane that made me move her ball out of a rut to help her beat Miss Rennie out of a party dress.

Well said Joe what of it?

Well I said it seems to me like these people have got a lot of nerve to pan Mr Crane and call him a sucker for doing what he done, it seems to me like $8000 and a swell dame is a pretty fair reward compared with what some of these other people sells their soul for, and I would like to tell them about it.

Well said Joe go ahead and tell them but maybe they will tell you something right back.

What will they tell me?

Well said Joe they might tell you this, that when Mr Thomas asks you how many shots he has had and you say 4 when you know he has had 5, why you are selling your soul for a $1.00 tip. And when you move Mrs Doanes ball out of a rut and give it a good lie, what are you selling your soul for? Just a smile.

O keep your mouth shut I said to him.

I am going to said Joe and would advice you to do the same.

Joe is a humorist of a sardonic turn of mind, with a sharp eye and tongue; the ladies are uncomfortable if he caddies for them. The writer of the diary has already succumbed to their corrupting example; but Joe is the moralist of the story. Shrewd, honest, and witty, he has seen through them all; but the job of a humorist is a thankless one. Joe's wit turns to weary contempt as he decides to keep his mouth shut. The character of Joe as a humorist and moralist is so carefully and deliberately built up that his comment becomes the point of the story.

The reviews of *How to Write Short Stories* were almost universally favorable. "The notices," he wrote to Fitzgerald, "have been what I might call sublime; in fact, readers might think I was having an affair with some of the critics. I'll send the most important ones when I get them all—Mencken, Bunny Wilson and Tom Boyd are yet to be heard from. But listen, if I do send them, will you please send them back? Burton (Rascoe) said I was better than Katherine Mansfield, which I really believe is kind of raw, but anyway it got him and Hazel an invitation to come out and spend Sunday with us. . . . Max Perkins and wife came out to dinner one night. Max brought along twenty-five books for me to autograph (not to sell) and it just happened on this occasion that I could hardly write my name once, let alone twenty-five times. I have promised to be sober next time I see him and her."

The critics were impressed most of all by Ring's use of the vernacular; it was generally recognized that he wrote like an artist, not merely a newspaperman. His satire was considered "good-natured"; it was somewhat later that his reputation for misanthropy became widespread. The reviews were all very much alike; the virtues of Ring's stories, isolated from the pages of magazines and put together in one volume, even with a title and an introduction that disclaimed any literary seriousness, were evident. Some critics seemed a little surprised that a writer of such supposedly low-brow origins should have turned out to be an artist. On the other hand, Edmund Wilson, reviewing the book for the *Dial*, chided Ring for the offhand manner in which he presented his best stories and for having fallen short of the artistic seriousness that might be expected of such a talent.

Mr. Ring Lardner is a popular journalist who writes for the New York American *and who also provides the text for a syndicated comic strip. It has therefore been thought appropriate to present his new collection of short stories as if it were a volume of popular humor. . . .*

The fact is that this new book of his, instead of belonging to the gruesome department of, say, Irvin Cobb's Speaking of Operations, *contains some of the most interesting work that Ring Lardner has yet produced. These stories, he observes in his preface, "will illustrate in a half-hearted way what I am trying to get at." But the stories are not half-hearted: it is the jokes that he intrudes among*

216

*them. The nonsense of his introductions is so far below his usual
level that one suspects him of a guilty conscience in attempting to
disguise his talent for social observation and satire. . . .*

Will Ring Lardner, then, go on to his Huckleberry Finn *or has he
already told all he knows? It may be that the mechanical repetition
of a trick that one finds in such a story as* Horseshoes *and the melodramatic exaggeration of* Champion *indicate limitations. But you
never know: here is a man who has had the freedom of the modern
West no less than Mark Twain did of the old one, who approaches
it, as Mark Twain did, with a perceptive interest in human beings
instead of the naturalist's formula—a man who lives at a time when,
if one be not sold irredeemably into bondage to the* Saturday Evening Post, *it is far easier for a serious writer to get published and
find a hearing than it was in Mark Twain's day. If Ring Lardner has
anything more to give us, the time has now come to deliver it.*

This challenge went unanswered. Ring continued to write short
stories, and some of his best were yet to come; but he never had a
Huckleberry Finn on his mind, and when he sought to extend his
work, it was in the direction of the theater, because it gave him
greater satisfaction than writing fiction.

Ring was genuinely pleased by the reviews. But he had already
adopted a character in which he showed himself to the public, and
he stuck to it. He kept on shrugging off literary laurels and pretending that he did not understand what the "high-brow" critics
were talking about. It was not an evasion of the responsibility of a
man of letters; he did not think of himself as one, however gratifying he found the praise of Mencken, Franklin P. Adams, and Wilson. The literary life as exemplified in the twenties by cocktail
parties, autographing bees, and bookish gossip columns which ex-
ploited authors' personalities had no attraction for him; it provided
him with material for some hilarious burlesques of the lives of
geniuses, interviews with authors, and literary diaries. He obviously
thought that the professional, public literary life was silly. He continued to write as he could write, and to guard his privacy. Unmoved by the exhortations of critics and friends, he published his
next book of short stories with a nonsense preface that only re-
emphasized the skepticism he felt about the value of his own work.

As a humorist, he was well aware of his own situation, and he
had no illusions about it. He could be very proud of being a humorist; when one of his sons asked him if he was a humorist, he replied
that describing oneself as a humorist was like saying one was a

great third baseman. But he never thought he was good enough. He also saw the disadvantages of being a humorist, or a satirist: like the caddy Joe Bean, who was keeping his mouth shut. He certainly had no faith in the salutary effects of satire; and he also knew that people would always be urging him to be funnier, or to stop being funny and get serious.

How to Write Short Stories was not merely a critical success; it sold far more than Ring had expected—over twenty thousand copies, which for a book of short stories at that time was an excellent sale. But whatever satisfaction he got from the critics' and the public's recognition of him as a literary man, it did not alter his opinion of himself.

Between "The Golden Honeymoon" in 1922 and "Haircut," which appeared in 1925, Ring wrote no short stories. His magazine articles were largely miscellaneous burlesques for *Cosmopolitan* and *Liberty,* modernized fairy tales in Lardner dialect, and the articles on Europe. A collection of these odd pieces was published under the title *What of It?* in 1925, the year in which Scribner's also reissued *You Know Me Al, Gullible's Travels,* and *The Big Town. What of It?* is an amusing, uneven book, notable chiefly for the first appearance in book form of Ring's great nonsense plays, which properly belong with his theatrical work since most of them were written to be played. This miscellany had only a mild critical success but, for such a haphazard collection, a fairly good sale. The reissued books, on the other hand, gave critics an opportunity to consider Ring's major work as a whole and they quickly saw the importance of the earlier books, which, while they had been favorably reviewed at their first appearance, had not commanded much interest or respect. The old titles had a negligible sale; but they made possible a general critical appraisal of Ring which established him as one of the major writers of his day. Certain points of that appraisal are still open to controversy; but on the whole it was a just one and remains valid.

Ring's stories for the next two years were published in *Cosmopolitan* and in *Liberty,* of which his brother Rex was an editor. "Speaking of Liberty," Ring wrote to Fitzgerald in November 1925, "John Wheeler has been removed as editor. J.M. Patterson of the Chicago Tribune has come to New York to run it and the Daily News. Harvey Deuel, a Chicago newspaperman, will succeed Jack as editor of Liberty. I guess my brother Rex is all right for a while, but if they do anything to him, I'm going to jump to Cosmopolitan."

When Ray Long had seen Ring in London in 1924, he had made him this offer: "For your next six short stories, $3000 each, or, for your next twelve short stories, to be delivered at intervals of not more than 45 days, $3500 each." Shake-ups at *Liberty* were frequent. When Rex was removed, Ring went over to *Cosmopolitan* with all his short stories, and Rex went along as an associate editor. Ring's stories were in great demand, and he could use his influence in behalf of Rex.

As always he remained very close to his family and old friends. His sister Anna and her children visited him, and so did Ellis's many brothers and sisters. "Went to see Ring and had a gay hour with his sister Mrs. Tobin," Franklin P. Adams noted in his "Pepys' Diary"; and on another occasion, ". . . So met with Mistress Ellis Lardner, and begged her for a lodging, so I and my wife to R. Lardner's, and had a pleasant time talking of this and that, and R. tells me his four sons and his little niece, Miss Anne Tobin, are writing a libretto called 'Skinafore,' which they will play Friday, and the musick will be good, being written by Sir Arthur Sullivan himself."

In spite of the fact that Ring and Ellis went out a great deal, traveled for weeks at a time in the winter, and entertained, Ring was very much a family man, devoted to his growing sons and interested in everything they did. Their pastimes were very much what Ring's had been in his childhood: music, sports, games, reading, putting on plays, editing a family newspaper; they seemed naturally to follow their father's bent.

Ring, when asked once to what he attributed his success, said, "To Home Run cigarettes and a family with extravagant tastes which always needs money." Actually the extravagance of the family's tastes was largely Ring's doing. He himself had been brought up in comparative luxury, and Ellis had come from a prosperous home. But Ring had his mother's flair for spending freely, and although his personal requirements were modest—he seldom bought himself anything and Ellis had to see that he bought new clothes occasionally—he wanted the best for his family. Their welfare and security were almost an obsession with him; they did not make the demands. They lived as Ring thought they should. Miss Feldmann, who had joined the household as David's nurse, remained as governess to the boys; Ring thought it important that they should have a trained nurse. He always worried when any of the family were out in the car, so he engaged a chauffeur, Albert, who was to stay with the family for thirty years, and Ellis never drove the car again. Servants came and went—there were generally two or three others at a time—but Miss Feldmann and Albert constituted a sort of permanent staff.

The older boys went to private schools at an early age, and all of them attended Andover later. When John, the eldest, was going to Greenvale School, Ring engaged a football coach and invited boys from the school to play on the grounds back of the Great Neck house. None of Ring's sons turned out to be a distinguished athlete, possibly to his disappointment; but he encouraged them in sports. He certainly did not have the illusion that it built character, but he believed it was important for their health, which was a matter of great anxiety to him, the more so as his own health was failing.

All of the boys showed a precocious talent for journalism. The three elder ones started a newspaper, edited by John, and their father was frequently importuned for contributions. He instructed them in sound reporting and good writing; they had the benefit of his fanatical perfectionism as a reporter and writer, and his insistence on accuracy; later he watched with pride the start of John's career as a journalist. All of them became writers, although Jimmy's greatest interest was in music. He inherited his father's passion for song writing, as well as many traits of temperament: his reticence, his intent silences, his extreme sensibility. Once when Jimmy was a small boy, he ran a needle into his arm while he was playing. Ring took him to the doctor and suffered more than anyone else while the needle was being extracted; the spectacle of pain was always agonizing to him. Jimmy was always his particular care and worry. There seemed to be a special understanding between them.

While the children were young, Ring treated them with an awkward tenderness; as they were growing up, his health was getting worse, he saw less of them, and since reticence was a family characteristic, a painful shyness grew up between them. It was partly caused by the strict regimen they followed, partly owing to the fact that, after Ring discovered that he had tuberculosis, he deliberately kept himself away from his family. Because of this he didn't enjoy his family life as much as he might have. He had a craving for affection and a great deal to give, but his own shyness and his concern for the children's health inhibited much of it.

In the columns of the "Wake" he had often written sentimental poems about his boys, and in his weekly letter, which had so much in it that was really personal, he sometimes wrote of family life:

220

Now friends the paragraph I am now writing is supposed to ring tears from the reader a specially the male parent of male offspring. It ain't no secret by this time that I am the father of 4 boys and I have made it a rule that as soon as each of them got to be 7 yers. old I would cease from kissing him good-night as boys of such advanced age don't relish being kissed by parents of their own sex. Well 3 of them has been over the age limit for some time and I only had one left on who to vent my osculatory affection namely David who was 6 yrs. old in May. Lately I noticed that he did not return my caress with any warmth and one night he held out his hand to shake like the others boys and then run upstairs and told his brothers gloatingly that he had escaped Daddy's good-night kiss. Naturally this remark was repeated to me and naturally it meant the end as far as I am conserned being a man of great pride and I suppose in time the wound will heal but mean wile hardly a evening passes when I don't kind of wish down in my heart that one of them had been a daughter.

As he had written verses about his older boys for the "Wake," Ring continued to write them about his youngest, introducing one of his miscellanies in *Cosmopolitan* with:

DAVE'S IMPERTURBABILITY

*When Davey, my kid, takes a tumble
And gets and abrasion or two,
If you dare sympathize, he coolly replies:
"It's what I was trying to do."*

*When he smashes a toy he was fond of
Or bursts a balloon that's brand new,
He'll throw it away and brazenly say:
"It's what I was trying to do."*

*That's Dave's philosophical system,
And I think I will follow it, too;
When I foozle and err, I will boldly aver
It's what I was trying to do.*

*So, ye who don't like these two pages,
Don't think I'll be angry with you.
If you say to me, "Fool, you have written plain drool"—
That's what I was trying to do.*

Almost every family occasion was marked by a verse. On one of David's birthdays Ring wrote, to accompany a gift of money:

> *Here's wealth for you, David.*
> *You'll spendid?*
> *How splendid!*
> *I feared you would savid.*

And, to welcome their parents home from a trip, the children wrote:

> (To the tune of Yankee Doodle)

> *Daddy and Mother went away down south*
> *Along with Thornes and Rices*
> *And now their coming home again*
> *No matter what the price is*

> *We're glad that they are home once more*
> *Because they made us lonesome*
> *We hope that being with us again*
> *Will make them stay at home some*

Ring worked at home a great deal in spite of distractions. Ellis, who liked to remodel and redecorate the house, included a study for him.

. . . So anyway we are in the throws of alterations and the main idea of same seems to be to provide a kind of private ward for the master which I don't never half to poke my head out of same even for meals and I can be kept an absolute secret from both friends and morbid curiosity seekers and will be living under practically the same conditions as Mrs. Haversham or the guy's wife in Jane Eyre.

As luck would have it I was brought up on morning newspapers and have never been able to get over the habit of doing my best sleeping between 8 a.m. and noon and it seems that those is the same hours when carpenters does their loudest work and while our house ain't no police booth, still and all neither is it big enough so as you can be rooming in any one corner of it and not know that they's 17 carpenters giving a concert elsewhere on the premises. So that is why I been kind of anxious that they would hurry and get through so as I could get some sleep and I made a remark to that effect to the madam yesterday.

"It won't be much longer," she says. "They are going at it hammer and tongs."

"Well," I says, "I wished they would get to the tongs solo."

Was it not for my training with my kiddies it would of certainly been impossible for me to tour the house lately without serious accident. Children, or at least my children, uses chairs for only one purpose, to stand on the rungs of same to see if they will break. When they want to read or play some sedentary game, they lay or set on the floor.

So I have just naturally acquired the habit of watching my step in roaming from room to room so as not to scrunch no bodies and only for that practice why in the last few wks. they's no telling how many brave union men I would have trampled under ft. while patrolling my baronial halls which a former Marine told me reminded him of Belleau Wood in late July, 1918, as far as human hazards was concerned.

Ellis knew how to guard Ring when he wanted seclusion, answering the telephone and keeping away outsiders who sought Ring's company or his largess; and the children were well trained not to distract him. Sometimes he and Ellis would sit up late in the evening while Ring tried to think of an idea for a short story. He would ask Ellis for suggestions, and she would talk to him. Then he would go into his study and the typewriter would start, slowly. Sometimes he worked all night on a story. When it was finished, it seldom had anything to do with what he and Ellis had talked about.

Despite Ring's family affections his home in Great Neck in the twenties was a long way from the Lardner home in Niles in the 1890's. Ring and Ellis traveled a great deal, Ring was often away in New York, and when he was home his hours were irregular. The children's lives were strictly supervised by their governess, they went early to school, and early to bed. The time Ring had to enjoy his family life was short. As the children grew up, Ring's health got worse, they had less contact with him. Yet, when the traveling and the social life were over, Ring's sons remained his constant concern and deepest pleasure.

Ring and Ellis went out together often, but Ring also went out by himself, sometimes staying away from home for several days at a time. Sometimes he stayed at a hotel in New York, either to work or simply to rest; and other times he drifted around in search of entertainment, and he was a familiar figure in restaurants, clubs, and speak-easies, or backstage at theaters. He was not only restless, he also had an insatiable craving to be amused, to talk, to listen silently to music, to sing, or merely to be someplace where something was going on, however aloof he remained from it.

He once wrote a piece for *The New Yorker* that described his nocturnal wanderings with more accuracy than his readers might have suspected:

On this occasion I was taking one of my sitting-up exercises which hardly ever last less than forty-eight hours and in fact I hold an unofficial record of sixty hours at the Friars' Club, but it has never been allowed by the A. A. U. because it was done in dinner clothes and the only people that get up in such costumes are those who are called on for speeches. I might state four uninteresting facts in connection with this Friars Club sitting: One was that five of the best music-writers in New York played their latest stuff and it all sounded good (at the time); another was that I and whoever happened to be with me at the moment ordered five meals and rejected them as fast as they were brought in; the third was that in this era they had kind of silly traffic laws in New York (not that that differentiates the era from any other era)—the code being that your car could face east for twelve hours and then must face west for twelve hours—and it was necessary to find a couple of bellmen capable of making the desired alterations at six A.M. and six P.M.; and the fourth was that though I was not even a neophyte when I entered the monastery, my long sojourn made me a regular member and I have been a Friar from those days and nights to this, probably because of some obscure squatters' law. Will say in conclusion of this interminable paragraph that the function occurred in June and I had no topcoat and the urge to get home and weed the bathtub came at high noon, and it was kind of embarrassing passing all those policemen in dinner clothes instead of the conventional pajamas. . . .

So the next night at eight I ran into Dorothy ("Spark Plug") Parker and we went places until I got tired of her and I landed at the stagedoor of the Broadhurst hoping I could pick up somebody and it was Harry Rosenthal who his press agent said his left foot had just been insured for sixty-two cents so there would be no temptation for him to fool with the soft pedal. Harry left me with two girls on my hands and I took them to Reuben's hoping the last-named would at least have the grace to christen one layer of a sandwich in my honor, but all the waiters acted as if I were still living in Niles, Michigan, and the girls soon joined another party and the only person in the joint that seemed to recognize me was Rosie

224

Dolly who hadn't seen me for nine years, but she got up and shook hands and said, "I am Rosie Dolly," and I said, "You don't have to tell me that because I can always tell you girls apart the instant you say you are Rosie Dolly." This went over with a bang and I was quickly out in the street with nobody to talk to but a taxi man and I gave him my home address though I wasn't at all sleepy and when I got home I took some paraldehyde and plunged into the vacant bathtub thinking it was breakfast and along about noon my patella began to hurt and we had to call Dr. Tyson and after five days he persuaded me to go down to St. Vincent's where they could take an X-Ray, but I didn't give in until he promised to have me sent there in an ambulance.

This funny and bewildering nightmare is not purely imaginary. Ring's séance in the Friars Club is one of the most famous of the innumerable stories told about him, and, unlike most of them, it is authentic. Ring went there one night after the theater and sat drinking and listening to various people play the piano. With the excuse that he did not want to go home in evening clothes he stayed through the next day, sometimes talking to whoever came along, but mostly sitting alone in a melancholy mood. The second day passed the same way. At the end of the third day someone approached him and said, "Have you heard the one about the——" Ring got up abruptly and left. A few minutes later an actor came in and said, "My God, the statue's gone!"

It was on another occasion that he and a friend ordered meal after meal and refused them. Ring seldom ate while he was drinking, a considerable factor in undermining his health. He had not much palate for food at best, he drowned everything in Worcestershire Sauce, and also killed his appetite by excessive smoking. On one long trip he is said to have gone three weeks eating almost nothing, yet never becoming drunk or losing his poise.

The Lambs club was another of his haunts, and many stories about him there have achieved the magnitude of legend. He would sometimes sit alone for hours at the piano playing chords. Or he would, if he were in a sociable mood, play at his favorite game of telling long and pointless stories to a friend, who would roar with laughter. This always drew a crowd. On one occasion, seeing a captive audience assembled, one of the members brought out a piece of verse which he said had been written by his brother who was twenty years dead. This fooled nobody. He asked Ring to read it

225

aloud and give his opinion of it. Ring read it and said, "Did he write it before or after he died?"

One time when Ring was sitting alone at the Lambs, an actor was reciting at the bar an endless and stupefying scene from a play in which he was appearing. When he had finished, Ring asked him to come over and recite it again. The actor eagerly obliged. Ring then asked for a third performance. The actor, delighted, asked, "Do you really like it?" "No," said Ring wearily, "but I was a bad boy last night and this is my penance."

Ring was sitting with Paul Lannin, a composer and musical director, in the Lambs club one evening when a Shakespearean actor with a head of wild, unruly hair passed by to the bar. When he came by a second time, Ring stopped him and asked, "How do you look when I'm sober?"

Ring sometimes dropped in on sessions of the Thanatopsis Literary and Poker Society, in the Algonquin, where members of the Algonquin Round Table met to play cards evenings. Nearly everyone in this circle was a good friend of Ring's—Franklin P. Adams, Marc Connelly, George Kaufman, Heywood Broun, Alexander Woollcott, and many others—all of them had a nearly fanatical admiration for Ring as an artist, and many of them owed a good deal to his influence. Ring did not lunch at the Round Table, much as he liked most of the people who did. It was a clique, and a fairly self-conscious one, and its members were required to perform. Ring did not care for cliques as such, and he certainly would not be compelled to perform. But the Thanatopsis was less demanding, and he enjoyed an occasional poker game. There he was noted chiefly for his long but amiable silences, and for the rare, terse, apposite remarks that seemed to say all there was to be said.

But most of the time he wandered. One night he drifted into a party at Dorothy Parker's, where he pretended to be a Pole who did not speak English. This spared him the necessity of saying anything at all. The pose is significant; he wanted to be in places where people were, but he still felt himself an alien.

Ring's drinking spells were characterized by a monumental stubbornness. When he wanted to drink, nothing could stop him, and he was perfectly candid about it. One time in Florida he and Ellis went to a club with the Rices, and a friend joined them. Everyone ordered drinks. The friend looked at Ring and said, "Don't you think you've had enough?" "Make mine double," Ring said. Once in Great Neck, where a friend had driven out to visit Ellis, Ring asked her for a ride into town to the Lambs club. Her driver

226

dropped her off at her home, then proceeded to take Ring to the club. On the way the driver was forced to make a sudden stop in traffic, and Ring, thrown against the glass partition behind the front seat, cut his head. The driver took him to the nearest hospital, and called the Lardners' friend. She arrived and found Ring seated in the center of a circle of anxious nurses and interns, refusing any aid. He wanted to be taken directly to the Lambs. He persisted, the driver finally took him there, and called a doctor to attend to the wound.

But his stubbornness gave way to remorse. Then he would call friends on the telephone, berate himself, and finally go home to taper off, to rest, and try to begin to eat and work again, and the house would smell of paraldehyde. He came out of these spells in a dreadful state of physical weakness but with his mind clear enough. He always knew where he was and how to get home; at home they always knew where he was, even though he might stay away for several days. He did not try to disappear.

Sometimes he made himself so ill that he would have to go to the hospital to recuperate. At first it was St. Vincent's, where the sisters adored him and often indulged him. One time he took a double room there and invited Paul Lannin, the composer with whom he wrote a musical comedy, to spend the weekend with him. Lannin did, they entertained many visitors, and filled in the intervals with talk about baseball and music. Another time Arthur Jacks, who as a banker handled some of Ring's financial affairs, hauled him out of St. Vincent's to renegotiate a business deal. Ring had bought a tract of land near Great Neck as an investment. ("Ellis and I have bought a farm four miles southeast of here," he wrote Fitzgerald. "We don't intend to farm, but if possible, to hold onto it for five or ten years and sell it at a big profit, the theory being that New York City will grow out to it by that time. We are doing it as a memorial to the kiddies. After I get it all paid for, in two or three more years, I hope, I'm going to quit saving money and drink in a serious way.") The investment required refinancing, and it was necessary for Ring to sign the documents by a certain date. Arthur Jacks called for him at St. Vincent's, Ring eluded the nurses (it was not his only unauthorized departure from a hospital), and they went uptown to an office where Ring found himself surrounded by admirers, who broke out a bottle of whiskey and concluded the negotiations in high spirits. Ring got back to the hospital safely, only a little behind in his cure, and potentially somewhat richer. When later he sold the land at considerable profit, he sent Jacks, who was not entitled to any commission but had only acted as a friend, a check for $2000.50. The $.50, he explained, was for telephone calls.

Ring spent long periods on the wagon and made heroic efforts to resist the compulsion to drink, placed himself in the hands of doctors, and even tried psychiatric treatment with Dr. Gregory at Bellevue. But it was ineffective, and he had little faith in it. He drank for escape, and he needed it often and badly; when he got sober, he still faced the same world he had tried to escape from, with the same acute sensibility he had always had, and a little less physical stamina. Later, when his health was ruined and the parties and the wandering were over, he wrote a story called "Cured!" The exclamation point in the title is significant. It is about a cartoonist who is happily married, with a fine job as a comic-strip artist for a syndicate, which gives him a good deal of time to indulge his thirst. He is not content with a drink or two but likes to drink steadily, and he realizes that he becomes tedious to his host and hostess at dinner parties. And "it was no great fun for him to sit around, cold sober, from half-past seven to midnight, and listen to anecdotes, jokes and stories which he had heard a score of times before, and watch the normal husbands and wives toy with one highball for an hour, enough time for him to have got rid of nearly a dozen."

Now, when a person is a cartoonist, he gets to know people whom his wife never meets; or if she does meet them, she doesn't like them. Dick had a number of pals who, queerly enough, found him bright and amusing when he was drinking, and a bore when he wasn't. It was natural that he should seek out those pals when he started on a bender. They sang with him; they laughed at what he said; and they saw nothing odd about a person's ordering another highball all around while the glasses were still half full of the last one.

. . . They all had a deep affection for their wives and if they didn't get home for a day or two, it was merely because the trip was too much of an effort. Dick, for example, lived up in Westchester County, nearly thirty miles from town. It was a tedious and expensive trip in a taxi, and the trains always left just ten minutes before you could catch them.

After one of Dick's benders his wife engages a psychiatrist, who says that drinking is a disease, not merely a bad habit. Dick engages a hotel room in town, the psychiatrist calls on him at four o'clock every afternoon, always finding him sober. At five Dick goes back to the bar, drinks until 4 A.M., goes back to the hotel, takes a sleeping pill, gets a good sleep, and sees the psychiatrist again. After three weeks he misses his wife and goes home sober, and the cure looks permanent. It is not a very convincing story, but it suggests some of the motives that lay behind Ring's apparently aimless drifting in search of easy companionship, part of the milieu he frequented when he wandered around New York; and it surely suggests that he did not have much faith in psychiatry as a cure for drinking. For him drinking ended only when his health was too far gone to permit it.

Ring began traveling as a young baseball reporter, and he continued all his life. There was not much variety to it; he kept going to the same places each year, Florida, California, or Nassau, and his coverage of sporting events took him back to the same towns he had already known as a young man. It was not curiosity that moved him to travel about, and it was only partly the lure of warm climate; it seems to have been part of his general restlessness, the need for a change followed by the need to get back to New York, from which he never liked to stay away very long.

Ring's travels are reflected in his stories: his characters are a footloose lot, they meet on trains, they come from Michigan and are going to California or Florida; they are stenographers on vacation, sportsmen, businessmen, athletes on tour, old folks coming from St. Petersburg, rich people at luxurious resorts, or ordinary men talking in Pullman smokers. The very rhythms of Ring's prose catch the ways in which people talk all over America: the Midwest, the East, the South; the educated, the badly educated, and the illiterate of many classes and places turn up in his stories and articles. He had heard them all.

One of Ring's constant traveling companions was Grantland Rice, whom he had known since his earliest days as a sports writer. There could hardly have been two close friends of such different temperament: Rice was gregarious, talkative, enthusiastic, full of a universal good will, optimistic, and outgoing. He was the champion of sports, while Ring was a skeptical critic of them. Rice liked almost everybody, while Ring had reservations about almost everybody. Yet they were devoted friends and after years of traveling together built houses side by side in East Hampton.

For years they played golf together, and Rice took Ring to Washington to meet President Harding and play golf with him. Rice wanted to get a story, while Ring was there only for the trip. "I want to be appointed ambassador to Greece," Ring said. "Why?" Harding asked. "My wife doesn't like Great Neck," Ring replied.

When they played golf, Harding drove first from the tee, then walked ahead. Ring's drive knocked a branch off a tree which struck Harding. Ring walked up to him, but instead of apologizing, said, "I did all I could to make Coolidge president." Harding liked the joke, coming from Ring.

They covered many sports events together, including the 1919 World Series, which sickened both of them, and the Series of 1925 at Pittsburgh, long after Ring had got tired of Series. "I had forgotten what terrible things worlds series were so I consented to cover this year's," Ring wrote to Fitzgerald. "I got drunk three days before it started in the hope and belief I would be remorseful and sober by the time I had to go to it. But when I got to Pittsburgh it seemed that I was the only newspaperman in America who had reserved a room; all the others moved in with me and there wasn't a chance to eat, sleep, work or do anything but drink. The result was two fairly good stories and seven terrible ones out of a possible nine, including rainy days." Rice came to Ring's room and found him tapering off from this celebration with a bottle of scotch which Rice tasted and pronounced to be poison. He told Ring not to drink any more of it while he went in search of some good whiskey. When he returned, he found that Ring had drunk a good deal of the bad scotch and was extremely ill. Rice took care of him until he recovered.

One time Ring and Arthur Jacks made a trip to South Bend to visit Ring's sister, who was ill in the hospital there. At their hotel they had a stock of liquor which included some good Canadian whiskey and some raw Midwestern corn moonshine of very recent date. After a heavy night Jacks awoke first, in need of a drink. He tried some of the Canadian whiskey, but it promptly came up. Undaunted, he tried again, with the same result. After he had made three or four unsuccessful attempts, Ring opened one eye and said:

"Arthur, if you're just practicing, would you mind using the corn?"

Every winter Ring and Ellis and Mr. and Mrs. Rice took a trip to Florida, California, or Nassau, and sometimes all three. In Florida they stayed at Belleair, while Ring and Rice played golf. Both of them knew so many people that they found old friends wherever they went. One time Ring improvised a formidable male quartet composed of himself, Paul Waner, Max Carey, and Reinald Werrenwrath. These trips were largely vacations for Ring, but on one of them, having a specified number of stories to write for *Cosmopolitan,* he shut himself in his hotel room and wrote two short stories in three days, dropped them in the mail, and went on playing golf. Sometimes he had to go back to New York on business before the Rices and Ellis left for California; he would rejoin them en route at Montgomery and resume his vacation.

The Lardners and Rices spent the winter of 1926 on a tour that took in Florida, New Orleans, and California. Ring wrote to Fitzgerald:

> *Hotel Del Coronado*
> *Coronado Beach, Calif.*
> *Feb. 23, 1926*
>
> *Heap Big Zelda and Scott:—*
> *I am in the Indian and Mexican country and am learning the language rapidly.*
> *The elegant picture, "The Fitzgeralds' Christmas," was forwarded to us here and we really did and do like it. We agree that Scotty is the second best looking one in the outfit, or shebang, to use the colloquial.*
> *We and the Rices, including their daughter, went to Belleair, Florida, the first week in January and staid there three weeks. Then I had to go home for a few days and view a Tommie Meighan picture, to which I was engaged to write the titles. . . .*
> *On the tenth of February, if you are still interested, we set out for New Orleans, stopping fifteen minutes in Montgomery, where we shed a tear. (But I almost forgot to say that while in New York, Ellis and I saw "The Great Gatsby." . . . we thought the show was great and that Rennie was just about perfect. . . . Every now and then one of Scott's lines would pop out and hit you in the face and make you wish he had done the dramatization himself.)*
> *Well, anyway, we got to New Orleans for the Mardi Gras and were rushed by a bunch of morons and I couldn't stand it and fell off the wagon and we all got the flue and had a very sick trip from New Orleans to this place, where we are resting. From here we go to Los Angeles (including Hollywood), Monterery and San Francisco; then home, arriving there the first week in April. The Rices have been with us right along and we are still all speaking.*
> *Write soon, both of you. You, Zelda, come home and show up the Charleston dancers. You, Scott, also come home and write a play.*
> *And Oh, yes, we had two long and entertaining sessions with Sherwood Anderson and wife in New Orleans. We took them along with us on one of the dinners given, for no reason, in our honor and*

The New Orleans visit was hectic, and Ring was subjected to the kind of boredom he hated most—elegant parties, pretentious people. Grantland Rice took him to an exclusive club where he was waylaid by the scion of an old Southern family who told him at appalling length about his distinguished ancestry. When he asked Ring about his family, Ring said, "I was born in Niles, Michigan, of colored parents. . . ." The man left him quickly.

To escape the fashionable bores who wanted to lionize him, Ring called up Sherwood Anderson and asked him to dinner. Anderson, a great admirer of Ring's work, arranged a dinner party for Ring and Ellis and the Rices at a small French restaurant. Even the chef was a Lardner fan and took special pains with the dinner. Anderson described the evening in an essay, "On Meeting Ring Lardner," in which he records his remarkably sensitive impressions of Ring:

There was something loose and free in the little room. How shall I describe it? It was Ring. What we all felt for him was warm affection. I had never known anyone just like him writing in America. He awoke a certain feeling. You wanted him not to be hurt, perhaps to have some freedom he did not have.

I dare say that the tragedy of Ring Lardner . . . that gorgeous talent of his so often smeared . . . is our common tragedy, the tragedy of every creative man, big or little, in our day. No one of us escapes it. How can he?

Just the same, Ring Lardner did often escape. He had a marvelous technique. He could always get behind the mask, and then, too, he must always have had a great deal of what he was getting that night at dinner; that is to say, warm affection from many people. We poured it over him as we poured the wine down our throats. We loved him. I cannot help thinking it was a rich and rare evening in his life. He laughed. He talked. He drank the wine. He told stories. It was a good evening for him. It was something more than that for the rest of us. Two years later, I was in the same little restaurant, and the chef, that fat Frenchman, came to my table. I was alone and he brought a bottle of wine. He had come in from the kitchen and had on his white apron. He stood beside my table and poured wine for us both. "To that man you brought here that time . . . to Ring Lardner," he said, lifting his glass.

The second evening Ring spent with Anderson he had been invited, with the Rices, to a dinner party where he expected to be bored. He phoned Anderson and asked him to come and get him away.

When I arrived [Anderson wrote] there was a swarm of people and Ring was busy. He was putting on a show. He sat in the middle of a big room at a piano and they were all gathered about him and he was singing and making them sing with him. He sang "Two Little Girls in Blue" . . . "Just Tell Her That You Saw Me and That I Was Looking Well" . . . "There'll Be a Hot Time in the Old Town Tonight," and several others. He made them sing.

The people were crowded in close about Ring, who sat at the piano wearing his mask. He could look at a man or woman with strangely impersonal eyes. "Sing," he said and the person so looked at sang.

It was quite a long time before Ring saw me that night, but when he did he made for me, the singing having stopped abruptly . . . he had them all going right . . . they had been throwing their heads back, drinking the liquor and stepping into it. He pushed me through them, brushing them aside. Now and then he stopped to introduce me to a man or woman. The mask on his face was well adjusted. He introduced me as an author, his fellow author, the author of The Great Gatsby . . . The Confessions of a Young Man . . . Tess of the d'Urbervilles . . . *the man who wrote* Moby Dick.

Ring had a plot to make a quick getaway with some of the host's liquor and to continue the evening elsewhere without the tiresome people who had been lionizing him. He and Anderson went into a butler's pantry. Anderson got three or four bottles and rushed out to hail a taxi. But the host saw them and insisted on driving them all back to Ring's hotel. Anderson sat in the back seat with the clinking bottles, and as soon as they reached the hotel he got out, hiding the liquor under his coat, and went to the door and waited.

Our host had got out of his car. It was a Rolls-Royce. He was doing his own driving. "Your friend, your fellow author—where is he?" he said, looking about. He seemed extraordinarily small and pale, standing there before Ring. It was like a big dog and a little dog and the little dog was wagging his tail. He didn't care a hang about the liquor we had got. He knew we were going somewhere to sit and drink and talk quietly, and I think he wanted to come along,

233

but he was too polite to ask, and I think also that Ring was, for a moment, tempted to ask him to come.

Ring was looking down at the man. I could see it all. There was an overhead light shining down on them. I saw something happen. Ring had been wearing his mask all evening, but, for a moment, it dropped. He started to ask the man to come with us, but changed his mind. I saw his lips tremble. I know what happened. He wanted to ask the man to come along, but was afraid I wouldn't like it, and so he said nothing, but stood there, looking down at the man, his lips trembling. This was a different Ring Lardner from the one I had seen in the room with all those people.

This one was a shy man and so was the little banker. The two men stood like that, looking hard at each other, and then, as if by a common impulse, they both began to laugh. They laughed like two young boys, or for that matter like two girls, and then the banker ran quickly and got into his car and drove away, but as he did so he took a shot back at Ring. "I hope your friend got plenty of good stuff . . . I hope he got enough," he said, but Ring was not looking. He was a man whose habit it was to wear a mask, and it had slipped off, and at the moment I was like a man standing in the dressing-room of a theater and watching an actor at work on his make-up. I saw him put the mask back on his face and he wore it for the rest of the evening.

Ring's solemn, immobile face and his wondering eyes had always looked like a mask. Now he knew how to use it as a defense and as an escape. Anderson had caught a glimpse of how it worked.

The Love Nest and Other Stories was published in the spring of 1926, with an introduction which indicated that Ring had not been touched at all by any adverse criticism of the joking self-deprecatory presentation of *How to Write Short Stories*. The joke misfired in some quarters. Ring wrote to Fitzgerald: "Reviews of 'The Love Nest' have been perfectly elegant. I don't know whether you've seen the book, but I had an introduction to it written as if I were dead. The Sunday Times ran a long review and played up the introduction strong, saying it was too bad I had died so young, etc., and the result was that Ellis was kept busy on the phone all that Sunday evening assuring friends and reporters that I was alive and well. It just happened that I was at home and cold sober; if I'd been out, she might have worried a little. Or maybe not."

The introduction was purportedly by Sarah E. Spooldripper, who "lived with the Lardners for years and took care of their wolf. She knew all there was to know about Lardner, and her mind was virtually blank. It was part of her charm." The account of the "Master's" life which follows is a burlesque of all introductions, of intimate memoirs, of literary scholarship. One of the high points is this:

It was in the middle of this work that the rivalry between Lardner, Scott Fitzgerald, and Opie Reade for the love of Lily Langtry reached its height. During a dinner party at which the then raging beauty and her raging suitors were all present, the toastmaster, Gerald Chapman, asked Miss Langtry to rise and drink to "her favorite." The muscles of Fitzgerald and Reade were taut; Lardner's were very flabby.

After a pause that seemed to endure all night but really lasted only half that long, Miss Langtry got up, raised her glass and said: "I drink to Red Grange. Heston may have been his superior on the defense, and Coy, Thorpe, Eckersall, and Mahan more versatile, but as a common carrier I take off my hat to the Wheaton icemonger."

All of the nine stories of *The Love Nest* were written and published in magazines within a period of less than two years. Four of them are among Ring's best, and the collection as a whole increased his reputation for misanthropy. These stories demolished a few rosy conceptions about American life that had long been cherished in the popular mind: the title story blasts the rich, romantic movie marriage; "Haircut" exposes the hearty practical joker as a callous monster; the nurse in "Zone of Quiet" shatters the sentimental idea of the angel of mercy; "Mr. and Mrs. Fix-It" hints that helpful friends can be meddling bores.

"The Love Nest," considered one of Ring's most brutal satires, was based squarely on actuality; the characters were people whom Ring knew well and whom he did not dislike; yet it is one of his most unsparing and devastating stories. Ring made no bones about who the models for the story were, although they were probably the last to suspect it. It is about Lou Gregg, a movie magnate who has married one of his young stars. A reporter, Bartlett, visits his home to get a story about him. The house is enormous and ostentatious. Mrs. Gregg is still pretty, and so are the doll-like children. They present a perfect picture of marital contentment. Gregg has to leave for a while, and Mrs. Gregg shows Bartlett around the house:

"It is wonderful! I call it our love nest. Quite a big nest, don't you think? Mother says it's too big to be cosy; she says she can't think of

*it as a home. But I always say a place is whatever one makes of it.
A woman can be happy in a tent if they love each other. And miserable in a royal palace without love. . . ."*

Mrs. Gregg begins pouring out whiskey and quickly gets drunk,
while the embarrassed Bartlett remains sober.

*"The trouble with you, Barker—do you know what's the trouble
with you? You're too sober. See? You're too damned sober! That's
the whole trouble, see? If you weren't so sober, we'd be better off.
See? What I can't understand is how you can be so sober and me so
high."*
"You're not used to it."
*"Not used to it! That's the cat's pajamas! Say, I'm like this half
the time, see? If I wasn't, I'd die!"*
"What does your husband say?"
*"He don't say because he don't know. See, Barker? There's nights
when he's out and there's a few nights when I'm out myself. And
there's other nights when we're both in and I pretend I'm sleepy
and I go up-stairs. See? But I don't go to bed. See? I have a little
party all by myself. See? If I didn't, I'd die!"*
"What do you mean, you'd die?"
*"You're dumb, Barker! You may be sober, but you're dumb! Did
you fall for all that apple sauce about the happy home and the con-
tented wife? Listen, Barker—I'd give anything in the world to be
out of this mess. I'd give anything never to see him again."*
"Don't you love him any more? Doesn't he love you? Or what?"
*"Love! I never did love him. I didn't know what love was! All
his love is for himself!"*
"How did you happen to get married?"
*"I was a kid; that's the answer. A kid and ambitious. See? He was
a director then and he got stuck on me and I thought he'd make me
a star. See, Barker? I married him to get myself a chance. And now
look at me!"*

Mrs. Gregg gets to bed before her husband comes home, and the
next morning they carry on the farce of pretending they are happily
married. It is a complete and shocking revelation, and as in all of
Ring's best stories the characters give themselves away almost entirely through dialogue. Even when Ring wrote in the third person,
he never got far away from the first-person dialect story; common
speech was his medium. The banality of Mrs. Gregg's silly delusion
about love-in-a-tent and Gregg's pompous and self-assured clichés

236

and conversational tags are what characterize these people. Their lives are loveless and false, and there is no way out of their situation.

"The Love Nest" was made into a play by Robert E. Sherwood and presented in 1927. "This ain't my play," Ring wrote to Fitzgerald, "though of course I will share in the receipts. (There won't be many.) I saw a dress rehearsal last night. Bob has done some very clever writing and the second act is quite strong with June Walker great as a drunk. But I'm afraid most of it will be over people's heads. This, of course, is under your hat."

The story is too slight for a three-act play, and it was necessary to provide a resolution by having Mrs. Gregg elope with the butler. The device is too flimsy, and it begs the question: the butler can't make a star out of her, and there is nothing in her character to suggest that she can be happy in a tent. The play ran only three weeks, after indifferent notices.

"Haircut" is a favorite anthology piece, a classic example of Ring's first-person dialect stories, and it shows all of his indignation at cruelty, stupidity, and callousness. A small-town barber, garrulous in the time-honored tradition, tells the story of one of his late customers, Jim Kendall, an all-round practical joker and "card." He is a ne'er-do-well, incompetent scapegrace, but popular with his fellows for his sense of humor and his pranks.

Jim had a great trick that he used to play w'ile he was travelin'. For instance, he'd be ridin' on a train and they'd come to some little town like—well, like—we'll say, like Benton. Jim would look out the train window and read the signs on the stores.

For instance, they'd be a sign, "Henry Smith, Dry Goods." Well, Jim would write down the name and the name of the town and when he got to wherever he was goin' he'd mail back a postal card to Henry Smith at Benton and not sign no name to it, but he'd write on the card, well, somethin' like "Ask your wife about that book agent that spent the afternoon last week," or "Ask your Missus who kept her from gettin' lonesome the last time you was in Carterville." And he'd sign the card, "A Friend."

Such are Kendall's wit and the barber's level of appreciation. Kendall's last joke involves a young doctor and a young woman, Julie Gregg, who is hopelessly in love with him. Kendall, imitating the doctor's voice, phones Julie and asks her to come to the doctor's office. When she does so, eagerly, Kendall and some fellow jokers mock and tease her. When Paul, a village boy who is mentally retarded but adores the doctor and Julie, tells the doctor about the prank, the latter says that anyone who'd do that shouldn't be allowed to live. Soon after, Kendall takes Paul duck-shooting, and the boy "accidentally" shoots and kills him.

Personally [says the barber] I wouldn't never leave a person shoot a gun in the same boat I was in unless I was sure they knew somethin' about guns. Jim was a sucker to leave a new beginner have his gun, let alone a half-wit. It probably served Jim right, what he got. But still we miss him round here. He certainly was a card!
Comb it wet or dry?

The practical joker, traditionally a beloved small-town figure, turns out to be miserable, brainless, and cruel; and the barber who admires him is just as bad. Ring was exposing the witlessness of a whole vein of the American comic tradition—the small-town wag who is a degenerate descendant of the frontier hell-raiser, and is generally accepted as a genuine humorist. Actually he is degraded and perverse; but there are still innumerable jackasses to laugh at him. Not even what commonly passes as a "sense of humor" has much saving grace in it, offers any release or any leavening of the sordidness of the small, meager, impoverished world that Ring evokes so skillfully in the barber's monologue.

Practical jokes are the basis of much of the humor in Ring's baseball stories; Jack Keefe is almost always the dupe of them. But these are harmless, they are even sometimes funny, and in any case Jack Keefe is too thick-skinned to be hurt by them. This kind of humor is fairly shallow at best, as Ring knew; but in "Haircut" it is not funny any more. Humor itself has become corrupt. It is a bitter and appalling story.

There is nothing else quite so grim as this in the collection. "Zone of Quiet" is about a talkative, featherbrained nurse who recounts to a helpless patient all the details of her amorous conquests, taking her girl friend's boy friend away from her in spite of her protests of loyalty. Ring knew all too much about hospital life and nurses; he probably found the story ready-made for him. At least one passage of dialogue was:

"What's that you're reading?" [the nurse asks].
" 'Vanity Fair,'" replied the man in bed.
" 'Vanity Fair.' I thought that was a magazine."
"Well, there's a magazine and a book. This is the book."
"Is it about a girl?"
"Yes."

"I haven't read it yet. I've been busy making this thing for my sister's birthday. She'll be twenty-nine. It's a bridge table cover. When you get that old, about all there is left is bridge or cross-word puzzles. . . ."

"Mr. and Mrs. Fix-It" is not a very remarkable story; it is reminiscent of one of the early "Gullible" pieces; but it is amusing in connection with a paragraph in the introduction. It concerns a couple in Chicago who meet another couple, the Stevenses, who are inveterate arrangers of other people's affairs. They insist on getting their new friends an apartment they don't want, new clothes they don't need, tickets to the wrong football games, and finally railroad tickets to Florida. At last, tired of the well-meant but exasperating favors of the Stevenses, the couple slip off alone to Biloxi. The Stevenses are quite recognizable as types who can be found anywhere, but especially in the Midwest or the South where social life is informal and neighborliness can become a downright invasion of privacy.

In the introduction Ring burlesqued a literary note on the source of the story:

Publication of this story in Liberty *caused an estrangement between the Master and the Grantland Rices, who were unmistakably the parties inspiring it. So accurately were their characters and idiosyncrasies depicted that they recognized themselves and did not speak to Lardner for a week. This was considered a triumph by the Master.*

"But the lesson was all lost," he told me afterwards, when a conciliation had been effected. "They knew I was writing about them and now they are right up to their old tricks again, dictating where we shall buy our shirts, how to discipline our kiddies, what roads to take South, what to order for breakfast, when to bathe in what kind of bath salts, and even how often to visit the chiropodist. It is an intolerable example of maniacal Southern hospitality."

"Who Dealt?" is a monologue expertly calculated to produce in the reader just the bearable amount of embarrassment, agony, and suspense, topped with a fatal climax. The speaker is a bride of three months whose husband, Tom, has brought her to see his oldest friends, Arthur and Helen Gratz. During a bridge game the young wife rattles on, paying no attention to the cards. It becomes obvious that Helen was the childhood sweetheart of Tom, but has married Arthur instead. The bride cheerfully exposes their private life—

239

Tom has gone on the wagon at her request; he wears pajamas now instead of nightshirts. Over his protests she tells the plot of a story Tom has written; it is plainly autobiographical—the story of how Helen jilted Tom and eloped with Arthur, who is richer. Then the wife recites a sentimental love poem she has found among Tom's papers. The story ends:

"Isn't that pretty? He wrote it four years ago. Why, Helen, you revoked! And, Tom, do you know that's Scotch you're drinking? You said—— *Why, Tom!*"

At the end of this agonizing recital one is sure that a marriage has been shattered. One can see the suburban living room, the characters, the very expressions on their faces, and the whole course of Tom's life which has brought him to marriage with this dreary, insensible, rattlebrained girl. In the course of her monologue she has unconsciously told everything about their fundamental incompatibility, the kind of lives they are doomed to; and the hosts' embarrassment and the husband's dismay are nearly intolerable.

The Love Nest reinforced the opinion of the critics that Ring was a formidable satirist. Some of its satire is good-natured enough; some is cold fury. It led to the general impression that Ring hated the human race; actually he hated only people who were brutal or phony; the stupid he felt sorry for.

He kept on pretending he was not a satirist and that he was not a serious fiction writer, although he knew he was both. But there is a note of pessimism in the very playfulness of his burlesque introductions. The device of presenting the book as if he were dead is not without macabre overtones; the note of futility could hardly have been unintentional. Writing of the Master's last days, Sarah Spooldripper says:

But he was always trying to tune in on Glens Falls and it was only in his last illness that he found out there was no broadcasting station at that place. His sense of humor came to his rescue in this dilemma.

"Junior," he said to his wife, "they tell me there is no broadcasting station at Glens Falls."

"Am I to blame for that?" retorted the little Nordic, quick to take umbrage. (Junior was an inveterate umbrage-taker and frequently took more than was good for her.)

"No," he answered. "It's Glens Falls'."

This recalls the introduction to *How to Write Short Stories:* the mule in the Grand Canyon that watches the trains come in and wonders who is going to ride him but never finds out. However effective these introductions may be as burlesques, they express a profound sense of isolation; and the "sense of humor" was no help at all. The final irony was that his last long illness was not far off.

Ring was in 1926 at the peak of his fame as a columnist and short-story writer; this was only twelve years after the publication of his first stories; he was forty-one years old. He was tired of writing in character, and he got little pleasure out of writing short stories, whatever the praise he received. He still liked to write songs and plays, and he kept on trying, in a desperate effort to get some satisfaction from his work. This was a crucial year in his life, and he knew it. For one thing, he found out for a certainty that the state of his health was precarious. He decided to give up newspaper work entirely and to devote himself as much as possible to music and the theater.

CHAPTER SEVEN

Ring was born stage-struck. He was also born with perfect
  pitch, and his love of music was the deepest and most constant interest in his life. His greatest ambition was always to be a
song writer, and he wanted most to write music for the theater. He
never achieved any notable success as a song writer, and only one
as a playwright, and this came long after he had been discouraged
by many failures. Still, the pleasure he got from writing songs and
plays was rewarding, and he kept on writing them nearly to the end
of his life. For him music and theater became a single interest. He
would have preferred to spend all his time and energy on it than on
the journalism that was his living or the short stories on which his
fame rests.

Dramaturgy was Ring's meat almost from infancy. He found a
good deal of theatrical inspiration at home. The repartee in the
Lardner family was swift and uninhibited by the rules of classical
drama. Their favorite kind of humor was part of Ring's heritage as a
writer. They were always amused by the kind of incorrect grammar
and diction that characterizes the speaker; they played with words,
and the more outrageous their puns, the funnier they were. Mrs.
Lardner and the three youngest children were gifted with a wild kind
of free association, and much of their conversation culminated in mad
irrelevancies that resembled the dialogue of Ring's later nonsense
plays. The Lardner family had a style; its influence on Ring's own
style is marked.

Ring's native gifts as a musician came from his mother. His elder
sister Lena was also a musician of professional caliber and helped

243

to give the younger children a sound musical education. The Lardner home attracted and welcomed the talented musicians of the locality. There was hardly any kind of music in which Ring did not have some knowledge or training; but he had a bent for improvisation and never submitted to too rigorous a discipline. Instead, music was his pleasure, and his surpassing interest was in popular songs. The musical culture of his home was of a high order; but music in the West, for one of Ring's generation, meant music for singing. The pleasure was not in listening but in participation. Ring grew up in the era of the barbership quartet and the last days of the minstrel shows. These were not considered "folk art" then; they were part of the fabric of social life. And so, although Ring lacked no opportunity for the higher intellectual discipline of music, it was mainly a social pastime, and it was the popular kind that appealed to him. In music, as in writing, being a popular artist was the condition of his being an artist at all.

Ring and Rex sang in the choir, organized quartets and musical shows. They saw a great many minstrel shows in the Niles Opera House. These had become a stereotype and they were passing along with the era that had fostered them. The spirit of high burlesque had departed. But the forms of the minstrel tradition had been carried over into vaudeville and variety shows, and Negro artists became the exponents of the ballads and comic acts which had had their origins in blackface minstrelsy. Of these artists the greatest were Williams and Walker, for whom Ring and Rex had an overwhelming admiration. When the Lardner boys went to Armour Institute in Chicago for the ostensible purpose of studying engineering, they spent all the time they possibly could watching the Williams and Walker revues at the Great Northern Theater. This preoccupation was one reason for their untimely withdrawal from higher education. It also led to Ring's friendship with Bert Williams and their subsequent collaboration on songs. Ring had more than admiration for Williams as an artist; there was a deep fellow-feeling between them and some telling similarities in their attitudes as comedians and entertainers.

Bert Williams and George Walker made a break with the minstrel show tradition, which was mainly carried on by white performers in blackface, and in which the stage Negro was a standard character, so circumscribed by convention that it required no particular originality to portray it. Williams and Walker were both performers of exceptional and distinctive personal gifts, and they shattered the cliché of the stage Negro for all time, even though much of their

244

material derived from the old tradition. Walker was noted for the most stylish cakewalk ever seen, and Williams was one of the most versatile comedians of the American theater, a singer, dancer, and clown whom no one has surpassed. A great personality himself, he and Walker established the dignity and individuality of the Negro actor in the theater and did a great deal to demolish the conventions that had inhibited Negro talent. Ring's enthusiasm for Williams was not a passing youthful admiration; it lasted all of Ring's life. His love of Williams' songs and comic style is a touchstone to Ring's own song writing; and his sympathy for Williams as a man and an entertainer reveals a great deal about Ring himself.

The songs that Williams sang were Ring's all-time favorites, and are still affectionately remembered by a whole generation: "Nobody," "You're in the Right Church but the Wrong Pew," "I Don't Like No Cheap Man," "All Goin' Out and Nothin' Comin' In," and "My Castle on the Nile." The last was by J. Rosamond Johnson, one of Ring's favorite composers and later a personal friend.

As a young sports reporter in Chicago, Ring saw much of Williams, on and off the stage. He went to all of Williams' shows not merely to watch him with pleasure, but to study his technique and his comic style. He liked to take Williams to Stillson's tavern, the hangout of *Tribune* reporters, and to other newspapermen's haunts. But Williams did not feel at ease in such places; he rather sadly accepted discrimination, and even in later years when, as a Ziegfeld *Follies* star, he was invited to stay in the same hotels as the rest of the cast, he used back entrances to avoid embarrassment. So more often he and Ring went to a saloon at Thirty-first Street and South State—the same saloon where Shelton Brooks, pianist and composer, wrote "Some of These Days." There Ring and Williams drank together and talked about songs, and Ring began to write material for him. Although Williams had come a long way from the old-time Negro, he still sang "coon songs" and one of his most famous numbers—the impersonation of a Negro preacher in a haunted house visited by large black cats who keep saying, "We can't do nothin' till Martin comes"—is a variation on the trite theme of the alleged proneness of Negroes to superstitious fright. When Ring began to write for Williams, he was following Williams' style, and he wrote a comedy piece about a colored servant sent on an errand to a lodge room where one of the brothers is laid out for burial:

Now dey tell me dat de white I seed was nothin' but a sheet,
Dat's use' sometimes to cover up de gran' exalter's seat;

245

An' dey tell me dat de eyes I seed was jes' my own, dat's all,
Reflectioned from a mirror dat was hangin' on de wall;
An' dey tell me dat de noise I heared was probably a rat,
An' de things I seed a wavin' was de plumes on Jedge Lane's hat.
    Yes, sir.

But dere ain't no lookin'-glass with eyes as big as buggy wheels,
An' dere ain't no sheet dat reaches out an' grabs a person's heels,
An' dere ain't no plums ur udder kin's of veg'tables dat flirt,
An' dere ain't no rat dat knows me well enough to call me Bert.
I guess I'm big enough to know de things I hear an' see,
Yes, sir! Yassir! Yes, sirree!

This was plausible enough material for Williams, although it is commonplace and shows nothing but a facility for versifying, and a thoughtless acceptance of outworn stage conventions about Negroes. Ring was not at his best when he was writing to strict specifications. But he kept on trying. After he had become sports editor of the Boston *American* and Williams had become a star of the *Follies*, Ring wrote another song and sent it to him. Williams answered:

New York, March 17, 1911

Hello there Big Boy:
   Thanks so much for the laying out. But it was deserved. Have revamped the song so I'm sure it's a positive hit. Will write the music this week while I am in Baltimore. It's not so cold here now, but it's not time yet to leave the overcoat home. Please during this Spring practice get the kinks out of your arms because I'm going to beat you bowling and beat you good. I know you're having a good time "mongst the Pines" and when you see Bro. Dorey, my regards——This week Baltimore, next, Syracuse. If I hear from you there shall send you all the route into Frisco. Good luck and health are the worst I can wish you.

Bert Williams

This is all that remains of their correspondence; and there is nothing to indicate that the early songs Ring wrote for Williams had any conspicuous success, if they ever reached the stage at all. Williams' material had to be tailored to the somewhat baffling requirements of Florenz Ziegfeld, and much of it was dropped or altered beyond recognition before it got to Broadway. It was not until 1917 that the *Follies* program credited Ring for the words and music of a song, "Home, Sweet Home (That's Where the Real War Is)," sung by Williams, and later recorded. So except for the satisfaction of

246

their friendship their collaboration brought little reward. Williams felt stifled in the *Follies,* and Ring was to meet with continued frustrations in all the subsequent work he did for Ziegfeld.

Williams died in 1922; he had been a popular star for two decades, but his popularity was waning. With the twenties a whole new style of entertainment arrived and eclipsed even such unique talents as Williams', which had come to fullness in the prewar era and were superseded by performers of quite another quality and pace. Ring himself, formed in an older school, never quite fell in with the tastes of the twenties in popular songs. But he was better qualified than almost anyone else to estimate Williams' place in the theater.

Heywood Broun, writing in the New York *World,* devoted a column to Williams just after his death. For Broun, Williams symbolized the harshness of the struggle of Negro performers for recognition in the theater, and the injustice of the public attitude that all Negroes were born singers anyway and just naturally comic. Broun's point in general was well taken, but he missed the specific point about Williams entirely; Ring wrote to him, and Broun published the letter:

When I read your line "It did not seem to us that Williams was a great comedian and certainly not a great clown," I thought to myself——

But then I thought, "This guy ain't stupid so the answer must be that he never saw a Williams and Walker show, and judging Bert by Bert in the Follies, well, sir, you might just as well judge Babe Ruth's pitching on his 1920–1921 showing with the Yankees."

And besides being the greatest comedian and one of the greatest clowns I ever saw, Bert was a great natural musician and a masterly singer of "coon songs," and when I say singer I mean singer.

The people who wrote the Williams and Walker shows knew how to write for Bert. The Follies people didn't, and he lacked the energy to write for himself. Besides, he was under the impression, the delusion, that Follies audiences were drawn by scenery and legs and didn't want to laugh. He used to say, "I'm just out there to give the girls a chance to change."

In my early Chicago days, Williams and Walker played long runs, mostly at the Alhambra and Great Northern theaters. My allowance for spending money was about $5 a month. I used to spend $3 of it on their show, going once a week at 75 cents a trip. It was Williams who drew me and he meant to me a sacrifice of sixty beers a month. He had a song—My Castle on the Nile—in the chorus of which there *wasn't a funny line; yet they (we) made him come out and sing, or dance, that refrain twenty-one times in one show.*

Speaking about his dancing, if you'd seen him just dance in the old days, you'd have pronounced him comedian and clown as well as the champion eccentric hoofer of all time.

In my record book, he leads the league as comedian and can be given no worse than a tie for first place as clown, pantomimist, story-teller, eccentric dancer and a singer of certain types of songs. Otherwise, he was a flop.

Ring was interested in Williams as an artist, and he understood how he felt, smothered in the overdressed inanity of the *Follies*, working with indifferent material, required to be funny whether he felt like it or not, in the face of increasingly less appreciative audiences.

It was through Williams that Ring got his first professional experience in the theater. He knew almost all the foremost theatrical figures of his time, but no one else ever left a deeper impression on him.

When Ring was traveling with the White Sox at various times from 1908 on, he was friendly with Guy Harris ("Doc") White, a pitcher with a musical bent, and Ring's first published songs were written in collaboration with him. One of them, "Little Puff of Smoke, Good-Night," subtitled "A Southern Croon," is a pleasant lullaby whose melody is reminiscent of any number of other Southern lullabies. Ring's lyrics are not remarkable, yet it is the lyrics that make the song, and they are quite skillfully wrought, if not highly original. Another Lardner-White song, "Ain't It a Wonderful Game!" never superseded in popularity the already well-established "Take Me Out to the Ball Game," although it is far more ingenious; but it is not as simple or singable, and it certainly does not lend itself so well to the requirements of a loud brass band. A third song, "My Alpine Rose," is a sentimental love song which had the moderate success of the others; that is to say, it was published but never widely played. All of these are good songs, although they are in well-worn traditions; they are written, not merely borrowed, and they have a distinction that many a more successful song lacks. But the competition in their fields was overwhelming, and they remained obscure.

Ring had better luck with "Prohibition Blues," which he wrote for Nora Bayes in 1919, for the show *Ladies First*. Having a famous musical-comedy star introduce the song was an advantage. Ring wrote the lyrics, and while Nora Bayes is credited with the music, Ring actually wrote it. The song's success was unexpected, and Nora Bayes wrote that it was being published by Remick and that Ring would receive $250 advance royalty.

Here is Ring's lyric for "Prohibition Blues":

> *"What ails you, brown man,*
> *What makes you frown man,"*
> *I asked my man so mis'-ra-ble—*
> *"You look so winnin'*
> *When you is grinnin'*
> *With all them gold teeth vis-a-ble.*
> *But now you's always threat-nin'*
> *To bust right out and cry.*
> *Does yo' dogs fret you?*
> *What has up-set you?"*
> *Then he made his reply—*

CHORUS

> *"I've had news that's bad news about my best pal*
> *His name is Old Man Alcohol but I call him Al.*
> *The doctors say he's dyin'*
> *As sure as can be*
> *And if that is so*
> *Then oh oh oh*
> *The difference to me*
> *There won't be no sun-shine*
> *No stars   no moon*
> *No laughter   no music 'cept this one sad tune*
> *Good-bye forever to my old friend 'Booze'*
> *Dog-gone I've got the Prohibition Blues."*

Two hundred fifty dollars does not seem a staggering advance for a successful song, but it was just ten times what Ring had expected in 1910 when he signed a contract with the firm of T. B. Harms & Francis Day & Hunter for three song lyrics which would, if published, have brought him an advance of $25 each. They were never published, and probably not all were ever written. One of them had a promising title: "I Wonder What My Stomach Thinks of Me."

It is impossible to say how many lyrics Ring wrote. He had begun back in Niles to write verses to familiar airs for his own amusement and his friends'; and he dashed off a number of lyrics for which no music was ever written. Altogether only about a dozen of his songs were published, and none has a permanent place in the repertory of American songs which are still played and sung. Between 1919 and "June Moon" in 1929, none of his songs was published, although he was always at work on lyrics for musical shows that were never produced. He never gave up hope, and he was a little bitter about the failure of his songs. He was without envy, but he could not help noticing that song writers with no musical talent and with vulgar and insipid ideas were enjoying the greatest popularity. He did not begrudge them their success, but he despised the debased standards of the craft.

He had often contributed sports articles to the *American* magazine, which specialized in success stories by famous men in various fields. Ring was asked to write his story; and if he had written of himself as a journalist and short-story writer, he could have produced, probably to his dismay, an article that conformed to the standard pattern.

But the success story had already sickened him. He had written a collection of parodies on it entitled "Little Sunbeams of Success," for *Cosmopolitan*. One of his subjects, Ernest L. Zopple, wrote verses that sold to newspapers all over Iowa, and had a home in Pittsburgh. His success story in verse began:

> *Before we had money, we lived in a flat,*
> *The dear little woman and I.*
> *There wasn't no danger of us getting fat,*
> *And the cellar was painfully dry.*
> *But though we now boast of a house in Duluth*
> *And go there in passenger coaches,*
> *That house, it don't seem like the home of our youth,*
> *For a home ain't a home without roaches.*

The same issue of *Cosmopolitan* featured a poem by Edgar A. Guest, and ran Ring's "Little Sunbeams" under a caption which must have made him wince: "By Ring W. Lardner Who Makes Sunbeams Pay Real Money."

So when *The American* asked for Ring's account of his career, he wrote of himself as a song writer, and, measuring the time he had devoted to it against the returns, he estimated that he was out $10,000. The editor of *The American* rejected the article.

In Chicago Ring wrote songs and vaudeville skits, usually with his eye on Bert Williams, and he found opportunities to widen his acquaintance among theatrical people. His first meeting with George M. Cohan was to result in an intermittent association, the climax of which was Cohan's production of *Elmer the Great* in 1928. Mutual friends of Ring and Cohan wanted them to meet. Cohan had never heard of Ring (this was early in Ring's career) and, accustomed to meeting young people with theatrical ambitions, tried to fend him off. He said to a companion, "They've got a local comic here named Lardner. I don't want to meet him, he'll tell me funny stories. Let's duck."

But Ring was introduced to Cohan, while the latter's companion waited for him to get rid of what he thought was another importunate amateur.

"Mr. Cohan," Ring said earnestly, "you've been in the theater twenty years. You write songs and sing them. You dance. You write plays and produce them. You know everything there is to know about the theater. You're the one man who can tell me what I want to know. Mr. Cohan, how the hell does a guy get on the water wagon?"

Cohan dismissed his waiting friend and spent the evening with Ring.

Cohan became a great admirer of Ring and when Ring asked him to read his scripts, Cohan agreed and gave them his personal attention and advice. Although Ring was a master of dialogue, he was clearly at a loss when it came to constructing a full-length play. Cohan sent him scripts of *The Miracle Man* and *Seven Keys to Baldpate*, both of which had been hits, to guide Ring in matters of action and stage business. Ring sometimes wrote Cohan or his partner Sam Harris anxious queries on scripts he had written. In April 1917 he went to New York with a completed script of a baseball comedy for Cohan's consideration. Cohan finally rejected it, saying it contained too much baseball. "Your central character as a character is great but there is too much of him. Think he would appear to far better advantage as a bit and not as a steady diet. My experience has been that comedy like that should only be relief comedy. . . . I do not think the general public would be interested in so much baseball." Cohan was putting his finger almost exactly on what was wrong with *Elmer the Great* some ten years later after he had got through revising Ring's script.

Sometimes Ring found himself unexpectedly collaborating on a theatrical sketch. Shortly after he came to New York he met an old friend from Chicago, Charles Washburn, a newspaperman he had known on the *Tribune*. Washburn was writing a vaudeville turn for

Gallagher and Shean, who were to open at the Star and Garter in Chicago in a burlesque revue called *Joy Belles*. He drew Ring into it and finally Ring wrote about two thirds of a comedy scene. After the opening Shean sent Washburn a telegram saying that his first entrance failed to get a laugh—a situation nearly fatal to a comedian of his caliber. Washburn asked Ring to help him devise an effective entrance.

They met in a speak-easy on Park Row near the offices of the Bell Syndicate, for which Ring was writing his weekly column. It was an Italian restaurant, with a bar in the back room. The front room was dirty and nondescript, and Ring nicknamed it "the della Robbia Room." While he and Washburn were sitting there, a man came in from the back room, followed by a burst of laughter. He looked back and said, "These bootleggers are jolly fellows." Everyone in the front room roared. Ring suggested to Washburn that he have Shean come on with a burst of laughter off stage and say the same line. Washburn telegraphed the idea to Shean, who used it; for some reason it was a great success and it stayed in the revue while it ran a whole season in New York. Washburn got $500 for the sketch and offered to split it with Ring, but Ring refused. He had done it only as a favor.

Washburn later became George M. Cohan's press agent, and handled the publicity for *Elmer the Great*. This play was based on Ring's story "Hurry Kane," which appeared in May 1927, and in which Cohan—though he had once objected to a script that had a baseball player as a central character—must have seen great possibilities. He engaged Ring to write the stage version and Walter Huston to play the leading role.

Ring wrote Fitzgerald in December of that year: "My thing with Cohan is supposed to go into rehearsal in February, but you never can tell." Ring had by this time suffered a good many disappointments from producers, and he was due for another. The play did go into rehearsal in the spring of 1928.

"Hurry Kane" is not one of Ring's best baseball stories. Elmer Kane is unrelievedly dull, obtuse, and wrongheaded. He is a promising player, and the team and the manager try to keep up his morale, even to the extent of sending for his home-town girl. (This plot was getting a little thin.) But he becomes infatuated with a shady ex-chorus girl who induces him to throw a Series by telling him she will marry him if he has twenty thousand dollars. This makes it easy for the gambler—"a black-haired bird with a waxed mustache," as he is characterized—to arrange the fix. Elmer pitches badly during the first inning, but when he learns that the gambler is the girl's lover, he changes his mind and wins the Series. His sudden reform is not caused by moral enlightenment, but to chagrin and vindictiveness. He even keeps the five thousand dollars down payment the gambler has given him. Now Jack Keefe was dumb but endearing; but he would have been destroyed as a character if he had even thought of attempting to throw a game. Elmer suffers irreparably from that lapse. The narrator of the story absolves him of villainy by saying, "Besides, they ain't nothing crooked about him. He's just a bone-headed sap"; but Elmer hasn't enough stature to survive his attempt. A dumb ball player can be sympathetic, but not a crooked one. Elmer started out with two strikes on him; by the time Cohan got through with him, he was out. It is hard to believe that Ring had his heart in the story when he wrote it; but he was very anxious to write a play. There was a prolonged struggle between Ring and Cohan before the script was finished, and then it was not at all what Ring had meant it to be.

The metamorphosis of Elmer was so drastic that hardly a trace of Ring remained in the play. There are two versions in typescript in existence; the first, an intermediate stage in Elmer's transformation, still bears Ring's mark. In plot it follows the story almost exactly, and all of the dialogue of the story is carried over into the play. The scenes, all but two, are baseball training quarters, a Pullman car, and the dugout at the ball park—the backgrounds Ring knew well and depicted realistically. The scenes away from the baseball background are the least convincing; and one scene, in a saloon where Elmer succumbs to the show girl's wiles, is quite incredible and without any sort of merit. Elmer is whitewashed a little; he does not take any money for himself, but has it paid to the show girl. Otherwise the script conforms to the story; Elmer reneges on the gamblers when he learns of the perfidy of the show girl and sees his true sweetheart in the grandstand. He remains the stupid and easily tempted prize boob of baseball; he also has a little sentiment in his love affairs that is not apparent in the story. But in the end it is not ball players who win or lose games, it is the women in the grandstand—a chilling commentary on both women and ball players. The dialogue has the humor and color of Ring's better baseball stories, and the character of Elmer is made at least tolerable on the stage, although he is still as exasperating to his teammates as Ring originally meant him to be.

But a baseball player who even once agreed to throw a game could never be a hero to an American audience, Cohan suspected;

and that was the basic reason for the long battle over the rewriting, in which both Ring and Cohan were losers.

Cohan and Lardner had their rewriting troubles during the rehearsals of "Elmer the Great" (Ward Morehouse wrote in his biography, George M. Cohan). Lardner was living in Great Neck. So were George Holland and Dorothy Noland Holland, Cohan's sister-in-law. In the middle of the night, Holland got a call.

"Come on over here, George," pleaded Lardner. "We're going to fix this damn play and we're going to fix it right!"

For the next two hours with scissors and paste, they went to work on "Elmer the Great," pasting third act speeches over first act speeches and second act dialogue through third act scenes. They did a thorough job slicing up three scripts to get one as they wanted it.

"Now show up at rehearsal," said Lardner, as they finished, "and we'll beard the little bastard."

[Presumably Ring, in this uncharacteristic speech, was referring to Cohan.]

When Cohan arrived for the morning rehearsal Lardner was waiting for him. "Now this, George," he said, "is the way I want this comedy played."

Cohan took the script, turned a few pages, looked at Lardner, looked at the script, and roared. Then he called off rehearsals for the day.

People weren't in the habit of laughing in Ring's face; but there is no doubt that there was a great deal of antagonism between Ring and Cohan over Elmer. After Cohan got through with the character, he was unrecognizable.

For Elmer was to come out, not merely a lovable fellow, but actually the hero who, singlehanded, saves the national pastime from the gamblers. The baseball background, by far the most original element of the play, was cut to a minimum, only two scenes. The long scene in the dugout which in Ring's version was the climax of the play—Elmer's performance in the crucial game was dramatized in the dialogue of his teammates and over the radio—was eliminated completely. Every satirical touch, every bit of humor, was wrung out of the play line by line. Hurry Kane was deposed by Frank Merriwell.

The billing read: "George M. Cohan presents Walter Huston in Ring Lardner's American Comedy *Elmer the Great*," but it was not Ring's comedy any more. Act I takes place in the Kane home in

Gentryville, Indiana; Elmer, who drives a delivery wagon for the general store owned by Nellie Poole, his sweetheart, is shown eating breakfast—steak, potatoes, ham and eggs, and flapjacks, etc. The notion that a hearty eater is essentially lovable, not to mention wildly funny, is worked to the limit. It was also assumed that mere stubbornness and egotism are beguiling as well as hilarious. When Elmer refuses to sign with a New York ball club because he would rather stay home near Nellie than play ball, Nellie has to jilt him in order to make him move onward and upward in the sports world. This accomplished, it takes only a few evil machinations on the part of some gamblers to deceive Nellie into honoring some fake I.O.U.s allegedly signed by Elmer to pay gambling debts. But Elmer is on to the gamblers in no time, he takes their bribe money only to bet it on himself to win, and calls in the cops. The game takes place off stage between scenes, and by the end of Act III, Elmer and Nellie are back in Gentryville, a nationwide gambling ring is behind bars, Judge Landis is smoothing his hair, and Elmer is foxing the New York club out of ten thousand a year on a new contract, and is being sought for vaudeville appearances and cigarette testimonials. The play doctors had turned "Hurry Kane" into a heavy-handed vehicle for a good actor, Walter Huston, whose performance seems to have been the only notable thing about the play. That must have been a triumph, for there was hardly any character left to portray. Cohan's misunderstanding of Ring's story and his kind of humor was total.

Originally entitled *Fast Company*, *Elmer the Great* opened in Boston in the spring of 1928, and Ring, weary and ill as he was, attended the opening and even made a gala occasion of it. He and Charles Washburn, who handled the publicity, invited a number of sports writers to cover the opening, and Ring gave a party in his hotel suite the afternoon before the performance. Washburn had ordered a case of whiskey to be delivered to the office of the Tremont Theater, and had promised Ring two bottles. Ring got there before Washburn did and had no trouble wheedling the whole case away from the theater manager and transporting it to his hotel, where the sports writers gathered. Some of them got too drunk to write their stories, so Ring wrote them and sent them out under the proper names. Ring remained quite clearheaded, but Cohan knew that a party was going on and was concerned for Ring, since he knew he had been ill. He sent two nurses to the hotel to take care of him.

As curtain time approached, Ring had not yet arrived at the

theater, and Cohan began to be anxious. Ring finally arrived, sober and upright, supporting the two reeling nurses.

Ring was of course disappointed with the play and skeptical of its success. He hated to have his material rewritten, but he had permitted it for two reasons: one was that he was genuinely humble about his own talents as a playwright; he had never had any success. Besides he was not good at quarreling with people, and he was too tired and ill to try. He disclaimed, unofficially, the authorship of the script; but he stuck with the play and went to Chicago for its opening there. It had a fair reception, and the critics considered it promising. It came to New York in the fall, opening at the Lyceum Theater September 24, and ran for forty performances. In spite of its failure on the stage the motion-picture rights were sold to Paramount, and it was made into a film called *Fast Company,* with Jack Oakie. Both the property and the script underwent further changes and in 1933 it was again made into a film called *Elmer the Great* starring Joe E. Brown, who appeared as a home-run king instead of a pitcher. By that time the story had so little resemblance to the original that it didn't matter. It was moderately successful as a film, although the reviews were not enthusiastic.

After the violent treatment given his own story and script Ring was quite justified in disclaiming any part in the final version of the play. Nevertheless he had made grave compromises. He was obliging by nature and not contentious, and he yielded to Cohan. Cohan did not mind argument; he often quarreled with the people he liked best. Their differences did not impair their personal friendship. *Elmer* was their only joint theatrical venture; it was typical of many of Ring's experiences as a playwright.

The first Ziegfeld *Follies* had come to Chicago in 1907, and Ring saw it and every annual edition of it thereafter. Ziegfeld found a formula that worked for years: big-name stars, and what is fulsomely called feminine pulchritude; and he introduced into the musical revue the element of fashion, keeping pace each year with changes in style and sometimes starting fads. Costume seemed to be the framework of the shows. From Emma Carus to Marilyn Miller, his female stars were the most beautiful and most lavishly dressed women in the theater; and he surrounded his stars with the now legendary chorus girls. It was Ziegfeld who perfected the production number, the top-heavy, back-breaking, overloaded dance routine composed of literally everything that could be got on the stage. In retrospect the *Follies* would seem to have been only extravagant girl shows with statuesque beauties going through dance steps designed not to overtax the ingenuity of a three-year-old, and with emphasis on seminudity, dry goods, and feathers.

Actually Ziegfeld was as lavish in hiring real comic and musical talent, although he had little feeling for either. Considering how prodigal he was of the material he paid for and wasted, one of his greatest extravagances was hiring writers. The roster of Ziegfeld comedians is famous: Bert Williams, Will Rogers, W. C. Fields, Ed Wynn, Fannie Brice, Al Jolson, Eddie Cantor, and others; and among his best-known composers were Victor Herbert, Vincent Youmans, Irving Berlin, and Jerome Kern. The writers he engaged are less known, and deservedly. Ring Lardner was the only great one, and he never did his best work for Ziegfeld.

The *Follies* of 1922 was the first Ziegfeld show to which Ring made a considerable contribution. The top star was Will Rogers, who had risen to fame in vaudeville with his monologues and his lariat-twirling act; there were also Gilda Gray, originator of the "shimmy," and Gallagher and Shean, who introduced the interminable and nerve-racking song that bears their names. The book for the revue was written by Ring and by Ralph Spence. One of Ring's sketches, "The Bull Pen," a baseball scene in the vein of the "Busher's Letters," is true and unmistakable Lardner in spite of some interpolations. The star in it was Will Rogers. He did not think it was very funny, and said so. Ring did not think Will Rogers was very funny either, but was more discreet.

Ring's other sketch was called "Rip van Winkle Jr.," and its chief character was Hnery Wtz, a typographical error. Three other sketches Ring wrote were eliminated entirely. Ring took all of this with mingled good humor and exasperation, and wrote the history of his experiences with this revue in an article called "Why Authors?"

I don't suppose they's anybody that even seen the Follies or read articles in regards to same but what they realize that the production must of cost a bbl. of money. It ain't no secret neither that thousands of marks and rubles is spent on scenes which is throwed in the ashcan as soon as the producer has saw them in dress rehearsal. But I wonder if many people knows how much dough is just plain wasted in paying royalties to lyric writers, composers and authors, a specially the last named.

I hope Mr. Ziegfeld is out fishing when this article is published because if he seen it he might start thinking and here is what he would think:

"Why should I be sending checks once per wk. to these birds that poses as writers of wds. and music and etc. when it is plain to see that the actors and particuly the ones recruited from the ranks of vaudeville can write so much better themselfs? Because if they couldn't, they would quit changeing and rewriteing and improveing everything that has been wrote for them."

They's no denying the fact hinted at in that last sentence. It don't apply so much to the lyrics, as about the only change made by singers in the wds. of songs is putting in wds. they can pronounce in place of wds. they can't. And the tunes is generally always altered in just 1 or 2 spots where the original composer had slipped in a couple of strains which the audience might not recognize. . . .

However the biggest waste is the royalties slipped to the boys that writes the original script of what some gay Mary Andrew has nicknamed the comedy scenes. Let a author tend a performance say 6 wks. to 2 mos. after the opening when he has heard the lines then being used in said scenes he will wonder why is his name attached to them on the program. And between you and I he genally wishes it wasn't. . . .

Like for inst. they's a scene in one Follies called Rip Van Winkle Jr. in which a man sleeps for 20 yrs. and wakes up in 1943 to find the country quite a bit changed. He asks his butler who is President and the butler names a well-known Jewish gentleman. He asks who is Vice-President and another Jewish gentleman is named.

RIP—*But are they Democrats or Republicans?*

BUTLER—*Neither. They are Jewish. Everything is Jewish; even the Knights of Columbus.*

That line was stuck into the scene by Al Shean, who plays the butler, and is what us professionals could call a WOW. And the party that wrote the scene 1st. hereby admits that it wouldn't of occurred to him.

Then they's a baseball scene where 2 old time pitchers and a busher is down in the bull pen at the Polo Grounds dureing a game. The busher which is played by Andy Tombes is warming up. One of the old timers, played by Bill Rogers, is supposed to be kidding him. The busher says he would like to get a chance to pitch against this man Cobb.

ROGERS—*Who?*

TOMBES—*This Cobb.*

ROGERS—*Irvin?*

That one goes good and was thought up by Mr. Rogers. But just the same I would as leaf spare it as some of the ones that was left out last time I set through what used to be my scene. For inst. the name of Babe Ruth is broughten up and the busher, who belongs to the Yankees, says he thinks he could fool him.

ROGERS—*How would you pitch to him?*

TOMBES—*High and on the outside.*

ROGERS—*Yes, and that is just where it would go.*

TOMBES—*All right, but I bet the Babe's glad I ain't on some other club.*

ROGERS—*He don't know you ain't. . . .*

Wile those lines was still in the scene even the audience appeared to think they was O.K. though they didn't have the passion for them which the author felt. However that is either here or there. The actors has got that nag of knowing what to put in and what to leave out which a writer can't never seem to learn and that is what makes it seem so silly for a producer to keep sending checks wk. by wk. to people that ain't got no more to do with the show than Jane Addams. Personally will state in this regard that I wouldn't cash the checks neither if it wasn't for the wife and kiddies.

The 2 scenes referred to ain't the only scenes which the undersigned made of 1st. draft of them for the Follies. They was one about a fake seance but it was throwed out after the 2nd reading because nobody's part was better than anybody else's which everybody seemed to take as an insult. Each one went to the producer with the same story. "It may be all right but they's nothing in it for me."

Then they was a scene about a woman on trial for murdering her husband. In this scene 4 of the characters was supposed to be comical and the other 3 was straight. Unluckly 1 of the straight parts was assigned to a star who wouldn't lower himself to play straight for nobody. So he said the scene was l---y, a adjective very popular in the profession and derived from a little mammal which you might say was the only real winner in the European war. Well he said the scene was l---y so often that finely the scene believed him and jumped out of the show.

"The Bull Pen" was published in *Judge*, with the line attributed to Rogers included; but other lines of the original script were left out. One of the sketches omitted from the show reached print as "Not Guilty" in *Cosmopolitan*. It is not hard to see why it was dropped from the *Follies*; not only do the straight parts offer little for any actor, but the humor is rather strained and feeble, as if Ring

259

had felt obliged to write down to the level of the *Follies*. "The Other World," a tenuous satire on spiritualism, is also second-rate; there is something a little amateur about it. A good many of Ring's frustrations in the theater can be attributed to the egotism of actors and the whims of producers; but sometimes his own aim was faulty. But to have two sketches out of four included in the *Follies* was not a bad average.

Ring's association with Ziegfeld was probably the most galling experience of his professional career, yet he kept renewing it, breaking it off, then coming back again, almost to the end of Ziegfeld's life. Gene Buck, for years a librettist, lyric writer, and first assistant to Ziegfeld, collaborated with Ring on several projects, but none of them ever got far. Even before the *Follies* of 1922, for which Buck wrote lyrics, they embarked together on a show for Fannie Brice, an ill-fated effort of which only the vaguest traces remain.

Ring and Buck submitted a script to Ziegfeld, who apparently was not satisfied. Ring, who was then in Florida, got a wire from Buck that startled him into immediate protest. It informed him that Ziegfeld had engaged a team of writers to "reconstruct" his script. He wired Ziegfeld at once to return the script, and he would refund the five-hundred-dollar advance. Buck urged him to stay with the enterprise in view of the money in prospect and the fact that the other authors would not appear in the billing. This was even less satisfactory to Ring; he did not want his name on someone else's script. His decision was final, and his show for Fannie Brice was never produced.

Ring and Gene Buck next collaborated on a straight play called *Going South*, based on characters and situations drawn from Ring's book *Gullible's Travels:* episodes about a Chicago couple and the trouble they have finding a suitable husband for the wife's sister. The *raisonneur* of the play is the husband of *Gullible's Travels,* and it is here that Ring defined him as the "wise boob." But Ring was not so certain about the other characters, to judge from penciled alterations on the script. The wife in the play has a good deal more education and sense than in the book, and her social ambitions are only mildly satirized. The sister, who in the book is a rather unmarketable commodity, becomes a romantic ingénue in the play. She ends by marrying a millionaire, described as "A rich man's son. Father dead. A fine type of American youth; well bred, went to college; really studied, made the football team as quarterback and loves regular people; comes naturally to social position and neither likes nor dislikes it. Has millions of dollars, big interests, etc."—a rather hollow idealization the like of which never appears in any of Ring's stories, and is set down here without a trace of irony. The result of these alterations in characters was inevitably to denature Ring's original conceptions and their satiric bite and to produce a romantic comedy in which the kind of social ambitions which Ring and his wise-boob character really despised lead to an entirely conventional happy ending. When Ring allowed himself to pull his punches, to compromise his own vision of what people were like, he became trite. *Going South* is a well-constructed script with an adequate plot; but it is talky and insipid compared to the really funny stories on which it was based.

Ziegfeld did not rise to this opportunity, and the script was shelved until 1925, when Gene Buck revived his interest in it. Ring wrote to Fitzgerald:

Gene called up the other day and said he had sold the play "we" wrote for Ziegfeld, but that it would have to be written into musical comedy form. Ziegfeld had given him contracts for us to sign. There were clauses in them which I wouldn't sign even with a manager I could trust. I told Gene so and he cabled Ziegfeld, who is now in France, and said we objected to certain clauses. Ziegfeld cabled back that he wouldn't make any changes. Gene then wanted me to sign the contracts as they stood and I wouldn't. So that's that. I've got a story coming out in "Liberty" for October 3 of which Flo is the hero. When, and if, he reads it, he won't offer me any more contracts, even lousy ones.

However, Buck did not give up. In November Ring wrote again to the Fitzgeralds:

Well, in August Gene called up and said Ziegfeld was "hot" for the Palm Beach show "we" wrote two or three years ago; he wanted it rewritten into musical comedy form; he "had to have it" to put in the Cosmopolitan theater to succeed "Louis the Fourteenth," which was slipping. I said it was ridiculous to pretend the show could be fixed up by the first of September (which was the date set by Ziegfeld); besides, I didn't trust him and wouldn't even think about working on it till I saw a check. So then Ziegfeld extended the time limit to October first and gave us $500 apiece, with a written promise to give us $500 apiece more when the completed play was turned over to him, provided it was within the time limit. I got busy and rewrote the play into a musical comedy book; also wrote some lyrics which I thought were not bad. On the first day of Octo-

ber, Ziegfeld had not yet signed a composer, and as you know, it is impossible to turn in a complete book and lyrics these days unless you have a composer with whom to work on the numbers. On the second of October, Ziegfeld engaged Vincent Youmans to write the music. I showed him my lyrics and he didn't seem to care much for them. Neither did Gene. In fact, Gene wanted to write all the lyrics himself, though he didn't say so. Finally I said, "Well, I'm going to write the lyrics of three or four comedy songs and I want them to get a trial anyway." Then I went to the world's series and when I came back, not one tap of work had been done and Gene hadn't even turned over the book to Ziegfeld. Moreover, I think, though I'm not sure, that Youmans told Ziegfeld he had seen the book and didn't like it. Anyway, both Gene and I got telegrams saying we had broken the contract and I was so sick and tired of the whole proceeding that I was glad of it, but Gene said he was going to give Ziegfeld a terrible bawling out. He saw him and Ziegfeld softsoaped him and said that what he wanted to do was get rid of Youmans and when he did he would produce the show, probably about the first of the year. So Gene thinks that is what is going to happen, but between you and me, dear Scott and darling Zelda, Ziegfeld is not going to produce the show at any time, whether he wants to or whether he doesn't. And I have written him a letter, to the effect that my stuff was probably known to more people than was that of any of the popular song writers of the day with the possible exception of Irving Berlin and that said stuff would never have got before the public if magazine and newspaper editors had jazz composers engaged to pass on manuscripts. I guess that will make him think, eh, girls?

At present I am Americanizing Offenbach's "Orpheus in the Underworld," which, if I do it well, is supposed to be produced by the Actors' Theater with Otto Kahn's backing and under the direction of Max Reinhardt. I have no confidence that this will come to pass, but I am looking forward to some pleasure in the work because there is no other lyric writer concerned and the composer is dead.

Ring forgave Youmans for balking this project; they remained friends and worked together on a later Ziegfeld show, and Ring always admired Youman's songs.

Concurrent with this fiasco was an equally ill-fated effort to collaborate on a musical with Jerome Kern, one of Ring's favorite composers. Ring wrote to Fitzgerald: "Harry Frazee, who is making millions out of 'No, No, Nannette,' (with four companies in America, three in England and two in Australia) promises to stage a small revue, written by Jerry Kern and me, late this fall. But you know how those things go." After the Palm Beach play had fallen through, he wrote again:

Now, then, we come to my latest theatrical successes. Harry Frazee agreed to put on a revue by me and Jerry Kern if we could land Bill Fields. Bill said it was all right with him and I started to work, only to discover that Bill had already signed contracts (synchronous contracts) with Goodman, with Ziegfeld and with the Famous Players. He's going to spend the winter in court. Goodman is suing him for $100,000, Ziegfeld has him and he is supposed to be working for Famous Players and getting $6,000 a week.

If Ring had ever written a show for W. C. Fields, the result might have been fabulous. They were the two greatest comic spirits of their time, and there are some basic similarities in their kinds of humor. In the comedy of Fields, as in the fictional world of Ring Lardner, there are two types of people, knaves and fools. Fields had an uncanny knack of combining both in one character: at his most knavish he was also the dupe, and his sucker-traps had a way of backfiring to make him as ludicrous as his intended victim. So in many of Ring's stories his most calculating and ambitious characters are in the end the victims of their own folly.

Fields, like Ring, savagely punctured all kinds of pretentiousness. They had a similar hatred of success crowned by respectability, knowing that almost all advantage is achieved by chicanery. Fields hated fraud and humbug so much that he made them his stock in trade as a comedian. Despising affectations of culture, false social ceremony, hypocrisy in general, they both attacked them through the comic use of language: illiterate speech, mock-genteel speech, the high-flown cliché, the parody of the insistent, monotonous manner of the complacent bore, the irrelevant talk of mindless people. They also knew the value of the dead-pan pose.

They both had a profound sense of the cruelty of life, as men of extraordinary sensibility are bound to have. Fields, although somewhat paranoiac, had a tougher hide than Ring; he had endured a harder life than Ring had. But Ring's susceptibility to moral outrage made him no less vulnerable to cruelty than had Fields's actual experience. It played a large part in their humor; it is obvious enough in its larger aspects, in the practical jokes which Fields perpetrated in his role of scoundrel, in such Lardner stories as "Champion" and "Haircut." It also permeates their most innocent

263

comedy. In one memorable scene Fields appeared leading a very small dog on an immensely thick, heavy rope. Compare this with Ring's account of a World Series in which he proposed to kill his kittens to make a fur coat for his wife. In both situations the suggestion of cruelty is the essence of their humor. With Ring and with Fields this sense of the brutal ended in masochism: Fields was always landing in situations that were meant to be physically painful, ludicrous, and humiliating. The same kind of thing happens to Ring in the character he assumed for his "autobiography," *The Story of a Wonder Man,* in which he shows himself constantly beaten, duped, and degraded, in spite of the brash poses he strikes.

They were both deeply pessimistic, and both of them had reason to be skeptical of the role of the satirist in society. They knew that a satirist plays a dangerous game: he is tolerated only so long as he makes people laugh, and he is tolerated, not as a critic of society, but as a funny man. Perhaps that is why Fields was constantly in fear of losing his audience and Ring finally didn't care if he did lose his.

Ring and Fields were not close personal friends; they admired each other at a certain distance. Fields lived in Bayside for a time, while Ring lived in Great Neck. It was Fields's custom to come to the Great Neck railroad station with a shaker of martinis and dispense them to his friends among the commuters, and it is possible that Ring occasionally received a drink from Fields, who was acting, not out of benevolence, but from a simple wish to flout the law.

Ring might have had ideas about writing for Fields, and evidently Fields would have been willing to undertake a role in the revue which Ring proposed. But in spite of the resemblances in their humor there were great disparities of temperament which might have thwarted such a collaboration from the start. Fields had shared billing in the *Follies* with other top stars—Ziegfeld was opposed to having a single headliner in the show—and as a result he had become an expert scene stealer and ad-libber. If he did not like Ziegfeld's idea of how a scene should be played, he wasted little time arguing about it. He went on stage and played it the way he wanted. This was the kind of thing Ring as a writer hated in performers. Although a shared antipathy for Ziegfeld might have been a bond between them, it is just as possible that Fields would have rejected Ring's ideas as highhandedly as he did everyone else's. Writing for Fields, tempting as it may have seemed, might well have proved only another frustration for Ring.

Eventually Fields abandoned Ziegfeld and the stage for the films, thereby placing his audience at a safer distance. But Ring stuck doggedly to the theater, and even came back to Ziegfeld, who apparently hadn't read the story Ring wrote about him.

In the fall of 1930, Ziegfeld's last production, *Smiles*, went into rehearsal, with a book by William Anthony McGuire, music by Vincent Youmans, and lyrics by Clifford Grey and Harold Adamson. But while the show was still rehearsing in New York, Ziegfeld called Ring in to provide additional lyrics. In spite of his unpleasant experiences with the *Follies*, Ring agreed, although at the beginning the assignment was not a large one. Two of Ring's friends were working on the show, Vincent Youmans, and Paul Lannin, who was musical director. Ring was enthusiastic about Youmans' songs, especially "Great Day" and "Without a Song." Lannin was an old friend from baseball days; they had met in 1916 when Lannin was vice-president of the Boston Red Sox, of which his father was part owner. He had given up sports for music, and for a time had a band of his own, later becoming a musical director of Broadway shows. He had directed the orchestra for Youmans' *Hit the Deck*, and Ring frequently had visited the theater where it was playing to sit in the pit with the musicians for the pleasure of hearing the score at close range, the kind of pastime he loved.

The presence of Youmans and Lannin probably made Ziegfeld's offer more attractive than it would have been otherwise; at least he would find some fun in the work. But everything went wrong, and ultimately Ziegfeld quarreled with both Youmans and Lannin. With Ring he seems to have used persuasion rather than temper, and Ring patiently fulfilled his commitments in spite of the utter confusion of the whole affair. It became so fantastic that he got a good deal of amusement out of it.

He wrote to his son John, who was then in Paris:

The thing that took me to Boston and gave me a chance to visit Andover, and the Kitchells at South Byfield, was a summons from Ziegfeld to "help out" with the lyrics of the Marilyn Miller-Astaires show, "Smiles." While the company was still in rehearsal here in New York, the Astaires threatened to walk out because they didn't have a single song together and demanded two. I wrote them two, to Vincent Youmans' music, for a flat price, and thereby got myself into a world of trouble because one of the two was so very comical that, on opening night in Boston, it stopped the show. This was too much for Marilyn's temperament and she told Ziegfeld she would walk out unless I wrote her a comical one (she being as well equipped to sing a "funny" as Miss Feldmann). Ziegfeld called me up from Boston and asked me to come there and write a song for Marilyn and rewrite three other lyrics that were not so good. I knowing him well, asked for an unheard of advance royalty. He accepted my terms and I went to Boston and wrote eight songs instead of four, and have written two more since I came home (Youmans singing me his tunes over the long distance telephone). Your knowledge of mathematics will tell you that I have written twelve songs altogether (three of them purely production numbers), but there isn't a chance that more than seven of them will be used because there won't be room for even that many. My work in Boston was rendered quite feverish owing to the fact that it was next to impossible to get Youmans (who was quarreling with Ziegfeld) out of bed and to the piano.

The book of the show, by William Anthony McGuire, was unbelievably terrible as I saw it in Boston, but it may be better when it opens here next Tuesday night. I will send you my songs when, and if, they are published.

[The book of the show concerned four American Army buddies who adopt a French orphan girl and bring her back to the United States where she is brought up as a Salvation Army lassie.]

. . . Paul [Lannin] resigned his job as musical director at Youmans' suggestion (everybody knew there was something the matter with the show and picked on Paul, who was not at fault), but I gather from latest reports that he is reinstated and that some of the quarrels have been patched up. The real trouble is the book and the fact that the three stars are cutting one another's throats and each trying to help him- or herself instead of the production. For example, the best of my contributions, a duet and ensemble for the opening of the first act, will be left out through the protests of Fred Astaire—the number calls for the presence of some Park Avenue women in evening dress and he doesn't want anybody to appear dressed up before his own entrance.

All and all my trip to Boston was kind of wearing, but I wouldn't have missed it because it was so ludicrous. I got two hours of sleep out of each twenty-four and spent the rest of the time coaxing Youmans to the piano. One morning when I was retiring at four o'clock, Harland Dixon, who was directing some of the dances, came into my room and said, "I'm drunk and I'm going to tell you some tragic incidents in my life, though I know I'll regret it tomorrow." I said, "I know I will, too," but that didn't stop him and he went on

*relating tragic incidents until suddenly I had a bright idea—I drank
some paraldehyde and went to sleep with him still standing there
with his incidents.*

During a rehearsal a chorus girl came up to Ring and said, "Mr.
Lardner, I've just been rehearsing songs and I just found out that
your lyrics are wonderful."

"Wait till you hear the music," Ring said.

Besides countless telephone calls from Ziegfeld, Ring also got
two of his famous long-winded telegrams, which suggest the di-
sheveled state of the show only a few days before its New York
opening.

1930 NOV 7

MY DEAR RING I DO NOT WANT YOU TO FEEL THAT I AM
IMPOSING ON YOU BECAUSE OUR AGREEMENT READS THAT
YOU ARE TO WRITE THE NECESSARY LYRICS THE LYRIC I
AM MOST ANXIOUS TO GET AND TO FIT TO THE TUNE OF
THE SALVATION ARMY GIRL MARILYN MILLER THE LYRIC
TO CONVEY AS NEAR AS POSSIBLE WHAT HUGH MORTON
LYRIC IN THE BELLE OF NEW YORK DOES I HAVE JUST
BEEN TALKING TO WAYBURN & WE WANT TO SPEND SUN-
DAY IN ROUTINE THE SHOW PUTTING IN THE NEW SALVA-
TION ARMY NUMBER THE MILLER GREGORY DUET THE NEW
FINALE MARILYN MILLER FRENCH PANTOMIME & THERE
WILL BE NOT TIME TO GET TO THE OPENING OR THE BOW-
ERY SCENE I DONT THINK WE WILL GET TO THAT BEFORE
WEDNESDAY I WILL KEEP YOU POSTED BUT PLEASE RUSH
ME THE SALVATION ARMY GIRL LYRIC FOR THAT IS VITAL
TO THE SHOW IN THE MEANTIME I AM WORKING OUT THE
COSTUMES FOR THE OPENING OF THE BOWERY

ZIEGFELD

1930 NOV 9

LARNIER [Lannin] SAYS YOU LEFT OUT THE ENTIRE LINE
IN THE RALLY ROUND ME LYRIC MARILYN OBJECTS TO THE
LINE ABOUT THE DEVIL AND LINE I USED TO SHIRK MY
WORK ETC I KNOW IT IS HARD TO WRITE A LYRIC LONG
DISTANCE AND IT IS HARD ON ME SO NEAR OPENING THIS
IS A TOUGH BUNCH TO HANDLE WILL YOU PHONE YOU-
MANS TO GET THE MUSIC RIGHT I WAS FINALLY COM-
PELLED TO GET A COURT ORDER TO PREVENT YOUMAN
RUNNING THE SHOW THE ONLY THING HE FORGOT TO GIVE

ME A CHEQUE FOR 200,000 DOLLARS WE ARE GRADUALLY
GETTING INTO SHAPE AND WAYBURN IS DOING GREAT
WORK AND THE COURT ORDER KEEPS YOUMANS FROM IN-
TERFERING THAT IS A VERY IMPORTANT LYRIC PLEASE TRY
AGAIN I THINK YOU HAVE GOT TOO MANY RALLY ROUND
ME IN IT REGARDS

ZIEGFELD

Smiles opened in New York, incredibly enough, on November 18, and Ring's prophecy concerning the fate of his lyrics was substantially correct, optimistic as it had been. He had six numbers in the show: "Rally 'Round Me," sung by Marilyn Miller and the Salvation Army Lassies; "Time On My Hands" (refrain *What Can I Say?* by Ring Lardner), sung by Marilyn Miller and Paul Gregory, "Be Good to Me," sung by Fred and Adele Astaire; "Anyway, We've Had Fun," Marilyn Miller and the Astaires; "If I Were You Love (I'd Jump in the Lake)" by the Astaires; and "Why Ain't I Home?" sung by Eddie Foy, Jr. and the Girls. The fact that only one refrain of his lyrics was used in "Time On My Hands" irked Ring; he wanted to write all of a song or none. But by this time he was fairly philosophical about working for Ziegfeld; he knew what to expect. He endured Ziegfeld's badgering good-humoredly and came across with lyrics that were expected of him. One half of his efforts were successful, although the show was not, and gave up after sixty-three performances. Ring was not surprised or greatly disappointed.

After the Boston opening and the frantic revision of the show some of the principals involved gathered in Ring's hotel room to talk it over. Ring wearily lay down on the bed and apparently slept while the conversation around him went on until the early morning. Someone said, "If you want to know what I think, I think the Astaires are going to steal this show."

Ring roused himself to say, "That would be petty larceny."

The story "of which Flo is the hero" is "A Day with Conrad Green," included in the collection *The Love Nest.* It was written some time after Ring's experience with the 1922 *Follies* and before Ziegfeld had wriggled out from under the Palm Beach musical comedy; and it was not inspired by any immediate personal animosity, even though Ring took some pleasure in pointing out to Fitzgerald the original of its central character. It is coldly objective and aloof; Green could be any unscrupulous businessman; but the fact that he is a Broadway producer makes the story a significant commentary on what Ring thought of the type.

268

Conrad Green arrives at his office in the morning pluming himself on having been invited to the socially prominent Mrs. Bryant-Walker's tedious little soirée of the previous evening, and looks forward to seeing his name on the society page. He flies into an infantile rage when it is not. His browbeaten, forty-five-dollar-a-week secretary has just died. When he finds that the flowers for the funeral cost forty-five dollars, he keeps the last pay check due his secretary's widow. He sees a script writer and steals from him a scene which he tries unsuccessfully to put over as his own idea on his regular librettist. The unexpected arrival of his wife, who reminds him that it is her birthday, forces him to give her, with horrible expressions of connubial affection, a pearl necklace he had bought for his mistress. A visit from his mistress, who has come for the pearls, results in her breaking off their relationship. He gets out of going to his old secretary's funeral, and the end of the day finds him on the telephone with Mrs. Bryant-Walker, trying again to ingratiate himself.

No pity is wasted on Conrad Green, but he is anything but a triumphant villain. He succeeds only in his pettiest schemes. On the whole he has a dismal day. He gives the pearls to his unloved wife, he loses his unloving mistress, and he is exposed to the contempt of his employees. He does not even know why he feels defeated and unsatisfied; but his sense of power has not been diminished. There is little reward in it, though. He is left shivering, as if with cold.

There is a fine passage which shows how Conrad Green's mind works. He tells Martin, his librettist, a garbled version of the idea a writer has tried to sell him. "I couldn't sleep last night, and I just laid there and an idea came to me for a comedy scene . . ." and he outlines it.

"Listen, Connie," said Martin: "You've only got half the scene, and you've got that half wrong. In the second place, it was played a whole season in the Music Box and it was written by Bert Kalmar and Harry Ruby. Otherwise I can do a whole lot with it."

"Are you sure you're right?"

"I certainly am!"

"Why, that damn little thief! He told me it was his!"

"Who?" asked Martin.

"Why, that Blair, that tried to butt in here last year. I'll fix him!"

"I thought you said it was your own idea."

"Hell, no! Do you think I'd be stealing stuff, especially if it was a year old?"

269

That tells everything about Conrad Green, in its staggering lack of logic, its disingenuous air of wounded innocence, its revelation of an ego that has slipped, hastily trying to recover its poise.

In "Nora" (1928), Ring wrote of the treatment accorded the hapless writer by producers and composers. It is very close to his own experience. The writer, Hazlett, has written a straight play and taken it to Brock, a producer who immediately sees in it material for a musical comedy, and calls in a lyric writer and composer for a conference. Hazlett summarizes his book: Nora is the beautiful niece of an Irish contractor who is trying to get business from a politician. The politician's son falls in love with Nora's picture. Nora is imported from Ireland and falls in love with the young man, as her uncle had hoped. When the politician is exposed as a crook and ruined, the uncle tries to alienate the young couple, but true love triumphs.

The song writers have written two numbers that do not fit into this libretto at all, and they start to revise it.

"Where's your comic?" inquired Morris.

"Mr. Hazlett forgot to mention the comic," Brock said. "He's and old Irishman, a pal of What's-his-name's, a kind of Jiggs."

"People don't want an Irish comic these days," said Morris. "Can't you make him a Wop or a Heeb?"

"I'd have to rewrite the part," said Hazlett.

"No, you wouldn't," said Morris. "Give him the same lines with a different twist to them."

"It really would be better," Brock put in, "if you could change him to a Heeb or even a Dutchman. I've got to have a spot for Joe Stein and he'd be a terrible flop as a Turkey."

"And listen," said Morris. "What are you going to do with Enriqueta?"

"Who is she?" Hazlett inquired.

"The best gal in Spain," said Brock. "I brought her over here and I'm paying her two thousand dollars every week, with nothing for her to do. You'll have to write in a part for her."

"Write in a part!" exclaimed Morris. "She'll play the lead or she won't play."

"But how is a Spanish girl going to play Nora Crowley?" asked Hazlett.

"Why does your dame have to be Nora Crowley?" Morris retorted. "Why does she have to be Irish at all?"

270

"Because her uncle is Irish."

"Make him a Spaniard, too."

"Yes, and listen," said Moon. "While you're making the gal and her uncle Spaniards, make your boy a wop. If you do that, I and Jerry have got a number that'll put your troupe over with a bang! Play it for them, Jerry. . . ."

> "In sunny Italy,
>   My Spanish queen,
>   You'll fit so prettily
>   In that glorious scene.
>   You will sing me 'La Paloma';
>   I will sing you 'Cara Roma';
>   We will build a little home, a
>   Bungalow serene.
>   Then in the Pyrenees,
>   Somewhere in Spain,
>   We'll rest our weary knees
>   Down in Lovers' Lane,
>   And when the breakers roll a-
>   Cross the azure sea,
>   Espanola, Gorgonzola;
>   Spain and Italy!"

"A wow!" cried Brock. "Congratulations, Jerry! You, too, Frank! What do you think of that one, Mr. Hazlett?"

"Very nice," said Hazlett. "The tune sounds like 'Sole Mio' and 'La Paloma'."

"It sounds like them both and it's better than either," said the composer. . . .

"But we've got something else, hey, Frank?"

"You mean 'Montgomery'?" said Moon.

"Let's hear it," requested Brock.

"It'll take a dinge comic to sing it."

"Well, Joe Stein can do a dinge."

> "Take me to Montgomery
>   Where it's always summery.
>   New York's just a mummery.
>   Give me life that's real.
>   New York's fields are rotten fields.
>   Give me those forgotten fields;

I mean those there cotton fields,
Selma and Mobile.
I done been away so long.
Never thought I'd stay so long.
Train, you'd better race along
To my honey lamb.
Train, you make it snappy till
('Cause I won't be happy till)
I am in the capital,
Montgomery, Alabam'."

To accommodate these numbers, Brock, Moon, and Morris devise a few alterations in Hazlett's script. Nora becomes the cashier in a Spanish restaurant, and the boy, an Italian count incognito, falls in love with her. He takes her out on a yacht, where a scheming Frenchman has her falsely accused of the theft of a jewel, in order to disillusion the count. The second act opens in Saratoga, with twenty-four girls in jockey suits. The count learns of the Frenchman's perfidy; but the girl won't accept his apology until they go to Montgomery. The last scene has to be in Japan, because the song writers have a cherry-blossom number. They send Hazlett home to make a few changes in his script. "And I want to say that your book is a whole lot better than most of the books they hand us. About the fella falling in love with the gal's picture—that's a novelty idear."

This appears to be a rather broad burlesque, but a glance at the musical comedy librettos of the twenties will prove that it is really not very much exaggerated. And the songs, with appropriately borrowed tunes, could be sung without any humor at all in a musical comedy. Ring's straight lyrics are good; his parodies are masterpieces.

Neither realism nor individual characterization played any great part in these musical comedies. Tuneful, familiar music and gorgeous settings seemed to be the important ingredients. Consequently the idea of a modern adaptation of Offenbach's *Orpheus in the Underworld,* which Morris Gest proposed to Ring in 1925, did not seem an implausible one. Offenbach's music is still delightful, witty, and popular; and there is no reason why the Orpheus legend should not be capable of a new comic interpretation. Gest and Max Reinhardt probably had in mind a lavish spectacle; that was their specialty.

Recent Offenbach revivals somehow lead to the conviction that the very attempts were unpromising from the start. It seems to be felt that a drastic adaptation is necessary; what was witty and satirical under the Second Empire is not particularly pertinent now. Lyrics, jokes, costumes, and settings must be modernized; while the music remains the same. The perils are obvious.

Ring's book is not very funny. Orpheus is a Tin Pan Alley song writer—a tune stealer—and Eurydice is his long-suffering wife who wants to and does get rid of him to marry a prince. The gods and goddesses are largely low comedy figures whose lines are stale vaudeville jokes. Of course Ring meant them to be broad burlesques of standard comedy characters; but somehow the idea of the Olympians reduced to Broadway types is a little oppressive. The humor depends on every possible play on the word "Hell," on gags which may have been funnier during Prohibition than they are now, and on some fairly heavy references to the lusty nature of the gods. It sometimes sounds like the work of a man who is trying to approach a mildly risqué joke and doesn't know how; which, of course, was exactly the case.

In the lyrics, however, Ring showed great ingenuity and taste. Some are comedy numbers and others are unabashedly romantic. But the result had no distinctive style of its own; it is a hodgepodge of incompatible styles. Ring was limited not only by Offenbach but by the musical stage of the time; there was not much scope there for his kind of satire. The show was never produced.

Two other musical comedy scripts fared no better. One was a modern version of Cinderella, set on Long Island; the Prince is the Prince of Wales, whose visit to this country was sensational news at the time. Ring designated his heroine "just another Marilyn Miller type. Sympathetic, appealing. Good singer, good dancer." All of the characters are similar stereotypes. But this libretto is pleasant and amusing, and the dialogue really sounds as if Ring had written it; the lyrics are wrought with care and with the intention that they should be sung clearly and understood; they were meant to carry the story, not to stop the show, which made them nearly unique at that time. This was rejected by several producers. Another, a rather boisterous and busy romp centered around the difficulties of a young man running a paper at a New Jersey seaside resort, including a bathing-beauty contest which offered obvious possibilities for a big production number. This is sometimes quite funny, but it could have been written by almost anyone. It was also shelved.

In 1928 Ring and Paul Lannin got the idea of doing a musical comedy together, and they worked on it for several months, Lannin writing some pleasing tunes for some of Ring's best lyrics. The show

273

was to be called *All at Sea,* and the setting was on board a ship making a round-the-world cruise with stops at various European and Oriental ports. The plot concerns a gangster wanted for murder, and a young man suffering from amnesia who is mistaken for the gangster. There are also a young newspaperman and two ingénues for romantic interest, and some broad character parts. The familiar husband and wife from *Gullible's Travels* are barely recognizable in minor roles. Ring, largely because of his health at this time, did not feel equal to the task of working out the whole book, and called on George Abbott for his assistance. He also wanted Abbott to direct the show. His collaboration with Abbott amounted to only a few conferences, and then Joseph Santley, the writer and director, helped Ring to complete a script that seems to be quite finished as far as plot goes. The story is ingenious and the dialogue is sprightly if not exactly witty, and it is altogether the most professional and the cleverest of the musical comedies that Ring worked on.

But Ring's real interest was in the songs, and he and Lannin wrote a dozen first-rate numbers. They were well matched as lyricist and composer, and the hours they spent at the piano were sheer pleasure for both of them. They liked each other's humor, and took the same sardonic view of their profession; but their songs were not satirical. They were straight comedy or romantic pieces, and there is nothing startlingly original about them. Their distinction lies purely in their quality. They are worth hearing over and over, and both words and music have a polish and subtlety that do not wear out with repetition, and they still do not seem at all dated. They were never destined for wide popularity—they were never even published—but if they had been, they might have held up far better than the ordinary run of the songs of a season.

One of them, intended for this show but not included in the final version, is a mock-lugubrious song meant to be sung by a man with a deep voice and a solemn, expressionless face (Ring had Arthur Treacher in mind when he wrote it):

> *I feel just like poor Hamo-let*
> *Who said, "To be or not to?"*
> *To kill oneself is wrong, and yet*
> *I b'lieve I've almost got to.*
> *The girl I love is so unkind!*
> *When I am gone, she'll rue it.*
> *So I will die if I can find*
> *A pleasant way to do it.*

274

Refrain:

> *But cyanide, it gripes inside;*
> *Bichloride blights the liver;*
> *And I am told one catches cold*
> *When one jumps in the river.*
> *To cut my throat would stain my coat*
> *And make my valet furious.*
> *Death beckons me, but it must be*
> *A death that ain't injurious.*

2nd refrain:

> *A shot would make my eardrums ache*
> *And wake my niece, who's teething;*
> *A rope would wreck my classic neck*
> *And interfere with breathing;*
> *I can't take gas because, alas,*
> *The odor's unendurable.*
> *O Lord above, please tell me of*
> *A death that ain't incurable.*

Another song called "Sixth Avenue" has the refrain:

I love the roar of the "L" and the general smell of the street.
I love the mobs who are out of jobs, and who never overeat.
My chums are down and out bums from Morocco, Monaco and
> *Rome.*
Good old Sixth Avenue, I'm proud of havin' you for my home.

One of the duets is "A Wonderful Pair":

> *What a wonderful pair we two are!*
> *What a wonderful pair are we,*
> *If the words that we have spoken are so!*
> *If you're really as nice as you are*
> *And I'm really as nice as me,*
> *Won't the common folks feel blue when they know? Oh,*
> *It seems peculiar that on sea or on land,*
> *Just you and I should be so perfectly grand!*
> *But if the things that we say and do are*
> *Half so charming as we both swear,*
> *Surely we must be a wonderful pair!*

Lyrics without the music do not give an adequate idea of the song; but it is at least worth observing of these lyrics that they have style, they follow some principles of versification, and they are witty. If you compare them with almost any other popular lyrics, their distinction is obvious.

The last script of *All at Sea* is credited to George Abbott, Joseph Santley, and Ring Lardner. It is quite a good piece of work, but there is not much in it besides the lyrics that is strikingly characteristic of Ring. After the songs were done and the book had been got into shape, Ring became involved in *June Moon*, and it was not until early in 1930 that anything was done about having it produced. Lannin suggested the partners Alex Aarons and Vinton Freedley as producers and discussed it with them; but before a decision was reached, the partnership was dissolved. Joseph Santley was then called to the West Coast on a directing assignment and mentioned the script to Robert Woolsey, of the comedy team of Wheeler and Woolsey, who wanted it rewritten to fit their requirements. Ring was willing to leave the matter in Santley's hands, and the script was bought by RKO for the comedians. But their material had been planned far in advance, and the project was delayed. Finally RKO gave up the idea of filming *All at Sea* and nothing more was ever done about it.

The trouble with Ring's unproduced scripts was not that they were unlikely musical comedy material. It is rather that they do not seem to have much to do with Ring. He was not working in his own vein. Except for the carefully written lyrics, which are literate and clever, none of them has much character; they could have been turned out by any number of writers. They are good enough ideas, and they are well enough constructed; but the dialogue and the jokes are not like Ring's other work. He lacked assurance when he was writing for the stage; he seems to have been tailoring his ideas and material to conform to current styles and conventions. So far his attempts to work by himself had been disappointing, and his efforts with collaborators hardly less so. Yet he did need the assistance of someone with practical experience, and he knew it. He could write good dramatic dialogue and contrive an acceptable plot; but he did not know how to cope with that tortuous process by which a script becomes a production, and struggling with producers, directors, and actors was not congenial to him. He no longer felt capable of getting a play produced against all the opposition he had been accustomed to. Cohan had turned *Elmer the Great* into a Cohan play against Ring's better judgment; nothing of Ring remained in it. But in his next collaboration, *June Moon*, written with George S. Kaufman,

276

Ring's own material and his own unmistakable style were at last successfully translated to the stage.

Ring and Kaufman began to work on the play early in 1929. It was based on Ring's wonderful story, "Some Like Them Cold," in so far as it had the same characters and initial situation, but it was not a slavish adaptation of it. The play is a satire on the song-writing business, and Ring put into it all he felt about it, including some splendid examples of popular songs. Kaufman, an experienced playwright and director, provided a structure and a pace for the comedy that carried out Ring's intentions completely. Whatever the respective contributions of the collaborators, the result was all of a piece. Kaufman himself had a satirical turn of mind, he knew Ring well, and he understood his work.

Ring wrote the first draft scene by scene, and Kaufman read it, making suggestions for changes, which Ring accepted and incorporated in a new draft. He did not merely patch or revise the script. He rewrote it entirely each time even though it meant scrapping as much as sixty pages at once and starting all over. He repeated this process until a suitable version was completed. It was his way of working; with everything he wrote he had to be able to see it and put it down as a whole. It was a sound method; the play has a tight and even style and pace. Ring worked on it long hours each day all spring, and it was ready to be tried out in Atlantic City early in the summer.

The Atlantic City tryout was a disheartening setback. The first act was good, but the last two acts were inadequate, and Ring and Kaufman were faced with the prospect of having to rewrite them completely.

Ring was gloomy about it. He went out and paced the boardwalk, where he met a friend who was surprised to see him there.

"What are you doing down here?" the man asked.

"I'm down here with an act," Ring said.

He returned to New York, and, as he often did when he wanted to work undisturbed, took a suite in the Hotel Pennsylvania. He had a piano brought in; a spirit of conviviality overtook him, after the strain of a long period of work, and he began to call up friends, among them Paul Lannin, who with many others dropped in for a couple of days of drinking and music. He was completely blocked on the second act. During the musical party a window washer came in and washed the windows. It gave Ring the idea for the second-act curtain.

In the play a window washer comes into the music publisher's office and at the end of the act is left alone on stage.

The room belongs to the WINDOW CLEANER, and maybe he doesn't realize it. He scampers over to the piano and hits a few tentative notes. Resigning himself to a musical career, he drops his sponge on the window sill and startes picking out the notes of "Hello, Tokio!" Encouraged by his success with the first phrase, he starts again, this time singing it. Then he takes a long breath and starts again, louder this time. He is plunging recklessly into it, and oblivious of his surroundings, when MAXIE (the piano-player) comes in behind him. MAXIE stands perfectly still for a second, taking in the situation. Then he makes up his mind. Turn about, he decides, is fair play. He picks up the sponge and starts feverishly washing the window.

Ring telephoned Kaufman and told him his idea. Kaufman liked it. The party ended, and Ring went back to work. The play was not finished in one burst; it required the rest of the summer, with many rewritings and conferences with Kaufman. By the end of the summer it went into rehearsal with Kaufman directing, and a cast that included Linda Watkins, Norman Foster, Philip Loeb, Frank Otto, Jean Dixon, Lee Patrick, Florence Rice, and Harry Rosenthal.

June Moon has the two central characters of "Some Like Them Cold," the egotistical and naïve young song writer and the girl whom he has met casually; and the letters of the story, with all their affectations and clichés, subterfuges and insincerities, are transformed into the dialogue of the play. Fred strikes up a conversation with Edna on a train bound for New York, where he is going to be a lyric writer. They begin a shy, tentative romance until Fred is attracted by the transparent wiles of Eileen, mistress of Hart, a music publisher, who is tired of her. Eileen is the sister-in-law of Paul Sears, a composer who can't even play "Chopsticks" and is desperate for a hit. Fred and Sears write a song called "June Moon," which is so much like every other popular song that it is, to everyone's surprise but Fred's, a great success. Fred, who now has money, is trapped into a promise of marriage by Eileen and is going to throw over Edna. But Maxie, a kindly piano player who has failed as a composer because his tunes are too original, brings Fred and Edna together, while Sears tips off Fred about Eileen's shady past. The young couple fall into each other's arms as Fred begins to improvise a sickening lyric about a bungalow for two.

Sears has composed a song called "Montana Moon," with lyrics by

278

one Fagan. "Fagan isn't so bad," Maxie says. "Only he's using up his ideas too fast. He puts a state and a moon all in one song." And "If song writers always wrote about their home state, what a big Jewish population Tennessee must have." Another character is Benny Fox, "a song writer of the dangerous type." He has written a number called "Hello, Tokio," which contains a whole musical comedy.

> *Hello, hello, Tokio!*
> *Girlie, you'll excuse it please,*
> *If I no spik Japanese.*
> *This little call will leave me broke-o,*
> *But I simply had to say, "I love you so."*
> *Believe me, dearie, it's no joke-o;*
> *I'd gladly fly through fire and smoke-o*
> *To share with you the marriage yoke-o,*
> *Fairest flower of Tokio-okio-okio!*

But Benny surpasses himself with another one. "It's about a couple that have a baby without benefit of a clergyman, and you can dance to it."

> *Should a father's carnal sins*
> *Blight the life of babykins?*
> *All I ask is give our child a name—I mean a last name.*
> *I don't ask to share your life,*
> *Live with you as man and wife;*
> *All I ask is give our child a name—*
> *Not just a first name.*

The hit song of the show is "June Moon." "It's a tune that's easy to remember," Maxie says, "but if you should forget it it wouldn't make any difference."

> *June Moon, shining above.*
> *Will my true love come soon?*
> *June Moon, I am so blue;*
> *I know that you long for her, too.*
> *Sweet night-bird, winging aloft,*
> *Singing a soft love tune,*
> *Tell her to come to me here,*
> *To me and her dear June Moon.*

Both "June Moon" and "Montana Moon" were published after the play had opened, with the credit line "Eavesdropped by Ring Lardner and George S. Kaufman." They are both rather pretty songs in an ordinary way, and out of the context of the play could be taken quite seriously.

The characters of the play are true Lardner characters. They operate on a level of unawareness that gives them an odd appeal, like a boob baseball player. Fred and Edna are a sweet young couple and very boring; they are not so much disingenuous as merely unconscious. But the authors, in providing a happy ending for them, did not promise them salvation or weaken the satire. Percy Hammond, reviewing the play in the *Herald Tribune,* observed, "Plays are but incidental foothills approaching the mountains of event . . . and even so conclusive a comedy as 'June Moon' takes us but a short journey in the lives of its characters. I am sure the hick lyric-writer from Schenectady and the scheming little ingenue who blissfully falls in his arms as the story quits, are not so congenial by this time. He is probably a pompous composer of theme-songs impossible to live with, and she is flirting casually with strange gentlemen in Pullman cars and the Albany night boats."

Only the character of Maxie is wise. He has long ago caught onto the song-writing game and the other characters. Because he is the only one in the play who knows what is going on, he might seem to have been contrived only to serve as a commentator and precipitate the denouement. Actually Maxie is a natural. The role was played by Harry Rosenthal, who was a piano player at Joe Smallwood's restaurant at Garden City, where Ring had heard him play many times. Ring chose Rosenthal for the part, and insisted upon him over the objections of nearly everyone else concerned. Rosenthal was not an actor, as Ring knew. Ring only wanted him to act himself, and he adapted the part for him. Ring's judgment turned out to be exactly right. Rosenthal was virtually perfect in the part—the only one he ever played.

In spite of the arduous labor of rewriting and the discouraging failure in Atlantic City, Ring thoroughly enjoyed working on the show and got a deep satisfaction from having finally achieved an unqualified success in the theater. Taciturn and sophisticated as he seemed, he was still stage-struck enough to feel a boyish delight at seeing his name on the marquee, he liked to hang around backstage at the Broadhurst, where the play was running, and he was especially pleased to hear that someone had gone to see the show more than once. He entered into it with all his enthusiasm, writing some spoofing program notes for "Who's Who in the Cast": "Linda Watkins won instant recognition from the critics by her portrayal of Ibsen in the play of that name"; "Norman Foster, who portrays the role of Fred Stevens, is well qualified to act the part of a song writer, as he is the stepfather of Stephen Foster, who turned out such smash hits as 'Swanee River,' 'Celeste Alda' and 'Old Black Jolson.' Norman (as you begin to call him after a while) is married to Claudette (Peaches) Colbert, who cannot be with us but sends regards"; and "Florence D. Rice is the daughter of Grantland Rice, the taxidermist. Miss Rice's parents have no idea she is on the stage and every time she leaves the house to go to the theater she tells them she has to run down to the draper's to buy a stamp," etc.

The show, produced by Sam H. Harris, opened in New York on October 9, 1929, and ran for two hundred seventy-three perform-ances. A second company went on the road with great success. All the critics liked it, and the popular response was immediate. It was included in Burns Mantle's yearbook, *The Best Plays of 1929–30*, and published by Scribner's with one of Ring's irrelevant introduc-tions which dealt exclusively with traffic statistics: "In the year 1898 there were 201 fatal street accidents in the city of New York. Of these, eighty-eight were caused by horse vehicles and 113 by street-cars. In the latter total are included people who died of old age while waiting for cars that were not labelled 'Car Barn Only.'" This time the introduction was not intended as an apology, or as self-deprecation. Ring had had the kind of success he wanted, and he was having fun with it.

But he did not enjoy it long. He wrote to Fitzgerald:

> New York City
> February 27, 1930
>
> . . . "June Moon," the play I wrote with George Kaufman, will run about six more weeks here, I think; then will play Philadelphia, Boston and perhaps Pittsburgh before folding up. It is still doing all right, but nearly everyone will have seen it in a little while. We have no kick coming; it opened in New York on Oct. 9 and, until the first of the year, broke all records for a non-musical show. We put out a second company, which played a week in Cleveland and is now in Cincinnati, after ten weeks in Chicago, where it did well. It will play a week each in Milwaukee, St. Louis and Kansas City and then go to the Coast. The notices here and in the other towns were grand. George and I worked on the play nearly all last spring and summer and when the New York opening was over, I went on a bat that lasted nearly three months and haven't been able to work since, so it's a good thing the play paid dividends. I wish you had had George to collaborate with you on, or to direct, "The Vege-

table," and not Sam Forrest, who, to me, is one of the mysteries of show business. I'd like to hear first hand what your plans are and news of a personal nature; and I'm anxious to know all there is to tell about the premiere danseuse and her daughter, to both of whom I send love.

Ring was gratified by the fortunes of his play, but did not seem able to enjoy them. He permitted himself no saving touch of vain-glory. Once, after the show was well established, he called Kaufman from a speak-easy where he had been drinking for some time and asked him if he thought it would hurt the run of the play if he, Ring, were to commit suicide. It was not the first time he had thought of it; the idea came to him when he had been drinking and was plunged in melancholy. The success of his short stories had done nothing to mitigate his despair and the skepticism he felt about the value of his work; now, not even the kind of success he had wanted most could help him. By this time he knew that drinking would damage him seriously; yet he still had the same need to escape from despair, from fatigue, and insomnia. As always, it only made him hate himself worse. After the bat came illness; in the hospital remorse set in and he struggled to put himself back into working condition.

"Not to keep on going"—that seemed, after he had recovered, to be the worst mistake anyone could make, he wrote to a friend long after this, when the prospect of another play had roused him to an-other tremendous effort.

Ellis is in East Hampton and I am staying in town for two reasons —one is a long-delayed session with the dentist, which will last at least two weeks, and the other to plan with George the first two acts of our next collaboration. I am fortunate, I guess, to be one of the chosen to work with him. There are flocks of more experienced playwrights seeking his partnership and the only thing that wins consideration for me is the fact that he keeps promises and as soon as we had finished "June Moon," we agreed to do another one on a subject I had in mind—as soon as I got around to it, which has been a long, long time. I only hope I can stay well enough to work. If I can, I promise you and the rest of the world one thing: that never again will I take a vacation when I am through with a job. I think it is the biggest mistake a person can make—not to keep on going. I never felt better in my life than when I was working twenty hours a day, trying to get "June Moon" into shape, and never felt worse than afterwards, when it was in shape and I treated myself to a "layoff," which was mostly spent in the lovely atmosphere of hospitals.

In spite of the reaction that set in after his work was finished *June Moon* was Ring's one wholly satisfactory venture in the theater, and he enjoyed working on it. He had found a collaborator whom he could trust and to whom he felt grateful; Kaufman had shown an equal respect for Ring's material. The second play he looked forward to working on with Kaufman—the subject was, ironically, alcoholism—was never to be completed.

Ring's nonsense plays, sometimes called Dada plays, belong with his theatrical work, since some of them were written to be performed; and it was only after they had been successfully presented that they appeared in print. After that Ring wrote others of the same genre which could not possibly be acted because they consist largely of unexecutable stage directions. All of them make wonderful reading.

The first one to be produced was *The Tridget of Greva,* which was presented in a revue, *The Forty-Niners,* given by a group of actors and writers who were more or less associated with the Algonquin Round Table. It was an amateur production by professionals, the main purpose of it was to entertain the entrepreneurs, and it was a kind of gesture of defiance at the commercial theater. A previous revue, *Nosirree!* (the title was a take-off on *Chauve Souris,* not a very good one), had been a riotous success in the sense that everyone had fun. It turned up some fine original talent, too. The second, for which everyone lay in wait with a critical eye, was not greeted with the same enthusiasm, except for *The Tridget.* No one had seen anything quite like it before, and it immediately became legendary. It was never published, but Ring used some of its more notable passages in subsequent nonsense plays written for publication.

It is impossible to say that *The Tridget* is "about" anything. Three men are sitting in rowboats pretending to fish, talking in *non sequiturs.* They give the curious impression of being about to make sense, but when you stop to think of what they are saying, you find yourself looking into bottomless absurdity. It has a little more logic, of an ordinary kind, than the later plays: every once in a while the answers have some relation to the questions; then again, they don't.

BARHOOTER: . . . *What was your mother's name before she was married?*
CORBY: *I didn't know her then.*

LAFFLER: *Do they allow people to fish at the aquarium?*

(Barhooter and Corby ignore him.)

BARHOOTER (to Corby): *Well, then, what was your mother's first name?*

CORBY: *I don't know.*

BARHOOTER: *Do you mean to say that you don't know your mother's first name?*

CORBY: *Why, no. I always called her mother.*

BARHOOTER: *But your father must have called her something.*

CORBY: *I should say he did! Everything he could think of!*

(Laffler's and Barhooter's fishlines become tangled. Barhooter gets out of his boat, untangles the lines and resumes his place in the boat.)

BARHOOTER: *I wanted to ask you something about your sister, too.*

CORBY: *What about her?*

BARHOOTER: *What's the matter with her?*

CORBY: *Who?*

BARHOOTER: *Your sister.*

CORBY: *I'm not married.*

(After a pause, Barhooter and Corby both laugh.)

BARHOOTER (to Laffler): *Do you know what we were laughing at?*

LAFFLER: *No. What?*

BARHOOTER: *I thought you might know.*

CORBY (to Barhooter): *Which way is the wind from?*

BARHOOTER (moistens his finger and holds it up): *It's from off-stage.*

Just when you are expecting sheer nonsense, something logical, or at least explicable, comes out. You never know where you are. This compels the closest attention; part of the joke is on you, because you have rather seriously been looking for something.

Dinner Bridge, the most subtly disconcerting of these plays, was written for a Dutch Treat show in 1927, and Edmund Wilson, then literary editor of the *New Republic,* published it in that magazine, to the dismay of H. L. Mencken, who would have liked to have it for the *American Mercury.* It was performed by a cast composed of Will Irwin, Henry Clapp Smith, Robert Benchley, Percy Hammond, Rea Irvin, Percy Waxman, George S. Kaufman, and Robert Sherwood. The idea is simple: some laborers are being served dinner out of their lunch pails on the Fifty-ninth Street bridge, which is always being torn up for repairs. The principals speak "correct Crowninshield dinner English," except when they lapse into outrageous dialect. The dialogue, far from being illogical, is relentlessly literal:

LLANUZA: Why do you always have to keep repairing it?
CROWLEY: What do you mean, what's the matter?
LLANUZA: Why do they always have to keep repairing it?
AMOROSI: Perhaps Mr. Crowley has the repairian rights.
TAYLOR (*guffawing and slapping Hansen or Chamales on the back*): What did I tell you?
LLANUZA (*in dialect*): But down in Mexico, where I come from, they don't keep repairing the same bridge.
AMOROSI (*to Llanuza*): If you'll pardon a newcomer. Mr. ——, I don't believe I got your name.
LLANUZA: Llanuza.
AMOROSI: If you'll pardon a newcomer, Mr. Keeler, I want to say that if the United States isn't good enough for you, I'd be glad to start a subscription to send you back to where you came from.
LLANUZA: I was beginning to like you, Mr. Amorosi.
AMOROSI: You get that right out of your mind, Mr. Barrows. I'm married; been married twice. My first wife died.
HANSEN: How long were you married to her?
AMOROSI: Right up to the time she died.

There is a waiter who asks questions then exits hurriedly before he can hear the answers; Taylor imitates bird calls; Amorosi mimics public buildings. When the whistle blows, indicating that the dinner hour is over, Crowley rises and says, "Shall we join the ladies?"

"I Gaspiri (The Upholsterers)" was first published in the *Chicago Literary Times*, of which Ben Hecht was editor, and then in the *Transatlantic Review* in Paris, in 1924, with a note by the editor commending it to the attention of André Breton, a leading surrealist, hinting that Ring was doing what the Dadaists and the surrealists were trying to do, and doing it much better. It is a drama in three acts, adapted from the Bukovinian, and the characters are:

> IAN OBRI, a blotter salesman
> JOHAN WASPER, his wife
> GRETA, their daughter
> HERBERT SWOPE, a nonentity
> FFENA, their daughter, later their wife
> EGSO, a pencil guster
> TONO, a typical wastebasket

285

ACT I

A *public street in a bathroom. A man named Tupper has evidently just taken a bath. A man named Brindle is now taking a bath. A man named Newburn comes out of the faucet which has been left running. He exits through the exhaust. Two strangers to each other meet on the bath mat.*

FIRST STRANGER: Where was you born?

SECOND STRANGER: Out of wedlock.

FIRST STRANGER: That's a might pretty country around there.

SECOND STRANGER: Are you married?

FIRST STRANGER: I don't know. There's a woman living with me, but I can't place her.

(*Three outsiders named Klein go across the stage three times. They think they are in a public library. A woman's cough is heard offstage left.*)

A NEW CHARACTER: Who is that cough?

TWO MOORS: That is my cousin. She died a little while ago in a haphazard way.

A GREEK: And what a woman she was!

(*The curtain is lowered for seven days to denote the lapse of a week.*)

In *Clemo Uti—The Water Lilies*, the curtain rises on "the outskirts of a Parchesi Board. People are wondering what has become of the discs. They quit wondering and sit up and sing the following song:

CHORUS: What has become of the discs?
 What has become of the discs?
 We took them at our own risks,
 But what has become of the discs?

(*Wama enters from an exclusive waffle parlor. She exits as if she had had waffles.*)

ACTS II & III

(*These two acts were thrown out because nothing seemed to happen.*)

Performances of Ring's sketches at the Dutch Treat or at Lambs club shows reduced audiences to a state of almost insane enthusiasm. Robert Benchley, whose own kind of nonsense comes close to Ring's, was a raving admirer. Once Ellis attended a function at which one of Ring's skits was presented. Benchley did not know who she was, but he fell into conversation with her and praised

Ring's play almost breathlessly. Ellis said, "Do you really? I think it's terrible." Benchley coolly left her, but soon came sliding back across the floor, ending up on his knees before Ellis, saying, "Forgive me! I didn't know!"

Edmund Wilson compared the work of Benchley and Lardner to Dada: "Their non sequiturs and practical jokes seem the product of similar situations: in France the collapse of Europe and the intellectual chaos that accompanied it; in America what is perhaps another aspect of a general crisis: the bewildering confusion of the modern city and the enfeeblement of the faculty of attention. It relieves some anxiety to laugh at pointlessness." Other critics thought the plays were parodies of expressionism, and of the Moscow Art Theater. Gilbert Seldes preferred to believe that they were an "attack of sheer lunacy," and that is what they are essentially. *Cora, or Fun at a Spa,* is subtitled *An Expressionist Drama of Love, Death and Sex;* and *Quadroon—A Play in Four Pelts Which May All Be Attended in One Day or Missed in a Group*—is a take-off on O'Neill's *Mourning Becomes Electra* and consists largely of luncheon and dinner menus for the intermissions. But Ring had been writing this kind of wonderful nonsense long before he had heard of Dada or expressionism. Unlike Dada, whose solemn purpose was to destroy the meanings and relationships of traditional art, to enthrone chaos as the true reality, Ring's nonsense had no purpose at all, and it is only incidentally a parody of the drama.

It derives—if it matters at all—from Ring's own uninhibited flair for free association; some of the dialogue sounds like the wild conversations of the Lardner family, who had a gift for *non sequitur* and loved bad jokes and outrageous puns. Like everything Ring wrote afterward, it is foreshadowed in the columns of the "Wake," for which he wrote many little plays that bordered on nonsense. Those dialogues in Pullman smokers, the records of the conversations of relentless bores, all lead up to these fantasies. The long, pointless stories about Pat and Mike and their Lithuanian nurse which Ring used to tell to Joe Farrell in the Chicago Press Club, the stories about men coming out of bathtub faucets, about "queels" and "Lornas," all of these come from the same source as the plays. But what is compelling about them is not merely that they are hilariously silly and apparently without any anchor in reality: it is that they are familiar and very real indeed. They come directly out of Ring's own superior understanding of the way people talk and think. The truth is that people don't listen to what other people say, and so they make irrelevant answers; they are always trying to tell something that nobody wants to hear, so they interrupt desperately and repeat; they tell labored and pointless stories, half-remembered and misunderstood jokes, trying to recall what was funny about them; their minds wander and they can't keep on one subject for long ("the enfeeblement of the faculty of attention," Wilson noted). There is a good deal of acute realistic observation behind these plays. All the time we thought people were making sense, but this is really what they sounded like.

Ring wrote to Mrs. Rice one of those idle, charming letters about nothing of importance:

Well, what I started to say was that on Friday afternoon, I had to go way downtown to buy an algebra book for John, and I came uptown on a bus. I sat on the roof and a lady sat down beside me. Her costume looked as if it had been cut out of a wash cloth. She said: "What time is it?" I said: "It is half past three." She said: "Oh, I thought you were a Mexican."

Conversations like that can never be explained.

Tomorrow I am going under the knife. The doctor's name is Trembley, and so am I.

This is not nonsense; it's something that happened on a Friday afternoon when Ring was out buying an algebra book. His canny ear was always picking up something like this; he did not have to look far for nonsense. It looks easy; a good many humorists have tried it quite successfully—Benchley, Donald Ogden Stewart, Stephen Leacock, S. J. Perelman—and all differently; there is nothing in the world quite like Ring's own brand of nonsense. But it takes a fine and subtle talent. There is something ineffably right about the irrelevancies, the exaggerated jokes, the horrible puns.

Some of Ring's unproduced and unpublished sketches written for the commercial theater resemble these nonsense plays. But of the pure genre there are only eight or nine perfect examples; he did not write too many; they remain inimitable rarities, the essence of his humor, a commentary on nothing except the absurdity of everything.

Ring was not especially attracted by the movies; he did not think very highly of them, as his burlesques of movie scenarios and his sardonic comments on his visits to Hollywood show. The only film on which he really worked was disappointing.

He wrote to Fitzgerald in November 1925:

Please don't hold it against me, but I have just written a pictures scenario for Tom Meighan. The plot, which has to do with baseball *and Florida real estate, was originated by one of the Famous Players' regular men, but they wanted me to elaborate it or something. I didn't want to, so when they said $5,000, I said it wouldn't be worth my while, but I might do it for $7,500. They said that was fine. So I did it, taking four days to the job. They begin making the picture next week. After it's done, I am to write the titles. I suppose some would consider this easy money, but it was a damn bore and unless the picture is very good, I'll be sorry I did it. The reason I said $7,500 is that Tom gets that amount per week, work or no work, and I thought perhaps I could do it in a week and be as well paid as he.*

The following February he cut short a Florida vacation to go back to New York to write the titles: "The picture, I believe," he wrote, "will be the worst ever seen on land or sea, and the titles are excruciatingly terrible." And in a third letter to Fitzgerald he wrote: "When the picture came out, it was a complete surprise to me and one of the worst pictures I ever saw. But it seems to be going all right and I am told that it compares very favorably with most of Tom's recent releases."

The picture was *The New Klondike*. He wrote in his weekly column, ". . . 286 of the 288 titles I had wrote had been throwed into somebody's ash bbl. and they was a couple of baseball incidence in it that would make a ball player wonder if the author had fell out of a toy balloon in his infancy."

Ring was a little ashamed of this enterprise, or he would not have written so apologetically to Fitzgerald three times about it. No doubt he got into it in the first place because Tom Meighan was a friend. He also liked the idea of earning as much as a top film star, at least for one week. When he was approached next to do a script, he made the price high.

A couple of months ago [he wrote to Fitzgerald, October 13, 1926] the Metro-Goldwyn people asked me to write a baseball picture for Karl Dane, the man who made such a hit as "Slim," one of the doughboys in "The Big Parade." We talked matters over several times and finally the man asked me how much I would want. I told him I didn't know what authors were getting. He said, "Well, we are giving Johnny Weaver $7,500 and Marc Connelly the same," so he asked me again what I wanted and I said $40,000 and he threw up his hands and exclaimed, "Excuse me, Mr. Lardner, for wasting your valuable time!"

A few years later he had an idea for a comedy for Harold Lloyd, but nothing ever came of it. Some of his stories were made into films, but he did no more original scripts. He was far more interested in songs and the legitimate stage.

Long after columns and short stories had become wearisome, Ring kept on writing songs and plays. He was a good musician and a highly professional lyric writer, but he never found the formula for a hit song, although in some of his more derivative efforts he was obviously looking for one. Fashions in popular songs had changed since he first became enamored of them, and the success of songs depended on factors he could not calculate. He lacked the vulgarity that seems necessary to so much success in this field. All he had was taste, musicianship, and skill, and they were not at a premium. Scarcely half a dozen popular composers with all these qualities gained any fame or popularity in Ring's time. If he dramatized himself as a thwarted composer, he had a clear title to the role.

In the commercial theater nothing Ring achieved was an expansion of the work he had already done as a short-story writer; his successful pieces were only good translations of his individual style. The possibility remains that had he lived to write more plays he might have extended the scope of his vision to subjects he had not touched before; it is suggested by the fact that his next play dealt with far more complex personal relationships than he had ever written about in his stories. But that came too late, after he no longer had the strength to sustain the enthusiasm he had felt for the theater.

He was stage-struck and susceptible to the world of make-believe and of entertainment; that was his real interest, and he never ceased to find pleasure in it. But everything he wrote about that world shows that he had become just as disillusioned about it as about everything else. It was not that his frustrations had soured him; he was without envy of any kind. He went out of his way to praise good playwrights, producers, and actors; and he had a forthright admiration for many composers, Jerome Kern, Youmans, Richard Rodgers, and Gershwin. He had reservations about Gershwin; he liked his early popular songs but thought that with *Rhapsody in Blue* he had gone high-brow. Sophisticated as Ring was, he had at bottom a naïve distrust of highbrows, quite apart from his hatred of artistic or any other kind of pretentiousness. In a story, "Rhythm," he wrote about a popular composer who was nearly ruined by being taken seriously by intellectuals. It is amusing if not entirely convincing; and it is a clue to his own attitude about writers of any kind. If that attitude served as a defense, it was also genuine enough. For himself he chose to remain a popular writer in whatever field he worked.

It is significant that the most important development in music in Ring's time—jazz—seemed to have very little influence on his songs. This was not because jazz was taken up by intellectuals; it was rather that he did not have much taste for it. Musically he was, according to the taste of the times, a little out of date.

For a man who had cultivated a habit of silence and isolation from his youth Ring was strangely gregarious, although not always exactly sociable. He may have found in the theater what he had once found in a baseball clubhouse or a Pullman car, a feeling of companionship that did not violate his sense of privacy. The business of joining with other people who shared his interests and tastes in producing a show was more rewarding than the solitary task of grinding out articles and stories. Disenchanted as he was by the world of entertainment, he certainly tried hard to stay in it.

But he was not taken in by that rather inclusive and blowsy entity known as "show business." Show business, which comprises Tin Pan Alley, comes off badly in his stories; it is all vanity, sharp practice, unscrupulous ambition, mediocrity. He was much loved by theatrical people, and there were many he loved and admired for their talent and integrity. Others he regarded with the same aloof, aristocratic suspicion as he might have cast upon gamblers in a ball park. Partly from observation, partly from a native prudery, he thought that the theater was a little shady, and he was dubious about its morals. All the show girls in his stories are women of easy virtue, always a little underdressed. He really did not believe that the theater was a proper place for a nice young girl; when it was once suggested that a favorite niece of his go on the stage, he was firmly opposed to it. There was doubtless some basis for his misgivings, but they seem also to be a hangover from his late-Victorian upbringing. Ring always remained untouched by the revolution in sexual morality that took place in the early decades of the century. The theater was probably a good place to observe this phenomenon, but it never relaxed Ring's views. Solemn, dignified, remote, he moved about the theater intent on his business. He was the kind of man Follies girls respected.

CHAPTER EIGHT

In 1926 Ring's weekly column appeared in more than a hundred fifty newspapers; he was certainly among the ten most famous men in the United States, and easily the funniest. His clipping-service bills were enormous; his opinion on every subject was solicited; nothing he did or said passed unnoticed; he had become a genuine "notoriety," lionized and adulated to the point of nausea. His imitators were thriving. *The Love Nest* had received a just and laudatory acclaim from the best critics, and now Ring had the admiration of every level of a society that seemed impervious to the scorn he had expressed for it, either in his satirical short stories or in the deceptive character of the genial wise boob whose peculiar power lay in his ability to make every reader feel as though he himself might have just said what Ring was saying.

He was tired of it and he was almost through with journalism, as he told Fitzgerald in a letter that has a good many overtones of sheer ennui in it:

October 13, 1926

Fitzgeralds one and all—
I have said to myself a hundred times, "Ring, you just must write to those sweet Fitzgeralds," and then I have added (to myself, mind you), "Better wait, perhaps, until there is something to write about." But the days come and the days go and nothing happens—nothing may ever happen. Best not delay any longer.
Very, very glad to hear you are returning to God's Country and

the Woman. Don't you dare live anywhere but Great Neck, but if I were you, I'd rent awhile before I thought of buying. If you want me to, I will be on the look-out for a suitable furnished house.

Ellis had two babies this summer. They are both girls, giving us two girls and four boys, an ideal combination, we think.

May Preston reports that she saw you (not you, Zelda) on your way to the hospital, in Paris, and that you were carrying a bouquet of corsets to give your wife.

I enclose a copy (nearly complete) of the story I wrote about the "fight" in Philadelphia. Heywood Broun refused, at the last moment, to cover it and as a favor to Herbert [Swope, of the World], I said I would do it. We had terrible wire trouble on account of the rain and only about half my story got into the World. It broke off (the story) in such a manner that people must have said to themselves that I was very drunk. It made me so mad that I am going to quit newspapers as soon as the last of my present contracts expires, which will be in six months. After that I am going to try to work half as hard and make the same amount of money, a feat which I believe can be done. . . .

You ought to meet this guy Tunney. We had lunch with him a few weeks before the fight and among a great many other things, he said he thought the New York State boxing commission was "imbecilic" and that he hoped Dempsey would not think his (Tunney's) experience in pictures had "cosmeticized" him.

We have just had a world's series that neither club (St. Louis vs. the Yankees) had any right to be in, let alone win. . . .

I have been on the wagon since early in July, when Ellis' mother died. Before that I had a spree that broke a few records for longevity and dullness.

It might not be very lively for you, but why not come and stay with us a while before or after you go to Montgomery.

Keep me posted on your plans and accept the undying love of the madam and

        I.

Journalism, a championship fight, a World's Series, a long spree—all of them seem to have lost their enchantment for Ring; he was never again to regain his pleasure in them. The Dempsey-Tunney fight was a particular disappointment to him. After the Black Sox scandal of 1919, Ring had two enthusiasms left in sports—Dempsey and Notre Dame. He felt that Dempsey had let his fans down; for a long time afterward he never missed a chance to make a scathing remark about the fight. After Dempsey no other fighter had any appeal for Ring. Tunney was "about as popular as my plays," he said. Everything about the fight was wrong, including the wire trouble which had cut off his story. Grantland Rice also covered the fight.

Due to the rain [he wrote in his autobiography] it was impossible to use a typewriter. I dictated the description of the fight to my wire man. With me that night were Lardner and Benny Leonard, the lightweight champ from 1917–1925. Back at the hotel a raging sore throat and a hangover had me in bad shape.

"Take a slug of bourbon and lie down," said Lardner. "I'll file your overnight." Leonard, a Dempsey man, told Lardner that he suspected the fix had been in for Tunney to win. The story appearing next day under my byline blistered the hide off both Tunney and Dempsey. Neither spoke to me for several months. I couldn't blame either, but I couldn't open my mouth. I had a ghost.

As for journalism Ring stuck to his intention to quit his newspaper job, and he wrote his last weekly column in March 1927. The wire trouble the night of the fight was not the real reason. For a long time it had been a grind, and to judge from the columns of the last year, Ring was running low on ideas, repeating old anecdotes he had used as far back as the St. Louis *Sporting News* days. He had turned from commentary to reminiscence, and to spinning out tenuous trifles that were sometimes funny but often labored and hardly concealed Ring's boredom with his weekly stint. And he had got tired of writing in the same old character.

From July 1926 to the following January Ring filled the column with the chapters of a mock autobiography, which was later published in book form as *The Story of a Wonder Man*. The foreword is again by Sarah E. Spooldripper, who had introduced *The Love Nest:*

The publication of this autobiography is entirely without the late Master's sanction. He wrote it as a pastime and burnt up each chapter as soon as it was written; the salvaging was accomplished by ghouls who haunted the Lardners' ash bbl. during my whole tenure of office as night nurse to their dromedary.

Some of the copy was so badly charred as to be illegible. The ghouls took the liberty of filling in these hiatuses with "stuff" of their own, which can readily be distinguished from the Master's as it is not nearly so good. Readers and critics are therefore asked to bear in mind that those portions of the book which they find entertaining are the work of the Master himself; those which bore them or sound forced are interpolations by milksops.

Another request which I know the Master would have wished me to make is that neither reader nor critic read the book through at one sitting (Cries of "Fat chance!" and "Hold 'em, Stanford!") It was written a chapter at a time and should be perused the same way with, say, a rest of from seven weeks to two months between chapters. It might even be advisable to read one chapter and then take the book back to the exchange desk, saying you had made a mistake.

The Story of a Wonder Man is a wild burlesque on autobiography in general, on the idea that anyone is important—or egotistical—enough to write an autobiography; but since it is a work of untrammeled improvisation, it manages to be a burlesque on every topic which the process of free association can bring within the compass of a limited space. As it appeared chapter by chapter, it observed only a perfunctory chronological sequence. Otherwise Ring's fancy ranged hilariously from one freak juxtaposition to another, usually with an atrocious pun in view. He was writing in character, but this time a different one; he was the brash, precocious wonder boy, the compulsive joker playing for every laugh.

The first chapter tells of the Wonder Man's birth in Niles, Michigan, during what was later set aside as "Have a Baby Week," and shortly thereafter, "little Ring, au naturel, was bathed in pure alcohol, the guests afterwards dipping pipes into the tub and blowing soap bubbles." For a few paragraphs the story lapses into the vernacular so pointlessly that one suspects that Ring had no particular plan in mind when he started the series. "This autobiography started out to follow the style of Edward Bok and Henry (Peaches) Adams and refer to the hero in the third person, but the idea has been abandoned because in my case it would be confusing on account of two of my interminable brothers also being named Ring. . . ." The boy grows up and is abandoned in Seattle, whence his family had taken him for the Inaugural Ball, at which he danced with Dolly Madison. "Before the second encore, I was calling my partner 'Dolly' and she was calling me 'Lard' and that night marked the beginning of a friendship that soon ripened into apathy.

"Inside of seven years I was in San Francisco, playing a cornet, evenings, at Tait's on the beach, and in the daytime working in the park as a squirrel-tender. In those days there were no benches in the parks and a squirrel-tender's job was to keep the squirrels out of trees so the people would have some place to sit. . . . Outwitting them and keeping them on terra firma developed both my brains and speed and ten years later, when my three runs of the length of the field won Yale a championship game, 4 to 2, an Associated Press commentator said, 'Harvard was beaten in the parks of San Francisco.'"

The Wonder Man meets a Professor Ashley Snoot in a Pullman car. "'All right, Prof.,' I said. 'What do you think of biology?' 'It's a wonderful idea,' replied Prof. Snoot, 'but how can they enforce it? We have had it now since January 1920, and they tell me there is more drunkenness than ever; why, I understand that women, who never drank before, are now insisting on a cocktail before dinner.'"

He goes to medical school and passes his final examination:

"Q: Where is your appendix located? A: In Washington Park Hospital, Chicago, unless the cleaning woman has been in.

"Q: How does the stomach act when you eat regularly? A: Surprised.

"Q: What has been your hospital experience? A: Terrible.

"Q: What would you do in a case of an epileptic fit? A: Call a doctor.

"Q: What would you do if somebody had a stroke? A: See that they counted it."

Recounting his experiences in Polyandry Hospital, the Wonder Man says:

"Dr. Pine explained that Dr. Gasp had been drinking heavenly. (Editor's note: The author evidently means 'heavily.' Author's note: The editor is evidently a f--l.)

"The two doctors made me strip to my nightgown and went all over me with a horoscope. Their diagnosis was chronic alfalfa and they said I must be rushed to a hospital and tattooed.

"On the third day of October, 1896, I was ridden on a rail to the Polyandry Hospital and taken in charge by Dr. Barnacle, who immediately put me under the ether. The janitor found me there two days later and lifted me onto a bed. . . .

"My room which I shared with the Marx brothers, the Dolly sisters and the Fairbanks twins, was a veritable paunch of flowers. . . .

"We now come to my first marriage. The girl was a born Laplander and landed on my lap in the course of a quiet week-end party at the Curley estate on Long Island. I suppose I was fascinated by the music of her broken English as much as by the blonde perfection of 212 pounds of bubbling youth.

" 'Listen, hon',' were her first words: 'I'se mahty thusty. Is you-all goin' to fetch me some mo' dat dere gin?' . . .

"Now followed preparations for the wedding . . . I wanted the ceremony held at Old Trinity; Hugga said it was below her station—she usually got off at Columbus Circle."

Almost any selection of quotations would serve to illustrate the point of Sarah E. Spooldripper's foreword: the chapters are much better a week apart than all together; parts of the book are the Master's own, and others are "interpolations by milksops." Ring knew that it was uneven and did not seem to care. Sometimes his playful inanities, his elaborate build-ups to tottering anticlimaxes are very funny; often they are flat. Many of its allusions are not only too topical but too parochial to have outlasted the decade. Gags about Texas Guinan and Queen Marie of Rumania no longer have much humorous connotation; and the innumerable private jokes mean nothing to the reader. Ring indulged himself in easy jokes and laboriously made up bad ones on purpose, and mixed them all together. But there is one entirely consistent note throughout the book—one of utterly relentless burlesque carried to the point of exasperation; and the exasperation is not so much the reader's as Ring's own. He was perpetrating a joke on himself as a humorist, on the very idea of humor, and on the audience that thought it was funny. He seemed to be saying, "If this is what people think is funny, let them have it." He could give them all the stale old vaudeville routines, the tortured puns and Joe Millers they wanted without even trying. And so he parodied them all, not with equal success, and when he did bring it off, it was simply the triumph of style.

In a few passages Ring showed a controlled and deadly irony: "Not far from us, on Cow Lane, lived Ed Streeter, author of the 'Dere Mable' letters, for which I received many congratulations." And he was not merely being funny in his account of the Dempsey-Tunney fight:

It was for the purpose of adding to this [autograph] collection that I visited Philadelphia in September of 1926; notables from all over the country were there at the time to witness the great heavyweight championship prize-fight between Jack Dempsey and Gene Tunney, but it developed that very few of them could write their names. The fight went ten rounds and the judges gave the decision to Mr. Tunney and a lot of us boys thought it would have been a horse on Mr. Dempsey if they hadn't. It was reported after the fight

298

that the winner was considering an offer from C. C. Pyle to join the ranks of the professionals.

This was my first trip to the City of Brotherly Love since Gen. Smedley Butler was sent there to clean it up. The result of his work was a revelation. Unless you had brought your own liquor, you could no longer get a drink in Philadelphia without asking for it.

Philadelphia at that time had a boxing commission something like New York's (No offense meant). The commission, which was appointed by the Governor, named the judges that decided the outcome of fights. On this occasion Gov. Pinchot said he would like to see Mr. Tunney win and it may have been to save the commission and the judges from embarrassment that Mr. Dempsey acted as if the whole party was a big surprise to him. He seemed to have at last mastered the boxing style of Farmer Lodge who helped him prepare for his fight with Firpo some years before.

A man sitting right back of me kept insisting that Mr. Dempsey ought to be disqualified for violating Pennsylvania's boxing code, which barred the rabbit punch. I was not familiar with the rules, but Jack certainly punched like a rabbit.

Ring was writing a savage satire on the success story—his own in particular. He mimics the unctuous false modesty of many such memoirs, the egotistical complacency of Edward Bok, the revolting sentimentality of nostalgic recollections. He pictures the Wonder Man as a tireless exhibitionist, aggressive, conceited, and hollow. In the almost repellent hospital jokes he reflects his own squeamishness and his own humiliation. Except for a few of the sublime irrelevancies that recall the nonsense plays the book is rasping and frenetic. It is not that he let himself go, or that his flights of fancy got out of control. It is all perfectly deliberate. It shows not only strain but contempt for himself and for the audience at which this barrage of mixed comedy was hurled.

Its publication in book form added nothing to his literary stature, which did not concern him, and detracted nothing from his reputation as a humorist. "Mr. Lardner's knack of oblique humor," said the New York *Times Book Review*, "was never better revealed than in this burlesque autobiography. Its freshness has not suffered through weekly exposure in a Sunday supplement and if there be criticism to make it is of a certain laziness and repetitiousness on the part of this talented humorist. For Mr. Lardner is a humorist, not a satirist, nor even an ironist: his humor is harsh, wry and at times savage, but it is diffuse. It lacks the sense of morality which animates satire, the Olympian passivity which underlies irony. . . . But Mr. Lardner's humor, if general, is absolutely natural. It is his reaction to life."

But it was a reaction that displayed little amusement. The nonsense plays, which have something in common with the lunatic humor of *Wonder Man*, show some relish of the absurdity of life; here there is none. From this point on there is a marked change in Ring's work: his satire lost its edge in sentimentality on one hand, and mere asperity on the other. There was no change in the scope or direction of his work; but there was a slackening of creative power.

The despondency and boredom reflected in Ring's letter to Fitzgerald were only new depths of a despair he had felt for many years. A good many factors contributed to it. As far as his work was concerned he was now suffering the penalty of having been precocious. He had come early to the enjoyment of his pleasures and his talents and his social life; they had palled on him too soon. He was, like so many puritanical idealists, a perfectionist. He had been praised and rewarded for achievements which he himself did not think good enough, and so he was skeptical of his success. Since his work was never good enough to suit him, he found less and less satisfaction in it, and he had less and less respect for those who thought that his second-best was first-rate.

But now another factor set in. In the summer of 1926 he had gone to the hospital for a minor operation, and a routine checkup revealed that he had tuberculosis. It was not a severe case; but at that time tuberculosis was a good deal more serious even in its early stages than it is now. His health had never been sound. He had always lived up to the limit of his energy and there was nothing in reserve. He had never had a protracted serious illness, but he had had many minor ones; and an almost total disregard for his own health had certainly weakened his resistance. The diagnosis alarmed him; but only to increase his despair.

The immediate effect of the diagnosis should have been to force him to take care of his health; but he never resigned himself entirely to inactivity or obeyed the doctors' orders sensibly. In April he had gone on the wagon, theoretically for a year, but it was not until July that he got on it to stay for any length of time. The first indication he gave of curtailing his activities was his decision to quit his newspaper job. With characteristic reticence, Ring did not mention his illness to Fitzgerald; he kept his own counsel and covered his tracks. He was a fastidious man and the idea of having an infectious disease disturbed him. His early habit of self-deprecation grew in the years

300

of his illness to self-loathing. It is probable that his first case of tuberculosis was arrested. In the fall of 1926 he was well enough to go with Ellis and John to Andover, where John was entering school, and to cover the Dempsey-Tunney fight. But the disease recurred, and during the active phases he withdrew from his personal contacts, preferring to stay in the hospital even at times when he might have been as well off at home. After he knew he had tuberculosis, he saw less of his children. He even stopped shaking hands with them. Ellis and Miss Feldmann maintained an increased vigilance over the health of the boys. Ring was always afraid that his illness would dampen his family's pleasures, and he hated to have anyone think that he was seriously ill.

The following summer, 1927, the family went to Lake Placid with the idea that the air would be beneficial to Ring. But he did not spend much time there. He refused to take care of himself, and, unwilling to burden others with his illness, he would not let anyone else take care of him except when he was compelled to go to the hospital.

It was not merely the discovery of this illness that brought Ring to his mood of hopelessness, although it surely intensified it. He seemed even as a young man to have some foreknowledge of illness or infirmity; possibly because of the lameness of his childhood and his inability to distinguish himself as an athlete he had always identified himself with the sick or handicapped. His obsession with buying life insurance rather than increasing his wealth by investments that would pay off in his own lifetime bespoke some deep fear that he might die before his sons were able to support themselves. Tuberculosis was only one of several diseases he was to suffer, and he bore them with a courage which is amazing because it is evident that for himself, from then on, he expected nothing more than illness and such work as he could manage to do. The work now seemed the justification of an existence which he felt to have no other aim. Once he had made his family's future secure, he had little more purpose in living.

Not all the effects of chronic illness were immediately visible, possibly because Ring took such pains to conceal them. The amount of work he accomplished, his travels, his varied interests, his continuing fame would seem to belie his ill-health. His illnesses were periodic and he made many remarkable recoveries after severe crises. In such intervals he wrote *June Moon,* many magazine articles and short stories, and some humorous pieces that are among his best. Because he needed money, he undertook two journalistic assignments of the kind he had vowed never to do again. He and Ellis continued to travel in the winter; but finally these trips were made for the sake of his health rather than for pleasure. His stays in hospitals became longer and more frequent. He was no longer able to plan his work but was left completely at the mercy of his physical condition.

Ring's weekly column had brought him about $30,000 a year, and the loss of this income was not fully compensated by his increased production of short stories and articles. After *Elmer the Great* failed, he went back to newspaper work for a time.

In 1928, Joseph Moore joined a group of associates to buy the *Morning Telegraph,* a sports paper with emphasis on horse racing. The *Telegraph's* standing among dailies was not high, but it had a name and a local circulation, and it was Moore's idea to build it up into a national sports and theatrical paper by hiring a brilliant staff and adding many special features. Gene Fowler, former editor of *The American,* became managing editor, and assembled a distinguished staff. For a while the paper was spectacularly supplied with big names—Norman Hapgood, the crusading liberal editor, was engaged to write political commentary; James R. Harrison came from the *Times* to write baseball; Ben Hecht covered boxing; Richards Vidmer wrote on tennis; and Westbrook Pegler, whose sports column was syndicated by the Chicago *Tribune* but had no New York outlet, made his first appearance in New York.

The new *Telegraph* expanded its coverage of social and cultural events, hiring Whitney Bolton as drama critic, Charles D. Isaacson as music critic, and Martha Ostenso to write about books. Lois Long of *The New Yorker* wrote society news with a slightly raffish accent on sporting society, and Walter Winchell contributed a Broadway gossip column under the pseudonym "Beau Broadway."

Ring wrote a parody of this, called "Your Broadway, Beau, and You Can Have It." Some of the items were:

"Aleck Hamilton and Aaron Burr have phfft. . . . The Geo. Washingtons (she was Martha Lorber of the Follies) have moved into their Valley Forge snuggery for the Old Man Shiver Days.

"Recommended to diversion seekers: The Florida East Coast R.R. timetable . . . The Lynn Fontannes. . . . A Madison Square Garden phffight decision. . . .

"Danny Deever is halter bound. . . . What subscriber to the N. Y. telephone directory has got a cold? . . ."

Ring joined the staff of the *Telegraph* in December 1928 to write four articles a week at a reported salary of $50,000 a year, which made him for a time one of the highest-paid columnists in America. In spite of his books, plays, songs, and stories Ring had always regarded himself primarily as a newspaperman. But it was not nostalgia for printer's ink that brought him back to column writing, and he had little heart for it. His health was uncertain, his income had dropped, and he had three sons in school. ". . . I am a four-father," he wrote, "i.e., the patriarch of a male quartet of bambini, and three of them are senile enough to go to school, so each year I have to Hand over/ Four grand over/ To Andover."

Ring's advent to the *Telegraph* was heralded by this portentous announcement on the front page, December 1:

We are pleased to announce that Ring Lardner, a great writer who never went literary, has agreed to write for the Morning Telegraph, beginning next Tuesday. He is supposed to be writing around and about the news of the day, but he probably will write about anything. Sometimes he may write about nothing. We can imagine only one general topic more entertaining than Ring Lardner on ANYTHING: that is, Ring Lardner on NOTHING.

We do not expect that he will have our readers in hysterics every day. Our new fellow has a great change of pace. He wrote The Romance of Esther Fester, you may remember, but he also wrote "Golden Wedding," which was quite another story.

But we are not trying to introduce him to his own public.

We only mean to announce that he will be with us.

Company is coming for a long visit, and we are all of a flutter.

Mr. Lardner will conduct his column under the title of "Ring's Side."

This marked the New York debut of Westbrook Pegler, who never went literary either. The stories he referred to are "A Frame-Up" and "The Golden Honeymoon."

On December 4 the *Telegraph* came out with an entirely new format and typography, minus the ads of touts and bookies, which must have been an endearing feature of the old paper, not to mention a source of considerable revenue. Ring's first column appeared on the front page. He explained "in a few well-rounded gutterals" that he was back at work, and reported a conversation between the boss of the paper and his editor. "After all, a newspaper should have some news. Hire an old-fashioned go-getter, the kind that ain't too blaze, to register a scoop* (*A large ladle for dipping liquids; a utensil for bailing boats), the kind that takes pride in scoring a beat**. (**A biennial plant producing a root much used for food, and also for making sugar.) Tell him money is no object." It was not a very brilliant beginning.

The following day he wrote: "Letters and telegrams congratulating this paper and myself on our betrothal poured into the office yesterday and last night in such quantities that it took an armless copy boy nearly a minute to assort and distribute them. To print even half of them would crowd out the weather report, so the public must be content with a few of the more notable ones:

" 'Best wishes stop am sure you will last as long as elmer the great.'

" 'Hear you are writing a new play stop remember you promised me first refusal on your next work stop well comma this is it George M Cohan.' "

The failure of *Elmer the Great* still rankled. Something about the tone of Ring's first columns suggests that he had not undertaken the column with very high hopes. Before Christmas he wrote: "Note to Santa: Please bring this little Lardner boy a wastebasket and don't attach a card saying you hope he will make use of it."

It was a lame joke, and Ring knew it; still the effort he put into the *Telegraph* pieces was enormous. The paper had offices in a building which had once been a car barn, at Eighth Avenue and Fiftieth Street, across from Madison Square Garden. Ring occupied a small room alone, and the management tried to make it as nearly soundproof as possible. Eighth Avenue was being torn up for the building of the subway, and the noise was maddening. Ring, intensely nervous, was abnormally sensitive to noise. But he sat in his small office nearly all day to write a column which often was little more than five hundred words. A good deal of copy did go into the wastebasket.

He was free to choose his own subjects, and he contributed parodies of fellow columnists and burlesque sports stories. It was customary for sports writers to choose an All-American team, and Ring obliged:

VICTIM OF POISONED LIQUOR

Herman Balch, who has chosen this department's All-American football team for 1928, is a patient at Bellevue Hospital whither he was rushed last Thursday to recover from the effects of drinking a pint of milk, which he had mistaken for Lon Chaney. Mr. Balch's selections and his comments on same were obtained as soon as he was put to bed and while he was still in convulsions, with a temperature of 116 and a high fever. The first eleven follows:

Penczenick, Newport Naval Training School, and Trushowski,

304

Michigan, ends; Wilczewski, Boston College, and Pommering, Michigan, tackles; Steponovich, S.C., and Walterskirker, Gonzaga, guards; Nicellello, Syracuse, center; Adlernzini, Pittsburgh, Guarnaccia, Harvard, Fleishacher, Stanford, and Pieculervicz, Fordham, backs.

"There," said Mr. Balch, "is a 100 percent All-American team that a man might be proud to have in his home. Take that forward wall and place it parallel to the goal line as it would be in a game. Beginning at the left end, it would look like this:

"Penczenickwilczewskistoponovich etc.

"No space to get through and if you tried to run the ends, you'd be out of bounds."

He wrote of prize fights with a scorn that had little geniality in it; he rehashed subjects he had treated in his earlier columns; his verses and plays were the best things he wrote, and one of them, *Abend di Anni Nouveau*, is classic nonsense:

ACT I
A hired hall. It is twenty-five minutes of nine on New Year's Eve. A party, to which all the members of the cast were invited, is supposed to have begun at thirty-four minutes after eight. A WAITER *enters on a horse and finds all the guests dead, their bodies riddled with bullets and frightfully garbled. He goes to the telephone.*

WAITER (*telephoning*): I want a policeman. I want to report a fire. I want an ambulance.

(*He tethers his mount and lies down on the hors d'oeuvres. The curtain is lowered and partially destroyed to denote the passage of four days. Two* POLICEMEN *enter, neither having had any idea that the other would come. They find the* WAITER *asleep and shake him. He awakes and smilingly points at the havoc.*)

WAITER: Look at the havoc.

FIRST POLICEMAN: This is the first time I ever seen a havoc.

SECOND POLICEMAN: It's an inside job, I think.

FIRST POLICEMAN: You WHAT?

WAITER: The trouble now is that we'll have to recast the entire play. Every member of the cast is dead.

FIRST POLICEMAN: Is that unusual?

SECOND POLICEMAN: When did it happen?

WAITER: When did what happen?

SECOND POLICEMAN: I've forgotten.

But on the whole, the *Telegraph* column was far below Ring's standard. Still, his prestige was enormous, the staff of the paper held him in awe, and he could write what he pleased. When he wrote a funny article pretending to be against the use of tobacco, the paper received letters of warning from advertising agencies, as humorless then as they are now; but the agencies were rebuffed, although the paper was in need of advertising.

The *Telegraph* column was a full-time job; in fact four times as demanding as the weekly syndicate letter, which Ring had given up. He obviously had to reach pretty far for ideas. He can hardly be blamed for running short of ideas for satire or burlesque. He had already satirized almost all there was; but people went on writing the same things. He was left with nothing more to say.

The staff of the *Telegraph* was loaded with more high-priced talent than its revenue justified, and it began to dissolve. Ring's last column appeared February 5, 1929, just two months after it had begun. The end of it must have been a relief to Ring.

During the year 1929, Ring published more magazine pieces than in any other single year of his career—eight short stories and nineteen articles, most of the latter for *Collier's*. They were not all written that year; but since his material was in constant demand and he never accumulated a very large stock, it is probable that most of them were written within a two-year period marked by intermittent and severe illnesses, mental depression and anxiety; he was also working hard on *June Moon*. Even with uncertain health he was capable of sustained spells of intense activity; and his concern for his family in the event of his incapacity or death compelled him to overexertion.

The life of Great Neck was strenuous, and it was too close to New York. Ring was accessible to a great many people he no longer had time or energy to see. In 1928 he and Grantland Rice had bought a tract of land in East Hampton on Long Island, and built houses side by side on the ocean. Ring called his new, and last, home "Still Pond" —"no more moving." He had not abandoned social life; but in East Hampton it was limited to a closer circle of intimate friends—the Rices, the Percy Hammonds, the James Prestons, and the John Wheelers. He made fewer trips to New York and narrowed the scope of his interests. He was less and less preoccupied with sports in a professional way; songs, plays, and stories took up most of his time.

In 1929 Ring's collected short stories were published by Scribner under the title *Round Up*, which would have been more appropriate to a Western. He did not choose the title; it seemed a matter of in-

306

difference to him. The volume contained thirty-five of the sixty-five stories which Ring had published up to that time (excluding the busher series and the stories which make up *The Big Town*), and it was hailed as a monument to Ring's career and his elevation to the rank of a contemporary classic. It was made a selection of the Literary Guild, then a small book club whose accolade was judged to be a mark of literary distinction. Ring accepted the honor with his customary stoicism. One of the Guild's recent selections had been *The Cradle of the Deep* by Joan Lowell, a highly colored account of the author's seafaring childhood. Upon being told that the Guild had bestowed on him the same recognition accorded Miss Lowell, Ring remarked, "I guess I'll have to learn to spit a curve in the wind."

Round Up included all of *How to Write Short Stories* and *The Love Nest*. Ring never wrote anything to surpass them, and the other sixteen stories, which appeared from 1926 to 1929, are not among his best, although some of them are still his most popular. Of the thirty-five stories only five appeared originally in *The Saturday Evening Post*, where he had first become famous; and only nine were directly concerned with sports, which had provided the framework of his earliest fiction. He had, since 1914, ranged widely over American life; he had gone back to Niles for scenes and characters, and he had observed various aspects of the existence of the rich, the famous, the talented, and the mediocre in New York. *Round Up* belies the still common notion that Ring was "only a sports writer."

In the stories written after 1926 there are no surprises; the themes and characters are familiar. There is a vein of sentimentality that is lacking in the two earlier volumes, and two stories that could conceivably have been written by someone else. Many of the pieces are technically brilliant, but none has the artistry of "The Golden Honeymoon" or "Some Like Them Cold." Nevertheless they are distinguished by Ring's sure and convincing dialogue and his personal kind of irony. And they illuminate some of his attitudes in a way which his more objective and perfectly achieved stories do not. In many cases the very flaws in the stories are clues to his anger, his exasperation, his disappointments, his excess of sentimentality, his revulsion against his own life.

"Contract" and "Dinner" are funny if not very deep depictions of social behavior into which Ring put all the weariness and irritation he suffered from rude and boring people. The first of these shows the Lardner bridge-playing suburbanites at their worst; it also shows Ring getting back at them. Shelton, a young editor new to the suburb, and his wife are invited to play bridge with neighbors, and he is annoyed by the way his new acquaintances criticize everything he does during the game. He deliberately sets out to offend them in order to preclude any further invitations. After a few drinks he lets loose, correcting their bad grammar and their table manners with calculated insults until the women are in tears and the men in a rage. The Sheltons leave, and the next week find a new set of acquaintances, only to discover that they too insist on correcting his bridge playing. Shelton is irked by the very things that always irked Ring: unsolicited criticism, bad manners, bad piano playing, baby talk, affectation, the silliness of social life on this level. For the most part Ring endured all this in silence, or relieved his feelings by kidding people in a way that was inoffensive because it was over the heads of the people he was teasing. In this story he threw off some of his own repressed disgust.

"Dinner" is about a young man who reluctantly attends a dinner party to oblige the hostess, and is seated next to two rattlebrained, garrulous girls who never finish a sentence or listen to a word he says. Their minds run in circles; their talk is all of themselves. It is distressingly familiar. The young man baits them and needles them to no avail; they are impervious to everything but their own idea of themselves. With what pleasure Ring must have identified himself with the young man who kids them, then finally—after having had enough drinks—escapes the party with a triumphant sense of relief.

"Ex Parte" is another episode in the running domestic battle which figures so prominently in Ring's fiction. The narrator is a rather ordinary, well-meaning man who buys a house and furniture for his future wife before she has seen them. When he brings her home after their wedding, she is appalled to find a new house with heavy and highly polished Grand Rapids furniture. To make it worse, she has friends who live in a remodeled barn tastefully equipped with battered antiques. Her petulant complaints about the vulgar newness of their home drive her husband to get drunk and take an ax and blowtorch to the dining-room table. She leaves him. In a marriage like this there is clearly nothing to be done; the man is as childish as his wife is petty; it has all been based on the wrong values. There was a loving impulse behind his first gesture; but it was wasted.

In "Now and Then" Ring wrote about a marriage after the honeymoon. A wife writes letters to a girl friend describing her wedding trip to Nassau, during which her husband is charming, attentive, and considerate. Three years later she writes of a vacation trip to the same place, during which her husband, who has now taken to steady drinking, obviously cannot bear his wife's presence, leaving her alone to seek new companions and eventually urging her to go home by herself. She is as incapable of sharing his pleasures as he is of understanding her feelings. There will be no golden honeymoon for them.

In these stories Ring portrayed men caught in similar situations. They are bored by vacuous or querulous women, and, driven to exasperation, they drink to alleviate the boredom, then, finally, to escape the trap. These characters are all essentially the same; behavior in this world is terribly standardized. The stories are entertaining, but they are not funny; their appeal lies in the way in which the characters find an explosive release from boredom and frustration by losing their inhibitions and asserting themselves, however crudely. There is no question here of who is right or wrong; there is not much to be said in favor of any of the characters; in "Contract," Shelton, although he is intelligent and sympathetic, is rude and anti-social; there is no justification for his behavior. In the stories about marriage everything decent and kindly has been lost in the need for self-assertion. None of these people is really any good any more. Their only release is in anger and spite. In writing these stories Ring, one suspects, also got a kind of release: his own exasperation shows through them.

Ring's pictures of married life never show women to any advantage. Idealizing women as he did, he seemed more appalled by their shortcomings than by men's. He did not think them any more tiresome than their husbands; he only wished them not to be tiresome at all. Avarice, meanness, and vulgarity were so much more unbecoming to women; like profanity in children. Actually the husbands and wives in Ring's stories have very much the same faults. In "Anniversary" it is the husband who is abysmally self-centered, complacent, and kill-joy. He reads factual articles from newspapers aloud; he tells the same stories over and over; he is opposed to automobiles and liquor and to anything that might give any pleasure and variety to life. A woman friend stops into the Taylor home and tells a lurid but appealing tale of a wife whose husband drinks too much and while drunk accidentally hits her in the eye; but she loves him and forgives him. After the friend has left, Mrs. Taylor says, "Do you know what day this is?"

"Why, yes," Louis replied. "It's Tuesday."
"It's Tuesday, November twelfth. Our anniversary."

"Gosh! That's right! I wish I'd remembered it. I'd have bought you some flowers. Will it do tomorrow?"

"I don't want any flowers. But there is something I would like you to give me. And you don't have to wait till tomorrow."

"What is it?"

"A punch in the eye," said Mrs. Taylor.

"You're feeling kind of funny, aren't you? Did Florence have a shot of their home-made gin in her bag?"

"No. And I'm not feeling funny. I'm just sleepy. I think I'll go to bed."

Louis was reading again.

"It says: 'Experiments in the raising of sisal are being made in Haiti.' I don't suppose you happen to know what sisal is."

But Mrs. Taylor was on her way upstairs.

This sorry picture of a hopeless marriage is accentuated by the very flatness of the manner in which it is presented—a technique which Ring had often used to good effect but which in these later stories is mechanical, dry, and obvious. The story has more weight than power; it has a repertorial truth, a downrightness which in the angry and bitter stories of this period seems self-conscious.

The mood of such stories as these is not unrelieved. In the same years Ring was still writing stories in his old vein. "I Can't Breathe" is one of the most popular because it is funny. It is the literally breathless diary of an eighteen-year-old girl who is juggling with the affections of four suitors with little regard for anything but her own young rapture. She is quite brainless and without scruple, but rather endearing all the same. She is—and you know such things about Lardner characters without their ever being said—of the upper middle class, good family, pretty and amiable; and she writes in the speech of her kind, mingled with all the clichés of romance-smitten youth, in a spate of confidence which is at once naïve and canny. While she may eventually become one of those deplorable bridge-playing matrons, there is not a single accent of disapproval or adult condescension here. Ring used the girl's language as skillfully and as truthfully as he used the lingo of baseball players or song writers. This is satire, but of a gentle sort. Youth and beauty make egotism, fickleness, and light-mindedness tolerable.

So Edith Dole of "These Are Smiles" is the embodiment of feminine charm, and also of mindless irresponsibility. A good-humored traffic cop falls in love with her, and is suddenly and uncomprehendingly downcast when he learns that she has been killed in an auto accident—as she was bound to be, since she drove her car as if she were proof against fate. It is a thoroughly sentimental story, a little pat and tricky, the kind that caused Ring to be compared repeatedly to O. Henry. Nevertheless Ring wrote it with a good deal of pity, both for the attractive and insouciant people in this world and those whom they unwittingly hurt.

The first story in *Round Up* is "The Maysville Minstrel," another story about a practical joke, but otherwise quite unlike "Haircut." In that story Ring exposed the small-town joker; the villain of the Maysville piece is a city sophisticate who is even more contemptible because he ought to know better. Stephen Gale is a young man who works in the gas office in a small town on the Lackawanna Railroad, for a salary hardly sufficient to support his wife and children. He is not a very successful bill collector: "He couldn't blame other people for not settling when he was stalling off creditors himself." In his spare time Stephen writes poetry, his first effort being a birthday poem for his wife, beginning:

> Stella you today are twenty-three years old
> And yet your hair is still pure gold.
> Stella they tell me your name in Latin means a star
> And to me that is what you are
> With your eyes and your hair so yellow
> I rate myself a lucky fellow Stella.

The practical joker of this story is a traveling salesman: "Roberts was also a wise-cracking, kidding New Yorker, who, when at home, lunched where his heroes lunched, just to be near them, look at them and overhear some of their wisecracks which he could repeat to his fellow-drummers on the road. These heroes of his were comic-strip artists, playwrights and editors of humorous columns in the metropolitan press."

Roberts learns that Stephen writes poetry and persuades him to let him send the ode to Stella to a New York columnist. The columnist prints it with a caption the humor of which escapes the young poet, who now believes himself on the way to fame. Roberts follows up this triumph by sending Stephen a phony letter from a non-existent editor requesting more poems, and Stephen responds with one called "The Lackawanna Railroad."

> The Lackawanna Railroad where does it go?
> It goes from Jersey City to Buffalo.

311

Some of the trains stop at Maysville but they are few
Except the 8:22 . . .

In high hope Stephen quits his job at the gas office. But when his poems are returned undelivered, he realizes that Roberts has played a joke on him. He tears up his manuscripts and goes back to his job and the dreary round of bill collection. For just a moment—the story limps to a halt—he thinks of taking some sort of revenge on Roberts. "But even as he spoke, Stephen realized there was nothing he could do about it."

It is not the autobiographical reference of the story which has a particular significance; Ring often used his own experience to provide backgrounds. He did work in the gas office, and his employer there used to say that Ring was not a good bill collector because he was too softhearted. Perhaps Maysville is Niles, the Lackawanna is the Michigan Central, the Delaware River is the St. Joseph; it does not matter. What is more interesting is that all his life Ring was fascinated by local poets, the Sweet Singer of Michigan, the Poetical Policeman of Toledo, the Poetical Coroner of St. Paul, whose most memorable line in an ode to his mother was "If by perchance the inevitable should come." These poets and many others paid to have their work printed by small presses, sometimes with abominable cuts showing the old homestead and a gravestone or two; and Ring used to collect them and read them and laugh at them until he cried. They were illiterate, they were pretentious, they were funny; but they were also pathetic. They were the actual and authentic inspiration for the verse of the Maysville Minstrel. He had even more pathos; his verses are so earnest and so literal, yet he has the true local poet's feeling for place names.

Stephen's heroes range from Edgar Guest to Amy Lowell—it is hard to say which Ring himself hated worse; and Roberts' heroes are New York comic-strip artists, playwrights, and columnists—people like Ring and his friends. Ring seems to have been casting a doubting eye on his own profession, and a pitying eye on the guileless small-town boy. The story is not a very good one; it is excessively sentimental, and it lacks the sure touch of Ring's best stories. But he did write it, and some others which are equally sentimental; and there is no reason to think that these are any less characteristic of him than his most polished and objective stories.

"The Maysville Minstrel" is full of compassion for a whole race of struggling inarticulates left behind in small towns. And while there is no literally autobiographical figure in any of Ring's fiction

312

—and he could hardly be said to have been pitting the tank-town bards against the pundits of the metropolis—still, there is something about the stifled singer of the gas office that reminds one of Ring, the frustrated song writer.

The stories in *Round Up* that were written after 1926 are typical enough in their subject matter, characters, and dialogue. Ring's repertorial eye seems as shrewd as ever, but one feels that he was not observing his subjects afresh, but only remembering them from a previous scrutiny. He had seen clearly enough the first time, his memory was accurate, and nothing had changed. But the inimitable lively turns of phrase are fewer, the pace is a little flat-footed, and the characters, although they are set down sharply enough for the purposes of the immediate tale, are not memorable. It is situations rather than people that stand out, a kind of behavior rather than an individual.

These later stories arouse an easy kind of pity—as in "The Maysville Minstrel"—and sometimes an equally ready feeling of distaste. This is not because Ring in his later years developed a streak of sympathy for his characters that was lacking in earlier stories; he did not go soft because of suffering, ill-health, and disillusionment. He still saw things in the same way; he was still skeptical and pessimistic. He had always had compassion for people, and toward some a furious indignation. What is lacking in the later stories is detachment. The artistic process which had produced such masterpieces as "Some Like Them Cold" and "The Golden Honeymoon" was not working any longer. The raw material came out still a little raw. Ring was a fine storyteller, his ear was unimpaired, but his creative power had slackened. Whatever alchemy had given to Jack Keefe, Alibi Ike, Mabel Gillespie, and Chas. F. Lewis and the old couple in Florida an existence of their own did not transform the flat figures of the later stories. You feel like shouting at the ghastly card players of "Contract" and comforting the cop in "There Are Smiles"; but the Busher, My Roomy, and the caddy are out of reach of reprisals.

The later stories cost Ring as much effort as the earlier and finer ones; he was never entirely satisfied with anything he wrote, and he was not coasting. If he no longer created characters in the round, it was probably because he was no longer so interested in people. He had observed all he could, his eye was still clear, but the surfaces of the visible world reflected rather than refracted the light and did not show the depths of character. And he was not an imaginative writer in the sense that he could invent what he had not experienced or seen. He was bound to come to the end of his material. But whatever their artistic shortcomings, these later stories have a unique quality; all but a very few bear the imprint of Ring's powerful personality.

Ring's aplomb in the face of literary acclaim was never more needed. The opinions of the critics on *Round Up* would have bewildered a writer who took himself more seriously than Ring did. It was clearly the time to make a definitive estimate of Ring's literary stature. Ring's popularity was beyond question; there was general agreement as to his originality and his quality; and a few people had maintained for years that he was a genius. But there were vast disparities in the critical opinions that were called forth by his collected stories. The *Saturday Review of Literature*, once enthusiastic, printed a somewhat reduced estimate. Allan Nevins wrote that part of the volume was substantial and durable literature but that most of it was simply entertainment; he did not specify how much of it was both or whether or not the two categories were mutually exclusive. He credited Ring with skill in reporting and a thorough knowledge of the ordinary American and his mind; beyond this "Mr. Lardner's endowments are not remarkable"; and, curiously, he lamented the lack of "poignant artistry."

Lewis Mumford in the New York *Herald Tribune* granted Ring's work a lease on life, but not immortality: "The short stories brought together in 'Round Up' must be counted among the few that will be readable twenty years hence. . . ." and John Chamberlain in the *Times* said, "'Round Up' gives the full measure of his talent—a talent that is mature and sure-footed."

Harry Hansen in the *World* was warmer: ". . . When an author gets to this stage, it is comparable in modern days to having a bust placed in the Hall of Fame. . . . To many authors republication of this kind means literary eclipse, but I am confident that Mr. Lardner will survive.

"It will be harder for him to survive the opinions which his publishers, the Messrs. Scribner, have placed on the jacket of this book, for the very distinguished gentlemen who exude them seem intent on taking him away from the popular audience and elevating him to literary greatness. I even find on the jacket something I once wrote about Ring Lardner among testimonials from such learned and astute gentlemen as Carl Van Doren, Sir James Barrie, Edmund Wilson and H. L. Mencken. . . ."

The entire literary pantheon, from Parnassus to the Bowery, was

314

to be scoured for comparisons. Hansen said that Ring "gets his effects without Jim Tully's punch and Ernest Hemingway's carefully timed patter." T. S. Matthews in the *New Republic* reached higher in a review entitled "Lardner, Shakespeare and Chekhov." He pointed out that the last two had also been popular writers, that is, they had written potboilers too. "As if 'playing down to the audience' were not the whole duty of a writer. . . . I have chosen to compare him, not with the avowedly dedicated writers of his own generation, but rather with Shakespeare and Chekhov, writers whose attitude seems to have been as unpretentious, whose aims as sensible. For Lardner, like Shakespeare and Chekhov, has owed his literary existence (and has repaid it by writing for them) to the common people of his day, the people who have been talking prose all their lives, and will never know it."

This brought into focus the whole question of a writer's intentions, which, in the case of Ring and a good many other popular artists, have been argued bootlessly at great length. Ring wrote to make money, and the way to make money was to be entertaining. He was a conscientious craftsman, and he was also a genius. Some of his stories turned out to be works of art, but he did not think that this was any of his business. Some of the stories are also undoubtedly satire, but it is impossible to say just at what times Ring was conscious of being a satirist.

Referring to "Champion" and "The Love Nest," Mr. Matthews wrote: "This is real satire, for there is indignation behind it"; while Mr. Hansen said: ". . . indignation has no part in his feeling toward his material." It is hardly possible to overlook the indignation behind "Champion"; it accounts for its excessive melodrama. On the other hand it is equally difficult to see any indignation in "The Love Nest," in which the author seems entirely detached. There is no satirical intention in the busher stories, in the sense that they are informed by indignation; yet they fall within any definition of satire.

Ring was first a fine reporter; he could create character; and he was a humorist. His most effective satire, whatever his aim at the time he wrote it, came out of his strictest realism. He was willing to leave the question of art to the critics, and the question of satire to the reader.

The reviews of *Round Up* brought forth nothing new in the way of critical perceptions. Everything important had been said years before; on the whole the appraisals of Ring's work in his lifetime were thoughtful and just. Ring took a good deal of satisfaction from honest praise, he was amused by extravagance, and he was quite unimpressed by any efforts to award him a suitable rank. A good many graves were troubled: Mark Twain, O. Henry, Bill Nye, Artemus Ward, Finley Peter Dunne were invoked. Among the living Will Rogers, George Ade, Damon Runyon, and Irvin Cobb were sized up. The results were not conclusive, because Ring, in spite of superficial resemblances, really had nothing much to do with any of them. He had always gone his own way. Once he had hoped to be as good as his predecessor on the "Wake," Hugh E. Keogh; and when he was writing his first short stories, he measured himself against Charles Van Loan and Harry Leon Wilson. *Round Up* was evidence of a solid achievement, and it was gratifying to have it recognized. But Ring was as skeptical of immortality as he was of fame. Whether or not he realized it, all the efforts of his contemporaries to put him into good company only proved that he stood alone. He belonged to a line of American originals, Thoreau, Hawthorne, Melville, Whitman, and Mark Twain, each eccentric, unique, and unaccountable, owing nothing except to the demands of his own genius.

From the time he was discovered by the literary critics Ring had been hailed as the most ferocious satirist since Swift, the scourge of the Jazz Age, a hater of mankind. Because his most striking stories revealed a low opinion of various kinds of people, it was held that he was only himself when he was burning with an incandescent fury. A rather irrelevant difference of opinion arose over the question of whether Ring had any kindly feeling for his fellow men or merely hated them all with a cold impartiality. His more genial and sentimental stories were brushed off as being less typical of him than those which mercilessly exposed people as cheap and phony. Bitterness and indignation appealed more to the critical temper of the twenties than pity and sentiment. Even Ring's nonsense plays, in which his humor reached a peak of pure hilarity, were interpreted as a mordant commentary on the chaos of the modern world. When the decade passed and with it the taste for the moral nihilism it had managed to find everywhere, a new critical mood set in. Chastened by the Depression, the criticism of the thirties became touched with piety, and what had been a cause for acclaim became an accusation. The view that Ring fed only on hatred has persisted to this day. Every literary history, every introduction to an anthology echoes the same charge: ". . . he seemed to hate everything he touched"; ". . . a mood of bitter distaste and cruel tedium, a mood of contemptuousness so sharp as to be weary of itself . . . Never

316

again does Lardner relent to his *bête humaine*. Dreadful creatures
. . . poor clods in human shape . . . pretentious fools of a ghastly
emptiness . . . a hell of relentless dullness and cold cruelty." These
views have become so standard that literary historians are inclined
to pigeonhole Ring along with contemporaries they have equally
misunderstood. His "hard-boiled characters" are lumped with those
of Dashiell Hammett, although there is only one truly hard-boiled
character in all Ring's stories—Midge Kelly of "Champion"; the rest
are the most thin-skinned and vulnerable people in American fiction; and there is no essential point of resemblance between any
Lardner character and any Hammett character.

Certainly a number of Ring's stories show a marked disesteem for
various citizens of the republic; he was ruthless with fakers, brutes,
with all morally callous people. Whether he hated the people or
only their faults is worth considering. Against the body of critical
opinion which holds him to be an unalloyed misanthrope, there is
another school of thought whose claims have equal validity. Ring's
earliest admirers and many of his closest friends were journalists
and sportsmen who recognized his genius before he won literary
acclaim, and there is hardly one of them who did not know him as
an exceptionally magnanimous and loving man; they feel that his
strictures against the human race were directed only at particular
characters; that he did not hate people, but only meanness, falseness, and pretentiousness. The ball players he traveled with, the
people he befriended, his colleagues in journalism, sports, and the
theater reject the charge. "There will be many to talk of his bitter
hatred of the human race's selfishness and stupidity," Franklin P.
Adams wrote, "but he was filled with a mighty compassion for the
possessors of these qualities."

"When Lardner began to write his letters of the pitcher from the
bushes, *You Know Me Al,*" Grant Overton had written in the *Bookman* in 1925, "people said he was a humorist, which was fair enough
as definitions go. Later, and especially with the appearance of *How
To Write Short Stories,* all the Algonquin braves raised the war cry
that Lardner was a great satirist or ironist. . . . I gather from this
and some other comments that Gilbert [Seldes] and the rest picture
Ring as one filled with hatred for the baseball moron. The contrary
is true. Lardner assures me that he loves said moron and will any
time do even that thing he most detests, come into town, to spend
an evening with one of these bush men and listen to their modish
operandi."

As far as his stories are concerned it does not matter whether he hated people or only their follies, any more than it matters whether satire is motivated by indignation, ill temper, or sheer delight. But Ring himself was aware of the personal accusation against him, and he did not believe it was true. The most telling statement of the critical point of view was made by Clifton Fadiman in the *Nation*, in an article called "Ring Lardner and the Triangle of Hate." Fadiman admired the skill with which Ring flayed humanity, and he listed the particulars which revealed Ring's loathing of mankind. His selection of evidence is of a high legal proficiency and quite convincing:

> *In the face of Lardner's perfectly clear simon-pure, deliberate misanthropy it is a little difficult to understand how readers could ever have welcomed him as a popular humorist. The world he shows us—and it is one in which we feel not the slightest exaggeration or lack of balance—is a world of mental sadists, four-flushers, intolerable gossipers, meal-ticket females, interfering morons, brainless flirts, liars, brutes, spiteful snobs, vulgar climbers, dishonest jockeys, selfish children, dipsomaniacal chorus girls, senile chatterers, idiotically complacent husbands, mean arrivistes, drunks, snoopers, poseurs, and bridge-players. Funny? If these people are funny, so is "Gulliver's Travels."*

> *In his apparently burlesque introduction to "June Moon" Ring Lardner has condensed his confession of faith and his last word on the values of American society as at present organized:*

>> *It is estimated that if the horse vehicles and street cars had kept on fighting and maintained their early leadership over automobiles, by the year 1970 the entire population of New York City would have been wiped out and no harm done. The "World Almanac," from which this information was gleaned, gives us only one ray of hope. In New York's biggest borough, Brooklyn, there were a thousand fewer births and thirteen hundred more deaths in 1928 than in 1927.*

Ring, spending the winter of 1933 in California, read a summary of Fadiman's article in a newspaper, clipped it out, and sent it with a letter to his friend Mrs. Vereen. The clipping read:

HATE IS BACK OF RING LARDNER'S FUN;
HE HATES HIS CHARACTERS, SAYS WRITER

Ring Lardner, who is said to do his writing from a sick-bed somewhere in the west, is popularly regarded as a funny man. But hear

318

Clifton Fadiman's opinion in this week's The Nation. Fadiman says:

The special force of Ring Lardner's work springs from a single fact; he just doesn't like people. Except Swift, no writer has gone farther on hatred alone. I believe he hates himself; more certainly he hates his characters; and most clearly of all, his characters hate each other.

There is no mitigating soft streak in him as there is in the half-affectionate portraiture of Sinclair Lewis; and none of the amused complacency of H. L. Mencken.

He has found nothing whatsoever in American life to which to cling. Other writers who reveal this masochistic pattern in a less pure form are George S. Kaufman and F. Scott Fitzgerald. But neither of these is cursed with Lardner's intuitive knowledge of the great American swine. . . .

Read beneath the lines and you will see that everything he meets or touches drives him into a cold frenzy, leaving him without faith, hope or charity.

What Lardner, even in his simplest magazine stories, is interested in getting at is the core of egotism from which even our apparently most impeccable virtues spring.

Somewhere Lardner has a remark about "this special police dog" which "was like most of them and hated everybody." Lardner himself is the police dog of American fiction, except that his hatred is not the product of mere crabbedness but of an eye that sees too deep for comfort.

Ring sent two enclosures in his letter:

La Quinta, Calif.
Saturday, April first [1933]

Dear Myrt:—

The enclosed is not just a cash prize for you, but the Lardners will be much obliged if you will turn it over to your sister Kate [Mrs. Grantland Rice]. It is a debt we owe her and please tell her not to send it back again—That would simply mean returning it to her, and so on ad infinitum. . . .

The other enclosure (the one without Lincoln's picture) will tell you the latest news of me—and to me. The writer is evidently a fellow from whom you simply can't keep a secret. But I do resent being called a police dog, or dog of any kind.

I hope all the Hollises are well and that Mr. Crisp is much better. Love to everybody, including Mrs. Vereen.

A Born Hater

"George and I worked on the play nearly all last spring and summer," Ring wrote to Fitzgerald in February 1930, "and when the New York opening was over, I went on a bat that lasted nearly three months and haven't been able to work since, so it's a good thing that the play paid dividends." That year Ring spent a good deal of time in hospitals. There was always the danger of recurring tuberculosis; in addition he was beginning to show the symptoms of a heart ailment. One of the most painful was a swelling of his feet and ankles; he was unable to wear shoes for weeks at a time.

His financial situation had been somewhat eased by the success of *June Moon*. During 1930 his other sources of income were small. He published only two short stories. One of them, "Mama," is about a woman who is taken to Bellevue suffering from amnesia. She does not remember that her husband and children have died of flu. The story was based on a case which Ellis had observed while doing volunteer social work in the hospital. It is "true to life," no doubt, but somehow not true to Ring. It could have been written by any competent imitator of O. Henry. The other story, "Words and Music," is about a stenographer who is infatuated with a famous crooner. Posing as a reporter, she goes to interview him in order to meet him face to face; but she is permanently disillusioned when she overhears an unlovely colloquy between the singer and his vulgar mistress. Ring's disgust with the characters is apparent; they are uninteresting and trivial. He seemed to have lost for good his gift for creating characters in the round, and his satirical thrust was blunted by sentimentality or a feeling of revulsion. None of his fiction after 1929 is first-rate; and some of it is totally lacking in any kind of distinction.

But if his fiction declined, his purely humorous pieces remained as brilliant as ever. That year he contributed half a dozen occasional pieces to *The New Yorker*, a magazine he liked to write for. Its editor, Harold Ross, would have liked to engage Ring to write exclusively for him, but he could not afford to pay the prices Ring was accustomed to getting, and Ring needed money. The few short pieces he wrote for *The New Yorker* are among his best. Quite different from the stories and columns on which his reputation was based, *The New Yorker* pieces are reminiscent of the nonsense plays in style and a strictness of form which disciplines apparently uninhibited flights of sheer hilarity. Ring liked writing these, although they were not so effortless as they seem despite the effect of spontaneity he was able to achieve. In such pieces as these Ring rarely faltered. He still had the gift of "inextinguishable laughter."

By the autumn of 1930 he was well enough to go to Boston to write lyrics for Ziegfeld's "Smiles." Frustrating and tiring as the experience was, he found it ludicrous enough to be more amused than exasperated, and he wrote of it—in letters and a piece for *The New Yorker*—in high good humor. But shortly after that he had another relapse and was obliged to rest. He and Ellis went to Florida in January, and while he was there, he began to write a daily newspaper letter for the Bell Syndicate and the Chicago *Tribune* and New York *Daily News*. It was a kind of work he hated and had forsworn five years earlier. But he found short stories, plays, and long articles too difficult to write. He lacked the physical strength for sustained effort; he was weak, he could not sleep and sedatives had lost their efficacy; and he still had to bear the anxieties of illness and family responsibility. He thought that a short daily stint would not overtax his strength, and it might be profitable. The Depression had arrived. The market crash had not affected Ring directly, since he did not speculate much in stocks, his chief investment being in insurance policies; and it would be another year before the demand and the prices for his stories and articles showed signs of diminishing. But at the moment the problem was to find the kind of work he could do.

A story called "Insomnia," written about this time, reflects the difficulties Ring was having with work. It begins:

It's only ten o'clock, but I hardly slept at all last night and I ought to make up for it. I won't read. I'll turn off the light and not think about anything. I must go to sleep and stay asleep until breakfast time.

Then maybe I'll feel like working.

I've got to get some work done pretty soon.

It's all going out and nothing coming in.

That was a song of Bert Williams'. Let's see; it started:

> *Money is de root of evil, no matter where you happen to go. . . .*

Bert sang a song of mine once and I had it published; it was put on phonograph records, too, and I think the total royalties from sheet music and records amounted to $47.50. It's fun writing songs, but I never could make money out of things that were fun, like playing poker or bridge or betting on horses.

The only way I can earn money is by writing short stories. Short! By the time I'm half through with one, it's a serial to me.

I wish I were as good as O. Henry and could get by with a thousand or twelve hundred words. I could write a thousand-word short

321

story every day; that is, I could if my head were as full of plots as his must have been. I think of about one plot a year, and then, when I start writing it, I recall that it's somebody else's, maybe two or three other people's.

Just the same, plot or no plot, I'll have to work tomorrow. There's the insurance and notes and interest on mortgages— But I won't get to sleep that way. I mustn't think about anything at all, or at least, I must think about something that doesn't make any difference.

Sheckard, Evers, Schulte, Chance, Steinfeldt, Hofman, Tinker, Kling, Brown.

Twenty years ago I was a baseball nut and could recite any club's batting order. Nowadays I hardly know which Waner bats second and which third.

. . . Ten or eleven highballs or a shot in the arm would be an effective lullaby. The trouble is, the more habits you have, the more you have to snap out of. At that, I guess too much coffee is as bad as too much Scotch. Too much of anything is bad; even too much sleep.

These are evidently Ring's own thoughts during his sleepless nights. In the last part of "Insomnia" he throws away a fairly ingenious story plot by merely summarizing it. It gives a clue to the remorse and apprehension he felt about his own plight. It is about a young alcoholic who marries a rich girl whose family disinherits her because of him. He goes on the wagon for four years, makes a lot of money, and saves as much as his wife has. Then he begins to drink again and loses most of his money gambling. His wife refuses to see him again. In a desperate effort to repair his fortune he uses his wife's securities to play the stock market; then he goes abroad and drinks himself to death. The stocks he bought suddenly jump in value, and his wife is left with a huge profit, plus his insurance. She returns to her family feeling that she has "loved wisely and just about well enough."

This grim story is not really written, merely sketched out among the musings of an insomniac. The whole piece is a graphic indication of Ring's own state of mind, an actual record of one of his endless white nights, and the plot of the story is one he did not feel capable of writing. So it lies there, along with a wistful recollection of his youth: of how he and some other boys of the Episcopal choir went out drinking one night and serenaded a pretty girl, whose father chased them away. He—Ring—alone was blamed for the drunken disturbance because, being the tallest of the boys, he was readily recognized.

In spite of ill-health and the torment of sleeplessness Ring kept up a lively interest in many things. A letter to his son John, who after a year at Harvard had gone to Paris to study, is full of courage and good spirits:

In New York
3 A.M. Sunday, Feb. 15, 1931　　*The Vanderbilt Hotel*
8 A.M. the same day in Paris　　*Park Avenue at Thirty-fourth*
　　　　　　　　　　　　　　　　　Street
　　　　　　　　　　　　　　　　　New York

Dear John—
Keep a hold of this letter
For fear you won't get anything better.
It is written in the "wee small" hours of the morning
Without an instant's warning;
I just suddenly took a notion,
Having sworn off the nightly self-administration of a sleeping
　　　potion,
To get out of bed and use my Underwood portable
Rather than go out and walk the streets and perhaps court a belle.
We are back from the South and stopping at the Hotel V-nde-b--t,
A place that some goose or gander built.
The food here would annoy you and pain you
More than that procurable at the Pennsylvania,
And my opinion, which is seldom wrong,
Is that we won't be stopping here long.
If you should care to write us, through a sense of duty or pity,
Address us in care of the Bell Syndicate, 63 Park Row, N. Y. City,
Which, in association with the Chicago Tribune and New York
　　　Daily News,
Both of whom have plenty of money to lose,
Has engaged me to write a daily wire a la Will Rogers,
Designed to entertain young folks and old codgers.
I am supposed to write a hundred words or less per day
On timely topics, at very fair pay,
Though you are safe in betting
That I am not getting as much as Mr. Rogers is getting;
However, it keeps the wolf from the door
And while I may not be getting so much now, some day I might be
　　　getting more.

323

The reason I accepted this position
Was that my food was not giving me proper nutrition
And I seemed to lack the strength
To write short stories or plays or other works of any length.
When I am feeling fit again and everything is nice and tidy,
I intend to write the book of a musical show with a brand new idea.
A while ago I received a letter from a young man who, I am sure,
Had recently seen my own elegant signature,
And some time last autumn, ere the leaves were off the limb,
You had written my autograph and sent it to him;
He sent this autograph back and said he didn't want it;
By the vicious words of his accompanying letter I am still grieved
*   and haunted.*
David and your mother are in the next room,
Sleeping soundly, I trust, through the inexorable gloom.
The little one came in from school yesterday to meet us
And greet us with an advanced case of tonsilitis.
His throat is so sore that it irks him to swallow,
And if the ailment were to continue eight or ten years, his insides
*   would become hollow.*
Yesterday afternoon, your mother and I went to a matinee:
"America's Sweetheart," the new Fields, Rodgers and Hart musical
*   play.*
Gus Shy, John Sheehan, Jeanne Aubert and Inez Courtney are in it
And some of the songs are pretty enough to take home and play on
*   your spinnet;*
In fact, it is the best Rodgers score I have heard for a long time
And I'll send you the three best numbers when I think it is song
*   time.*
I thought you very deftly and wittily
Described your visit to s---y Italy.
This spring, if you have another holiday,
I wish you would spend it in Montpellier
Where my mother's niece Amy Serre
Lives unless she has moved from there.
She is a widow about seventy and has a daughter
Who grew old before a suitor caught her.
But they are nice and the daughter is a musician
Who prefers playing the pianoforte to going fishing.
I shall find out whether they're still there, yes or no;
Meanwhile, you inform me whether you'd like to go.

324

At Miami Beach, I saw very
Much of Paul Waner and Max Carey.
Paul is holding out for a larger salary
And poor Max is about through playing for a baseball gallery.
He is a free agent and would make a swell coach;
Barney Dreyfuss would keep him if he (Barney) were not a roach.
"June Moon" closed in Boston a week ago
After making quite a lot of money for such a small show.
I still think they were rather silly
To let it play four weeks in Philly,
But we beat Holiday records in Detroit,
Greatly to the stockholders' delight.
My experience with "Smiles" is too funny and too long to put in a
*   letter;*
When I see you I can tell you better.
And now when you think it isn't too much bother,
You might write a letter to sincerely your father.

Ring was not certain what his address would be in the months to come; because of his health he had been advised to go to Arizona for an indefinite period. His tubercular condition was complicated by digestive disorders and a weakening heart. Reluctantly he went alone to the Desert Sanatorium in Tucson early in March. His next letter to John was written from there.

Sunday, March 15 [1931]

Dear John:—
    Believe it or not, your letters are much better reading than the Arizona Star or the Tucson Daily Citizen. I have learned from the latter, however, that Old Homme Seine is running amuck and perhaps by this time your dormitory has become a house boat like the Lardners' hovel in East Hampton. . . . [A hurricane had damaged Ring's house that spring.]
    My wardens, not knowing I am a born rover, think I intend to stay here all spring and most of the summer, but right after the middle of April les Etats Unis will be placarded with announcements that I have escaped. As Lincoln said, you can stand Arizona part of the time, you can even stand Arizona some of the time, but you can't etc.
    My daily "night letter" is not in as many papers as it is out of. It would be more readable if I weren't always four or five days behind the news, but I do think it's as good as Bill Rogers' or Coolidge's stuff.

325

All my neighbors have radios (a recent invention) and just as I get ready for my sleeping potion at nine P.M. (Mountain Time) they turn on Amos and Andy, who, as you may not know, are now broadcasting twice per night. I can't hear them distinctly and wouldn't mind if I could, but what wrecks me is the kind of laughter with which one of said neighbors greets their gags. It is like the bleat of the coyotes in the surrounding mountains and keeps me awake long after it is hushed for the night. . . .

Write whether you feel like it or not and keep going to them concerts.

A Vagabond

Ring hated being immobilized, especially far from his home, his family, and all his interests, and he had no intention of following the doctors' advice. He wrote to Kate Rice's sister, Mrs. Luthy, in Americus, Georgia:

Wednesday, March 11 [1931]

Dear Millie:—

You are a nice girl to take time from your gardening and your games with Jane to write to me. Most of the letters I get are from lawyers or income tax agents who seem to think I am a born embezzler. Yours (your letters, I mean) take the curse off the others.

You had better not offer your services as nurse unless you are in earnest. I would give a fabulous sum (if I had it) for one like you, even though I know you would try to force those funny drinks on me. The nurses here are a hard-boiled lot and evidently selected for their ugliness. There is only one pretty one and she, strange to say, is from Georgia. Stranger to say, she is incompetent.

Something tells me I am not going to linger here long. The doctors know their business and the weather is perfect, but the Lord didn't intend me for sanatorium life two thousand miles from home. What I'd like and hope to find is a suitable place within easy telephoning and visiting distance of New York. I suppose it would be sensible to obey orders and stay here six months, but I'm just not sensible.

Ellis and I would have come to Americus and stayed there until we were driven out if Sister Kate hadn't objected to the idea so strenuously. I guess she wanted all the attention herself. We will come at a time when there is no danger of stealing the spotlight from anybody.

Love to you and your mother and all the other Hollises.

R.

Before Ring left for the East, he made a brief escape from his sickbed to visit an old friend. Mrs. India Moffett, whom Ring had known as India Gillespie on the Chicago *Tribune*, was living in Phoenix, and Ring wrote to her and asked to come to see her. Mrs. Moffett offered to drive to Tucson to bring him back, but Ring insisted upon coming to Phoenix alone, and asked to be met at the bus station. It was against the doctors' orders for him to leave the sanatorium, and he contrived his escape by stealth. Once Ring made up his mind to do anything, no obstacles were insurmountable. He arrived at the Phoenix bus station on schedule, bringing gifts—Mickey Mouse watches—for Mrs. Moffett's young children.

Mrs. Moffett realized that Ring's departure from the sanatorium was unauthorized and persuaded him to telephone to Tucson before the officials became alarmed. He looked ill and exhausted; but he obtained a bottle of bourbon and after he had had a few drinks—he had been on the wagon for months—he became relaxed and talkative, as he had been in his younger days. They spent a pleasant evening recalling Chicago days, and then Ring reluctantly returned to Tucson.

Ring wrote a piece called "A Slow Train Through Arizona," in which he told of his visit to Phoenix. Driving him from the bus station to her home, Mrs. Moffett was stopped for speeding. Ring wrote that she "disobeyed every motor-traffic law in Arizona and received the usual penalty accorded drivers of the society-editor sex —a bright smile from the cop." It is a mildly amusing piece, but it is also a little sad: Ring's boredom and restlessness are quite evident. He left the sanatorium after having spent less than two months there. Nevertheless, when he stopped in Niles on his way home, to visit his two sisters for a day, his health seemed somewhat improved. In any case, he was trying desperately to make it seem so, and because he was anxious to get back to New York he minimized his illness.

But back in New York he soon re-entered Doctors Hospital. He never found a suitable sanatorium near the city.

The Bell Syndicate-Chicago *Tribune-Daily News* "night letter" was in trouble almost from the beginning. Ring made an agreement with the syndicates before he went to Florida in January, and his first letter came from Miami:

Miami, Fla., Feb. 1. My dear public: If I come out and see my shadow tomorrow noon you will probably get a message from me every day for the next six weeks or more and if I don't come out and see my shadow the same thing will happen. I will leave the government in the capable hands of Will Rogers and confine myself to things with which I am more familiar, such as what is going on in society and different hospitals. I trust Mr. Rogers will not think I am intruding. After all we are both Indians only he ain't been scalped.

Ring kept away from serious political commentary but he continued to spoof politics in his familiar vein:

Miami Beach, Fla., Feb. 5. Democrats and gents: When I read in the papers that Owen D. Young had withdrawn from the presidential massacre of 1932 I immediately decided to do the same thing myself and suggest that all those who are dissatisfied with the present incumbrance of the White House concentrate on one man to succeed him. My notion of an ideal President is Al Capone. He would provide his own bodyguard and see that congress got good beer instead of whatever it is they have been drinking that makes them act so silly. If he just brought his baggage, the army's artillery strength would be doubled. As for his social standing, he is head of the racket club and his family can be traced back as far as Sicily. For Vice President I would nominate Judge Crater or Charles Levine, or somebody else you can't find.

Ring had not intended to follow the news; but he found himself at a loss for subject matter and unless he could comment on current events, he had to fall back on something casual and very often trivial:

New York, Feb. 8. Well, here I am back in old New York after a brief sojourn in the sunny climes of Florida and it brings a tear to my eyes when I compare my welcome down there amidst strangers to the way I was received today in what I have learned to call my home town.

I had hardly lighted from the train at Miami when I was photographed four times, interviewed three times and invited to make a speech before a junior Bible class. My reception committee at the Pennsylvania station today was composed of one black boy with a red cap and he didn't even have a pocket kodak or even ask me to autograph the dime I gave him for carrying my laundry to the waiting barouche.

Mar. 6. Today was the birthday anniversary of ye modest undersigned, who is now rapidly approaching par. The occasion was cele-

brated in South America, where a dinner dance was given at which the Prince of Wales was a guest. In Chicago and San Francisco the stores opened at nine and closed at half-past five. The New York stock exchange remained open only until 3 o'clock. The New York World did not publish, and the streets were filled with people enjoying an involuntary holiday. All the branches of the Bank of the United States stayed closed. In Niles, Mich., the hero's birthplace, a piece of confetti was picked up by a street cleaner, who mistook it for an aspirin tablet.

The note of self-deprecation is familiar enough, but now it is neither bitter nor very personal; it is merely a perfunctory device.

Ring knew that the letter was not selling and cast about for an idea which would distinguish the column from those of his colleagues. He invented another rookie pitcher.

Tucson, March 22. Word has been received from Willie Clough, the young Tucson semi-pro pitcher who hitch-hiked from here to Pas Robles, Cal., to try out with the Pittsburgh Pirates. He was much impressed by his first contact with the big league team and wrote: "All the players has each got their own glove. They have changed the ball by taking out the old crippled rabbit and putting in a young one that is really spry. I think the change makes things easier for a pitcher. For instance, last summer in Tucson I use to sometimes pitch four or five innings but yesterday Manager Ens took me out before I had pitched two whole innings against the first team though I had held them to twelve runs and most of them was waners."

By April 3, the letter was entirely about baseball and had been moved to the sports pages; but it was still not selling, and Ring was worried. The syndicate had reduced the weekly guarantee from $750 to $500; the Chicago *Tribune* had omitted two or three releases on the grounds that they were "inappropriate" to a series of this kind, and Ring took this to mean that they were thought to be in questionable taste. Because of rival columnists Ring's choice of subject matter was limited. And it was an inauspicious time to launch a new syndicate feature. The Depression had hit with full force.

Ring's comments on the Depression in his letter were not calculated to give much hope to readers or to compliment the government on what was being done for the unemployed. One of them ran:

New York, Feb. 16. While passing an apple vendor at Park Avenue and 34th street in New York City today, I got a swell idea,

329

which I suppose I will have to turn over to the government, just the same as I do everything else. The sale of apples on street corners is supposed to relive the unemployment situation. Well, if they sold watermelons instead of apples at the conventional price of five for a quarter, you would have to employ at least four more ladies or gents to help carry them home.

The trouble with this is not so much that it treats the Depression with something less than solemnity; it is just not funny—the only lapse for which a humorist is never forgiven. Another letter on the bonus for war veterans must have seemed even less acceptable:

Feb. 18. Back in 1917 and 1918 a bunch of young whippersnappers from this country went to France on a joy ride and forced dotards like myself to leave our pleasant firesides nights and go out dancing and carousing with debutantes who had not yet learned the facts of strong drink. Now congress is arguing the propriety of giving these truants and refugees a bonus. Don't give 'em nothing, is my slogan. Fine 'em a year's salary, even if they ain't getting it.

There is no doubt as to where Ring's sympathies lay; but such columns are not inspirational reading in the depths of a depression. It was not the time to be sardonic on matters which had become political. A new note of piety had entered politics, a subject on which Ring had never been very reverent.

On his return to New York, Ring found that the column had no future at all, and he abandoned newspaper writing for good. From Doctors Hospital he wrote to Ring, Jr., who was in the hospital at Phillips House in Boston, recovering from a fractured pelvis and shoulder, which he had got from falling off a ledge outside the fourth-floor window of an Andover dormitory while trying to get from one window to another:

Monday night, April 27 [1931]
Dear Bill:—
I don't intend to allow a son of mine to show me up. If you can live in a hospital, so can I. I would like to trade ailments with you, for I have no excuse not to write letters; you have, which means that I shall hear from you almost as often as before.

I am on the ninth floor of this structure so that if I ever take a notion to step out of the window and stroll along the walls, the X-rays are likely to show a couple of fractured fingernails as well as the conventional arm and leg breaks.

Out in Arizona, the gent in charge of me said I mustn't do any

330

work for six months at least, and preferably for a year. I had hoped for an order like that, from a competent physician, for a long, long while, but I didn't like it so well when it was actually issued. So I said I wouldn't do anything excepting for a daily syndicate "feature" of about one hundred words; it was no strain, paid very well and couldn't really be classed as work. He said anything I had to think of every day was sure to be a strain and a handicap. I said maybe that was true, but I intended to keep it up. Well, you can imagine my blushes when I got back to this city (New York) and discovered that the various newspapers throughout the country were in thorough agreement with my Arizona doctor; not only did they feel that I mustn't do any work, but also they doubted that I had been doing any. The only reason I can think of is that readers of the few papers to which my stuff had been sold were dying with laughter in such numbers that the editors were afraid the entire circulation would soon be in the col', col' ground. Anyway, massa is temporarily amongst the unemployed and awaiting offers from magazine editors. I presume I shall have to ask for a squad of mounted police to keep them in line at the door.

A very unfortunate thing just happened to you. Your mother called up and reported that she had received a letter from you, written on a one-armed typewriter. If you can write to one parent, etc. But don't do it if it tires you.

Sr.

In his "night letter" Ring had been content to avoid politics for the most part, leaving them to Will Rogers and Calvin Coolidge. Although political events had provided him with a good deal of copy, he had never, as a writer, taken them seriously. He never espoused a cause or a party, and he was profoundly skeptical of all politicians. He attended national political conventions regularly, covering many of them for the Bell Syndicate. In 1912 he had playfully set off demonstrations for Theodore Roosevelt and had even written a song, "Teddy, You're a Bear," but this indicated no particular predilection for Roosevelt as a candidate. He was sometimes a conspicuous figure at conventions and at the Republican gathering in 1920 he got a fraction of a vote for the presidential candidacy. In 1924, covering the Democratic convention, he invented a character named Abel Woose, the Neutral Delegate from Gangrene, Texas, and also Jovial Whee, whose qualification for the presidency was that his father was a right-thinking man who believed in God's great out of doors. "The boss of the press stand handed me a letter from an admirer in

Kansas to the effect that I should ought to be throwed in the ash can because I was trying to make a joke out of a serious convention. Coals to Newcastle is all I can think of to say in reply." He regarded all conventions as circuses; he thought that the platforms were evasive and disingenuous, the entire procedure dishonest, and the delegates low-grade clowns who had come to the city for a spree. While he called himself a Republican, it was only a joke; he cared no more for the Republicans than he did for the Democrats. In fact he did not think politics any of his business; his business was only to be funny about them.

He and H. L. Mencken had both attended the Republican convention of 1920 and had seen much of each other. Ring respected Mencken above almost all other contemporary critics. Both of them had the same contempt for the American politician, the same distrust of the democratic process and of the masses. Most of Ring's writing-in-character is really a kind of joke on the American boob; Ring did not think him capable of developing a very sound system of government.

On the major political issues of his time Ring remained noncommittal. When woman suffrage was the biggest issue of the day and his paper, the *Tribune*, waged a bitter fight against it, Ring remained silent. He was not interested. On the subject of the war he refrained from any writing that could be called political; but he quite pointedly avoided the xenophobia to which everyone else succumbed, and made fun of it; and his report on the war suggests nothing but disgust for it. He regarded the peace with suspicion and did not think that the crusade for democracy had succeeded. The actions of Congress seemed to him amusing at best, contemptible at their worst. He might have approved of an effective Prohibition law, even though he was opposed to any infringement of personal liberty; but the one which was enacted seemed to him merely farcical. He covered the Disarmament Conference in 1921 in much the same spirit as he covered political conventions. He had no faith in its accomplishments. He had a horror of war and doubts about the possibility of avoiding it. Along with the jokes he made about the conference there is a perfectly serious and deeply felt plea for peace.

He attacked the Ku Klux Klan with ridicule; he knew it was dangerous, and he hated its religious and racial bigotry as well as its infantile brutality. He found the Teapot Dome scandals fascinating and deplorable, but not very surprising. When the Sacco-Vanzetti case enlisted the passionate sympathy of almost all the writers in the country, many of them Ring's close friends, he kept still. He did

332

not think it was his place to take any public stand. When the Depression came, it was hardly possible to avoid comment on it; but it was just another phenomenon of American life, and Ring did not assign the blame or suggest remedies.

One of his friends was Heywood Broun, whom Ring liked and respected as a man, even though he was not particularly interested in his political schemes. When Broun ran for mayor of Hartford on the Socialist ticket, Ring endorsed him out of friendship, not out of any belief in socialism. It was only a matter of doing a personal favor for a friend. In 1932, at Broun's behest, Ring wrote a letter saying that he was going to vote for Norman Thomas, Socialist candidate for president—the other two candidates offered so little that he had nothing to lose. *The New Leader* solemnly published this as an endorsement of Thomas.

Broun tried to enlist Ring as a fellow crusader in the cause of humanity. He recognized Ring's genius, and he also knew that Ring had a ready sympathy for anyone who was troubled or oppressed. After Ring's death Broun claimed him as a proletarian writer because he wrote about little people. Actually Ring had no feeling for nor even awareness of the proletariat as such, and Broun's attempt to give him a Marxian sanction was an earnest failure. Broun seemed to have misunderstood Ring in many ways. It is said that his last words were, "Ring Lardner died a happy man because he wrote what he wanted to."

Sometimes political personalities fascinated Ring. He thought Harding a genial fellow and enjoyed playing golf with him, and he was really interested in Coolidge, possibly because he was the only man in the country more silent than himself. He met Coolidge at a White House press conference. Coolidge was amiable enough to say that he had heard of Ring, and Ring felt like saying "a horse apiece." Writing of it later, he said he had told Coolidge a funny story and Coolidge had laughed until you could have heard a pin drop. But Ring could easily have been impressed by Coolidge's refusal to exploit his personality, or rather, a personality he didn't have; and dignity and reticence were qualities of which Ring approved.

Ring made frequent visits to Washington, but most of them had nothing to do with politics. He went more often for a ball game or a play; and his companions were newspapermen rather than politicians. He was well known at the National Press Club. One time, with Everett Watkins of the Indianapolis *Star*, he visited Harvey's restaurant and stayed till closing time; then he hired the musicians, a pianist, and two violinists to come to the Press Club, where they played all night for Ring and the newspapermen who came in from their jobs on the morning papers at 7 A.M.

In so far as Ring had any political views at all, he maintained the conservatism of his forebears. He certainly was not ignorant of socialist theory or of liberal movements; but for him they held no hope. He always remained part of the class he was born in, and despite his independence of mind he clung to many of its conventions. Some of the stereotyped attitudes typical of his background lingered on in his habits of speech and thought. The characteristic xenophobia and racial attitudes of the Midwest of his time crop up surprisingly in his letters and his published writings. Sometimes he caricatured them; at other times he seemed unthinkingly to accept them. He never quite got over some of the generalized prejudices of the wise boob. Yet in his actual relationships he rose above clichés and conventions and made no class or racial distinctions among his many friends.

The only relationships he cared about were personal. He remained resolutely indifferent to any abstract or political relationships—it was another aspect of his total skepticism. All his life he had a wary distrust of governments. He once remarked that a nation could always be depended upon to do the most stupid thing. An arch individualist, he had no faith whatever in mankind's collective intelligence.

CHAPTER NINE

Ring's stays in the hospital were longer and more frequent
now, he suffered increasing pain and discomfort, and he
was never to overcome the insomnia which made his days and nights
of chronic illness seem interminable. Yet he kept up a variety of
activities, entertained more visitors than his doctors approved of,
and worked as much as his strength permitted. Baseball players,
sports writers, composers, actors, and authors, as well as other old
friends, amused and distracted him, and he still enjoyed seeing them.
   He wrote to Mrs. Luthy in the spring of 1931:

> *Doctors Hospital*
> *Tuesday evening*
>
> Dear Mildred:
> *A Mr. and Mrs. Lanier called on me yesterday morning. Mrs.*
> *Lanier claimed to be one of the Hollis family of Americus, but I*
> *couldn't quite believe it because I never saw anyone from Americus,*
> *least of all a Hollis, move so fast. Before I had a chance to say hello,*
> *they were saying good-bye and were gone. They seemed to be very*
> *nice people and I would have enjoyed a longer visit with them, but*
> *they evidently were under the impression that they were disturbing*
> *me. The only thing about a Hollis that can disturb me is its obsti-*
> *nacy. I have never met one I wanted to say good-bye to. If they*
> *are really relatives of yours, I wish you would ask them to come*
> *back and give me a chance to get acquainted with them before I am*
> *ordered out of here to make room for some one who is sick.*

335

The other night I had a visitation from five members of the Lambs Club. They were all in extremely high spirits and the house doctor refused them permission to see me. They pushed him aside and came in anyway. Among them was Gitz Rice whom you will re-member as composer of "Dear Old Pal of Mine." Chairs were plenti-ful, but Gitz preferred sitting on the floor, from which he arose at too frequent intervals to come to my alleged bed of pain, kiss me on top of the head and say, "You old sweetheart!" They had all given their names down at the office, and when they had gone, my nurse, who had witnessed the proceedings, said, "I had no idea Grantland Rice would act like that." Of course I immediately corrected her error, but it was too late to deny the rumor which she had spread all over the place and I am afraid Grannie will go down in Doctors Hospital history as a man who sits on the floor and springs up every little while to kiss the patient on top of the head.

Aside from the Laniers' split-second call, I have been pleasantly surprised here just once. Vince Youmans came in and a house doctor took it on himself to conduct us to the housekeeper's rooms, where there was a piano. I made Vince play everything he had ever written, and it was grand. If I could afford to hire a composer-pianist like him to stay with me all the time, I could laugh at doctors and nurses.

John gets home next Sunday. Ellis is going to meet him and bring him right up here. I hope he still speaks English.

Love to the family. (And to you).

R.

Youmans' impromptu entertainment was so successful that it was repeated on a larger scale, and a party which included Paul Lannin, Ohman and Arden, the two-piano team that Ring liked so much, and Harland Dixon, the dancer of *Smiles*, was held in the house-keeper's rooms at the hospital. Ring was so popular with the staff that he was accorded privileges which were not strictly consistent with hospital routine. The pleasure he got from them more than compensated for the physical strain they involved; and after his isolation in the Arizona sanatorium, he was glad to be back in New York.

To the friends who visited him in the hospital his physical decline was shocking. He had always had a gaunt and somber appearance; now he was wasted and hollow-eyed. He was good-humored and cordial, if somewhat quieter than he had ever been. Some of his guests he enjoyed; to others he was indifferent, yet he treated everyone with the same kindness and affability. He never lost any of his gift for inspiring affection in the most disparate kinds of people and for suppressing, out of natural good manners, any apathy or distaste he may have felt in personal relationships. There were doubtless some unwelcome visitors, but none of them ever knew it.

He was able to spend much of the summer at home in East Hampton. There he planned and began to write a series of six autobiographical articles which appeared in *The Saturday Evening Post* from November 1931 to the spring of the following year. It was his first work for the *Post* in almost ten years. After the rejection of "The Golden Honeymoon" Ring had found good markets and prices elsewhere. In fact *Cosmopolitan* allowed him more range in subject and treatment than the *Post*. But these articles, reminiscences of his days as a young baseball reporter, were particularly suited to the magazine through which he had won his first large popular audience. They are among the best straight non-fiction pieces Ring ever wrote.

From the story of how Ring began his career as a baseball reporter on the South Bend *Times* and official scorer for the Central League in the local ball park, through his misadventures as a would-be scout for Comiskey, his account of his early travels with the White Sox and the Cubs, to his picture of newspaper and sports circles in Chicago and the demimonde of politics and shady night life, they are a clear and authentic record of what he had seen; and Ring looked back on it with amused affection. It is the only real autobiography he wrote, and it is notably lacking in the bitterness and self-deprecation of his mock-autobiographical columns. He was writing about times and places he had loved, but the delight of these amiable recollections does not come from mere nostalgia. They are fine reporting; the scenes and the personalities are vivid and true. It is the exactness of his observation, the fidelity of his memory, the easy charm and gentle humor of the style, the radiance of his own youthful personality which make them such pleasurable reading. There are no depths, no shadows; written at a time of anxiety and despair, they have an unexpected calmness and sagacity.

Another relapse took Ring back to the hospital in September, but by early October he was able to move to a furnished apartment on East End Avenue, where he and Ellis and John and David were to spend the winter. John, after a year in Paris, was working as a reporter on the *Herald Tribune*, Jimmy had entered Harvard, and Ring, Jr., was at Andover.

Ring worked on his *Post* articles and short pieces for *The New Yorker* and looked for other tasks to do. At the same time he kept up a steady correspondence with his sons at school, and he amused himself by following the football season closely. He wrote to Jimmy at Wigglesworth Hall in Cambridge:

Sunday, October 31 [1931]

Dear Sir:—

I can recall a Wigglesworth who played on your team; otherwise I should have to keep asking Ronghild.

You may get up in the middle of Harvard Square and tell the Reds that I never wrote a picture for Chevalier and expect never to be asked to. If I were, I know I should swoon. At the present moment, I am awaiting a telephonic yes or no from Harold Lloyd as to whether I am to write the dialogue (not the scenario) for his new picture at an outrageous (not for Hollywood) price. If he says yes, I shall have to go out there in a couple of days and stay three or four weeks. If he says no, well and good. Again, if he says yes, I shall try to find some sappy Southern Californian who wants to bet against Notre Dame, so I can get even with my baseball sharpshooters. Otherwise, it will be necessary for me to back you vs. Yale.

Since starting this letter, I have had a telegram from Harold, who thinks my price is too high. I telegraphed back that I disagreed with him. He replied that he would give me a definite answer on Monday. I know he is right, so if we get into a conversation on the telephone, I shall bargain with him until we come to terms. I need the money to pay the galumps who moved our house back to Sag Harbor. [This refers to damage done to the house in East Hampton by a hurricane the previous spring.] I shall try to ease in a stipulation to the effect that he pay an extra fare out there and back, so I can have a compartment and work all the way going and coming. Your mother or older brother will let you know the result.

John is making good at the Herald Tribune and will probably be managing editor by the end of the year if the paper fails, as seems inevitable. He and Dicky Tobin went to the Princeton-Michigan game today. The game was for the championship of the slums and Michigan won, 21 to 0. If, as I presume, you depend on the Boston papers, you may not know this.

If King Howard wins the managership of the team and you are any kind of business man, you will strip him of enough tickets to pay your board, lodging and tuition.

The meals, nursing and beds here are much better than at the *hospital. The day I left there, Dr. Erdman, who works about five days a year, performed three operations, while fifteen doctors stood around and watched. His total fees were $25,000. One was the removal, manicuring and replacement of the stomach of a seventy-year-old rake, who is now able to go out and get cock-eyed again.*

Other East Hampton news is the death, by pneumonia, of Mr. Coppell. Why couldn't it have been she, is the question being asked in all the quail coveys.

Write to me here. If I'm gone, the letter will be forwarded by mail.

In a week or two, maybe this week, a series of mine will begin in the Saturday Evening Post. Save the covers.

Mrs. Coppell

The projected movie assignment for Harold Lloyd fell through, and Ring remained in New York. Late in November he wrote again to Jimmy:

Saturday, 3 A.M.

Dear James:—

As I told your brother at Andover in a belle lettre I wrote him yesterday morning about this time, I have a new habit; I grow very, very sleepy every evening at dinner, stay up after dinner, nodding and blinking, until your mother scolds me into going to bed, fall asleep at eleven, awake at 1:30, all through with sleep, and spend the balance of the night working or writing mash notes such as this. The habit has persisted ever since I left the hospital, where a kindly nurse gave me shots in the arm to insure me a night's sleep (thereby also insuring herself one), but I have a hunch that during the coming week, I shall return to something near normalcy and then my correspondents (God help them!) will wonder why they aren't even receiving postcards from me any more.

Now don't imagine for one moment that I am suffering from a delusion that I owe you a letter—well do I remember replying to your last one and advising you to take advantage of King Howard's appointment to the post of football manager and make yourself and family independently wealthy by scalping. (I judge from recent events, however, that no tickets will be sold for Harvard games after this fall; the public will be barred, as Husing was, for the use of naughty words or for other misbehavior—In passing, my child, I might say that if you weren't a Harvard man, I'd write a little piece for The New Yorker regarding your school's haughty attitude toward the outside world. I know Bill Bingham and like him, but his refusal to have anything to do with the benefit games for the unemployed, his high hat stand in the Husing case, etc.—these and other items of the same sort have kind of cooled my love for your institution.) Nevertheless I have tried all week to bet on you and only last night succeeded in finding anyone with more than ten cents in Yale money. I had to give 8 to 5 (nonsensical odds) and the amount of the wager is $80.00 to $50.00. I lost my shirt and underwear on the world's series and not through bad judgment either, but incredibly bad luck. The defeat of Earnshaw in the last game was nothing short of murder. There was only one real hit (Watkins' home run) made off him. . . .

Sunday, 4 A.M.

I presume I ought to kneel down and thank the Almighty for getting by as fortunately as I did yesterday. I am thoroughly convinced that your hero, Barry Wood, got his Phi Beta Kappa key from a locksmith and that Notre Dame's coach, Hunk Anderson, will be driving mules in an Indiana coal mine next fall.

Forgetting (if we can) that first scrimmage, in which Harvard had a first down on Yale's seven-yard line, and the selection of plays that couldn't have scored a touchdown against Niles High School, let us leap into the fourth quarter where all the allegedly bright boys (Wood Casey at Harvard and Anderson, Jackswhich and Schwartz at Notre Dame) suddenly became the victims of brainstorms.

In war or in football, the first lesson is that the attack is more wearisome than the defense. In football it is a cardinal principle that the team just scored against shall kick off and not receive the kick-off. If the man who kicks off is any good, the receiving team will have eighty yards to go for a touchdown. When it is finally forced to punt, your team will have the ball close to midfield. The blunder occurred only once at Harvard. At Notre Dame, it happened three times. And listen to this: when Notre Dame was leading 14 to 6, the broadcaster said, "Notre Dame wisely elected to receive the kick-off so it would be in possession of the ball," and on the first play after Notre Dame had received the kick-off, Schwartz threw a sixty-yard pass from his own twenty-yard line, and the pass was knocked down. He proceeded to get himself into a hole and finally made a bad punt that gave U.S.C. its chance for a second touchdown. Even at that, Notre Dame could have kept its one-point advantage if it had slowed up its play. What is a five-yard delay penalty compared with defeat? Or three or four penalties?

Oh, well, let's not get mad. But I did get mad yesterday afternoon. Your mother, John and I were listening to both games over

340

the radio (*a new invention*) and I am afraid your mother heard some "putrid" language.

In closing, I hated to see Harvard lose on your account and John's, and I hated to see those swell-headed Californians beat a superior team because it's Schwartz's last year.

There is one safe bet—that poor old Rock turned over in his grave at least three times yesterday P.M.

Remember me to the Howards and write.

A Second Guesser

Ring's betting luck during the World Series and the football season of 1931 was typical. With all his expert knowledge of sports he managed to bet on the losing teams. This had happened to him quite consistently since 1919, when he had bet on Willard and on the White Sox. But he never stopped trying; he enjoyed the business of figuring out odds and making predictions, and he wrote about sports to his sons and to his nephew, Richard L. Tobin.

Richard Tobin was a senior at the University of Michigan, and editor of the *Michigan Daily*. In October the *Daily* had uncovered a scandal in the Building and Grounds Department of the university and printed a story on it. It was no credit to the administration, and Tobin was suspended by the president. The press all over the country protested. Tobin was reinstated by the Board of Regents and continued to edit the *Daily* for the rest of the school year. The incident was widely publicized, and it was invariably mentioned that Tobin was Ring Lardner's nephew. This brought in a bale of clippings from the clipping service to which Ring subscribed, and Ring sent his nephew a bill for three hundred dollars. Ring was quite proud of it.

In December he wrote to Tobin, on a Postal Telegraph press telegram form:

Dec. 10, 1931, 2 A.M.

. . . I guess I told you that I don't sleep o' nights any more, and my ankles are so swollen and itchy that all I can do is sit in a scratching position and turn out words, either for publication or for some one's private ear. This press-telegram may be placed in the latter category and, as usual, what I write you is confidential. Mr. Rice's All-American team (to be in the Decemger 26 issue of Collier's, which, appropriately enough, goes on sale the 18th.) is composed of the following rugby stars: Ends—Dalrymple, Tulane, and Catnip Smith, Georgia; tackles—Schweger(?), Washington, and an unspellable Pittsburgher, something like Quoutchi or Pouchi; guards—

341

Hickman, Tennessee, and Munn, Minnesota; center, M-rr-s-n, Mich-
igan; backs—Wood, Schwartz, Rentner and Shaver. No team repre-
sented by more than one man and may God have mercy on my soul
and yours if you breathe a word even to your mother-in-law. There
is nothing, however, to prevent you from digging up pictures for
use at the proper time.

A few hours ago I did my annual raddio broadcast (with Grant-
land Rice). I called Morton Downey a soprano, which he is, but
when he sees me and starts to sock me in the jaw, I'll tell him I have
just been sick.

John has had five stories in the paper in the last three days and
one of them each day carried a by-line. We are all swollen up like
my ankles.

He (John) and I lost nothing on Notre Dame for the reason that
no one would bet on the opposition.

The Princeton-Columbia-Penn-Cornell round robin yesterday was
a terrific flop and the unemployed had to drive the visiting players
home in their Hispano-Suizas. John Philip Suiza's band is on the
Goodyear hour nearly every Tuesday and Saturday night. So are
the Revellers, under a pseudonym. I read in the Michigan Daily
that the Revs were in your town last week. Lah-de-dah.

In one of the next two or three New Yorkers will appear a comical
parody on "Mourning Becomes Elektra." ["Quadroon," Dec. 19,
1931] It was a tough thing to write as two-thirds of it is menu cards
which I copied from the program.

Love to Dean Yost.

A Cadaver

The *Michigan Daily* appeared on December 18 for the last time
before suspending publication for the Christmas holidays, with a
story on Grantland Rice's All-American football team, with pictures,
the same day *Collier's* got on the stands in Ann Arbor.

After leaving the hospital in October, Ring had given an interview to a *World-Telegram* reporter. It was to cause him some regret. Ring was quite easy about giving interviews; in fact he helped
many a reporter out in such cases. One time he was asked by a reporter in Charleston when he was going to write another *House-
boat on the Styx;* he parried the question so neatly that the reporter
never knew he was interviewing the wrong author. This time there
were repercussions. Some days later *Time* picked it up and ran the
following item (Nov. 9, 1931):

Slowly recovering from pernicious anemia, Ring W. Lardner was removed from hospital to home. In the course of an interview, said he: "The prince of all bad writers is Dreiser. He takes a big subject, but so far as handling it and writing it—why one of my children could do better." (Author Lardner has four children, all boys. Last summer the youngest, David Ellis Lardner, 10 [sic], was "humorous editor" of High Tide, *juvenile newspaper of East Hampton, L. I. Richard Lardner Tobin, nephew, is managing editor of the* Daily *at the University of Michigan (TIME, Oct. 19).*

The *Time* item made the interview seem a gratuitous attack on Dreiser, and Burton Rascoe, in a column in the New York *Sun,* commented on it; whereupon Ring wrote to him:

December 16, 1931

Dear Burton:—
   I believe that a great many football fatalities might be averted by the adoption of the following rule:
   "Before commenting on a statement attributed to an interviewee, the commentator must seek out the interviewee and ascertain what the latter really did say. Penalty—Loss of two paragraphs."
   Love and a merry Christmas to the Rascoe parents and progeny.
                                                                R.W.L.

Ring had been impressed by *An American Tragedy.* Dreiser had come to see him, at Ring's invitation, and Ring had told him so, adding that he still thought *Sister Carrie* his best book. Dreiser seemed pleased by this. Ring was obliging and generous with praise; but he would hardly have gone out of his way to compliment Dreiser on this occasion if he had not held him in some esteem. However, once an interview is printed, it is difficult to allay the suspicion that there was some ground for it, and at least part of the statement attributed to Ring sounds like him—". . . one of my children could do better." Ring, himself a purist in matters of style, had little patience with Dreiser's ponderous prose. He once wrote that he had sent in a manuscript from shipboard and ". . . the water ran the words together so that when Ray Long accepted the story he sent the check to Theodore Dreiser." It is also possible that Ring was misquoted. What is interesting is Ring's conscience over the incident. He had reservations about Dreiser, but he was not in the habit of delivering uncalled-for barbs. His opinions were firm, he did not back down on them, but with his extraordinary sensibility he was very delicate about other people's feelings. He was sufficiently disturbed to write to Dreiser, explaining that he had been misquoted. Unfortunately this letter is missing from what remains of the correspondence, and what Ring actually said in it can only be inferred from the interchange that followed. Dreiser replied:

> *Hotel Ansonia*
> *New York City*
> *Jan. 5, 1932*

Courtesy and good will shine through your explanation of the WORLD-TELEGRAM and TIME comments, and I thank you, though you need not have troubled. It is a long while since I have taken umbrage at any comment made either on myself or my work, since, good bad or indifferent, both are as they are, and, as for my work, the best I can do.

Surely only critics are intolerant of those who do the best they can in so trying a world.

None the less, the phrase "the prince of bad writers" cheers me. It is glistering irony that ought to be said if for no more than the saying. I am grateful to you for having called my attention to it.

> *Cordially and with assurances of my esteem,*
> *Theodore Dreiser*

Ring did not feel he had made his point, and he wrote again.

> *Wednesday, January sixth* [*1932*]

Dear Mr. Dreiser:—

When I was in my teens, schoolmates and other acquaintances used to say of some one they particularly liked (one who spent money lavishly for drinks, ready-made cigarettes, etc.) "He's a prince," and for some reason the phrase nauseated me so that I have always avoided the word "prince" except when referring to the Prince of Wales, a thing that I have seldom found occasion to do. So whether or not "The prince of bad writers" is glistering irony, it isn't my irony and I cannot accept credit for somebody else's glistering.

It is only fair to warn you that when spring comes, your hotel will be a hotbed of Giant and Yankee ball-players—unless they have decided to jump to the Waldorf.

> *Sincerely,*
> *Ring Lardner*

Dreiser graciously accepted this as a full apology, even though Ring was apologizing for only one phrase.

Hotel Ansonia
New York
Jan. 7, 1932

Dear Lardner:

Plainly I did not make myself clear. But you must believe that I accept—and did—fully your assurance of innocence. More, that I appreciated fully and gratefully your troubling to write me and explain. Can I make this more definite? At the same time I rejoice in the phrase "The Prince of Bad Writers." The newspaper man who concocted it should have a medal of some kind—a real one. Let's call it "the phrase of the year" or "the year's best bit of irony."

Anyhow you are a neighbor of mine. If you would trouble to walk so far we might drown this slight misunderstanding in hard likker. The mystic hour of five usually finds me turning from composition to speculation & drink.

Theodore Dreiser

As for the base-ball wonders,—at worst they can only drown out the tuneful Latins herein resident at this hour.

Ring closed the matter by writing:

25 East End Avenue
New York City
January 11, 1931 [sic: *1932*]

Dear Mr. Dreiser:—

On the contrary, you did make yourself plain and I am grateful to you for taking my word.

I want to ask you for a rain check on that hard likker invitation. It is my misfortune that when I get started, I seem to find it necessary to fight it out on those lines even if it takes all winter, and having spent a year among the unemployed, I must now work until I am somewhere near even.

We would be neighbors if I lived on West End Avenue, but as it is the whole width of Manhattan divides us. I am within wading distance of Welfare Island and hope to finish there.

Sincerely,
Ring Lardner
The Prince of Doltish Drinkers

This was far beyond anything that was called for in the way of apology. Whatever reservations Ring had about Dreiser as a writer, he had meant no personal slight; he had made amends and had received assurances of Dreiser's esteem. No harm had been done;

they had never been close friends. Ring's chief concern was over being misunderstood. His remorse, his self-reproach, the final turning of the detested "ironical" phrase upon himself could hardly have been induced by the unlucky interview alone. They seem rather symptoms of a pervading state of mind.

The whole uneasy correspondence between these two sincere and highly articulate men is a little melancholy—so much effort to correct an unintentional slight, so much good feeling lost. They never saw each other again.

In the spring of 1932 Ring began to write a new busher series for *The Saturday Evening Post*. The original busher, Jack Keefe, had vanished thirteen years before, never to reappear in Ring's stories. The new one, Danny Warner from Centralia, Illinois, was kin to him—egotistical, gullible, opaque, with an inexhaustible store of alibis for every shortcoming, and an undeflatable vainglory over his athletic prowess, which consists largely of being a daring, if not very canny, base stealer. He has another talent, too; he is a "grooner" and a song writer; his colleagues call him "Rudy" after Rudy Vallee, and he is unaware that he is being ribbed.

The six stories are in the form of letters from Danny to his sweetheart Jessie Graham, and her replies. Danny is an outfielder for the Brooklyn team, managed by Max Carey, and his roommate is Casey Stengel, who tries to keep him out of trouble. His first attempt at base stealing is a great success, and he tries it again, making a brief and scrappy acquaintance with Rabbit Maranville, the Boston Braves' second baseman. "So I says wear did you pick up that high school pitcher and he says wear did you ever see a high school or was your father the janiter and I says no your father was." Danny goes on to steal third. ". . . and I dont know if I would of been out or not but there 3rd base man made it sure by dropping the ball and Stengel turned a summer salt and I looked at Maranville and he was lane on the ground kicking his ft in the air. . . ."

"Well I dident have no chance to get in there today but we beat them and they still kept on trying to ride me and Maranville made faces at me on the bench but all I done was waggle my thums in my ears and holler rabbit at him and sqeek at him like I was a rabbit."

Carey and Stengel encourage "Rudy" to write a song to the tune of "Life Is Just a Bowl of Cherries," and he produces an imitation of it ending:

> *Life is just a game of baseball*
> *so win or lose with a smile.*

His next attempt at stealing a base is a failure, and Danny is put out of the game and threatened with banishment to the minors. But it does not repress his zeal for song writing, and he writes a number inspired by the currently popular "My Mom."

> *My dad I love him*
> *My mom she loves him.*
> *My sister Edna loves him my dad.*
> *He is a wonder*
> *Will live to be a hundred*
> *And never made a blunder my dad.*
> *When I was a lad*
> *If I act it bad mom would scold me.*
> *Then I would go to him*
> *And on his lower limbs he would hold me.*
> *Theys no one greater*
> *Than my old pater.*
> *He is my alma mater my pop.*

"Stengel made me put Ednas name in and told me about alma mater but he says the line about never made a blunder dont ring true. Alma mater and pater are greek and means the same thing."

Like Jack Keefe, Danny imagines himself a Lothario, and is easy game for the predatory women who inhabit so many of Ring's stories. A telephone operator from Florida follows Danny to Brooklyn. He takes her to a night club, stays out too late, drinks too much, and finds himself liable to suspension. He naïvely writes all this to Jessie, who is first indignant, then reproachful, but very tenacious.

"Well Danny I am afraid this is not the kind of letter you want from me, though why you want any kind is more than I can imajine. And Danny there was a time when you calling me 'dear' would have thrilled me through and through, but when you write it in the same letter which you write H——— twice and mention nightshirts like they were nothing at all or you were writing to another man, well Danny I just wish you had not written 'dear' in that kind of a letter."

After a few hangovers Danny's mind is not on baseball and he persistently disobeys orders. So he is sent to Jersey City for some seasoning, and after a futile protest accepts his fate. Jessie writes to him that she is coming to join him, although he has not given her much encouragement:

"Well dear I am coming and will arrive at the Penn Station at

9:40 in New York Saturday morning and please meet me as I will be scared to death if you dont. If you still feel like you felt last winter and spring, well dear this is leap year. So good-bye till Saturday morning and dont fail me dear."

So Danny is left with Jessie and a minor-league job, with the possibility of a future in baseball if he learns discipline. The stories were popular with *Post* readers, and it was suggested that Ring might write more about Danny the following year. He might have had this in mind, but the series was never resumed. As it stood, the ending was conclusive enough: the possibilities for people like Danny and Jessie are limited.

The stories were published in book form under the title *Lose with a Smile* in 1933. It is a repetition of *You Know Me Al*, with an echo of "Some Like Them Cold" in the character of Jessie, with her little flashes of wounded pride, her disappointments, her willingness to compromise. It is by no means one of Ring's major works, and there is nothing in it that Ring had not written before. But, as the *New Republic* review said, "*Lose with a Smile* may be a potboiler, but many an intelligent reader will find it a refreshing recovery from the self-conscious [ness] that seemed to endanger Lardner soon after his discovery by the dilettanti several years ago. . . . Lardner can repeat himself more profitably than some American writers do. . . . Nor is there any concession to popular-magazine form in the story's end, which is neither happy nor sad. It is simply real."

The new busher stories were still fresh and readable, if minor. But what is lacking in Danny Warner is the ebullience of Jack Keefe, whose braggadocio had a certain engaging style to it. Compared to him, Danny is a little dreary and only mildly amusing. He has all the characteristics of his prototype except the vitality and exuberance that made Keefe's follies almost monumental. In contrast Danny is less than average and a little contemptible. But he is perfectly real, and so are the backgrounds of the baseball training camp, the ball park, and Centralia, which are so naturally and effortlessly evoked through the power of language. But Ring could no longer see his busher as the exemplar of common human foibles which were tolerable just because they were universal. Danny is a particular boob, and Ring did not feel for him the amused affection he had felt for Jack Keefe.

In May 1932, Ring was back in Doctors Hospital, where he stayed for a month. He was still working on the new busher stories for the *Post* and in spite of the increasing difficulty of writing he was looking for more work. During his illness and intervals of enforced idleness he had become a studious radio listener. Now he proposed to Harold Ross, editor of *The New Yorker*, who visited him in the hospital, to write some pieces on radio for him. Ross had always welcomed Ring's contributions and he was sympathetic to his views. "Over the Waves" became a regular feature of the magazine.

Ring undertook it because he had formed some definite ideas on the standards of radio entertainment. It was avowedly a crusade from the start. He wrote to Ellis's sister, Mrs. Hendry:

July 7 [*1932*]

Dear Rube:—

Thank God for John, if only because he made you write. I thought I was the Hendry's Forgotten Man; Ellis evidently thought so, too, for when she saw your writing, she opened the letter—and read it.

Arthur Jacks used to have an exasperating (until you knew him) trick of always "topping" people. If I complained of a headache, he had a worse one. If Rex mentioned a sore throat, Arthur had all the symptoms of diphtheria. So I will proceed to annoy you by pointing out that Robin's present unemployment is not nearly as "bad" as my plight throughout 1931 and several weeks of this blessed year. There was work to be done, but the mere sight of a typewriter gave me heebie-jeebies. When I was able to subdue them and attempt to work, I was immediately overcome by sleeping sickness, though nothing short of chloroform would put me to sleep in bed. I would lie awake and think of debts and expenses; jump up determined to work; begin to work and either get the shakes or doze off, and then go back to bed and start the whole performance over again. I maintain that when a person is idle through no fault of his own, it is less irritating than when he realizes that "loose living" is "the cause of it all."

Dickie Tobin, having got through Michigan, is rooming in town with John. They are both, as you probably know, reporters on the Herald Tribune. They have the same off-day and will probably come out here about once every two weeks during the summer. David will be our contribution to Andover this fall; Jim will go back to Harvard and Bill will enter Princeton. IF the magazines don't "ask" the old man to take another cut. Magazines and newspapers are, of course, face to face with the Grim Reaper, their only consolation being that radio, which beat them out of a lot of advertising, is now as badly off as they.

The New Yorker, being a "class" publication, doesn't pay much, but it's kind of fun to be a radio critic. If I don't get fired, I will crusade against the vulgarity and stupidity of some of the comedians and the immorality and illiteracy of most of the songs. It won't do any good, excepting to my disposition, which is soured by listening to the atrocities perpetrated by jokers, lyric writers and alleged singers. . . .

The bus cure for insomnia would work on me with a vengeance. Once I rode in one from Miami to Palm Beach, a trip taking only a couple of hours. An hour more and I would have shot all the other passengers and gone to sleep permanently in the electric chair. Buses and berths were not designed for people over five feet eleven. When I go to bed in sleeping cars now (which I don't), I wonder how in the world I stood it an average of two or three times a week all those years. Probably I was encouraged by the knowledge that there were always four or five pitchers who couldn't get through a car door without crawling on their hands and knees.

Come and see us and I will cook you a meal such as only I can cook—lamb chops, potato salad, pie—just as I cooked for you in Brookline twenty-one (Good heavens!) years ago.

RWL

The illiteracy of song writers, inane sentimentality, musical ham, male sopranos, tiresome commercials and dishonest advertising, all of them irked Ring into hilarious and not always good-natured comments in his radio columns. On the other hand there were many programs which he enjoyed and praised with obvious satisfaction; and he showed an uncanny clairvoyance in picking out the performers with the talent and showmanship to survive the vagaries of popular fancy and the enthusiastic blunders of producers and advertising agencies—Burns and Allen, Fred Allen, Eddie Cantor, Jack Benny, Bing Crosby and Paul Whiteman, to name only a few who were new to radio at that time and have for more than twenty years justified Ring's early admiration. To his criticism of radio he brought the standards which he had applied to his own work all his life: professional skill, good taste, and decency. If his attack on the things he hated was more downright and even more ill-tempered than he had ever seemed to be before, the principles were not new.

As a purist in matters of language, Ring was offended by the lack of grammar in song lyrics as well as by their general foolishness. The words of popular songs are often a collection of nonsense syllables designed for easy utterance by poorly trained singers; Ring hoped that they might mean something, or even say what they meant. He had listened to enough common speech not to be surprised at its deficiencies, and he had a good time razzing Tin Pan Alley lyricists who sometimes made Jack Keefe seem a Ph.D. by comparison, and who also seemed to think that what they wrote to borrowed music was really lyrical. After *June Moon* no one could suppose him to have been newly disillusioned over this phenomenon. But it was with particular glee that he tripped up Cole Porter, who was not exactly a denizen of the music publishers' sweatshops:

You must know that Mr. Cole Porter, lyricist of "Night and Day,"
shares the mantle of W. S. Gilbert with Ira Gershwin, Lorenz Hart,
Irving Caesar, Irving Berlin, Joseph V. McKee, Howard Dietz, Bert
Kalmar, George M. Cohan, Primo Carnera, and George Herman
(Columbia Lou) Gehrig. Well, it seems to me that in this number,
Mr. Porter not only makes a monkey of his contemporaries but
shows up Gilbert himself as a seventh-rate Gertrude Stein, and he
does it all with one couplet, held back till late in the refrain and
then delivered as a final, convincing sock in the ear, an ear already
flopping from the sheer magnificence of the lines that have pre-
ceded. I reprint the couplet:
Night and day under the hide of me
There's an Oh, such a hungry yearning, burning inside of me.

He offered variations of his own, preserving wherever possible the impeccable five words "There's an Oh, such a . . ." and attributing the first two to his niece:

Well, then, here is the first variant from Little Ann's pen, with
spelling corrected by uncle:

Night and day under the rind of me
There's an Oh, such a zeal of spooning, ru'ning the mind of me.

And another, wherein she lapses into the patois:

Night and day under the peel of me
There's a hert that will dree if ye think aucht but a' weel o' me.

And now a few by uncle himself:

1. Night and day under the fleece of me
There's an Oh, such a flaming furneth burneth the grease of
me.
2. Night and day under the bark of me
There's an Oh, such a mob of microbes making a park of me.

351

3. *Night and day under my dermis, dear,*
   There's a spot just as hot as coffee kept in a thermos, dear.
4. *Night and day under my cuticle*
   There's a love all for you so true it never would do to kill.
5. *Night and day under my tegument*
   There's a voice telling me I'm he, the good little egg you meant.

It was not merely lyrical inanity but musical affectation that moved him to write of Bing Crosby (whom he liked otherwise):

For the benefit of the untutored I must explain that in the days before the Musical Depression, a singer ordinarily ended a song on the keynote, or tonic. If a song is in the key of F, F is the tonic. The "third" is A natural and the "fifth" is C. (Am I educated!) In those days it was the exception when a number was wound up on a third, and even more so when the vocalist fifthed at the finish. Bing and Russ [Colombo] use the fifth nine times out of ten, or at least, they nibble all around it. It must be part of the Crosby system, but I hope Bing doesn't claim it as original. If he does, he should accuse not only Russ, but Ruthie Etting, Artie Jarrett, Streetie Singer, Katie Smith, and countless others of stealing his stuff, and among the countless others is the late Giacomo Puccini, who put it in the script of an important tenor aria in "La Boheme," which was composed before the invention of static. At any rate, the "trick" has become more or less familiar and I have been tempted to write to both of the boys and say, "Take a tonic." (Oh, dear! as Harry Richman remarks after his gags on the Chase & Sanborn Oh Dear Hour, taking the words out of the indestructible audience's mouth.)

Two of his pet hates were the Irish tenor Morton Downey, whom he called a soprano; and Tony Wons—"that bit of old Dresden"—whose specialty was reciting sentimental verse in a syrupy voice.

The popularity of Mr. Downey is evidenced by the fact that WABC keeps him going three times weekly Camels or no Camels, but to me he can never be the same when deprived of his sweet-toned sidekick, Tony Wons, on whom I was developing such a crush that I started to write him a special cheer:
             "Tony Wons! Tony Twice!
             Holy, jumping . . ."
And that was as far as I had progressed when the flash came that he was temporarily through and at present reciting Edgar Guest's poetry to an audience of helpless Wisconsin pickerel.

352

He repeatedly railed against "request" programs, believing that a good musical director could construct a better program than the great insensible audience, who wanted to hear "Danny Boy" and "Mother Machree" over and over again—a waste of the talents of such singers as Grace Moore and Lawrence Tibbett. It seemed to him that the networks and advertising agencies were making every effort to degrade programs musically as well as intellectually in a misguided attempt to reach the lowest and broadest level of popular taste; but he also had a suspicion that the attempt was not entirely misguided. He kidded soap operas and fatuous commercials, announcers who mispronounced words, inaccurate sports broadcasters, and he had an especially riotous time with the Blue Ribbon Malt contest, which offered prizes for the last line of a Limerick, the first four lines of which could have been conceived only by an imbecile. To his delight the last lines submitted were so dreadful that the announcement of the winners of the contest had to be postponed repeatedly until it fizzled out in virtual silence. "Well, I don't expect to land much of a job as a seer just because I prophesied that the Malters would never ask B. Bernie or anybody else to taint Gosh's untoasted air with a line that would consummate any such atrocity as that."

Ring's crusade against illiteracy and sheer stupidity was marked by an irony that seems genial compared to the anger and indignation he vented on off-color comedians and songs he considered pornographic. Popular songs and comic sketches were the kind of entertainment he loved best. Now, virtually a captive audience—as a radio critic he was compelled to listen in early all day and evening—he found himself assaulted at every turn of the dial by what he thought to be obscenity. His attack on it was deliberate and calculated; it was probably what was uppermost in his mind when he proposed to write the column for *The New Yorker*. After a few mild references to his howling displeasure he let loose at the end of July with a direct offensive:

No Visitors, N. Y.
It would be anything but a relief to the Unemployment Situation if radio censors went to work. People in such a deep coma can't suffer much from hunger pangs, whereas if they woke up, it would mean starvation for the families of many a bad comedian, many a worse singer and nearly all lyricists who are not writing for the stage.
Somewhere in the book there must be a rule against rough cracks.

353

The good comics don't use them. The bad ones can be depended on to average three per broadcast. When anyone tells me I am looking great and ought to get out and mow the grass or play golf (I always thought the two were synonymous), I tune in on some guy who has been called a low comedian and wants to live down to the title; a few minutes of him and the danger of convalescence is over. I say these things at the risk of being considered queasy and a prude. At the risk and in the hope. The censors, if they are not in the coma for which I have given them credit, run no such risk and share no such hope.

Somewhere else in the book there must be a rule against songs that are suggestive or songs that are immoral. Well, you can't apply suggestive to the majority of them; if you do, you probably call "Electra" an amusing skit. Let's study for a moment the refrain of "As You Desire Me." That, of course, is the first line and the rest of it runs:

> So shall I come to you.
> Howe'er you want me, so shall I be.
> Be if forever, or, be it just a day,
> As you desire me, let come what may.
> I doubt not but you will do what you will with me;
> I give myself to you, for you're my Destiny,
> And now, come take me, my very soul is yours,
> As you desire me, I come to you.

Words and music by Allie Wrubel, confessed author of "Now You're in My Arms," the lyric of which has baffled bards and cryptogram experts for two years. Nothing about this one will bewilder you, unless it's the punctuation. A few of those last commas strike me as kind of reticent, even if Allie ain't. Her (I hope it's a her) phrase "I doubt not but" is one I dastn't criticize. A descendant of mine used it in an essay contest at Andover and won $15.00. Of course, he might have been first but for the but. "Let come what may," however, should read "leave come what may" or "let may what come"; otherwise, a person gets all mixed up.

Now my $2.00 dictionary defines suggestive as "tending to bring into the mind what is improper," but to me it implies something subtle in the method of bringing. "Now You're in My Arms" is as ingenuous and aboveboard as Senator McNaboe, and I doubt not but that it tempts many young girls and young men—particularly if it be true that Prohibition has started them drinking—to call up and find out whether their destiny is home and if so, will he or she let *come what may. I know that when I heard Mr. Downey blare it for the first time, I grabbed my hat and Mother Hubbard and told Nurse I was going out. She asked where and that stopped me. But I does claim that Allie's protagonist is not a promoter of good morals, for he, or she, certainly shows no fear of consequences and sings "Let come what may" just for a rhyme. She may not be a fool who hath said in her heart that there is no Golly, but she is pretty sure that Golly will forgive her if she claims that Destiny pushed her out of bounds.*

Ring went on to protest against "Paradise," which he found suggestive because the refrain was hummed and whistled, after a verse which left no doubt as to what the humming signified.

Ring had minor successes in his crusade: when he was annoyed at a quacking noise that Eddie Cantor made on his program, he asked him to stop, and Cantor, a friend and admirer, readily complied. In the case of "As You Desire Me," Ring at least managed to get it revised:

In fairness to the N.B.C. and as an item of possible interest to the invisible audience and my brother tilter, I will state here that someone connected with the broadcasting company asked Mr. (not Miss) Tinpan Allie Wrubel to clean up the "Desire" refrain. He complied and wrote me a note, thanking me for his trouble. "Listen in to the new version," he said, "and if you can understand it now, you are better than I am. As one man to another, let come what may." Well, I did listen in and I'll admit that it is unfathomable in its purified form. But heck's becks! That ought to make it a smash hit.

In other quarters Ring met the opposition he expected. Ray Perkins, a comic whom Ring had attacked for being vulgar, at the very least, rose to the bait, and was defended by "Mr. Aircaster," the radio reviewer of the New York *Journal*. Their defense was simply that there weren't any—or at least many—objectionable songs or jokes on the air; and that anyway the networks, the sponsors, and the advertising agencies exercised a threefold censorship. Ring countered by specifying Mr. Perkins' offenses and inviting him to repeat them for a jury composed of Franklin P. Adams, Gilbert Seldes, and George Jean Nathan.

He continued his crusade in spite of its unpopularity:

Perhaps you wonder why I revive this tedious subject when there is so little chance of a queasy crusader making headway. There are several reasons, and one is that Mr. Wrubel and the authors of

"Paradise" ought not to be the only boys criticized when scores of their fellow-geniuses are trying their worst (and with ever-increasing signs of ultimate success) to outsmut them. Another reason is that, queer as it may seem, I don't like indecency in song or story, and sex appeal employed for financial gain in this manner makes me madder than anything except fruit salad. Reason 3: A large percentage of the invisible audience is composed of old people who retain the faculty of being shocked and of children between the ages of nine and sixteen who are not morally damaged by the words Hell, damn and God, but can't help wondering what the heck when they hear songs that glorify defiance of the seventh amendment to Moses' constitution. Reason 4: A curiosity as to whether there is such a thing as radio censorship, and if so, whether those in charge of it are morons themselves or simply don't know what is what and what is not; and whether they will take the hint lying down when their attention is called to this squawk, as it shall be. Reason 5: A curiosity as to whether the sponsors and their advertising agencies are just plain dumb or as broad as the ocean and as lewd as the sky. Reason 6: Something happened on a very recent Sunday night which rekindled the smoldering ashes of offended prudery and forced me to mention the six-letter surname of a New Testament character with such volume that even the nurse woke up.

The stations I usually play are WEAF, WOR, WJZ, and WABC. Tuning in first on WABC, I found myself listening to a risque song. Tuning in on WJZ, I heard another one. Similar thrills were waiting on WOR and WEAF, and it was then that I lost control of my tongue and frightened poor Miss Graham out of her nap and her cap. An apology and an explanation were in order.

"Well," she said, "it's Sunday. They probably thought of that and now they're celebrating the Fourth Commandment which begins (she whisked out the midget Bible that she carries in her hypo case): 'Remember that thou keep holy the Sabbath Day,' and ends: 'Wherefore the Lord blessed the Sabbath Day and hallowed it.'"

Now, I won't put your credulity to a test by averring that there was nothing except risque songs on the four stations that night, but between the speeches and the risque jokes, the boys and girls managed to crowd in a flock of numbers that were questionable in title, or in one or more lines, or in toto. I took down a few titles and print them here so that when you go Christmas shopping, you can visit your favorite music store and buy something educational to read aloud to sing to the baby. Some of them may be classified as bedtime stories, as you will see when you get them. Ready?

356

"I'll Never Have to Dream Again," "You're Telling Me," "Good Night, My Lady Love," "Pu-leeze, Mr. Hemingway" (*a swell tune and a good idea, marred by two or three words*), *"You Little So-and-So," "Forbidden Love," "Let's Put Out the Lights and Go to Sleep"* (*just on the border. They say that in the original lyric, the last word was not "sleep"*), *"Love Me Tonight," "Horses Carry Tales"* (*sung by what I thought was a new Negro quartet which could make "Rock of Ages" sound nasty*), *"Bring 'Em Back Alive," "And So to Bed"* (*an ingenious finishing touch*), *"Please," "Take Me in Your Arms," "Here Lies Love,"* and *"What Did I Get in Return?"*

Others you might buy, if the kid is bored by those I have named, are "Ain'tcha Kinda Sorry Now?" and "Thrill Me!" The latter I have not yet heard on the air, but I expect to, for it probably touches a new low for the year. A copy of this number ought to be in every right-thinking, kiddy-loving American home. Why, the refrain goes: "Thrill me with a kiss that's vicious with love delicious . . ." No, I won't spoil a sale. And I'll try hard not to feel so comstocky next time.

But when Rudy Vallee, whom Ring liked well enough when he confined himself to singing a couple of rousing "U. S. Nasal Academy" tunes, undertook on his regular program to defend "Let's Put Out the Lights and Go to Sleep," the Comstock in Ring was again aroused. ". . . And here was Rudy all hot and bothered, saying it was perfectly decent, having been written by a friend of his, and that he (Rudy) was about to sing it, presumably as incontrovertible evidence of its purity, or perhaps to purge it with the hyssop of his immaculate larynx." Ring countered with several convincing testimonials as to the immodest intentions of the lyricist, and asked with some asperity, "Did you really go to Yale?"

Ring's anger was genuine, though he had very little hope of accomplishing much by his crusade. Nevertheless he got some satisfaction from the response of the lyricists and performers who wore an air of aggrieved innocence in the face of his accusations, although it was quite obvious even then that they knew what they were doing, that their exploitation of sex appeal was a calculated policy which has been consistently followed ever since. Networks and performers could vindicate their taste and their morals by dismissing Ring as a prude; but when he wrote the column headed "Lyricists Strike Pay Dirt," he scored a direct hit on radio's source of revenue, which was peddling the suggestive to the suggestible, an occupation too widespread and lucrative for any one man ever to influence to any important degree.

Even outside professional circles Ring's campaign did not enlist a great deal of sympathy. His fan mail was full of complaints about his prudishness, and even some of his friends and admirers discounted his radio criticism as a personal crotchet. Fitzgerald referred to it deprecatingly as an "odd little crusade" that stemmed from his sexual repression; and Ernest Hemingway, in an article, "Defense of Dirty Words," which deplored the lack of sex and four-letter words in Ring's writing and somehow implied that it was an almost fatal defect, called "Over the Waves" "those pitiful dying radio censorship pieces."

It is true that Ring's distaste for pornography and even for mild vulgarity was almost obsessive and his prudishness pathological. He was offended by harmless and trivial things to which most people are either oblivious or completely inured. This was nothing new, not the result of illness or growing irascibility; he had always had it; it came partly from a lifelong habit of repression, and partly from a fastidious regard for good form and an acute sense of social propriety. His illness may have intensified it; he certainly had less patience than ever with dirty stories and sexual innuendo. His attacks on popular songs were undoubtedly the expression of a deep idiosyncrasy.

He was not mainly concerned with the morals of the public. ". . . Not more than 2.75% of the Invisible Audience can be morally or mentally hurt by the vulgarities and obscenities they have to listen to, if they listen at all. You can't teach the Red Sox new methods of hitting into double plays." He was really concerned about the standards of a profession he loved, and with his own enjoyment of it.

By most people's standards the songs he condemned are no longer considered very shocking; at least in comparison with current popular hits. Some of them seem totally harmless, others are only slightly obscene, a very few are intentionally pornographic. Ring's strictures seem quite old-fashioned now. He even had misgivings about the completely innocuous "Tea for Two." But his crusade can hardly be dismissed as a personal crotchet. His contentions were based on the absolute social and moral code by which he lived and which had fallen into disuse. Although he had long since ceased to profess any religion, he could still invoke the Ten Commandments in support of his views. He was not merely unburdening his own distaste; he saw a larger context to the issue, and he was aware of the enormous influence that radio was to have on vaster audiences than had ever been reached by any other medium.

Whatever its personal motivations, Ring's prudishness and his concern for the future standards of popular entertainment were not unjustified. The deleterious effect on the speech and minds of a whole generation of illiteracy and inanity relentlessly broadcast for thirty years is not hard to trace; and the commercial exploitation of sex to an audience consisting largely of children and of adults of at least impressionable mentality has probably had no better effect on human personality and values. Anyone who listens thoughtfully now to radio or television, not to mention juke boxes, cannot help regretting that Ring's crusade failed so utterly.

But the crusade was only a minor aspect of "Over the Waves." Ring was just as zealous in commending good programs, offering constructive criticisms, and establishing canons of taste to which every subsequent critic of radio and television has been indebted. If the intellectual and artistic level of broadcasting does not seem to have risen much in the past twenty years, it could conceivably have been much worse than it is if its early critics had not brought some knowledge and authority to a pioneer attempt to evaluate the industry in its early years. Ring's standards of criticism are still valid and could still be profitably applied to all the fields of popular entertainment.

CHAPTER TEN

Ring's state of mind varied during the last year and a half
of his life. At times he seems to have been optimistic about
the possibility of feeling better and being able to work; at other
times a kind of resignation appears to have set in; and a persistent
note of nostalgia in his letters and stories suggests that he was more
inclined to look backward than forward. He put the best face possible on his situation. He took his illness seriously enough, but was
reluctant to admit that he had tuberculosis; when he referred to his
symptoms, which were painful, it was in a humorous way; and his
physical weakness was appalling. One time his friend and East
Hampton neighbor, Percy Hammond, who was suffering from
stomach ulcers, visited him. Ring was too weak to talk; but he
pointed to his stomach and shook his head to signify that, whatever
else he had, he did not have stomach ulcers.

In spite of fatigue he kept driving himself, and he even found
time and strength to show the same interest he had always had in
family and old friends. Even while he was still in the hospital, he
wrote a long, friendly letter to John McGraw, who had been forced
to retire as manager of the Giants because of ill health.

> *Doctors Hospital*
> *New York City*
> *June 4, 1932*

Dear John:
   *This is just to say that I'm terribly sorry to hear of your resigna-
tion as manager and of the serious nature of the illness that caused
it. Baseball hasn't meant much to me since the introduction of the*

TNT ball that robbed the game of the features I used to like best—features that gave you and Bill Carrigan and Fielder Jones and other really intelligent managers a deserved advantage, and smart ball players like Cobb and Jim Sheckard a chance to do things.

You and Bill Gleason and Eddie Collins were among the few men left who personified what I enjoyed in "the national pastime." Moreover your retirement has ruined my hope of a resumption of amusing (to me) relations with Frank Belcher when, and if, I am ever physically and financially able to go into the Lambs club-house again. Two or three years ago, when the Giants lost a game or a series, I used to torture him by saying that it was due to bad management. When I had him on the verge of tears, I would "break down and confess" that I was kidding and that I really considered you the greatest of managers, and it was honestly pathetic to see him brighten up at my sudden change of front. If you ever had a loyal supporter, he was and is it.

Often I have wondered whether you ever enjoyed the feeling of security and comfort that must be a manager's when the reporters assigned to his club are "safe" and not pestiferous—a gang such as Chance and Jones and Jim Callahan were surrounded with for a few years in Chicago, and I don't say that just because I happen to be one of the gang. We had a rule, and lived up to it, that none of us would ever act as assistant managers, would be worthy of whatever confidence was reposed and would never ask, "Who's going to pitch tomorrow?" The result was mutually beneficial. We were kept posted on whatever changes, deals and trades were "in the air" and therefore knew what we were talking about when the trade or deal was put through or called off. The managers referred to didn't wince when they saw one of us approaching. They were our friends and we were theirs. So far as I was concerned, Frank Chance knew that I was very close to Schulte and lots of times when Schulte was not "behaving," Chance would drop a hint to me, knowing that I would warn Schulte, and I am positive I was thus enabled to save Schulte money and Chance the unpleasant task of fining and suspending him. . . .

I do hope you get better soon and that eventually you get "back." I am lucky in that I have no physical pain. My chief trouble is an increasing hatred of work, and it happens that work is necessary. Please remember me to Mrs. McGraw, or, as the internes would call her, Mrs. "McGror."

Sincerely,
Ring Lardner

Along with the genuine compliment he paid McGraw he included a modest reminiscence of his own role as a baseball reporter, as if he hoped that McGraw would remember him, too, as a good fellow. He was recalling the days of his life he had really enjoyed most. In saying that he had no physical pain he was merely being stoical; if the pain was not acute, the discomfort and fatigue were enough for any man to have to endure.

Shortly after he left the hospital for East Hampton, he wrote to his nephew Richard Tobin:

Solomon Gr--dy

Dear Dickie:—

Attached are two or three documents of value to you and me. The envelope is sent in the hope you will see it to its way via the New York PO. I don't dare send it from here or Jerome Kern would have to put the lyrics enclosed into his farewell opus and while Jim is home for the week-end giving it to him is like sending it to the dead letter office.

Sherwood Anders-n and Rabbit Maranville paid calls before I left No Visitors, N. Y., for this bed o'pain. Anders-n and I got to talking why we'd ever left our small towns. Maranville says the Yankees are a cinch so he isn't putting anything on them. I've got what the boys call a yard and a half unless Doyle wiggles out, and he's trying.

Claudette Colbert was in town before I left and came up to say hello. I never knew they was so many interns in Doctors Hospital. Every five seconds a new one would come in and say, "Can't I get you some icewater, Mr. Lardner?" or "I'm going out, would you like anything from the drug store?" Her hair is now pink but she's cute, anyway.

Your aberrated mother hasn't sent me any of your clippings but I caught one Sunday under a by-line. Good stuff, congratulations. When you see my son John tell him we now have mail delivery in East Hampton.

Ring

(The documents enclosed were some lyrics which Jerome Kern never used, and some currency for Tobin.)

The brief reference to Ring's conversation with Anderson about their small towns is suggestive. Until 1931 there is nothing very nostalgic in Ring's frequent, jocular mentions of Niles, to which he returned seldom and for very brief visits; and his stories of small-town life do not indicate that he thought very highly of it. But he

363

never quite got over Niles, confirmed city dweller though he was.

He continued his desultory, pleasurable correspondence with friends, just as if he found writing easy and had nothing else to do. To Mrs. Luthy he wrote:

East Hampton
Bastille Day [1932]

Dear Millie:—

Two or three years ago I scolded you for using a comma where a semi-colon belonged (or something) and you were furious, so I'm afraid to tell you how your last letter impressed me, or, rather, depressed me. Honestly it sounded as if you considered me a perfect or imperfect stranger and when I had finished it, I was amazed that the salutation hadn't been "Dear Mr. Lardner" or "Dear Sir." I won't answer such questions as how do I like my house in its new position or is my interest in radio something new. Listen, Miss, I ain't Dr. Erdmann, with whom you are trying to make dinner conversation. I remember you quite well and can talk to you on much more familiar topics—Ovaltine, for example. Aren't you the lady who once recommended it as a cure for my Intractable Insomnia? Well, the other night (July fourth) I was listening in on Little Orphan Annie and the man said, "If you are going to stay up and see the fireworks tonight, take a glass of Ovaltine before supper and another glass an hour later, and it will keep you wide awake and fresh for the evening's entertainment. Now Millie, this man is employed by the Ovaltine company and he ought to know what the lovely stuff is good for. Yet I can scarcely believe you would try to coax me into consuming a beverage that not only must drive a person to beverages more pleasant, expensive, habit-forming and devastating, but also keep him wide awake and, above, all things, FRESH. I simply am too fond of myself to entertain the thought that you don't remember me a little, and if you do, you surely are aware that I seldom have an ambition to keep wide awake, unless there is a game of setback in prospect, and never fresh. I do think an explanation is in order.

Moreover, I have this against you: One of the reasons I left the hospital before my time was to be in a position to serve as a member of the reception and entertainment committee when you and Jane came to East Hampton. I don't believe the Rices are ever coming but Helga is here and so hard up for work that she insists on inviting our two Danes to have a meal with her once or twice a week. Ellis seldom goes out in the evening and I am afraid she gets quite lonely without Kate. Even when she goes out, I would insist on your staying home and entertaining Jim, Bill and me; I am not suggesting that you wouldn't be invited other places, but merely hoping that your attitude toward parties is the same as it used to be. Dave misses Jane, as also do Liz Wheeler and the other Lardner boys. If you ever did want to go out, I would love to serve as Jane's nurse because it would give me a comfortable sensation of having to do something that isn't work. Please think it over, Millie, and consider carefully that the summer will be over before we know it. . . .

I know a person doesn't always, or often, feel like writing. But please try it again, Millie, and don't treat me as if I were a silent policeman.

R.

There is little about illness or anxiety in such affectionate and inconsequential letters; there are overtones of loneliness. Ring was leading a restricted life now, far from the gregarious existence in which once he seemed to be trying vainly to assuage his profound sense of alienation. That summer he listened to the radio and wrote his columns and toiled over a long story which was to take him months to finish—in contrast to his old habit of writing a story at a single sitting. The drugs on which he had come to depend to help him work were no longer of any avail. He had taken morphine to make him sleep, and caffeine to keep him awake; but he said that they affected him in reverse—the morphine stimulated him, the caffeine put him to sleep. He was sometimes found asleep over his typewriter, his forehead bruised from having fallen on the machine.

In November he was again in the hospital, under more stringent care than ever before. Still he found time and energy to pursue his interests and follow the activities of his sons. Jim, who was at Harvard, shared his father's ambition to write popular songs and sent Ring a draft of one. Ring painstakingly corrected it and wrote his son a letter which shows not only paternal solicitude but a highly technical and professional knowledge of the subject:

Doctors Hospital

I enclose an amended version of your song. As I said in my telegram, I think your refrain begins on the wrong word and on the wrong beat—Anyway, it's unsingable as you have it, as you will find out if you try. Your music demands a two-syllable rhyme scheme (except in the middle eight bars, where you have written "ritardo" —Incidentally, you don't want any retard; it ruins the number as a dance tune.) If I were you, I'd rewrite the music to those middle eight bars, simplifying it; you can almost do it with a couple of monotones, allowing the harmony to embellish it, or you can go into an entirely different key—A flat for instance. . . .

In the third bar of the refrain, you will notice that I have changed the tune to get away from the resemblance to "River Shannon" and innumerable other songs. . . .

In my version, the title appears in the first and last lines of the refrain, which always helps a song commercially. However, you mustn't think this song is commercial in a "big way."—Very few are these days. But it's too good not to work on, and I may find one or two people who will introduce it on radio. . . .

It's good news that you have even a chance to get on that ole davil dean's list, but if you miss it this time, don't let it worry you.

Who were those ringers that posed as Harvard's team yesterday? There is one consolation—I won't have to give 3 to 1 on Notre Dame against the Army.

. . . Don't forget to wire me how you come out with the dean, and when you have fixed this song, send it back and I'll see what can be done with it.

Pa

He even found time to write several letters to a total stranger who had written a book on football that he admired, and to try to arrange for the Bell Syndicate to buy it for newspaper serialization—a matter which required considerable effort on his part and was an entirely disinterested favor. "But," he wrote, "I think your knowledge of the subject ought to bring you something besides compliments." It recalled his friendship with Walter Eckersall. "I have always been deeply interested in kicking. In high school I was a fairly good drop- and place-kicker, but my punting, with no instruction, was more or less of a joke. After Walter Eckersall was through with college football and he and I were working on the Chicago Tribune, I got full of courage at a party one night and challenged him to a kicking match for a $5.00 bet. I named the conditions, and I wasn't as foolish as I seemed, for I knew that Eckie couldn't place-kick to save his would. The 'events' numbered four: drop-kick for goal, kick-off for distance, punt for distance, and place-kick for goal. He won the drop-kick and punt, and I beat him kicking off and place-kicking for goal." The author of the book on football, Le Roy N. Mills, a former coach, paid a visit to the hospital at Ring's invitation. "My doctor has been very stingy about allowing me visitors—he contends that solitary confinement is the only thing that prevents my talking too much. However, he is beginning to be more lenient now and I should be gratified to have you call some day soon when you expect to be in the neighborhood with time on your hands. All I ask is a day's warning so I can be rid of my beard. Also, you must promise to do at least eighty per cent of the talking."

He longed for company—of his own choosing—and wrote to H. L. Mencken: "Your suggestion that we meet far too seldom has been in my head for years. If I ever escape from here I will see what can be done about it. Meanwhile, kindly publish another book." Mencken replied that he would be glad to visit him and would tell him some dreadful scandal. Ring wrote back, "I think the chiropractors will let up on me in about two weeks. If you will tell me what days you are in New York, I will telephone and insist that you keep your promise." But his optimism was unfounded; his condition grew worse and he was allowed even fewer visitors. He was still in the hospital at the end of January, and his doctors had advised him to go to California. His next communication to Mencken was a telegram on January 30, 1933.

HAVE SEVENTY FIVE HUNDRED WORD FICTION STORY SO GOOD THAT POST COSMOPOLITAN AND COLLIERS DONT WANT IT STOP WOULD YOU LIKE A CHANCE AT FOURTH REFUSAL STOP IF SO WHERE SHALL I SEND IT STOP PLEASE WIRE ME CARE DOCTORS HOSPITAL STOP AM LEAVING FOR DESERT RETREAT NEXT SATURDAY

The following day he sent Mencken the story with a letter.

Here's the one-part serial. The Post just didn't seem to care for it, Bill Lengel said it was swell, but he ain't the boss, and Collier's objected to its length and tenuousness. What can you think of? I really advise you not to return it because I am leaving (by boat) Saturday for the Mojave Desert and it doesn't look to me as if it would stand a trip that long, or even one as far as the waste-basket.

Please don't imagine that I didn't appreciate your offer to come and see me here. To begin with, I was no treat; besides, the doc wouldn't permit visitors for quite a while though God knows you would have done me good, whereas some of the boys and girls who crashed the gate set me back weeks in half an hour, finally forcing me to take advice and arrange the impending hegira.

The same day he wrote to his sister Lena in Niles: "The doctors think it is necessary for me to get out of this climate and into the desert. So Ellis and I are leaving next Saturday by boat, via the

367

Panama Canal, for California (on borrowed money) and will stay for three months . . . in a dry quiet place, hoping my condition will improve enough to permit me to work again. It is hard to leave John and not to see the other boys occasionally, but I think it will be best in the long run." At the same time he wrote regretfully to several friends whom he had not been allowed to see in the hospital.

Mencken, although he would have liked publishing Ring in the *American Mercury* and was eager to help him now, declined the story, which he did not find suitable; but he suggested to Ring that he try the *Delineator*. Ring took his advice, and the story was accepted. Ring was troubled by the difficulty he had in selling it. It had taken him from June to January to write it, and although he realized the length was a drawback and that magazines were not buying as heavily as they had before the Depression, he was unaccustomed to rejections, and besides he needed the money. It weighed on his mind and he mentioned it repeatedly in letters to his friends. Shortly after he arrived in California, he wrote to Mencken:

Dear H.:—
You ought to be a literary agent and I a designer of gowns. I followed your advice about Mr. Graeve of Delineator—in sheer desperation, I must admit, and not with any idea that you were right —and he accepted the story with the comment that it was so unsuitable to his publication that he just couldn't resist it. Thanks.

Inasmuch as I always write on subjects familiar to me and am not at all with either fornication or treachery, I don't see how I can crash the Mercury. But when the Post rejects the next one, I'll at least ask you to find a sucker.

The story was "Poodle," which was published in the *Delineator* for January 1934, after Ring's death. It concerns a young married man who loses his job because of the Depression, but dreads telling his nagging wife about it. Instead he leaves home each morning as if to go to work and spends the day job hunting. While he is relaxing in a movie after a discouraging day, he is spotted by an amiable madman who insists that he must be a young man named Poodle from his home town. The elderly maniac hires him to be his companion and keeper at a salary higher than the one he had been getting, but he still does not tell his wife, being a little self-conscious about his odd profession. His wife calls his old office, finds he has not been working there for weeks, and jumps to the conclusion that he has been spending his time with another woman. She leaves home in outrage, and Poodle philosophically awaits her ultimate return, meanwhile passing his leisure hours drinking.

The characters are typical Lardner suburbanites, the language is authentic and highly amusing, and the plot is O. Henry. The talkative, gloating, mercenary wife is a familiar figure, and so is the henpecked Poodle, who accepts his humiliation without complaint and finds solace in liquor. It is characteristic enough, but it is not one of Ring's best stories, and it is not surprising that even with Ring's name it should have been rejected by magazines which were reducing their inventories and not paying top prices for second-rate stories. Ring was finally ironically amused at ending up in a woman's magazine.

From California, Ring regularly wrote full accounts of his activities to his boys.

February 28, 1933

Bill, John (and Dickie), David, James:—

This is a circular canary. A what, Baron? An orbicular crow; a spherical sparrow. Baron, are you sure you don't mean a round robin? Why, yes, of course, Charlie! What did you think I meant?

I adopt this method of writing to you little ones because I won't have time to write to you separately; besides, I should hate to say something comical to one of you and forget to say it to the others. The order indicated in the salutation is probably the best from a standpoint of speed in transmission. When Bill has read, and, perhaps, memorized these words, he is supposed to send them on to John, who, after mumbling them to Dickie, will forward them to David, and the last-named (in every way) will mail them to Jim, or, as some call him, the dead letter office. If this procedure is agreeable to you, I will write once a month, possibly oftener. If it isn't, you can take the consequences. I trust that Bill, John and David will vindicate my judgment in routing by being prompt to re-address and re-mail.

Well, let me tell you that boat-ride was okeh after a storm had laid Mrs. Lardner low the second day out, and would have been more okeh if my feet, unshod since last April, had not swole to elephantine proportions. All the girls on the ship dubbed them the Giant Redwood trees of California. Yes, the boat-ride was okeh, but don't ever take it just to have a look at the Canal. It is little more than a glorified Sault St. Marie, and when you have seen one lock, you have seen two locks, or my hair.

One afternoon I sat on the prowl pack—Pardon me, Baron; the what? The sauntering fifty-two cards. Why, Baron, I believe that you are trying to say the promenade deck. That's it, Charlie! The promenade deck—and I was reading Van Loon's Geography and the deck steward remarked that it was a great book. Being a democratic fellow, I replied to him and observed that one of my sons had given it to me for Christmas. "Isn't that queer, Mr. Lardner?" he said. "Because I was planning to give it to one of my sons for his birthday. That's a paradox." So now you know what a paradox is. Personally I had always thought it meant two physicians in consultation, or just two physicians.

Warner Baxter was a shipmate and walked twelve or fourteen laps around the deck each evening before dinner. This is called the Baxter Mile. Mrs. L. pretended she didn't know who he was, but she followed him with her eyes every time we turned our Baxter. Another mate was Mr. Collins, treasurer of the Curtis Publishing Company. He introduced himself to me and I tactfully said, "Oh, have they still got a treasurer?" This may result in the S.E. Post's rejecting a story I mailed last Thursday. I recall telling some you chaps that the story before this one was rejected by the Post, Cosmopolitan, Collier's and the Mercury, the two middle ones saying that it was too long, as it certainly was, and Mencken saying that it was not his style. But he suggested that I try Delineator, adding that the women's magazines were the only ones making money. I didn't know whether Delineator was a weekly or a college year book, but I followed Mencken's advice and tried it, and it accepted the story, the editor remarking that it was so unsuitable for his magazine that he couldn't bear to turn it down. He paid, or is going to pay, one-fourth of the Post's price, and according to him, four or three times as much as Mencken would have paid. So, fellows, we have crashed Delineator and there are no more worlds to conquer.

The boat landed at San Diego at noon of Friday the 17th. and stayed there long enough to permit the madam and myself to go to the races at Agua Caliente. At that dismal joint the finishing touches were put to my feet by a half-mile walk almost straight up hill. We would have quit even on the day but for the presence in the seventh race of a horse named June Moon. Golden Prize or something was favorite and I would have played him but for the June Moon hunch, as favorites were doing pretty well. Little Ellis, always timid, wanted me to play June Moon for show, she urging that June Moon had been a show. I urged right back that it had also been a straight play. For one instant I had a flash to bet on Golden Prize to win and June Moon to show, but I neglected Golden Prize and played June

Moon across the board, and the show money barely paid for itself.

If I could afford the trip, I would go in to Los Angeles, now that Vidmer's here and shoot him. They would never suspect me, because I would have to go barefooted and they would think I was a Hollywood boy. Don't get chesty, John, for winning arguments from your sports department, unless you win one from George Daley, who Sees Everything, Knows Everything, Is Everything. I done tol' your ol' mammy that you had written most of Bill Macbeth's Corbett stuff. Jim was really a good old soul who made good in vaudeville because he had sense enough to act as straight man instead of trying to be the comic; the team of him and Billy Van was actually worth seeing. His eating habits, such as two helpings of coffee, doughnuts and wheat cakes in the Lambs at one or two in the morning, were not conducive to longevity.

I was sorry (still addressing John) that Gannett appeared to like your book [The Crowning of Technocracy by John Lardner and Thomas Sugrue]. I was hoping he would pannett. But you can bet that F. Adams wouldn't have said it was funny if he hadn't thought so, and he is anything but a bad judge. However, I will do my own judging when, if ever, I see the book. I presume, and hope, that I'll get most of the reviews in my clippings. Remember my advice and don't give first refusal rights to any of those publishers, unless they pay you for them, and even then, don't tie up for more than one or two books with a decent firm, such as Farrar and Rinehart or Simon and Schuster.

Bill, how about finishing in Group 1 or Group 2 this semester? They tell me it's almost impossible not to at Princeton.

Dave, for my sake and dear old Andover (sometimes they call her Nancy) get a new picture taken so I can destroy the one of the noseless Jap which now makes our parlor table a living Bedlam on horseback.

Jim, we received one, not two, cables from you and what we'd like to receive is a letter stating what marks you got in each and every subject. Soon I shall write to Tom Shaw or Jack Doyle and ascertain the pre-season odds on the clubs in each league (some of them, I mean) and possible parlays such as the Yankees-Pittsburgh, the Yankees-Cubs. I wish some one would tell me whom Brooklyn got in exchange for Vance. Brooklyn, my lads, is not out of the race yet. It came pretty close last year without much help from the Doozler.

We are expecting a visit soon from Claudette [Colbert] and Norman [Foster], and possibly from Jean Dixon.

371

Meanwhile, the play's the thing
Which is worrying the life out of your

Shoeless Uncle Ring

The play was the one on which he proposed to collaborate with George S. Kaufman, and apparently his health had improved to the point where he could work on it regularly and at the same time continue his radio column for *The New Yorker*. He had sketched out the first act in the hospital, to judge from fragmentary notes on hospital stationery, and by the end of March he was rewriting the first draft. He wrote again to the boys:

March 29, 1933

Bill, John, Dickie, David and James:—Would you like to know what I have been doing lately? (Oh, goodness, what has father dad unk popsie wopsie been doing lately?) Well, occasionally working on the first draft of the first act of a play, and now I am on the 23rd page of rewriting, which is just about one-third of the way through. For this first act, my burdens, is nearly an hour and a half long in its present plight, which will give Mr. Kaufman the opportunity he lacked in "June Moon" of masticating and spitting out five and six pages at a time. I would have been in the midst of Act 2, the comical act, if hell hadn't popped loose a fortnight ago. Possibly as an aftermath of the temblors (if you think you're pronouncing that word right, look it up) things began happening in La Quinta and as they are things that might happen to anybody named Mr. and Mrs. Ring Lardner who came to the place called La Quinta in search of absolute La Quieta, I will outline them by way of warning (via Warneke):

Vincent Lawrence, former playwright, now Hollywood scenarist, and Dorothy Speare, novelist, entered our hut uninvited and wanted to know whether I had an idea for Harold Lloyd. Mr. Lawrence wrote his last picture, "Movie Crazy" or something; it was a flop, so Harold came back to him for more. I said I had no idea, but would try to think of one. I did think of one and it was a good one; so I thought and so Mr. Lawrence thought. However, it is well-known (to me, at least) that I can't tell things in synopsis form, or any other form—I have to write them out at length.

Well, a week ago Sunday came. The Rices were visiting us, I think. So was Phillips Holmes. So, suddenly, were Mr. Lawrence, Miss Speare, Harold Lloyd, Sam Harris, some anonymous girl, and Louella O. Parsons and her latest husband, one Dr. Martin, who says he knew me in Chicago, which he did not if I am any judge.

Louella also said that when she was working on the Chicago Trib-une, she and I used to go on lots of parties together, which we did not if I am any judge.

Harold was all steamed up over my having an idea, and I was all steamed up over the same miracle, but when he and I managed to get a moment alone, it developed that all he wanted was the bare idea, told in two paragraphs (as he phrased it) and his scenarists and gag men would attend to the rest. Well, to be modest, this was like sending Babe Ruth to bat and letting him stand there till the umpire had called one ball, then taking him out and substituting a good hitter. Harold and I both steamed down as quickly as he had up—and I had wasted two or three days of thinking and writing. Unless, as Mr. Lawrence suggests, Buster Keaton can be caught sober and interested in the same idea, which remains, yours sin-cerely, a good idea, reeking with gags that Harold and his gag men wouldn't think of in a month of Sundays, and if there were a month of Sundays, you could all call yourselves Little Orphan Annie.

Now Louella's interview with G. B. Shaw at the Hearst ranch may have been printed in papers to which you have access. If not, you are much obliged to me for the following excerpt from it, to ap-preciate which you must know that if Louella is fifty-five years old, she's fifty-six: "'Mr. Shaw,' I said, 'is it true that Gene Tunney was the original of Cashel Byron?' 'Young woman,' he replied, 'Cashel Byron was superannuated before you and Tunney were born.'"

Bill—Does this projected publication promise you or anyone else a living wage? Would you room and board at the Swopes'?

John—What's this I hear about you and one Sorghum having written a tune or a book called "The Crooning of Telegraphy"? If there is such a product, who is hoarding it?

Dickie—I imagine that Mr. Daley did Mr. Vidmer an injustice. The latter probably wrote a story about a ball game and it sounded like a story about an earthquake. All your baseball writers are tricky.

David—Please rush me a photograph of yourself. Ellis is mad and I am glad because I tore up a caricature of a noseless Jap which she was telling the waiters was sa jungest kind.

James—If you get a bronze medal for defaulting to a Swiss in a consolation bout, why not stay away from the meets and win a Cecil Pulitzer scholarship?

Anxious

The lighthearted tone of the letters from California does not necessarily mean that he felt well; he generally wrote in this vein to his family; he was always afraid that his illness would dampen their spirits or spoil their fun. But he was far more optimistic than when he had left New York. He seemed to enjoy his visitors, after his solitary hospital life, even though they interrupted his work. He was not at all abashed at his failure to come to terms with Harold Lloyd on a picture idea. If he was usually humble about his work, he could also be curiously arrogant about it; this was not always a sign of self-confidence, but rather a means of self-reassurance. In any case, he seemed to be in high spirits, and he was working on a play, which he really enjoyed.

He cut short his stay in California, where he had planned to stay three or four months, possibly because of the restlessness he always felt whenever he was away from New York for any length of time. He and Ellis stopped in Niles and in Detroit on their way home, then Ellis went to East Hampton while Ring stayed in New York to consult George Kaufman about the first two acts of the play. It was toward the end of May that he wrote, "I only hope that I can stay well enough to work. If I can, I promise you and the rest of the world one thing: that never again will I take a vacation when I am through with a job. I think it is the biggest mistake a person can make—not to keep on going." For the time being he was trying to keep on going.

Ring's last play remained unfinished. He left the manuscript of Act I complete, but obviously in need of cutting and revision, one scene of Act II, and some fragmentary notes which indicate that he had radically changed his early conception of the plot and probably had further changes in mind. The collaboration with George Kaufman apparently did not get very far. The script as it stands is full of repetition and slow expository passages. Written under the most adverse circumstances, it contains few of the old Lardner touches.

What is interesting about it is the problem that preoccupied Ring over the period of several years while he was thinking about the play and working on it. He was dealing here, far more earnestly than ever before, with the subject of alcoholism; but deeper than that is his concern with family relationships, which are only highlighted by the fact that the central character is an alcoholic.

This character is John Haskell, an attractive young man of twenty-five, who is a reformed drunkard. He is engaged to Marian Freeman, who belongs to a family which bears some resemblance to the family in an early story, "The Facts." Grandfather Freeman is a prosperous, self-made New York businessman of Midwestern back-

374

ground, who has got where he is by unflagging punctuality, industry, and dreary middle-class virtue. He dominates his wife and his son Taylor, who is Marian's father. Marian worships her father, whose wife divorced him years ago. Both the Freemans have retired from the family business, leaving it to John Haskell in the hope that the responsibility will keep him on the wagon and make him a suitable husband for Marian. John suspects that they are testing him and is wary of the trap they are laying to bring him into their own tight, restricted, and loveless world. The conflict is between John, who is warm and sympathetic, and the Freeman family, which is the epitome of stiff Bible Belt probity and an inhuman conformity to bourgeois values.

Marian is putting pressure on John to go to a psychoanalyst who can cure him of his compulsion to drink by finding out the roots of it. John scorns this solution; he says he is too bright for psychoanalysis and has only contempt for anyone who would babble out his secrets on a couch. He chooses to get along on his own strength.

Into this situation comes Julie, a friend of Marian's, who is as different from the Freemans as John is; it is obvious that they are immediately attracted to each other. Julie is engaged to a young man who has never taken a drink because he idolized his mother, who in turn idolized her father, who was a drunkard. Significantly, all the stuffy characters in the play have inordinate attachments to one parent or the other; the more sympathetic ones seem to drink.

John is about to leave on an important business trip to Brazil for the Freemans; he knows it is not important at all, that they are only putting him on trial. Nevertheless it is his big chance. In the course of a gathering at the Freeman home, as family tensions mount and the sordid side of the Freeman family life is revealed, John, in a gesture of defiance, goes off the wagon, gets drunk and walks out. The scene potentially has dramatic impact, and psychologically it is perceptive. It is at just such a moment that a reformed alcoholic might lapse, from the very fear of succeeding in an enterprise about which he has secret misgivings, or of being finally enclosed in a circle of personal relationships from which there would be no escape other than alcohol.

This is as far as the plot goes in the unfinished script; but it is not the plot or its possible resolution that matters. It is the questions raised and the attitudes disclosed in the character of John Haskell. Plainly Ring admired John as much as he despised the Freemans. John is unique among Lardner characters in that he seems to have the approval of the author, who has missed no chance to stress his virtues and withhold any condemnation of his single weakness. In John are expressed attitudes toward which Ring was sympathetic: his determination to live by his own strength, his warmth and understanding, his rejection of the Freemans' family discipline.

John himself has qualms about his potential capacities as a husband and father. All through the play there is a significant emphasis on men's failures: Mr. Freeman bullies his wife and dominates his son; Taylor has been a weak and inadequate husband, a father's boy who has little understanding of women; and in the background are other fathers who have been delinquent in some way. Ring seemed to be questioning whether or not a man could succeed in his family role.

Inordinate family attachments as a threat to a happy marriage were Ring's chief preoccupation in this play. In the character of John he embodied a spirit of revolt against many aspects of middle-class life. The revolt is not against conventional morality; it is against an inhuman rigidity, the denial of love and understanding, and the deceptions by which the Freemans seek to guard their safe, unbending, and restricted way of life. But most of all it is a revolt against those baleful family affections which blight and inhibit all others.

Ring himself lived all his life in a close family circle, first in the Lardner home in Niles, a sheltered, isolated, love-locked world; then in his own home, where a more formal atmosphere prevailed. Neither bore any resemblance to the world of the Freemans, and it would be useless to look back into Ring's own experience to find prototypes of the characters or situations in the play, despite the tempting similarities between John Haskell and Ring himself. The Lardners' childhood world was an enchanted one, of benevolence and indulgence; but it was an exclusive one and within it they gave and received a special trust and affection that could never be found again outside the fenced-in yard. Ring had known the pressures of family life, both those of extreme devotion and those of great responsibility; and he had sometimes expressed misgivings about them. Perhaps John Haskell's rebellion against the confinement of such a life, the routine entailed by obligation, and the suffocation of close family attachments is a remote reflection of Ring's need to escape from time to time, through drinking, from his personal situation.

At the end of May, Ring seemed hopeful that he could continue to work on his play. He spent a few days in New York, staying at a

West Side hotel, seeing his doctor and dentist, and conferring with George Kaufman. He went about in slippers because he could not get shoes on his swollen feet. Then he returned to East Hampton for the summer. But he wrote little more—two or three stories, not among his best; four more radio columns and a parody of O. O. McIntyre for *The New Yorker*. Although this last piece must have been written with difficulty, it is one of his funniest parodies, and he took a particular pleasure in it. He had always been scornful of McIntyre's absurd affectations; but there might also have been just a touch of personal malice in it. The cosmopolite from Gallipolis, Ohio, had once called the boy from Niles, Michigan, a hick, and it rankled.

He retained many of his old interests, theater, cards, music. But he seldom played the piano any more. This time he was home for good, and he saw few people except his family and the Rices. His three youngest sons were there; Ring watched them on the beach and worried about them when they were in swimming. Among his familiar amusements were two kittens which he called The Wedding Guest and The Loud Bassoon. Characteristically he worried about them because one of the neighbors had a large dog.

Sometimes he was observed alone, with his face in his hands, sobbing. Whether it was *lacrimae rerum* or only sheer exhaustion that broke him down it is impossible to know; he had always lived close to tears. He no longer had the strength to support such aspirations as remained to him, or whatever grief or disappointment he felt.

He had often suffered remorse over the ruin of his health, believing that his own immoderate habits were to blame, and he punished himself with work and anxiety. By now he could hardly have believed that he had long to live, yet he went on working, having relapses and coming out of them, as if illness were merely to be the normal condition of his life for an indefinite period.

Lose with a Smile had been published in book form that spring, and in the *American Mercury* for June, H. L. Mencken had written a review full of praise, reiterating his old prophecy that the professors of literature would eventually have to reckon with Lardner. Ring wrote him the last letter that can be found in his correspondence, August 24, 1933: "It is almost time I thanked you for that piece about the baseball book, which you know perfectly well did not deserve any of the space you gave it. Believe it or not, I appreciated it more than the check it brought from Brother Lorimer." It was very much what he had replied to the first praise he ever received for the "Busher's Letters."

Miss Feldmann, the boys' former governess, came to East Hampton to visit the family and found Ring failing fast and still exerting himself perilously. She proposed to take care of him, and at first he protested, as always; finally he yielded, and she stayed as his nurse.

The evening of September 24 he played bridge with Ellis, Kate Rice, and his son Bill, sitting up in a chair that was heavily padded because he was so thin. He seemed weak, as he had been for a long time; aside from that there was nothing to mark that particular evening as his last. The next morning he had a heart attack and fell into a coma from which he never regained consciousness, and he died that evening. He was forty-eight years old.

Many people close to Ring believed that long before he died he had lost any will to live. Fitzgerald wrote in an obituary that a dozen years earlier Ring had become cynical about his work, had deliberately formed a habit of silence and repression; he was "getting off"; and he called Ring's death a prolonged suicide. If so, it was a difficult one, in the face of a relentless drive to keep going that was sustained by his love of family, his sense of duty, the play that had absorbed him for so long, the few small diversions that still afforded him some pleasure even at the end of his life. But he had always needed escape, too, and the kinds of escape he could find had worn him out. Under the strain of that need, and of some remaining will to live that entailed too desperate a struggle, his health gave way.

He had more than once thought of death as the means of escape. He had said that the way he wanted to die was to pass by a street fight and get a stray bullet in his back. The final irony of his life was seven years of tormenting illness.

The day after he died, his body was taken away and, according to his own wish, cremated without ceremony—as if the proud and solemn man who did not believe in the value of his own work and had remained silent about the things that concerned him most deeply had chosen to cover his tracks to the very last.

LIST OF RING LARDNER'S PUBLISHED WORK

This is a chronological list of Ring Lardner's books, magazine stories, and articles, indicating dates of first publication and volumes in which the magazine pieces were collected. The following abbreviations are used:

YKMA, *You Know Me Al*
GT, *Gullible's Travels*
TER, *Treat 'Em Rough*
OYOH, *Own Your Own Home*
TRD, *The Real Dope*
TBT, *The Big Town*
HTWSS, *How to Write Short Stories*
WOI, *What of It?*
LN, *The Love Nest*
RU, *Round Up*
LWAS, *Lose with a Smile*
SEP, *The Saturday Evening Post*
SS, short story

BOOKS

With Edward C. Heeman, *March 6th; The Home Coming of Charles A. Comiskey, John J. McGraw, and James J. Callahan.* Chicago: The Blakely Printing Co., 1914.

Bib Ballads. Chicago: P. F. Volland and Co., 1915
You Know Me Al. New York: George H. Doran, 1916
Gullible's Travels. Indianapolis: Bobbs-Merrill Co., 1917

Treat 'Em Rough. Indianapolis: Bobbs-Merrill Co., 1918
My Four Weeks in France. Indianapolis: Bobbs-Merrill Co., 1918
Regular Fellows I Have Met. Chicago: Wilmot, 1919
Own Your Own Home. Indianapolis: Bobbs-Merrill Co., 1919
The Real Dope. Indianapolis: Bobbs-Merrill Co., 1919
The Young Immigrunts. Indianapolis: Bobbs-Merrill Co., 1920
The Big Town. Indianapolis: Bobbs-Merrill Co., 1921
Symptoms of Being 35. Indianapolis: Bobbs-Merrill Co., 1921
Say It with Oil. New York: George H. Doran, 1923
How to Write Short Stories. New York: Charles Scribner's Sons, 1924
What of It? New York: Charles Scribner's Sons, 1925
The Love Nest and Other Stories. New York: Charles Scribner's Sons, 1926
The Story of a Wonder Man. New York: Charles Scribner's Sons, 1927
Round Up. New York: Charles Scribner's Sons, 1929
With George S. Kaufman, *June Moon.* New York: Charles Scribner's Sons, 1930
Lose with a Smile. New York: Charles Scribner's Sons, 1933
First and Last, edited by Gilbert Seldes. New York: Charles Scribner's Sons, 1934
The Portable Ring Lardner, edited by Gilbert Seldes. New York: The Viking Press, 1946

MAGAZINES

1912

The Cost of Baseball, *Collier's,* March 2

1914

A Busher's Letters Home. SEP, March 7, ss (YKMA)
My Roomy, SEP, May 9, ss (HTWSS)
The Busher Comes Back, SEP, May 23, ss (YKMA)
The Busher's Honeymoon, SEP, July 11, ss (YKMA)
Sick 'Em, SEP, July 25, ss
Horseshoes, SEP, August 15, ss (HTWSS)
A New Busher Breaks In, SEP, September 12, ss (YKMA)
The Busher's Kid, SEP, October 3, ss (YKMA)
The Busher Beats It Hence, SEP, November 7, ss (YKMA)

1915

Tour No. 2 (in two parts), SEP, February 13 and February 20, ss
Own Your Own Home, *Redbook,* January, ss (OYOH)
The Busher Abroad (in four parts), SEP, March 20, April 10, May 8, May 15, ss
Braves Is Right, *American,* March
Some Team, *American,* April
Welcome to Our City, *Redbook,* May, ss (OYOH)
Tyrus, *American,* June
The Busher's Welcome Home, SEP, June 5, ss
The Last Laugh, *Redbook,* July, ss (OYOH)

Alibi Ike, SEP, July 31, ss (HTWSS)
Matty, *American*, August
Harmony, *McClure's*, August, ss (HTWSS)
Uncivil War, *Redbook*, September, ss (OYOH)
The Poor Simp, SEP, September 11, ss
Where Do You Get That Noise?, SEP, October 23, ss
Oh, You Bonehead, SEP, October 30, ss

1916

Carmen, SEP, February 19, ss (GT)
Three Kings and a Pair, SEP, March 11, ss (GT)
Good for the Soul, SEP, March 25, ss
War Bribes, *Redbook*, April, ss
The Crook, SEP, June 24, ss
The Swift Six, *Redbook*, July, ss
Gullible's Travels, SEP, August 19, ss (GT)
Champion, *Metropolitan*, October, ss (HTWSS)
The Water Cure, SEP, October 14, ss (GT)
A One-Man Team, *Redbook*, November

1917

The Facts, *Metropolitan*, January, ss (HTWSS)
Three Without, Doubled, SEP, January 13, ss (GT)
Tour-Y-10, *Metropolitan*, February, ss
The Hold-Out, SEP, March 24, ss
Ring Lardner—Himself, SEP, April 28 (autobiographical)
Fore!, *Redbook*, May, ss
A Friendly Game, SEP, May 5, ss
Ball-A-Hole, SEP, May 12, ss
The Yellow Kid, SEP, June 23, ss
A Reporter's Diary (in eight parts), *Collier's*, September 29, October 13,
        November 3, November 17, December 1, December 15, 1917; and
        January 12, January 19, 1918, reprinted in *My Four Weeks in France*
The Last Night, *Redbook*, November, ss

1918

The Clubby Roadster, *Redbook*, February, ss
Call for Mr. Keefe, SEP, March 9, ss
Jack the Kaiser Killer, SEP, March 23, ss (TER)
Corporal Punishment, SEP, April 13, ss (TER)
Purls Before Swine, SEP, June 8, ss (TER)
And Many a Stormy Wind Shall Blow, SEP, July 6, ss (TRD)
Private Valentine, SEP, August 3, ss (TRD)
Stragety and Tragedy, SEP, August 31, ss (TRD)
A Chip off the Old Block, *Redbook*, September
Decorated, SEP, October 26, ss (TRD)
Sammy Boy, SEP, December 21, ss (TRD)

1919

Simple Simon, SEP, January 25, ss (TRD)
The Busher Reenlists, SEP, April 19, ss
The Battle of Texas, SEP, May 24, ss
Along Came Ruth, SEP, July 26, ss
The Courtship of T. Dorgan, SEP, September 6, ss
The Busher Pulls a Mays, SEP, October 13, ss

1920

The Young Immigrunts, SEP, January 31, also published as a separate volume
Quick Returns, SEP, March 27, ss (TBT)
Beautiful Katie, SEP, July 10, ss (TBT)
The Battle of Long Island, SEP, November 27, ss (TBT)

1921

Only One, SEP, February 12, ss (TBT)
What Is the "American Language"?, *Bookman*, March
General Symptoms of Being 35, *American*, May (WOI)
Comic, SEP, May 14, ss (TBT)
A Frame-Up, SEP, June 18, ss (HTWSS)
Some Like Them Cold, SEP, October 21, ss (HTWSS)
The Battle of the Century, SEP, October 29, ss

1922

East Is East and Michigan Is Michigan When It Comes to Dogs, *Wheeler's Magazine*, February
A Caddy's Diary, SEP, March 11, ss
The Golden Honeymoon, *Cosmopolitan*, July, ss (HTWSS)
The Bull Pen, *Judge*, July 29
My Week in Cuba, *Cosmopolitan*, August
You Know Me Al, *Cosmopolitan*, September
For He's a Jolly Good Fellow, *Cosmopolitan*, October
Let's Go!, *Cosmopolitan*, November
Say It with Oil, *American*, November, also published as a separate volume
Little Sunbeams of Success, *Cosmopolitan*, December
What I Don't Know about Horses, *Trotter and Pacer*, December

1923

Not Guilty, *Cosmopolitan*, January
Bringing Up Children, *Cosmopolitan*, February
The Dames, *Hearst's International*, March (WOI)
Why Authors?, *Hearst's International*, April (WOI)
In Regards to Geniuses, *Hearst's International*, May (WOI)
The Big Drought, *Hearst's International*, June (WOI)
Enoch Arden, *Bookman*, June
Bedtime Stories (How to Tell a Princess and Bluebeard), *Hearst's International*, July (WOI)

Cinderella, *Hearst's International*, August (woi)
What I Ought to of Learnt in High School, *American*, November

1924

I Gaspiri, *Chicago Literary Times*, February 15 (woi)
A Close-Up of Domba Splew, *Hearst's International*, June (woi)
What of It?, *Liberty*, June 7 (woi)
In Conference, *Liberty*, August 16 (woi)

1925

The Other Side (in five parts), *Liberty*, February 14, February 21, February
    28, March 7, March 14 (woi)
Haircut, *Liberty*, March 28, ss (ln)
Mr. and Mrs. Fix-It, *Liberty*, May 9, ss (ln)
Sea Island Sports, *American Golfer*, May 16
What You Will Encounter in Nassau, *American Golfer*, May 30
Cora, or Fun at a Spa, *Vanity Fair*, June
Zone of Quiet, *Cosmopolitan*, June, ss (ln)
Women, *Liberty*, June 20, ss (ln)
The Love Nest, *Cosmopolitan*, August, ss (ln)
A Day with Conrad Green, *Liberty*, October 3, ss (ln)
Reunion, *Liberty*, October 31, ss (ln)

1926

Who Dealt?, *Cosmopolitan*, January, ss (ln)
Rhythm, *Cosmopolitan*, March, ss (ru)
Travelogue, *Cosmopolitan*, May, ss (ru)
I Can't Breathe, *Cosmopolitan*, September, ss (ru)
The Jade Necklace, *Cosmopolitan*, November, ss

1927

Sun Cured, *Cosmopolitan*, January, ss (ru)
Hurry Kane, *Cosmopolitan*, May, ss (ru)
Then and Now, *Cosmopolitan*, June, ss (ru)
The Spinning Wheel, *Cosmopolitan*, July, ss
Dinner Bridge, *New Republic*, July 20
The Venomous Viper of the Volga, *Cosmopolitan*, September, ss
Miss Sawyer, Champion, *The New Yorker*, September 10
Man Not Overboard, *Cosmopolitan*, November, ss (ru)

1928

Anniversary, *Cosmopolitan*, January, ss (ru)
Nora, *Cosmopolitan*, February, ss (ru)
Liberty Hall, *Cosmopolitan*, March, ss (ru)
The Battle of Palm Beach, *Collier's*, March 24
There Are Smiles, *Cosmopolitan*, April, ss (ru)
With Rod and Gun, *Collier's*, April 7
Mr. Frisbie, *Cosmopolitan*, June, ss (ru)

Laugh Clown, *Collier's,* June 23
Wedding Day, *Cosmopolitan,* July, ss
Dante and ————, *The New Yorker,* July 7
The Maysville Minstrel, *Cosmopolitan,* September, ss (RU)
Dinner, *Harper's Bazaar,* September, ss (RU)
Just Politics (in two parts), *Collier's,* September 1 and September 15
Can You Keep a Secret, *Collier's,* October 6
Ex Parte, *Cosmopolitan,* November, ss (RU)

1929

Old Folks' Christmas, *Cosmopolitan,* January, ss (RU)
Adrift in New York, *Collier's,* January 12
With Rope and Gun, *Collier's,* February 2
Onward and Upward, *Collier's,* February 16
Absent Minded Beggar, *Cosmopolitan,* March, ss
Contract, *Harper's Bazaar,* March, ss (RU)
Boy Entertainer, *Collier's,* March 2
Pluck and Luck, *Collier's,* March 16
Paul the Fiddler, *Collier's,* March 23
Reuben, the Young Artist, *Collier's,* April 13
Keeper of the Bees, *Collier's,* May 11
High Rollers, *Cosmopolitan,* June, ss
Ringside Seat, *Collier's,* June 16
Stop Me if You've Heard This One, *Cosmopolitan,* July, ss
Why We Have Left Hands, *Collier's,* July 6
Tee Time, *Collier's,* July 27
Oh, Shoot, *Collier's,* August 10
Nice Quiet Racket, *Collier's,* August 31
Pity Is Akin, *Cosmopolitan,* September, ss
Bad News for Pitchers, *Collier's,* September 14
Large Coffee, *The New Yorker,* September 28
Any Ice Today, Lady, *Collier's,* September 28
Cubs Win World Series, *Collier's,* October 12
That Old Sweetheart of Mine, *Cosmopolitan,* November, ss
Jersey City Gendarmerie, Je T'aime, *The New Yorker,* November 2
Army Black and Navy Blue, *Collier's,* November 30
Great Blessings, *Cosmopolitan,* December, ss
Bobby or Bust, *Collier's,* December 21

1930

Second-Act Curtain, *Collier's,* April 19
Sit Still, *The New Yorker,* April 19
Mama, *Good Housekeeping,* June, ss
X-Ray, *The New Yorker,* July 15
Words and Music, *Good Housekeeping,* August, ss
Bre'er Rabbit Ball, *The New Yorker,* September 13
Asleep on the Deep, *The New Yorker,* October 4
Tables for Two, *The New Yorker,* October 18
The Higher-Ups, *The New Yorker,* November 1
From a Zealous Non-Worker, *The New Yorker,* November 29

1931

Old Man Liver, *The New Yorker,* January 3
Cured!, *Redbook,* March, ss
Insomnia, *Cosmopolitan,* May, ss
All Quiet on the Eastern Front, *The New Yorker,* June 27
A Slow Train through Arizona, *Cosmopolitan,* September
Meet Mr. Howley, SEP, November 14 (autobiographical)
Me, Boy Scout, SEP, November 21 (autobiographical)
Quadroon, *The New Yorker,* December 19

1932

Caught in the Draft, SEP, January 9 (autobiographical)
Heap Big Chief, SEP, January 23 (autobiographical)
Chicago's Beau Monde, SEP, February 20 (autobiographical)
Alias James Clarkson, SEP, April 16 (autobiographical)
One Hit, One Error, One Left, SEP, April 23, ss (LWAS)
When the Moon Comes Over the Mountain, SEP, May 7, ss (LWAS)
Lose with a Smile, SEP, June 11, ss (LWAS)
Over the Waves, *The New Yorker,* June 18 (radio column)
Heavy Da-Dee-Dough Boys, *The New Yorker,* June 25 (radio column)
The Truth about Ruth, *The New Yorker,* July 2 (radio column)
Meet Me in St. Louis, SEP, July 2, ss (LWAS)
The Crooner's Paradise, *The New Yorker,* July 16 (radio column)
Allie Bobs Oop Again, *The New Yorker,* July 30 (radio column)
Holycaust, SEP, July 30, ss (LWAS)
Deacon Gets Tilt for Tat, *The New Yorker,* August 20 (radio column)
An Epistle of Paul, *The New Yorker,* September 3 (radio column)
The Ides of June, SEP, September 5, ss (LWAS)
Life of the Boswells, *The New Yorker,* September 17 (radio column)
Pu-leese! Mr. Hemingway, *The New Yorker,* October 1 (radio column)
The Crucial Game, *The New Yorker,* October 22 (radio column)
Eckie, SEP, October 22
The Lor and the Profits, *American Spectator,* November
Herb and Frank Panic 'Em, *The New Yorker,* November 5 (radio column)
Lyricists Strike Pay Dirt, *The New Yorker,* November 19 (radio column)
Announcer's Prep School, *The New Yorker,* December 3 (radio column)
Some Short-Selling, *The New Yorker,* December 17 (radio column)

1933

Ring In! (Two Weeks Late), *The New Yorker,* January 14 (radio column)
Rudy in Irate Mood, *The New Yorker,* February 4 (radio column)
An Infant Industry, *The New Yorker,* February 25 (radio column)
I Am a Fugitive from a National Network, *The New Yorker,* March 18 (radio column)
The Old Man Shows His Air Mail, *The New Yorker,* April 8 (radio column)
We're All Sisters under the Hide of Me, *The New Yorker,* May 6 (radio column)
Hail to the Chief, *The New Yorker,* May 27 (radio column)
Some Champions, SEP, June 3

Radio's All-American Team for 1932–1933, *The New Yorker*, June 17 (radio column)

Comic Faces Starvation as Gag Men Near Wits' End, *The New Yorker*, July 8 (radio column)

Ricordi to the Rescue, *The New Yorker*, August 5 (radio column)

The Perfect Radio Program, *The New Yorker*, August 26 (radio column)

Take a Walk, *American*, October, ss

Odd's Bodkins, *The New Yorker*, October 7

Bob's Birthday, *Redbook*, November, ss

1934

Poodle, *Delineator*, January, ss

Via the Canal, New York *Sunday News*, January 7, ss

Greek Tragedy, *Esquire*, February

1935

Widow, *Redbook*, October, ss

Freedom of the Press, *Pictorial Review*, November, ss

How Are You?, *Redbook*, December, ss

1954

Claude Diphthong, Student of Crime, *Ellery Queen's Mystery Magazine*, August

INDEX

387

Allen, Fred, 350
"Allie Bobs Oop Again" (Lardner), 385
"Along Came Ruth" (Lardner), 382
Altrock, Nick, 49, 50, 53
American Golfer, The, magazine, 198
American League, 90
American magazine, 134, 136, 162, 250, 302
American Mercury magazine, 190, 198, 284, 368, 370, 377
American Minstrels (Niles, Mich.), 30–33
American Tragedy, An (Dreiser), 343
America's Sweetheart (Fields-Rodgers-Hart), 324
Amos and Andy, 326
"And Many a Stormy Wind Shall Blow" (Lardner), 381
Anderson, Miss, 199
Anderson, Hunk, 340
Anderson, Margaret, 140
Anderson, Sherwood, 119, 130, 140, 231–34, 363
Anderson, William (Goat), 39, 40, 41
"Anniversary" (Lardner), 309–10, 383
"Announcer's Prep School" (Lardner), 385
"Any Ice Today, Lady" (Lardner), 384
"Anyway, We've Had Fun" (Lardner: *Smiles*), 268
Archer, Jimmy, 62, 93
Arizona *Star,* 325
Arlen, Michael, 198
Armour Institute (Chicago), 28–29, 74, 244

"Army Black and Navy Blue" (Lardner), 384
Artle, Al, 100
"As You Desire Me" (Wrubel), 354–55
Ashford, Daisy, 165
"Asleep on the Deep" (Lardner), 384
Associated Press, 93
Astaire, Adele and Fred, 265, 266, 268
Attell, Abe, 160–61
Atz, Jacob, 50–53
Aubert, Jeanne, 324

"Bad News for Pitchers" (Lardner), 384
Baker, Frank, 105
"Ball-A-Hole" (Lardner), 381
Barnes, Jess, 174–75
Barrie, Sir James, 165, 188, 314
Barthelmess, Richard, 198
"Battle of the Century, The" (Lardner), 382
"Battle of Long Island, The" (Lardner), 382
"Battle of Palm Beach, The" (Lardner), 383
"Battle of Texas, The" (Lardner), 382
Baxter, Warner, 370
Bayes, Nora, 248–49
"Be Good to Me" (Lardner: *Smiles*), 268
Bean, Joe (in Lardner's "A Caddy's Diary"), 213–15
"Beau Broadway" (Winchell column), 302
Beautiful and Damned, The (Fitzgerald), 193
"Beautiful Katie" (Lardner), 382

391

Gallagher and Shean, 252, 257
Gandil, Chick, 160–61
Gannett, Lewis, 371
Ganzel, John, 39–40
Gehrig, Lou, 351
"General Symptoms of Being 35" (Lardner), 382
George V, King of England, 127
George, W. L., 139
Gershwin, George, 290
Gershwin, Ira, 351
Gest, Morris, 168, 272
Gibbons, Floyd, 60, 147–48
Gibbs, Jack, 54–56
Gillespie, India, *see* Moffett, Mrs. India
Gillespie, Mabelle (in Lardner's "Some Like Them Cold"), 211–13, 313; *see also June Moon*
Gish, Lillian, 199
Gleason, Bill, 159, 160, 362
Glyn, Elinor, 137
Going South (Buck-Lardner), 260–61
Goldberg, Irma, 182, 197
Goldberg, Rube, 126, 156, 158, 182, 197
Golden, John, 193
"Golden Honeymoon, The" (Lardner), 185, 193, 205, 209–11, 218, 303, 307, 313, 337, 382
"Good for the Soul" (Lardner), 381
Gotch, Frank, 45, 46
"Gotham Gets Ready" (Lardner), 102–3
Graham, Miss, 356
Graham, Jessie (in Lardner's *Lose with a Smile*), 346–48
Grange, Red, 235
Gray, Gilda, 257

Gray, Harold, 61
"Great Blessings" (Lardner), 384
"Great Day" (Youmans), 265
Great Gatsby, The (Fitzgerald), 181, 189–90, 200, 231, 233
Great Northern Theater (Chicago), 244, 247
"Greek Tragedy" (Lardner), 386
Green, Conrad (in Lardner's "A Day with Conrad Green"), 268–70
Green Hat, The (Arlen), 198
Gregg, Lou (in Lardner's "The Love Nest"), 235–37
Gregory, Dr., 228
Gregory, Paul, 267, 268
Grey, Clifford, 265
Gross, Fred (in Lardner's *Own Your Own Home*), 134–35
Guest, Edgar A., 250, 352
Guinan, Texas, 298
Gullible's Travels (Lardner), 135–37, 143, 177–78, 218, 239, 260, 274, 379, 381

Hackett, Francis, 140
"Hail to the Chief" (Lardner), 385
"Haircut" (Lardner), 218, 235, 237–38, 263, 311, 383
Hammett, Dashiell, 317
Hammond, Percy, 47, 60, 156, 280, 284, 306, 361
Hansen, Harry, 141, 314, 315
Hapgood, Norman, 302
Harding, Warren G. (President), 229–30, 333
"Harmony" (Lardner), 206, 381
Harms, T. B., & Francis Day & Hunter, Inc., 249
Harris, Bucky, 124

394

399

403

Rice, Kate (Mrs. Grantland), 288, 319, 326, 364–65, 372, 377, 378

Richie, Lew, 68, 70, 124

Richman, Harry, 352

Richter, Charles, 47

"Ricordi to the Rescue" (Lardner), 386

Ring, Blanche, 200

"Ring In! (Two Weeks Late)" (Lardner), 385

"Ring Lardner—Himself" (Lardner), 381

Ringgold, Rear Admiral Cadwallader, 10

"Ring's Side" (Lardner column in *Morning Telegraph*), 303

"Ringside Seat" (Lardner), 384

"Rip van Winkle Jr." (Lardner: 1922 Ziegfeld *Follies*), 257–59

Risberg, Swede, 160–61

Robinson, Miss, 193

Rodgers, Richard, 290, 324

Rogers, Will, 169, 200, 257, 259, 316, 323, 325, 331

Roosevelt, Theodore, 156, 331

Rosenthal, Harry, 224, 278, 280

Ross, Harold, 320, 349

Rothstein, Arnold, 161

Round Up (Lardner), 306–16, 380

Ruby, Harry, 269

"Rudy in Irate Mood" (Lardner), 385

Runyon, Damon, 316

Russell, Lillian, 60, 64

Ruth, Babe, 170, 174–75, 247, 373

Ryan, James E., 41, 52

Sacco-Vanzetti case, 332–33

Sager, Lillian, 41

St. Louis Cardinals, 102, 105, 294

St. Louis *Sporting News*, 81, 87, 295

St. Vincent's Hospital, 225, 227

"Sammy Boy" (Lardner), 381

Samuels, Arthur, 197

Sanborn, Cy, 72, 85

Sandburg, Carl, 140, 141

Santley, Joseph, 274–76

Saturday Evening Post, The, 10, 111, 113–14, 121, 126, 134, 136, 149–50, 156, 162, 201, 209, 307, 337, 338, 339, 346–48, 367, 368, 370

Saturday Review of Literature, 314

Say It with Oil (Lardner), 380, 382

Schang, Wally, 101

Schmidt, Harry, 31

Schulte, Frank, 61, 62–63, 69, 93, 106–10, 111, 124, 145, 322, 362

Schulz, Germany, 86

Scott, Jim, 84, 127

Scribner's, Charles, Sons, 188, 189–90, 218, 281, 306, 314

"Sea Island Sports" (Lardner), 383

"Second-Act Curtain" (Lardner), 384

Seeman, Billy, 197

Seldes, Gilbert, 210, 287, 317, 355, 380

Seven Keys to Baldpate (Cohan prod.), 251

Seymour, Charlie, 81

Shaw, George Bernard, 373

Shaw, Tom, 371

Shawkey, Bob, 174

Shean, Al, 252, 257, 258

ABOVE: Mr. and Mrs. James Crusinberry
with Ellis and Ring about 1913.

RIGHT: F. Scott Fitzgerald
and daughter Scotty, in 1928.

BELOW: Ring, Ellis, and the boys,
Great Neck about 1923.